DUNGEONS & DRAGONS®

PLAYER'S HANDBOOK® 2

ROLEPLAYING GAME SUPPLEMENT

Jeremy Crawford · Mike Mearls · James Wyatt

CREDITS

Design
Logan Bonner, Jesse Decker,
Mike Mearls, Robert J. Schwalb,
Stephen Schubert, Stephen Radney-MacFarland,
Peter Schaefer

Development
Richard Baker, Andy Collins,
Jeremy Crawford, Mike Donais,
Andrew Finch, David Noonan, Matthew Sernett

Writing
James Wyatt

Mechanical Concepts
Rob Heinsoo

Editing
Jeremy Crawford (lead),
Michele Carter, Greg Bilsland

Managing Editing
Kim Mohan, Torah Cottrill

Director of D&D R&D and Book Publishing
Bill Slavicsek

D&D Creative Manager
Christopher Perkins

D&D Design Manager
James Wyatt

D&D Development and Editing Manager
Andy Collins

Art Director
Jon Schindehette

Graphic Designer
Soe Murayama

Cover Illustration
Daniel Scott

Interior Illustrations
Steve Argyle, Eric Belisle, Michael Bierek,
Devon Caddy-Lee, Mitch Cotie, Thomas Denmark,
Eric Deschamps, Brian Despain, Vincent Dutrait,
Steve Ellis, Wayne England, Howard Lyon, Mike
May, Raven Mimura, William O'Connor, Hector
Ortiz, Wayne Reynolds, Chris Seaman, John Stanko,
Matias Tapia, Franz Vohwinkel, Eva Widermann,
James Zhang

D&D Brand Team
Liz Schuh, Scott Rouse, Kierin Chase, Sara Girard,
Martin Durham

Publishing Production Specialist
Angelika Lokotz

Prepress Manager
Jefferson Dunlap

Imaging Technician
Carmen Cheung

Production Manager
Cynda Callaway

Game rules based on the original DUNGEONS & DRAGONS® rules
created by **E. Gary Gygax** and **Dave Arneson**, and the later
editions by **David "Zeb" Cook** (2nd Edition); **Jonathan Tweet,
Monte Cook, Skip Williams, Richard Baker,** and
Peter Adkison (3rd Edition); and **Rob Heinsoo, Andy Collins,**
and **James Wyatt** (4th Edition).

620-21898720-001 EN
9 8 7 6 5 4
First Printing:
March 2009
ISBN: 978-0-7869-5016-4

U.S., CANADA, ASIA, PACIFIC,
& LATIN AMERICA
Wizards of the Coast LLC
P.O. Box 707
Renton WA 98057-0707
+1-800-324-6496

EUROPEAN HEADQUARTERS
Hasbro UK Ltd
Caswell Way
Newport, Gwent NP9 0YH
GREAT BRITAIN
Please keep this address for your records

WIZARDS OF THE COAST, BELGIUM
Industrialaan 1
1702 Groot-Bijgaarden
Belgium
+32.070.233.277

VISIT OUR WEBSITE AT WWW.WIZARDS.COM/DND

CONTENTS

INTRODUCTION

GET READY for the next level!

Player's Handbook 2 is the most significant expansion yet to the 4th Edition DUNGEONS & DRAGONS® game. The *Player's Handbook*® presents eight races and eight classes. This book introduces five more races and eight more classes, including a mix of all-new material and some old favorites, along with a wealth of new options for any character.

Chapter 1 presents five additional races. The gnome and the shifter make the journey from the *Monster Manual*® to this book. The goliath (introduced in 2004's *Races of Stone*) and the half-orc return to the D&D® game in updated form. Devas are a new race of reincarnated immortal spirits striving for the perfection of their souls. This chapter also includes racial paragon paths for the races in this book as well as ones in the *Player's Handbook*.

Chapter 2 is the heart of the book, with eight new classes. Longtime D&D players will recognize some of these classes from past editions, but you've never seen them presented like this before. The arcane classes expand to include the bard and the sorcerer. The invoker and the avenger join the roster of divine classes. The primal power source makes its debut with classes of all four roles: the barbarian, the druid, the shaman, and the warden. The chapter ends with six new epic destinies.

Chapter 3 introduces the concept of backgrounds, a new game element you can use to customize your character and help expand his or her personality and history. If you're using the *FORGOTTEN REALMS Player's Guide*, you're familiar with the idea of choosing a home region for your character and gaining a benefit from that origin. The backgrounds in this chapter offer you dozens of ideas for expanding your character's story, and a choice of related benefits. This chapter also includes new feats, equipment, and magic items, including armor, weapons, and implements designed for use with the new classes in this book. The chapter ends with a group of new rituals.

At the end of the book is an important appendix of rule updates. It contains an updated explanation of how to read a power description, including new rules that apply to many of the powers in this book—in particular, rules about keywords such as beast form, spirit, and summoning. The appendix also contains the new version of the Stealth skill as well as updates to rules related to that skill in the *Player's Handbook*.

The D&D game is constantly evolving. *Player's Handbook 2* is the second book in a series that will continue adding new options for your characters for years to come. But the game changes in smaller ways as well, and the best way to keep up with those changes is to visit the Wizards of the Coast website.

YOUR PART IN THE STORY

One of the Dungeon Master's jobs is to be a narrator—to describe what's going on in the world of the game as you explore it along with your fellow adventurers. When your party enters a room, the DM tells you what it looks like and what's in it. However, narration isn't exclusively the DM's job: You describe your own character's actions, and even during an intense combat encounter, you have a chance to take part in telling the story of the game.

The flavor text included in every power description is a starting point you can use when narrating your part in the action. When your barbarian attacks, you can just say, "Krusk uses *howling strike*. I get a 24." Or using the flavor text as a cue, you can say, "With a blood-freezing scream, I throw myself into the fray! Does a 24 hit?"

A power's flavor text is only a starting point. You can modify that flavor however you like, as long as you don't change the power's game effects. Maybe you would rather think of the barbarian power *macetail's rage* as channeling the World Serpent, a primal spirit that appears in some shaman powers. You might say, "The earth shakes beneath my feet as the World Serpent stirs, knocking my foe to the ground!"

Choosing a background for your character can also be a great opportunity to take part in shaping the story of the game. After you've looked at the "Backgrounds" section of Chapter 3, talk with your DM about the background elements you want for your character.

The D&D game is all about telling an adventure story. If you take a more active part in telling your character's part of the story, everyone has more fun.

Four of the classes introduced in this book—the barbarian, the druid, the shaman, and the warden—use the primal power source. Some primal powers are more overtly magical than others, but they all draw on the spirits of nature that pervade the world and, to some extent, the echo plane known as the Feywild.

According to legend, when the gods made war against the primordials at the dawn of time, the battles raged across the cosmos for uncounted centuries. The gods slowly gained the upper hand, successfully imprisoning or banishing many of the primordials. However, this war threatened the very existence of the world, as the primordials who brought it forth from the Elemental Chaos clashed with the gods who sought to fix the form of the world in permanence. In the last days of the war, a new force made itself known in the cosmos: the spiritual expression of the world itself. These primal spirits declared an end to the conflict, asserting that the world would no longer be a battleground for the two opposing forces. The gods and the primordials were banished to their home planes, and the primal spirits of the world decreed a balance: The world would remain a place where matter and spirit mingled freely, where life and death proceeded in an orderly cycle, where the seasons changed in their unending wheel without interference. The gods and the primordials could still influence the world, but they could not rule it.

These primal spirits are beyond number, ranging from spirits too weak to have proper names to the mightiest incarnations of nature's power: the Primal Beast, the Fate Weaver, the Great Bear, the World Serpent, and others. They are spirits of winds and weather, of predators and prey, of plains and forests, of mountains and swamps. As the people of the world have come to know these primal spirits and live in harmony with them, some mortal spirits have joined their number after death, just as some mortal souls pass to the dominions of their gods. These great ancestors are among the most potent of the primal spirits.

Characters who use the primal power source stand firmly rooted in the world, between the divine power of the Astral Sea and the primordial churning of the Elemental Chaos. They have some affinity with the native inhabitants of the Feywild, who share their love and respect for the natural world. They are staunch enemies of aberrant creatures whose very existence is a blight on the natural world, as well as of demons that seek to destroy it, undead that violate life's natural cycle, and (to a lesser extent) those who seek to despoil the wilderness in the name of progress and civilization.

That doesn't mean that a primal character must be a sworn enemy of the gods, or of a character such as a paladin of Erathis who seeks to settle and civilize the world. There might be some conflict and disagreement between such characters, but they also have many common foes. A primal character's greatest concern is with creatures and forces that threaten the stability of the world and the balanced cycles of nature. In a broad view, the cities and civilizations of humans and other races are just as much a part of nature as are primeval forests and mountains, and just as worthy of protection.

Many primal characters do hold the gods in great respect. Without the gods' intervention, the primordials would have left the world in an ever-changing state not much different from the Elemental Chaos, hostile to natural life. In general, even evil gods would rather rule the world than destroy it.

For that reason, characters who wield primal power sometimes worship gods as well. As god of the wilderness, Melora is sometimes seen as an ally of the primal spirits. Kord is occasionally called the lord of the storm spirits, and both Corellon and Sehanine have ties to the Feywild that make them friendly with nature spirits.

Primal powers are called evocations, because primal characters evoke primal spirits to make attacks and effects in the world. Some characters channel primal spirits through their bodies in order to transform themselves and thereby make their physical attacks more formidable. Barbarians invite primal spirits to take residence in their bodies, entering a trancelike rage in which a spirit's ferocity overwhelms the barbarian's own reason. Wardens draw on the primal spirits of earth, trees, and beasts to transform their bodies, giving them strength to stand against their enemies. Druids call on the Primal Beast to transform their bodies into animal forms, taking on different aspects of the Primal Beast's nature.

Other characters evoke primal spirits to create external effects. Shamans use spirit companions as their primary link to the spirit world. A spirit companion might attack an enemy, or a shaman might conjure another spirit to create an effect—and afterward, the spirit's power lingers in the shaman's spirit companion. Druids, too, can evoke primal spirits to create terrain effects, buffet foes with thunder and wind, or create bursts of fire.

CHAPTER 1

CHARACTER RACES

THE EIGHT races described in the *Player's Handbook* are the most common heroic races in the world of the DUNGEONS & DRAGONS game, but they are by no means the only ones. This chapter introduces five new races, from the humble gnome to the exalted deva.

Two of these races—the gnome and the shifter—appear in the *Monster Manual*, but here they're fleshed out and presented with an eye toward their use as player characters. (The information in this book supersedes what's in the *Monster Manual*.) The other races—the deva, the goliath, and the half-orc—are new additions to the game and the world.

This chapter also includes racial paragon paths for the races in this book as well as ones in the *Player's Handbook*.

The races in this chapter follow the same format as the ones in the *Player's Handbook*. When you create a character, you can choose one of these races instead of one of those.

Devas are noble, virtuous beings who strive to perfect themselves through an apparently endless sequence of reincarnations. Once immortal spirits who served the gods of good, devas are now bound in flesh, the better to wage war against the forces of evil in the world and beyond.

Gnomes are small and stealthy fey who value a quick mind and the ability to escape notice. Gnomes are drawn to illusion and trickery. They explore the world with a sense of curiosity and wonder.

Goliaths dwell high in mountainous regions, traveling with the migrations of elk and other game. They view life as a grand competition and call on primal power to enhance their considerable physical strength and endurance.

Half-orcs combine the best qualities of humans and orcs and are strong, fierce, decisive, and resourceful. They savor the simple pleasures of life, from feasting and revelry to the thrill of battle.

Shifters carry a touch of lycanthropic blood in their veins. In the heat of battle, they tap into the power of the beast within, unleashing the savagery that lurks beneath their surface. They are predators by nature, defining the world in terms of hunter and prey.

STEVE ARGYLE

Immortal spirits who embody virtue, born and reborn to mortal life in the world

RACIAL TRAITS

Average Height: 6′ 1″–6′ 6″
Average Weight: 175–280 lb.

Ability Scores: +2 Intelligence, +2 Wisdom
Size: Medium
Speed: 6 squares
Vision: Normal

Languages: Common, choice of two others
Skill Bonuses: +2 History, +2 Religion
Astral Majesty: You have a +1 bonus to all defenses against attacks made by bloodied creatures.
Astral Resistance: You have resistance to necrotic damage and radiant damage equal to 5 + one-half your level.
Immortal Origin: Your spirit is native to the Astral Sea, so you are considered an immortal creature for the purpose of effects that relate to creature origin.
Memory of a Thousand Lifetimes: You have the *memory of a thousand lifetimes* power.

Memory of a Thousand Lifetimes	Deva Racial Power

The dreamlike memories of your previous lives lend insight to aid you.

Encounter
No Action **Personal**
Trigger: You make an attack roll, a saving throw, a skill check, or an ability check and dislike the result
Effect: You add 1d6 to the triggering roll.

Deep in the recesses of memory, devas recall what they once were: immortal servitors of the gods of good, spirits who chose to bind themselves to the world in mortal flesh. For millennia, their souls have been reborn to wage an endless war against the forces of darkness. Most devas are fiercely committed to the cause of good, because they fear what they might become if they turn to evil: A deva whose soul becomes corrupted risks being reborn as a rakshasa.

Play a deva if you want . . .

✦ to have dimly remembered connections to a thousand heroic lifetimes.

✦ to embrace the cause of good and strive for perfection in all you do.

✦ to be a member of a race that favors the avenger, cleric, invoker, and wizard classes.

PHYSICAL QUALITIES

In appearance, devas are very similar to humans, but with an unearthly beauty and an uncanny stillness about them. They are almost as tall as dragonborn, but much more slender.

Devas' coloration distinguishes them most strongly from humans. All devas have patterns of light and dark colors on their skin. The light portions are chalk white or pale gray, and the dark areas range from blue or purple to dark gray or black. In any individual deva, either light or dark can be dominant, with the opposite shade appearing in simple, elegant patterns on the face, chest, and shoulders. A deva's hair is typically the same color as these skin patterns.

When sitting or standing at rest, devas remain almost perfectly still, except for the occasional blink of the eyes. They don't fidget or twitch, and their eyes move only when they are actively examining something.

Devas do not have children. When a deva dies, his or her spirit is reincarnated in a new, adult body that appears in some sacred place, such as a mountain peak, a riverbank, or a desert oasis. The new deva retains enough memory of past lives to speak and understand multiple languages and offer the proper prayers and sacrifices to the gods of good.

PLAYING A DEVA

Devas are refined and polite. They follow the highest moral standards, but they are not afraid of violence. They believe that the pursuit of good is an eternal war with the forces of evil, embodied in rakshasas, demons, devils, and the evil gods and their servant angels. Devas wage that war in their hearts as well, constantly vigilant lest evil take root and corrupt their souls, transforming them into the creatures they most despise.

Because they remember, at least dimly, a life in the Astral Sea spent in close company with the gods, most devas are devout worshipers of the gods of good, especially Bahamut but also Moradin and Pelor. Devas seek to achieve a personal connection with the gods rather than approach them through temples and priests. They worship at meals in their homes, setting an empty place for the absent gods, and strive through meditation and prayer to become more like the gods they serve. Deva adventurers are commonly avengers, clerics, and invokers, who savor the experience of divine power flowing through them without any intermediary.

Devas do not have cities or societies of their own, and their numbers are so small that a deva can spend entire lifetimes without ever meeting another of his or her kind. They live among other races and, at least to some extent, adopt their ways. However, all devas remember elements of the life they had before their incarnation in flesh and the beginning of their cycle of rebirth, and they share some common cultural elements of dress, religion, and habits. Devas favor flowing clothes of fine silks, polished metal armor with winglike shoulder ornaments, and headdresses or helmets that suggest crowns or halos. In other ways, they prefer to live simply, without extravagance.

Deva Characteristics: Dedicated, devout, elegant, enlightened, introspective, mystical, refined, righteous, spiritual, thoughtful

Male Names: Adiah, Ansis, Ayab, Bavak, Beriah, Eben, Elyas, Galad, Gamal, Hiyal, Iannes, Kerem, Mahar, Marach, Mathas, Natan, Nehem, Oris, Raham, Ronen, Samel, Sered, Tavar, Vered, Zachar

Female Names: Abea, Adara, Asha, Chana, Danel, Darah, Davi, Elka, Eranah, Hania, Hava, Idria, Isa, Jael, Kana, Kayah, Lihi, Mahel, Marek, Noma, Navah, Paziah, Ravah, Riya, Sada, Shara, Tirah

DEVA ADVENTURERS

Three sample deva adventurers are described below.

Galad is a deva wizard who believes that the goal of his existence is to attain perfect knowledge of the universe. He believes that his arcane power is a manifestation of all he has learned throughout all his past lives, and that in this life or perhaps the next he will achieve perfect mastery and become a demigod, freed from the cycle of reincarnation.

Eranah is an invoker who wields the power of Bahamut. Just as Bahamut warred with Tiamat when the world was young, Eranah believes that her calling in this incarnation is to fight against the evil dragons and dragonspawn that pollute the world. Words of power resound in her mind like an echo of the Platinum Dragon's voice when she invokes his wrath upon her enemies.

Raham is a shaman who has embraced his life in the world, abandoning all thought of his previous astral existence. The primal spirits of the world are his patrons and allies, not the gods he left behind. He sees his endless rebirth as a part of the cycle of nature and has no desire to escape it.

GNOME

Slight, sly tricksters of the Feywild who excel at avoiding notice

RACIAL TRAITS

Average Height: 3′ 4″–3′ 8″
Average Weight: 50–75 lb.

Ability Scores: +2 Intelligence, +2 Charisma
Size: Small (see the sidebar)
Speed: 5 squares
Vision: Low-light

Languages: Common, Elven
Skill Bonuses: +2 Arcana, +2 Stealth
Fey Origin: Your ancestors were native to the Feywild, so you are considered a fey creature for the purpose of effects that relate to creature origin.
Master Trickster: Once per encounter, you can use the wizard cantrip *ghost sound* (*Player's Handbook*, page 158) as a minor action.
Reactive Stealth: If you have any cover or conceal-ment when you make an initiative check, you can make a Stealth check.
Trickster's Cunning: You have a +5 racial bonus to saving throws against illusions.
Fade Away: You have the *fade away* power.

Fade Away · Gnome Racial Power

You turn invisible in response to harm.

Encounter ✦ Illusion
Immediate Reaction   **Personal**
Trigger: You take damage
Effect: You are invisible until you attack or until the end of your next turn.

In the Feywild, the best way for a small creature to survive is to be overlooked. While suffering in servi-tude to the fomorian tyrants of the Feydark, gnomes learned to hide, to mislead, and to deflect—and by these means, to survive. The same talents sustain them still, allowing them to prosper in a world filled with creatures much larger and far more dangerous than they are.

Play a gnome if you want . . .
✦ to be curious, funny, and tricky.
✦ to rely more on stealth and deception than on brute strength and intimidation.
✦ to be a member of a race that favors the bard, sor-cerer, warlock, and wizard classes.

Physical Qualities

Gnomes are smaller even than halflings, rarely exceeding 4 feet in height. Apart from their size, they resemble elves or eladrin, with pointed ears and chiseled facial features such as high cheekbones and sharp jaws. They have a more wild look than eladrin do, though, particularly in the hair that sprouts from their heads in random directions. Some male gnomes sprout tufts of hair from their chins, but they otherwise lack body hair.

Gnome skin tone ranges from a ruddy tan through woody brown to rocky gray. Their hair can be virtually any color, from stark white to blond and various shades of brown to autumnal orange or green. Their eyes are glittering black orbs.

Gnomes are as long-lived as eladrin, living over 300 years, but they show more of the effects of age. A gnome over the age of 100 has gray or white hair and skin that shows the wrinkled and weathered lines of a century of laughter, but even the oldest gnome retains the strength and agility of youth.

Playing a Gnome

In quiet forests of the Feywild and remote woodlands in the world, gnomes live out of sight and mostly beneath the notice of larger races. Gnomes dwell in homes dug among the roots of trees, easily overlooked and cleverly concealed by camouflage and illusion. They are fond of the burrowing mammals that share their habitat, such as badgers, foxes, and rabbits, and have a sense of kinship with these small animals that share their forests.

Unobtrusiveness is a virtue among gnomes. They grow up on games of stealth and silence, in which the winner is the last to be discovered. An adult gnome who draws attention in a crowd is considered dangerously rude. Gnome folk heroes are not mighty warriors, but tricksters who slip out of captivity, play great pranks without being detected, or sneak past magical guardians. They deflect both aggression and attention with humor, and they guard their thoughts with friendly laughter.

Gnomes also value a quick mind and the ability to come up with a clever solution to any problem.

Being Small

Small characters follow most of the same rules as Medium ones, with the following exceptions.

✦ You can't use two-handed weapons, such as greatswords and halberds.

✦ When you use a versatile weapon, such as a longsword, you must use it two-handed, but you don't deal additional damage for doing so.

They appreciate witty conversation, especially rapid-fire repartee. They are inventive and resourceful, although they have little interest in or aptitude for the kind of technology found in human cities. They have an innate talent for magic and a love of illusion, music, poetry, and story.

Eager to see what the world has to offer and willing to be awed by its wonders, gnomes greet the world with open curiosity. Gnomes who are drawn to adventure are most often driven by curiosity and wanderlust above any desire for wealth or glory.

Gnomes were once enslaved by the fomorian rulers of the Feydark, the subterranean caverns of the Feywild. They regard their former masters with more fear than hatred, and they feel some degree of sympathy for the fey that still toil under fomorian lashes—particularly the spriggans, which some say are corrupted gnomes. Gnomes are not fond of goblins or kobolds, but in typical gnome fashion, they avoid creatures they dislike rather than crusading against them. They are fond of eladrin and other friendly fey, and gnomes who travel the world have good relations with elves and halflings.

Gnome Characteristics: Affable, clever, crafty, curious, funny, guarded, inconspicuous, inventive, secretive, sly, tricky

Male Names: Alston, Alvyn, Brocc, Eldon, Frug, Kellen, Ku, Nim, Orryn, Pock, Sindri, Warryn, Wrenn

Female Names: Breena, Carlin, Donella, Ella, Lilli, Lorilla, Nissa, Nyx, Oda, Orla, Roswyn, Tana, Zanna

Gnome Adventurers

Two sample gnome adventurers are described below.

Kellen is a gnome bard with a grim sense of humor and a ready blade. He was thrust unwillingly into an adventuring career when cyclopses raided his village and took him captive. He labored as a slave to a fomorian king for a decade before finally making his escape and fleeing the Feywild entirely. Though he longs to return one day to free the members of his family he was forced to leave behind, fear of what awaits him in the Feywild keeps him in the world.

Orla has lived in the world her entire life. She was born in a forest among elves, but an encounter in the forest one evening changed her life. She found herself face to face with a fey spirit of such power that she was unable to move or speak and could only acquiesce to its unspoken demands. Her life belongs to that spirit now, she knows. She wields its power as a fey pact warlock, but she feels its desires and pursues its goals without fully understanding where they might lead her.

GOLIATH

*Tribal nomads of the mountains,
strong as the rock and proud as the peak*

RACIAL TRAITS
Average Height: 7´ 2˝-7´ 8˝
Average Weight: 280-340 lb.

Ability Scores: +2 Strength, +2 Constitution
Size: Medium
Speed: 6 squares
Vision: Normal

Languages: Common, either Dwarven or Giant
Skill Bonuses: +2 Athletics, +2 Nature
Mountain's Tenacity: You have a +1 racial bonus to Will.
Powerful Athlete: When you make an Athletics check to jump or climb, roll twice and use either result.
Stone's Endurance: You have the *stone's endurance* power.

Stone's Endurance	Goliath Racial Power

Your foes' attacks bounce off your stony hide.

Encounter
Minor Action   **Personal**
Effect: You gain resist 5 to all damage until the end of your next turn.
  Level 11: Resist 10 to all damage.
  Level 21: Resist 15 to all damage.

Goliaths are mountain-dwelling nomads who see life as a grand competition. Their scattered bands have never been major players in the politics of the lowland world, but they have wandered the mountain ranges of the world since the primordials first shaped the peaks and valleys. Tall and massive, goliaths revere the primal power of nature and use it to enhance their own strength.

Play a goliath if you want . . .
+ to be tougher and stronger than nearly anyone else.
+ to master the rugged mountain slopes.
+ to be a member of a race that favors the barbarian, fighter, and warden classes.

PHYSICAL QUALITIES

Goliaths tower over even dragonborn, standing between 7 and 8 feet tall. Their skin is gray or brown, mottled with darker patches that they believe hint at some aspect of each goliath's fate or destiny. Their skin is speckled with lithoderms, coin-sized growths of bone that appear like pebbles studding their arms, shoulders, torso, and head. A bony ridge juts over their gleaming blue or green eyes. Male goliaths are bald, and females have dark hair they typically grow long and wear in braids.

Goliaths have life spans comparable to those of humans.

PLAYING A GOLIATH

Goliaths are driven by a fierce love of competition. Anything that can be conceived as a challenge invites goliaths to keep score, tracking their progress against both their comrades and themselves. A goliath fighter might remark on how many times he has drawn first blood in battle within a particular dungeon compared to the party's rogue, and he's certainly mentally tracking his own performance against his last adventure. This competitiveness takes the form of good-natured rivalry among goliaths. As a race they have no patience for cheaters, gloaters, or sore losers, but goliaths can be very hard on themselves when they fail to measure up to their own past accomplishments.

Daring that borders on foolhardiness is also a common trait among goliaths. They have no fear of heights, climbing sheer mountain cliffs and leaping great chasms with ease. Their nomadic lifestyle of hunting and gathering instills in them an inquisitive interest in whatever lies over the next ridge or at the head of a canyon. To a wandering hunter's mind, that curiosity can lead to better hunting grounds or a good water source that would otherwise go undiscovered.

Goliaths respect and revere the natural world, and goliath adventurers commonly draw on the primal power source. Druids and shamans are more common among them than clerics, and goliath priests—called skywatchers—invoke the spirits of nature and their ancestors far more often than they call on the distant gods of the Astral Sea. Some goliath tribes also honor Kord, Melora, and Avandra, particularly those tribes that have frequent contact with other races. Tribes that regularly trade with dwarves sometimes offer sacrifices to Moradin as well.

Goliath Characteristics: Competitive, daring, driven, inquisitive, powerful, reliable, restless, trusting

Male Names: Aukan, Eglath, Gauthak, Ilikan, Kavaki, Keothi, Lo-Kag, Maveith, Meavoi, Thotham, Vimak

Female Names: Gae-Al, Kuori, Manneo, Nalla, Orilo, Paavu, Pethani, Thalai, Uthal, Vaunea

GOLIATH ADVENTURERS

Three sample goliath adventurers are described below.

Kavaki was injured in an avalanche as a young man and exiled from his tribe because he was unable to walk with them when they moved to a new hunting ground. His tribe lamented his loss, celebrated his accomplishments, and then left him for dead. However, a ram spirit sheltered him through blizzards and storms until his injury healed, and he now evokes the power of that ram spirit to fuel his barbarian rage. Still cut off from his tribe, Kavaki has found a new family—a group of adventurers—and is determined never again to be in a position where he cannot carry his own weight.

Nalla was a tent-mother for her tribe, caring for infants and toddlers while their parents performed their own tasks on the tribe's behalf. When her own child died in an orc raid, however, Nalla felt that she could no longer bear to care for children, and she soon exiled herself. As a fighter, she has fallen in with a band of adventurers she now guards with her life, almost as if they were the children of her tribe.

Lo-Kag was a trader for his tribe, interacting regularly with a nearby dwarf clan. As a warden, he was interested in the traditions of the dwarven defenders—determined fighters and paladins sworn to the defense of their clanhold—and learned much from a mentor trained in their ways. On his last trip to the dwarf clanhold, however, he found it deserted. Corpses lay strewn around the citadel, but he saw no sign of violence or looting. Instead of returning to his tribe, Lo-Kag set out into the world to investigate the mystery of the dwarves' demise.

HALF-ORC

Fierce warriors who combine human resolve with orc savagery

RACIAL TRAITS
Average Height: 5´ 9˝–6´ 4˝
Average Weight: 155–225 lb.

Ability Scores: +2 Strength, +2 Dexterity
Size: Medium
Speed: 6 squares
Vision: Low-light

Languages: Common, Giant
Skill Bonuses: +2 Endurance, +2 Intimidate
Half-Orc Resilience: The first time you are bloodied during an encounter, you gain 5 temporary hit points. The temporary hit points increase to 10 at 11th level and to 15 at 21st level.
Swift Charge: You gain a +2 bonus to speed when charging.
Furious Assault: You have the *furious assault* power.

Furious Assault	Half-Orc Racial Power

Your monstrous wrath burns inside you, giving strength to your attack.

Encounter
Free Action   **Personal**
Trigger: You hit an enemy
Effect: The attack deals 1[W] extra damage if it's a weapon attack or 1d8 extra damage if it isn't.

An obscure legend claims that when Corellon put out Gruumsh's eye in a primeval battle, part of the savage god's essence fell to earth, where it transformed a race of humans into fierce half-orcs. Another story suggests that an ancient hobgoblin empire created half-orcs to lead orc tribes on the empire's behalf. Yet another legend claims that a tribe of brutal human barbarians chose to breed with orcs to strengthen their bloodline. Some say that Kord created half-orcs, copying the best elements from the human and orc races to make a strong and fierce people after his own heart. If you ask a half-orc about his origin, you might hear one of these stories. You might also get a punch in the face for asking such a rude question.

Play a half-orc if you want . . .

✦ to be big, strong, and fast.

✦ to harness anger into resilience and combat power.

✦ to be a member of a race that favors the barbarian, fighter, ranger, and rogue classes.

STEVE ARGYLE

PHYSICAL QUALITIES

Half-orcs favor their human lineage in appearance, but are distinguished by skin that tends to various shades of gray, broad jaws, and prominent lower canine teeth—though these are still a far cry from the jutting tusks of orcs. On average, they are taller and stronger than humans as well. Their hair is usually black, though it grays quickly with age. Most half-orcs who live among humans favor human styles of clothing and hairstyle, but a few adopt orc traditions, tying small bones or beads into long braids or bunches of hair.

Half-orcs don't live quite as long as humans do. They mature quickly, reaching adulthood at about 16 years, and rarely live past the age of 60.

PLAYING A HALF-ORC

Half-orcs combine the best qualities of humans and orcs, though some would argue that the good qualities of orcs are few and hard to find. From their orc blood, half-orcs inherit great physical strength and toughness. They are fierce warriors, fleet of foot as they charge into battle.

Their human blood makes half-orcs decisive and bold, resourceful and self-reliant. They are adaptable and able to make their way in almost any circumstance. Although half-orcs often live on the fringes of society in human towns and cities, they still find ways to prosper in a world to which they don't fully belong.

For all their good qualities, many half-orcs exhibit characteristics that polite society finds uncouth or undesirable. Half-orcs have little patience for complicated rules of etiquette or procedure and find little value in hiding their true opinions in order to spare someone's feelings. They enjoy the simple pleasures of food and drink, boasting, singing, wrestling, drumming, and dancing, and they don't find much satisfaction in more refined or sophisticated arts. They're prone to act without much deliberation, preferring to overcome obstacles as they arise rather than consider every possible outcome and make contingency plans. These qualities lead some members of other races to consider them rude or crass, but others find their brashness refreshing.

Half-orcs generally live among either human or orc cultures—some in bustling human towns or cities, others among remote human or orc tribes. Most half-orcs have two half-orc parents, but sometimes half-orcs marry and have half-orc children with humans or orcs. Orcs show grudging respect to half-orcs for their considerable strength and for their cunning intelligence, which sometimes allows half-orcs to rise to leadership positions in orc tribes.

Although possessed of many strengths, half-orcs frequently encounter prejudice in human communities. Thus, most half-orcs gravitate to careers involving physical labor or violence. For some, the life of an adventurer is either a natural extension of that trend or a way to throw off the weight of prejudice. The adventuring life also means finding a place in a group of allies and equals—a simple pleasure that is all too hard for many half-orcs to find in the world.

Half-Orc Characteristics: Brash, ferocious, hedonistic, impulsive, short-tempered, tough, uninhibited

Male Names: Brug, Dorn, Druuk, Gnarsh, Grumbar, Hogar, Karash, Korgul, Krusk, Lubash, Mord, Ohr, Rendar, Sark, Scrag, Tanglar, Tarak, Thar, Ugarth, Yurk

Female Names: Augh, Bree, Ekk, Gaaki, Grai, Grigri, Gynk, Huru, Lagazi, Murook, Nogu, Ootah, Puyet, Tawar, Tomph, Ubada, Vanchu

HALF-ORC ADVENTURERS

Three sample half-orc adventurers are described below.

Tarak, a half-orc rogue, is at home in the city. He grew up in the rough-and-tumble wharf quarter and ran with street gangs and rough sailors. Everything changed when a sailor dropped dead at his feet, leaving a mysterious box in Tarak's possession. The box brought chaos into his life until he fled the city and fell in with some adventurers on the road. Tarak doesn't know what's in the box—its strange lock has defeated every attempt to open it, and its hard metal sides resist breaking. But goblins and doppelgangers have proven themselves willing to kill to get the box for themselves, piquing Tarak's interest.

Murook is a warden, born and raised among an orc tribe. She was a staunch defender of her tribe for years, but her ties to the primal spirits of wood and stone slowly coaxed her away from the worship of Gruumsh and led her to question the brutality the orcs performed in his name. She made her way to human lands and has struggled to fit in, trying to leave behind the barbarian ways of her tribe and adopt at least a veneer of civilization, but she is still far more comfortable among the trees and mountains than confined in a city or village.

Dorn is a half-orc ranger who prefers not to talk about his birth and his family. He spent most of his life in a hut at the outskirts of a farming village, hunting and trapping in the surrounding forest, keeping to himself and asking only to be left alone. His life turned upside down on his thirtieth birthday, when a group of adventurers stopped in the village looking for directions to an ancient ruin. The villagers steered the adventurers to Dorn, who agreed to guide them through the forest. He never returned home, because that first adventure led him into many more.

*Ferocious heirs of the wild,
the perfect fusion of civilized race and wild beast*

RACIAL TRAITS
Average Height: 5´ 7"-6´ 0"
Average Weight: 130-180 lb.

Size: Medium
Speed: 6 squares
Vision: Low-light

Languages: Common, choice of one other

LONGTOOTH SHIFTERS
Ability Scores: +2 Strength, +2 Wisdom
Skill Bonuses: +2 Athletics, +2 Endurance
Longtooth Shifting: You have the *longtooth shifting*
  power.

RAZORCLAW SHIFTERS
Ability Scores: +2 Dexterity, +2 Wisdom
Skill Bonuses: +2 Acrobatics, +2 Stealth
Razorclaw Shifting: You have the *razorclaw shifting*
  power.

Longtooth Shifting   Shifter Racial Power
You unleash the beast within and take on a savage countenance.

Encounter ✦ Healing
Minor Action   **Personal**
Requirement: You must be bloodied.
Effect: Until the end of the encounter, you gain a +2 bonus
  to damage rolls. In addition, while you are bloodied, you
  gain regeneration 2.
  Level 11: Regeneration 4.
  Level 21: Regeneration 6.

Razorclaw Shifting   Shifter Racial Power
You unleash the beast within and take on a savage countenance.

Encounter
Minor Action   **Personal**
Requirement: You must be bloodied.
Effect: Until the end of the encounter, your speed increases
  by 2, and you gain a +1 bonus to AC and Reflex.

Shifters are fierce hunters strongly influenced by
their animal nature. Though they can't fully change
shape as their lycanthrope ancestors can, shifters do
become more bestial during the heat of battle, calling
on the primal power of the beast within.

Play a shifter if you want . . .

✦ to tap into bestial strength or speed in battle.

✦ to be a character in tune with your primal savage
  nature.

✦ to be a member of a race that favors the druid,
  fighter, ranger, and warden classes.

PHYSICAL QUALITIES

In broad strokes, shifters resemble humans with animalistic features. Their bodies are lithe and strong, and they often move in a crouched posture, springing and leaping along the ground. Their faces have a bestial cast, with wide, flat noses, large eyes and heavy eyebrows, pointed ears, and long sideburns. The hair of their heads is thick and worn long. Shifter skin and hair are usually some shade of brown.

Longtooth shifters claim werewolves as ancestors and have a vaguely canine cast to their features that becomes much more pronounced when they use their *longtooth shifting* power. Razorclaw shifters are descended from weretigers and are more catlike, particularly when using *razorclaw shifting*.

Shifters live about as long as humans.

PLAYING A SHIFTER

Shifters are strongly influenced by their animal natures. They think and act like predators, conceiving of most activities in terms of hunting and prey.

Longtooth shifters are drawn to a pack of companions, whether that's a family group or an adventuring party. They work well as part of a team in combat, coordinating their attacks with their allies and coming to the aid of beleaguered friends. They're drawn to the leader and defender roles, and they make excellent clerics, fighters, paladins, and wardens.

Razorclaw shifters are more independent, self-reliant, and adaptable. They're no less devoted to their adventuring companions, but they trust their allies to take care of themselves, and they strive to carry their own weight in the group. They're more inclined to be strikers or controllers, and they favor classes such as avenger, druid, ranger, and rogue.

Historically, most shifters dwelled in nomadic bands in plains and forests far removed from cities and towns. Since the fall of Nerath, however, the increasing dangers of the wilds have driven many shifters into closer proximity to human and elf communities. Some shifters have adapted smoothly to this change, carving niches for themselves as trappers, hunters, fishers, trackers, guides, or military scouts. Others have a much harder time fitting in. Shifters who feel alienated from the plains and forests they love sometimes take up the adventuring life as a way of escaping the confines of city walls and returning to nature. Some shifters, though, turn to a life of crime, preying on the residents of their new homes like the hunters they are.

Shifter Characteristics: Active, alert, fierce, free-spirited, intuitive, perceptive, predatory, self-reliant, unrestrained, wild

Male Names: Ash, Brook, Claw, Cliff, Flint, Frost, River, Rock, Storm, Thorn, Tor

Female Names: Aurora, Autumn, Dawn, Hazel, Iris, Lily, Rain, Rose, Summer

SHIFTER ADVENTURERS

Three sample shifter adventurers are described below.

Ash is a proud longtooth cleric devoted to Melora. His clan moved from the open plains into a nearby city shortly after the fall of Nerath, and most of them have adjusted smoothly to an urbanized life. Even during his childhood, though, Ash felt a calling to the wild places of the world, and he ventured far from the city on his wanderings. As a personal rite of passage when he turned 18, he traveled ten days from the city into the wilds and stayed there for ten more days, spending his time hunting, gathering food, and praying to the god of the wilderness. He had planned to return after those ten days but decided that Melora had a different plan in mind. He avoids cities and towns now unless he has no choice, spending his time wandering the wilds, exploring ancient ruins, and fighting the monsters that make the wilderness unsafe.

Summer is a razorclaw druid whose tribe still wanders a pristine forest far from any human cities. She was her tribe's moonspeaker, a religious leader who traveled among the different clans of her tribe. In the summer of one year, she went to visit the northernmost clan and never found them. She traveled farther and farther afield until she found a hobgoblin city. While sneaking into the city, she discovered that the surviving members of the clan were now slaves of the hobgoblins. She plans to return to that city one day to free her people, but in the meantime she is very interested in the power she has gained through adventuring.

Storm is a razorclaw avenger dedicated to the Raven Queen. He knows no tribe except the remote monastery where he was raised and trained. For many years, he never knew another shifter, and he believed himself to be a human who was specially blessed for the work of the Raven Queen—endowed with speed, stealth, and strength to make him more perfect in her service. On reaching adulthood, he left the monastery and ventured into the world on his first major undertaking for his order. There he discovered others of his race and has begun to question fundamental assumptions of his identity. Disillusioned about his god's work, he has taken up with a group of adventurers while he sorts out his place in a world that is much different from anything he previously imagined.

Most paragon paths are specific to particular classes. This section presents racial paragon paths, which are specific to races included in this book and in the *Player's Handbook*. The only prerequisite for any of these paths is that you be a character of the appropriate race. Only a dwarf can be a firstborn of Moradin, for example, and you must be a half-orc to take the bloodfury savage path. A racial paragon path is an exemplar of a race's defining characteristics. A scion of Arkhosia is not just any dragonborn hero: He or she is one of the finest examples of certain qualities that set dragonborn apart from other races.

Exemplars of the half-elf race do not pursue a paragon path; instead, they take the Versatile Master feat in Chapter 3.

Choosing a Racial Paragon Path: When you reach 11th level, you can choose a racial paragon path instead of another paragon path (see *Player's Handbook*, page 53). You gain the features and the powers of the path at the levels specified in the racial paragon path's description.

Implements: If your racial paragon path includes powers that have the implement keyword, you can use your class's implements, as well as implements you can use because of a feat, with those powers. When you wield a magic version of such an implement, you can add its enhancement bonus to the attack rolls and the damage rolls of your racial paragon path powers that have the implement keyword. Without an implement, you can still use these powers.

ADROIT EXPLORER

"Turn back? Now? But we don't know what's on the next floor!"

Prerequisite: Human

The unknown has an inexplicable hold on you. Your greatest ambition is to discover, to unearth, to explore. You are the perfect expression of the human tendency to comb the world in search of knowledge and power, infused with an almost superhuman determination. This determination is central to your nature—a drive that propels you to work harder, fight longer, and strive for more than you should be able to attain through your own merits. You are not satisfied until you have achieved complete victory in your endeavors, and you develop powers to help you achieve your goals. Your will only grows stronger when your back is against the wall, and you fight all the harder, making sure you win the day.

Whether you are motivated by a thirst for knowledge of the world's most ancient civilizations, a hunger for long-lost secrets of arcane power, a drive to conquer and settle the world in the name of Erathis, or a lust for gold and glory, you're willing to face great danger to achieve your goals. Thanks to your single-minded dedication, you usually manage to escape from danger in one piece, even if you survive only by the skin of your teeth.

ADROIT EXPLORER PATH FEATURES

Ambitious Effort (11th level): Choose an encounter attack power of 7th level or lower from your class. You gain that power. If you choose an encounter attack power that you already know, you now have two uses of that power per encounter. At 21st level, you can replace this power with an encounter attack power of 13th level or lower from your class.

Bloody Determination (11th level): The first time you are bloodied during an encounter, you gain a +5 power bonus to your next attack roll before the end of your next turn against the enemy that bloodied you.

Heroic Action (11th level): When you spend an action point to take an extra action, you also gain resist 10 to all damage until the end of your next turn. The resistance increases to 20 at 21st level.

Champion of Humanity (16th level): After each extended rest, you have 2 action points instead of 1.

ADROIT EXPLORER POWERS

Destined for Greatness	Adroit Explorer Utility 12

Despair is never an option.

Encounter ✦ Healing
No Action — **Personal**
Trigger: You fail a saving throw and you are not dying
Effect: You reroll the saving throw with a +4 power bonus. In addition, you can spend a healing surge.

Bloodied Greatness	Adroit Explorer Attack 20

Your enemies' attacks push you over a threshold, and you tap into a fresh reserve of strength. You unleash one of your mightiest attacks, fueled by your pain.

Daily
Immediate Reaction — **Personal**
Trigger: An enemy bloodies you
Effect: You use one of your encounter attack powers against the triggering enemy. That power can already be expended, and if it is not, using it through this power doesn't expend it.

ANCESTRAL INCARNATE

"It looks as if you spent a lifetime learning that technique. I humbly counter—with a technique that took a dozen lifetimes to master."

Prerequisite: Deva

All devas have at least a tenuous connection to their past lives, and they see themselves as spiritual descendants of their previous incarnations. For you, the connection to your past lives is more tangible. As an ancestral incarnate, you can call forth your own spirit as it existed years or centuries ago to advise you, protect you, and confound your enemies. Those who have the temerity to face you in battle learn that they aren't fighting just the present-day incarnation of you, but also every incarnation of you that has ever been.

ANCESTRAL INCARNATE PATH FEATURES

Resurgent Action (11th): When you spend an action point to take an extra action, you can regain the use of an encounter attack power that you have already used during this encounter. The power's level must be no higher than your level – 4, and you must use the power when taking the extra action.

Serene Countenance (11th): You gain a +2 bonus to saving throws to end effects that make you dazed or stunned.

Past-Life Acolytes (16th): When you perform any ritual, you can make three ghostly incarnations of your past lives step out of your body to help you. Each incarnation either grants you a +2 bonus to the ritual's skill check or contributes a healing surge to help pay the ritual's healing surge cost, if any. The number of incarnations increases to four at 20th level, five at 25th level, and six at 30th level.

ANCESTRAL INCARNATE POWERS

Past-Life Guardian	Ancestral Incarnate Attack 11

A translucent deva spirit steps out of your body and interposes itself between you and an enemy.

Encounter ✦ Conjuration, Implement
Standard Action   **Ranged** 5
Effect: You conjure a spectral guardian that occupies 1 square within range. The guardian lasts until the end of your next turn. The guardian makes the following attack when it appears, and it can repeat the attack as an opportunity attack.
Target: One creature adjacent to the guardian
Attack: Wisdom vs. Reflex
Hit: 3d8 + Wisdom modifier damage.

Past-Life Servant	Ancestral Incarnate Utility 12

A spirit resembling one of your past incarnations steps out of your body, bows briefly, and moves as you direct.

Daily ✦ Conjuration
Minor Action   **Ranged** 20
Effect: You conjure a spectral servant in an unoccupied square within range. The servant can perform one of these tasks when it appears:
  ✦ Move 6 squares.
  ✦ Pick up an unattended object adjacent to it that weighs up to 20 pounds.
  ✦ Manipulate an unattended object adjacent to it.
Sustain Minor: The servant persists, and it can perform another task from the list above. You can spend multiple minor actions in a round to have the servant perform multiple tasks.

Past-Life Vanguard	Ancestral Incarnate Attack 20

Spirit after sword-wielding spirit leaps out of your body Each stabs a nearby enemy; then they all leap back inside you, invigorating you as they return.

Daily ✦ Healing, Implement
Standard Action   **Close** burst 5
Target: Each enemy in burst
Attack: Wisdom vs. Reflex
Hit: 4d8 + Wisdom modifier damage.
Effect: You regain 5 hit points for each target.

Bloodfury Savage

"I'll tear out your heart and make it my feast!"

Prerequisite: Half-orc

In the veins of your people flows the mingled blood of orcs and humans, a perfect union of ferocity and adaptability. In general, half-orcs manifest the best traits of humans and orcs. In your heart, though, orc drums beat a call to war, stirring a savage craving for violence. You brim with fury you can barely contain, and in the thick of combat it overflows into a raging torrent. Only battle can feed the hunger in your soul, for you were born to the bloodfury.

For your entire life, you have felt the stirrings of war within you, the conflict between the human and orc halves that define your divided nature. From the battle raging inside, you derive great power, great strength, and above all, a great capacity for destruction. In combat, you lose yourself to the storm, unleashing your bloodfury in a frothing display of violence that inspires fear in all who fight you.

Bloodfury Savage Path Features

Eager Action (11th level): When you spend an action point to take an extra action, you also gain a bonus to speed equal to your Dexterity modifier until the end of your next turn.

Fearsome Disposition (11th level): When you make an Intimidate check, you can roll twice and use either result.

Savage Resilience (16th level): When you use your Half-Orc Resilience racial trait, you also gain resist 10 to all damage until the end of your next turn.

Bloodfury Savage Powers

Unbound Assault — Bloodfury Savage Attack 11

You tear across the battlefield, eager to feed fresh kills to your weapon.

Encounter ✦ Weapon
Standard Action   Melee weapon
Effect: Before the attack, you shift 3 squares.
Target: One creature
Attack: Strength or Dexterity vs. AC
Hit: 3[W] + Strength or Dexterity modifier damage, and you gain a +4 bonus to damage rolls against the target until the end of your next turn.
Special: When you gain this power, choose Strength or Dexterity as the ability you use when making attack rolls and damage rolls with this power.

Frothing Madness — Bloodfury Savage Utility 12

Something erupts inside you, turning you into a relentless force of destruction.

Daily ✦ Stance
Minor Action   Personal
Effect: Until the stance ends, you gain a +2 bonus to damage rolls and a +5 bonus to saving throws.

Murderous Rage — Bloodfury Savage Attack 20

You swear that your foe will not survive this battle, as you focus your steadily growing fury on it.

Daily ✦ Weapon
Standard Action   Melee weapon
Target: One creature
Attack: Strength or Dexterity vs. AC
Hit: 4[W] + Strength or Dexterity modifier damage.
Miss: Half damage.
Effect: Until the end of the encounter, you gain a +1 bonus to damage rolls against the target. Whenever you hit the target with a melee attack, this bonus increases by 1.
Special: When you gain this power, choose Strength or Dexterity as the ability you use when making attack rolls and damage rolls with this power.

Fey Beguiler

"Now you see me—but not for long!"

Prerequisite: Gnome

The gnome race has learned to survive in a danger-ous world by remaining unnoticed, staying out of sight and wielding magic to become invisible. As a fey beguiler, you take that a step farther, using magic to cloud and confuse your enemies' minds while you perfect your own talents for stealth and secrecy.

As you progress along the path of the fey beguiler, you learn an array of methods to move around unseen while bedeviling your foes. You can turn invisible, blast your foe with a globe of fey light and dash away unseen, or dumbfound an opponent, leaving it vulnerable to your allies' attacks. To supple-ment the powers of your path and your class, you also learn skills and utility powers typically available to rogues and wizards, either magical or mundane tricks to enhance your stealth, movement, or other

capabilities. The key to your success is to escape notice, and you have an arsenal of techniques to do just that.

You can be sly and sneaky, moving quietly and skulking through the shadows. Subtlety is a valuable tool, and secrecy can save your life. But sometimes a forthright attack on an enemy's mind is just the right tool for the job.

Fey Beguiler Path Features

Skill Learning (11th level): You gain training in a skill from the rogue or wizard class skills list.

Disappearing Trick (11th level): You can spend an action point to become invisible until the end of your next turn or until you attack, instead of taking an extra action.

Clever Versatility (12th level): You gain a util-ity power of 10th level or lower from the rogue or wizard class.

Sneaky Gnome (16th level): You roll twice whenever you make a Stealth check and use either result.

Fey Beguiler Powers

Bedazzling Orb	Fey Beguiler Attack 11

As you disappear from view, an orb of bright fey light streaks toward your opponent, then erupts in a dazzling flash that leaves that foe dazed.

Encounter ✦ Illusion, Implement, Radiant
Standard Action   **Ranged** 10
Effect: Before the attack, you become invisible until the end of your turn.
Target: One creature
Attack: Intelligence or Charisma vs. Reflex
Hit: 2d8 + Intelligence or Charisma modifier radiant damage, and the target is dazed until the end of your next turn.
Special: When you gain this power, choose Intelligence or Charisma as the ability you use when making attack rolls and damage rolls with this power.

Beguiling Bolt	Fey Beguiler Attack 20

Your mental assault leaves your foe bewildered and vulnerable to attack, as you draw on fey power to regain your ability to vanish.

Daily ✦ Implement, Psychic
Standard Action   **Ranged** 10
Target: One creature
Attack: Intelligence or Charisma vs. Will
Hit: 4d10 + Intelligence or Charisma modifier psychic damage, and the target grants combat advantage (save ends).
Miss: Half damage, and the target grants combat advantage until the end of its next turn.
Effect: You regain the use of your *fade away* racial power if you have already used it during this encounter.
Special: When you gain this power, choose Intelligence or Charisma as the ability you use when making attack rolls and damage rolls with this power.

FIRSTBORN OF MORADIN

"My strength is the eternal endurance of the mountains. I will not break."

Prerequisite: Dwarf

At the dawn of creation, dwarven myths say, Moradin made the race of dwarves. His firstborn had bones cut from bedrock, souls wrought from iron, and hearts carved of gleaming diamonds. These firstborn were the models after which all other dwarves were patterned.

Although the firstborn of Moradin's making vanished in servitude to the giants, their fighting techniques and mystical traditions have not been lost. A new era of dwarven heroism has arrived, and the legacy of the firstborn continues. Those few who most skillfully follow the paths of the ancient firstborn are slowly transformed into the image of Moradin's firstborn.

As one of the present-day firstborn of Moradin, you forge a deep connection with the earth, tapping into the power that courses through the bedrock beneath your feet. You draw on the strength of the mountains to resist injury, expand your senses through rock and stone, and root yourself in the bones of the earth. You are the stuff new legends are made of.

FIRSTBORN OF MORADIN PATH FEATURES

Stonebones (11th level): Whenever you take a critical hit, roll a d20. If you roll 10 or higher, the critical hit turns into a normal hit.

Strength of the Earth (11th level): When you spend an action point to take an extra action, you can also spend a healing surge.

Dwarven Resurgence (16th level): When you use your second wind, you make a saving throw against each effect on you that a save can end.

FIRSTBORN OF MORADIN POWERS

Receive the Charge	Firstborn of Moradin Attack 11

You ready yourself for an approaching enemy, deftly maneuvering to a better position and striking before your foe strikes you.

Encounter ✦ Weapon
Immediate Reaction   Melee weapon
Trigger: An enemy enters a square adjacent to you
Effect: Before the attack, you shift 1 square.
Target: The triggering enemy
Attack: Strength vs. AC
Hit: 2[W] + Strength modifier damage.

Earthsense	Firstborn of Moradin Utility 12

Your connection with the earth allows you to sense even the faintest tremors in stone, letting you see what others cannot.

Daily ✦ Stance
Minor Action   Personal
Effect: Until the stance ends, you gain tremorsense 10.

Mountain Stance Strike	Firstborn of Moradin Attack 20

You call on the weight of the mountains to crash down on your foes and to ground yourself against your enemies' attacks.

Daily ✦ Stance, Weapon
Standard Action   Melee weapon
Target: One creature
Attack: Strength vs. Fortitude
Hit: 2[W] + Strength modifier damage, and you knock the target prone. If the target stands up before the end of your next turn, you can make a melee basic attack against it as an immediate interrupt if you are adjacent to it.
Miss: Half damage.
Effect: You assume the mountain stance. Until the stance ends, you gain a +2 bonus to AC, and you can ignore being pulled, pushed, slid, or knocked prone.

HALFLING SCOUNDREL

"The bigger they are, the easier they topple."

Prerequisite: Halfling

The greatest heroes of halfling legend are those who defeat giants, dragons, or other oversized threats to their homes and communities, using their wits, their agility, and a hefty dose of audacity. These heroes aren't necessarily armored warriors wielding legendary swords, and they don't have lands or noble titles. They are ordinary folk who rise to the challenge of the times, proving that size and strength aren't needed to come out on top. You're one of these heroes.

Like most halflings, you have found that the best way to get by in a world full of much larger creatures is to stay out of their way. Doing that might mean keeping out of their sight or staying on their good side. It might also mean keeping out of their reach, or dodging their attacks. Stealth and trickery might not be weapons and armor by themselves, but they are a useful supplement to the finest steel. Coupled with your natural daring and determination, these strengths are enough to bring you victory against any foe, no matter how large.

Compared to the legendary heroes of other races, you might come across as a scamp or a scoundrel. But the fact that you're crafty, resourceful, and sometimes sneaky doesn't make you any less of a hero. Avandra has blessed you with courage beyond question, ingenuity sufficient for any challenge, and the stealth you need to survive.

HALFLING SCOUNDREL PATH FEATURES

Fearless Scoundrel (11th level): Whenever you are affected by a fear effect that a save can end, you can make a saving throw against the effect at the start of your turn. If you don't save, you can make another saving throw against the effect at the end of your turn.

Resourceful Action (11th level): You can spend an action point to gain a +5 bonus to an attack roll, a saving throw, or a skill check you have just rolled, instead of taking an extra action.

Crafty Combatant (16th level): When you use your *second chance* racial power and the enemy's attack misses after the reroll, that enemy grants combat advantage to you until the end of your next turn.

HALFLING SCOUNDREL POWERS

Sly Offensive — Halfling Scoundrel Attack 11

Your weapon ends up exactly where the enemy didn't expect, leaving that foe off balance.

Encounter ✦ Weapon
Standard Action   Melee weapon
Target: One creature
Attack: Dexterity or Charisma vs. Reflex
Hit: 2[W] + Dexterity or Charisma modifier damage, and the target takes a -2 penalty to attack rolls against you until the end of its next turn. If the target misses with any attack during its next turn, you can shift a number of squares equal to your Dexterity or Charisma modifier as an opportunity action.
Special: When you gain this power, choose Dexterity or Charisma as the ability you use when making attack rolls and damage rolls with this power. You use the same ability to determine the number of squares you shift.

Problem Solver — Halfling Scoundrel Utility 12

You find solutions to the thorniest problems.

Encounter
Immediate Interrupt   Ranged 10
Trigger: An ally within 10 squares of you fails a check with a skill in which you're trained
Target: The triggering ally
Effect: The target can reroll the skill check with a +2 power bonus.

Halfling's Taunt — Halfling Scoundrel Attack 20

You enrage your foe with a chuckle and a taunt. That foe's fury swells as its attacks miss you and you whack it in response.

Daily ✦ Weapon
Standard Action   Melee weapon
Target: One creature
Attack: Dexterity or Charisma vs. AC
Hit: 5[W] + Dexterity or Charisma modifier damage.
Miss: Half damage.
Effect: Until the end of the encounter, if the target attacks, it must include you as a target if none of your allies are nearer to it than you are. You gain a +2 bonus to all defenses against the target's attacks. If the target misses you with an attack, you can make a basic attack against it as an opportunity action.
Special: When you gain this power, choose Dexterity or Charisma as the ability you use when making attack rolls and damage rolls with this power.

STEVE ELLIS

MOONSTALKER

"I can see my destiny in the face of the moon, and I call to it in greeting."

Prerequisite: Shifter

Shifters harbor a bestial nature inside themselves. When a shifter is under duress, this nature reveals itself in his or her features and prowess. This innate savagery is the gift of shifters' lycanthrope ancestors, the quality passed down through the generations that gives the shifter race its identity. Most shifters can call on their legacy when needed, but you enjoy a closer kinship to your lycanthrope forebears.

You take the name moonstalker for the strong lycanthropic heritage you have awakened in your spirit. You have always had an animalistic side, manifested in your physical features and sometimes through your behavior, but at some point you learned that you were different, and that the gift from your ancestors was greater than you could have believed. You are still able to shift your form, physically expressing shifter traits, but you can take that power a step farther and use your bestial nature to fully transform into a wolf or a tiger. This ability accompanies a host of other changes, and your tactics and behavior leave behind civilized methods for those of an untamed predator.

MOONSTALKER PATH FEATURES

Hunter Action (11th level): When you spend an action point to make an attack, you can shift a number of squares equal to your Wisdom modifier as a free action before or after the attack.

Go for the Throat (11th level): When you hit a prone target with a melee attack, the attack deals 1d6 extra damage. The extra damage increases to 2d6 at 21st level.

Pack Tactics (16th level): While you are adjacent to a prone enemy, you and your allies add your Wisdom modifier to damage rolls against that enemy.

MOONSTALKER POWERS

Call to the Moon	Moonstalker Attack 11

A bloodcurdling howl escapes from your throat, announcing that the hunt has begun.

Encounter ✦ Fear, Psychic
Minor Action   **Close** burst 5
Target: Each enemy in burst
Attack: Wisdom + 4 vs. Will
   Level 21: Wisdom + 6 vs. Will
Hit: 1d8 + Wisdom modifier psychic damage, and the target grants combat advantage until the end of your next turn.

Unleash the Silent Predator	Moonstalker Utility 12

Your body contorts as you transform into the creature lurking inside you.

Daily ✦ Polymorph
Minor Action   **Personal**
Effect: You assume the form of a gray wolf or a tiger of your size until the end of the encounter, until you fall unconscious, or until you drop to 0 hit points or fewer. In this form, you add your Wisdom modifier to your speed. In addition, whenever you walk as a move action, you can shift 1 square as a free action before doing so.

Circle the Prey	Moonstalker Attack 20

You stalk around your enemy, searching for an opening to make a killing blow.

Daily ✦ Weapon
Standard Action   **Melee** weapon
Target: One creature
Attack: Strength or Dexterity vs. Reflex
Hit: 3[W] + Strength or Dexterity modifier damage, and ongoing 10 damage (save ends). In addition, you knock the target prone.
Miss: Half damage.
Effect: Before or after the attack, you shift a number of squares equal to your Wisdom modifier. After the attack, the target grants combat advantage to you until the end of your next turn.
Special: When you gain this power, choose Strength or Dexterity as the ability you use when making attack rolls and damage rolls with this power.

SCION OF ARKHOSIA

"By the blood of Io, you will fall!"

Prerequisite: Dragonborn

Scions of Arkhosia are the descendants of the noble dragonborn heroes of the fallen empire of Arkhosia. In the years since that empire fell, its heirs have scattered across the world, their lineage and heritage confused or lost in the darkness of the present age. Most dragonborn spend their lives unaware of what sort of potential lies within them, but a few manage to awaken and master their hidden reserves of power.

You are one of these scions, and you have begun the long and arduous process of unlocking the power of your noble blood. Your ancestry places you closer to your dragon kin than other dragonborn are. As a result, you gain a greater mastery over your *dragon breath*, able to alter its substance at will.

The clearest sign of your noble heritage, though, is the draconic wings that begin to form on your back as soon as you adopt this paragon path. They take some time to grow strong and large enough to sustain short bursts of flight, but they mark you unmistakably as what you are: a hero of your people reborn.

SCION OF ARKHOSIA PATH FEATURES

Versatile Breath (11th level): Whenever you attack with your *dragon breath* racial power, choose one of the following damage types: acid, cold, fire, lightning, or poison. The attack's damage is also that type.

Draconic Outburst (11th level): When you spend an action point to make an attack, each enemy adjacent to you takes damage equal to 5 + your Constitution modifier when you resolve the attack. This damage is the same type you initially chose for your *dragon breath* racial power.

Blood of Io (16th level): You gain overland flight with a speed of 12.

SCION OF ARKHOSIA POWERS

Dragon's Wrath — Scion of Arkhosia Attack 11

You exhale draconic energy that detonates at a distance.

Encounter ✦ Varies
Standard Action   **Area** burst 2 within 10 squares
Target: Each enemy in burst
Attack: Strength, Constitution, or Dexterity + 4 vs. Reflex
   Level 21: Strength, Constitution, or Dexterity + 6 vs. Reflex
Hit: 3d6 + Constitution modifier damage.
Special: This power uses the same ability as your *dragon breath* racial power, and it uses the same damage type you initially chose for that power.

Dragon Wings — Scion of Arkhosia Utility 12

Fully formed dragon wings protrude from your back, giving you the ability to fly.

At-Will
Move Action   **Personal**
Effect: You fly a number of squares equal to your speed. You must land at the end of this movement.

Clinging Breath — Scion of Arkhosia Attack 20

Your breath weapon clings to creatures before you, eating them alive.

Daily ✦ Varies
Standard Action   **Close** blast 3
Target: Each creature in blast
Attack: Strength, Constitution, or Dexterity + 6 vs. Reflex
Hit: 3d6 + Constitution modifier damage, and ongoing 10 damage (save ends).
Miss: Half damage, and ongoing 5 damage (save ends).
Special: This power uses the same ability as your *dragon breath* racial power, and it uses the same damage type you initially chose for that power.

Shiere Knight

"By the court of the Summer Queen, you shall pay for your transgressions!"

Prerequisite: Eladrin

Most noble eladrin, including bralani and ghaeles such as those described in the *Monster Manual*, are prominent figures in their houses, lords and ladies who have positions of authority over the lesser members of their houses. A few eladrin heroes, however, champion the cause of their race as a whole, rather than of any particular house. Though they are often anointed by house nobles, these shiere knights are free agents, beholden to no particular house and dedicated to protecting the eladrin from fomorians, spriggans, and other hostile denizens of the Feywild.

Becoming a shiere knight involves more than attaining a title. As a champion of your race, you become a living embodiment of the power of the Feywild. Your appearance is marked by a sign of the fey power within you: a faint glow that outlines your frame and burns in your eyes, an eldritch wind that constantly stirs the air around you, or some other manifestation of your otherworldly nature. You can channel this power to beguile your foes or drive them off in fear.

Shiere Knight Path Features

Blessed of the Fey (11th level): Whenever you are affected by a charm effect that a save can end, you can make a saving throw against the effect at the start of your turn. If you don't save, you can make another saving throw against the effect at the end of your turn.

Fey Leap Action (11th level): You can spend an action point to teleport 10 squares, instead of taking an extra action.

Cloaked in Magic (16th level): Whenever you teleport, you gain a +2 bonus to all defenses until the start of your next turn.

Shiere Knight Powers

Ensorcelled Mind — Shiere Knight Attack 11

You fill your foe's mind with haunting images of the Feywild's wonder and beauty, with the result that the enemy cannot bear to see you harmed.

Encounter ✦ Charm
Standard Action   **Ranged** 5
Target: One creature
Attack: Intelligence, Wisdom, or Charisma + 4 vs. Will
  Level 21: Intelligence, Wisdom, or Charisma + 6 vs. Will
Hit: Until the end of your next turn, the target can't attack you. In addition, when any creature within the target's reach hits or misses you, the target makes a melee basic attack against that creature as a free action, with a +2 bonus to the attack roll.
Special: When you gain this power, choose Intelligence, Wisdom, or Charisma as the ability you use when making attack rolls with this power.

Fey Escape — Shiere Knight Utility 12

As your foe draws near, a swirling storm of leaves spins around you and whisks you to safety.

Daily ✦ Teleportation
Immediate Interrupt   Personal
Trigger: An enemy enters a square adjacent to you
Effect: You teleport 5 squares.

Imperious Presence — Shiere Knight Attack 20

Filled with the power of the Feywild, you drive your enemies away in fear, sapping them of their strength.

Daily ✦ Fear
Standard Action   **Close** burst 2
Target: Each enemy in burst
Attack: Intelligence, Wisdom, or Charisma + 6 vs. Will
Hit: The target is weakened (save ends). The target then moves away from you at its speed as a free action.
Miss: The target is weakened until the end of your next turn, and you push the target 3 squares.
Special: When you gain this power, choose Intelligence, Wisdom, or Charisma as the ability you use when making attack rolls with this power.

STONEBLESSED

"There are secrets in the peaks, mysteries I have unraveled and embraced."

Prerequisite: Goliath

There can be no understating the kinship that goliaths share with their mountain homes. Like the mountains, goliaths stand tall despite the hardship of life amid the wind, snow, and ice of the highest crags. Most goliaths are proud merely to draw strength from their upbringing amid the towering peaks, but a rare few come to embody the spirit of the mountains.

You are such a hero, a stoneblessed goliath who has an uncommon connection to stone and earth. Rock beneath your feet emboldens you, and the elements nourish you, until you become the personification of your homeland's peaks. As a stoneblessed, you draw power from the stone itself, allowing you to transcend the bounds of your mortal form and achieve astonishing acts of strength. Your attacks strike with the weight of the mountain behind them. When you reach the pinnacle of this path, you can transform yourself into an entity of stone, crushing those who stand against you.

When you take the first step on this path, your features and form begin a slow transformation, revealing the depth of your mountain connection. Your skin gains the texture of sandstone, thickening to protect you from harm. Your eyes lose their moisture until they eventually shine like diamonds, reflecting light in a rainbow. The lithoderms that stud your shoulders and elbows transform into crystalline growths. Among goliaths, these features mark you as a true champion, a chosen hero of your kind.

STONEBLESSED PATH FEATURES

Stonehide Action (11th level): When you spend an action point to take an extra action, you also gain a +2 bonus to AC until the end of your next turn.

Unusual Reach (11th level): Your melee reach increases by 1.

Mountain Crush (16th level): Whenever you score a critical hit with a two-handed weapon, the attack deals extra damage equal to twice your Constitution modifier.

STONEBLESSED POWERS

Mountain Sweep	Stoneblessed Attack 11

You sweep your weapon in a terrible arc, slicing through your foes as if they were wheat before the scythe.

Encounter ✦ Weapon
Standard Action   Melee weapon
Target: One or two creatures
Attack: Strength vs. AC
Hit: 2[W] + Strength modifier + Constitution modifier damage.

Summit Advantage	Stoneblessed Utility 12

Focusing your awareness, you ready yourself to lash out at any enemy in reach that gives you an opening.

Encounter
Minor Action   Personal
Effect: Until the end of your next turn, you have threatening reach.

Avalanche Assault	Stoneblessed Attack 20

With the power of an avalanche, you rain blows on your enemy. The strength of the mountains lingers in your limbs while you remain in this stance.

Daily ✦ Stance, Weapon
Standard Action   Melee weapon
Target: One creature
Attack: Strength vs. Fortitude
Hit: 4[W] + Strength modifier damage.
Miss: Half damage.
Effect: You assume the stance of the avalanche. Until the stance ends, you can move through an enemy's space if that enemy is your size or smaller, and you gain a bonus to the damage rolls of your at-will attacks equal to your Constitution modifier.

TURATHI HIGHBORN

"The error of my ancestors was in dealing with evil powers they couldn't control."

Prerequisite: Tiefling

The sins of Bael Turath lie exposed in the sinister appearance of its tiefling descendants. Each pair of horns, every sinewy tail, and every set of glowing red eyes reminds the world of the perils of dealing with devils and the evils that result from such fell bargains. Many tieflings rise above the darkness clouding their souls, but a few find it far harder to divorce themselves from their sinister heritage, largely because of their familial connections to those first tieflings who forged pacts with Asmodeus and other archdevils of the Nine Hells.

As a Turathi highborn, you bear a heavier burden than your kin, for it was your ancestors who damned the tiefling race. For better or worse, you retain a stronger connection to the Nine Hells than most of your race. You loose bursts of hellfire on your enemies when enraged, and infernal power undergirds your other talents. Drawing on the lore of Bael Turath's ancient nobility, you can unhinge the minds of your foes or make them your slaves—even as you engulf them in hellfire.

TURATHI HIGHBORN PATH FEATURES

Turathi Frenzy (11th level): You gain a bonus to damage rolls against bloodied enemies equal to 1 + your Charisma modifier.

Hellfire Action (11th level): When you spend an action point to make an attack, that attack deals 2d6 extra fire damage on a hit.

Kneel before the Turathi (16th level): When you hit with an attack benefiting from your *infernal wrath* racial power, you also knock the target prone.

TURATHI HIGHBORN POWERS

Bolts of Bedevilment — Turathi Highborn Attack 11

Twin bolts of black fire leap from your hands to swirl about your enemy, tricking the foe into attacking one of its allies.

Encounter ✦ Charm, Fire
Standard Action   **Ranged** 10
Target: One creature
Attack: Charisma, Constitution, or Intelligence + 4 vs. Will
  Level 21: Charisma, Constitution, or Intelligence + 6 vs. Will
Hit: The target makes a basic attack against a creature of your choice as a free action. The target gains a +2 power bonus to the attack roll, and on a hit, its attack deals 2d6 extra fire damage.
Special: When you gain this power, choose Charisma, Constitution, or Intelligence as the ability you use when making attack rolls with this power.

Infernal Nova — Turathi Highborn Utility 12

You are wreathed in red and black flames that erupt to sear your foes when you are hit in melee.

Daily ✦ Fire, Stance
Minor Action   **Personal**
Effect: Until the stance ends, whenever you take damage from a melee attack, each enemy adjacent to you takes 5 fire damage.

Thrall of Turath — Turathi Highborn Attack 20

You wrap your foe's mind with hellfire, burning the enemy even as it follows your commands.

Daily ✦ Charm, Fire
Standard Action   **Melee** 1
Target: One creature
Attack: Charisma, Constitution, or Intelligence + 6 vs. Will
Hit: 2d6 + Constitution modifier fire damage, and the target is dominated and takes ongoing 5 fire damage (save ends both).
Miss: Half damage, and the target makes a basic attack against a creature of your choice as a free action.
Special: When you gain this power, choose Charisma, Constitution, or Intelligence as the ability you use when making attack rolls with this power.

TWILIGHT GUARDIAN

"Despoiler! Feel nature's wrath!"

Prerequisite: Elf

Among the elves, a rare few embrace the splendor of the natural world and draw power from its bountiful life in ways that others cannot begin to understand. Such elves champion nature in all its forms, placing the needs of the wilderness above their own. These heroes are called twilight guardians, for they preserve the wilderness from the encroaching darkness, safeguarding the natural world from destruction at the hands of the incautious and the malevolent alike.

Though it might seem that the twilight guardian chooses to champion the cause of nature, most twilight guardians would say that the world chose them. The world responds, they believe, to an uncommon reverence for nature, an awareness of the true power of life, and an understanding of the need for a harmonious balance to ensure the world's survival. These qualities arise most commonly among the elves, and thus the path of the twilight guardian is unique to that race.

As a twilight guardian, you evolve into a physical conduit of natural power, channeling the life force of the earth itself to better combat your enemies. The power flowing though you sharpens your senses and attunes you to your surroundings. Protecting the wilderness is your paramount concern. You are not required to safeguard a particular region, but instead to protect nature wherever you go in your travels. As long as you remain a stalwart protector, the natural world will aid you in your crusade, lending you its strength to ensure your triumph over those who would contaminate the land.

TWILIGHT GUARDIAN PATH FEATURES

Elfsight (11th level): You ignore the –2 penalty for attacking an enemy that has concealment. Also, your racial bonus to Perception checks increases to +4, and the racial bonus to Perception checks that you grant through your Group Awareness racial trait increases to +2.

Accurate Action (11th level): When you spend an action point to make an attack, you can make two attack rolls for that attack and use either result.

Twilight Walk (16th level): You ignore difficult terrain.

TWILIGHT GUARDIAN POWERS

Bonds of Life	Twilight Guardian Attack 11

Tendrils erupt from your target's body, entwining it and holding it fast.

Encounter
Standard Action   **Ranged** 5
Target: One creature
Attack: Intelligence, Wisdom, or Charisma + 4 vs. Reflex
   Level 21: Intelligence, Wisdom, or Charisma + 6 vs. Reflex
Hit: 1d10 + Wisdom modifier damage, and the target is restrained until the end of your next turn.
Special: When you gain this power, choose Intelligence, Wisdom, or Charisma as the ability you use when making attack rolls with this power.

Twilight Stealth	Twilight Guardian Utility 12

With a thought, you vanish into your surroundings.

Daily ✦ Illusion
Minor Action   **Personal**
Effect: Until the end of your next turn, you are invisible to any creature against which you have any cover or concealment.

Nature's Rage	Twilight Guardian Attack 20

The world reflects your outrage, coming to life with sudden and entangling ferocity.

Daily ✦ Zone
Standard Action   **Close** blast 3
Target: Each enemy in blast
Attack: Intelligence, Wisdom, or Charisma + 6 vs. Reflex
Hit: 2d10 + Wisdom modifier damage, and the target is restrained (save ends).
Effect: The blast creates a zone of writhing plants that lasts until the end of the encounter. Any enemy that enters the zone is restrained (save ends).
Special: When you gain this power, choose Intelligence, Wisdom, or Charisma as the ability you use when making attack rolls with this power.

CHARACTER CLASSES

YOUR CHARACTER'S class is the most important factor in determining what your character can do. Your class determines what armor and weapons you start off knowing how to use, what skills you can learn, how many hit points you have, and—most important—the class features and powers you wield. These, in turn, determine what role you're best suited for in combat encounters as well as in some noncombat encounters.

This chapter introduces eight classes to the D&D game, representing three power sources and all four character roles. The bard and the sorcerer take their place alongside other arcane classes. The avenger and the invoker expand the roster of divine classes to all four roles. The primal power source is represented here by one class for each role: barbarian, druid, shaman, and warden.

Every class dabbles in functions related to another role. Some classes have one secondary role, whereas others incline toward one of two secondary roles based on an individual character's choice of class features and powers. The role entries for the classes in this book note each class's secondary role or roles.

Here you'll find descriptions of the following eight classes, along with four new paragon paths for each one. The chapter concludes with six new epic destinies.

Avenger (page 32): A divine striker trained in secret rites to bring divine justice to the gods' foes.

Barbarian (page 48): A striker who rages with primal fury.

Bard (page 66): An arcane leader who inspires and empowers with magic song and verse.

Druid (page 82): A controller who is a master of primal magic and can take on animal forms.

Invoker (page 100): A controller who wields raw divine power, the magic the gods used to fight the primordials.

Shaman (page 118): A mystic leader who channels primal power through a spirit companion.

Sorcerer (page 136): A striker who is an open floodgate of unshaped arcane might.

Warden (page 152): A staunch defender who channels the power of earth and root.

WILLIAM O'CONNOR

"Everything my god needs to say to you can be said with my weapon."

CLASS TRAITS

Role: Striker. Your oaths bring divine wrath upon the enemies of your god. With methodical devastation, you eliminate one foe at a time. You lean toward controller as a secondary role.

Power Source: Divine. You practice mysteries forgotten or forbidden by most religious orders, yet the power you wield is a gift from your god.

Key Abilities: Wisdom, Dexterity, Intelligence

Armor Proficiencies: Cloth
Weapon Proficiencies: Simple melee, military melee, simple ranged
Implements: Holy symbols
Bonus to Defense: +1 Fortitude, +1 Reflex, +1 Will

Hit Points at 1st Level: 14 + Constitution score
Hit Points per Level Gained: 6
Healing Surges per Day: 7 + Constitution modifier

Trained Skills: Religion. From the class skills list below, choose three more trained skills at 1st level.
Class Skills: Acrobatics (Dex), Athletics (Str), Endurance (Con), Heal (Wis), Intimidate (Cha), Perception (Wis), Religion (Int), Stealth (Dex), Streetwise (Cha)

Class Features: Armor of Faith, Avenger's Censure, Channel Divinity, *oath of enmity*

In secret temples far from bustling cities and priestly hierarchies, orders of esoteric warriors train their initiates in ancient traditions now forgotten or forbidden by most religious organizations. The champions of these orders are avengers—deadly weapons in the hands of their gods, imbued with divine power through secret rites of initiation. In battle, avengers swear to execute divine vengeance, entering a mental state that gives them unerring focus on a single enemy.

As an avenger, you were trained in a monastery, initiated through secret rites, and imbued with the power to smite your god's foes. You might be a disciple of Ioun, sworn to hunt and exterminate the minions of Vecna until you one day face the Maimed God. You could be an agent of the Raven Queen, bringing death to those who would defy your mistress. Or perhaps you serve Bahamut as an agent of justice, bringing ruin to tyrants and oppressors. The organizations devoted to your god might view you as a heretic or a hero, but you answer only to your god and to the vows you swore upon your initiation as an avenger.

Where will those vows lead you? One thing is certain: Doing the will of your god is never easy and never free of peril.

WILLIAM O'CONNOR

Avenger Class Features

Avengers have the following class features.

Armor of Faith

The favor of your deity wards you from harm. While you are neither wearing heavy armor nor using a shield, you gain a +3 bonus to AC.

Avenger's Censure

As an avenger, you train your mind, body, and soul toward one purpose: destroying the enemies of your faith. To that end, you gain divine aid in pursuing a single target, though the way you eliminate that enemy varies. Do you pin your foe down and keep other enemies away, or do you pursue your foe across the field of battle?

Choose one of these options. Your choice provides bonuses to certain avenger powers, as detailed in those powers.

Censure of Pursuit: If your *oath of enmity* target moves away from you willingly, you gain a bonus to damage rolls against the target equal to 2 + your Dexterity modifier until the end of your next turn. The bonus increases to 4 + your Dexterity modifier at 11th level and 6 + your Dexterity modifier at 21st level.

Censure of Retribution: When any enemy other than your *oath of enmity* target hits you, you gain a bonus to damage rolls against your *oath of enmity* target equal to your Intelligence modifier until the end of your next turn. This bonus is cumulative.

Channel Divinity

Once per encounter, you can use a Channel Divinity power. You start with two Channel Divinity powers: *abjure undead* and *divine guidance*. You can gain additional Channel Divinity powers by taking divinity feats.

Oath of Enmity

Your god gives you the power to strike down your chosen prey. You gain the *oath of enmity* power.

Avengers and Deities

Choice of Deity: Each avenger chooses a single deity from the pantheon and gives his or her exclusive service to that deity (see "Deities," *Player's Handbook*, page 20). Most avengers are trained at secret temples or monasteries where they learn esoteric doctrines and hidden legends that often suggest the superiority of their deity over all others.

A ceremony of investiture at your home temple, which culminated in an experience that seemed like a manifestation of your deity, granted you the ability to wield your divine powers. Your investiture complete, you left your temple to travel the world in the service of your deity and your order—or perhaps you fled your order and now seek a way to serve your god beyond the order's strictures. Whatever relationship you have with your order, nothing can remove the spark of divine power within you. What you do with that power is yours to decide.

Choice of Alignment: You must choose an alignment compatible with the deity you serve. Good avengers serve good deities, lawful good avengers serve lawful good deities, and so on. However, if you are unaligned, you can serve any deity, for avengers' work often leads to a certain level of disillusionment and detachment that prompts them to be unaligned.

Implements

Like clerics and paladins, avengers use holy symbols to help channel and direct their divine powers. When they make their own holy symbols, the symbols are often different in some detail from the symbols used by other characters, yet avengers can use the same holy symbols used by clerics and paladins.

When you wear or hold a magic holy symbol, you can add its enhancement bonus to the attack rolls and the damage rolls of avenger powers and avenger paragon path powers that have the implement keyword. Without a holy symbol, you can still use these powers.

Creating an Avenger

The three key ability scores for an avenger are Wisdom, Dexterity, and Intelligence. Avengers typically choose feats, skills, and powers to complement the ability score related to their choice of Divine Censure.

Avenger Overview

Characteristics: Swinging a melee weapon in combat, you wield devastating divine power against your foes. You have a secondary assortment of ranged and close implement powers that let you draw your foes closer to you, teleport near them, or scorch them with divine wrath from afar.

Religion: An avenger might serve any deity, but an avenger is more likely to worship an unaligned deity than a god of good or lawful good. Avengers of Ioun are among the most common, fighting a war of knowledge against the servants of Vecna. Unaligned avengers often revere the Raven Queen, Erathis, or Sehanine, and evil avengers often serve Asmodeus, Lolth, Tiamat, or Zehir.

Races: Elves and razorclaw shifters make excellent pursuing avengers, and devas excel as isolating avengers. Many avengers are human, because most of the hidden monasteries that produce avengers are of human origin.

ISOLATING AVENGER

After you swear an *oath of enmity*, you keep your enemy beside you and drive other foes away. Your powers help you isolate one creature at a time and bring it down quickly and let you take vengeance when that creature's allies get past your defenses. Your attacks use Wisdom, so it should be your best ability score. Choose Intelligence for your second-best score, reflecting your keen tactical awareness. Select powers that help you sequester your foe from its allies.

Suggested Class Feature: Censure of Retribution
Suggested Feat: Toughness
Suggested Skills: Athletics, Intimidate, Religion, Streetwise
Suggested At-Will Powers: *bond of retribution, overwhelming strike*
Suggested Encounter Power: *avenging echo*
Suggested Daily Power: *temple of light*

PURSUING AVENGER

Once you swear an *oath of enmity* against an enemy, you pursue that creature wherever it goes. As much as it might try to escape your wrath, your powers let you follow it and punish it for trying to flee. Make Wisdom your highest ability score, and make Dexterity your second-best score to help you nimbly pursue your foe. Select powers that prevent your foe from moving away from you or that let you shift or teleport to the foe's side.

Suggested Class Feature: Censure of Pursuit
Suggested Feat: Invigorating Pursuit
Suggested Skills: Acrobatics, Perception, Religion, Stealth
Suggested At-Will Powers: *bond of pursuit, radiant vengeance*
Suggested Encounter Power: *angelic alacrity*
Suggested Daily Power: *oath of the final duel*

AVENGER POWERS

Your avenger powers are called prayers. Many avengers describe the experience of calling on their gods' powers in combat as a state in which prayers are uttered almost instinctively, as if their gods were controlling their actions.

CLASS FEATURES

Each avenger has the power *oath of enmity* and the Channel Divinity powers *abjure undead* and *divine guidance*.

Oath of Enmity — Avenger Feature

You focus your wrath on a single foe, giving your attacks against it extraordinary accuracy.

Encounter (Special) ✦ Divine
Minor Action   Close burst 10
Target: One enemy you can see in burst
Effect: When you make a melee attack against the target and the target is the only enemy adjacent to you, you make two attack rolls and use either result. This effect lasts until the end of the encounter or until the target drops to 0 hit points, at which point you regain the use of this power.

   If another effect lets you roll twice and use the higher result when making an attack roll, this power has no effect on that attack. If an effect forces you to roll twice and use the lower result when making an attack roll, this power has no effect on that attack either.

   If an effect lets you reroll an attack roll and you rolled twice because of this power, you reroll both dice.

Channel Divinity: Abjure Undead — Avenger Feature

You send a brilliant ray of radiant power at an undead foe, compelling it to stagger toward you.

Encounter ✦ Divine, Implement, Radiant
Standard Action   Close burst 5
Target: One undead creature in burst
Attack: Wisdom vs. Will
Hit: 3d10 + Wisdom modifier radiant damage, and you pull the target a number of squares equal to 1 + your Wisdom modifier. The target is also immobilized until the end of your next turn.
   Level 5: 4d10 + Wisdom modifier damage.
   Level 11: 5d10 + Wisdom modifier damage.
   Level 15: 6d10 + Wisdom modifier damage.
   Level 21: 7d10 + Wisdom modifier damage.
   Level 25: 8d10 + Wisdom modifier damage.
Miss: Half damage, and you pull the target 1 square.

Channel Divinity: Divine Guidance — Avenger Feature

You lend your deity's guidance to an ally's attack against your foe.

Encounter ✦ Divine
Immediate Interrupt   Close burst 10
Trigger: An ally within 10 squares of you makes an attack roll against your *oath of enmity* target
Target: The triggering ally
Effect: The target makes a second attack roll and uses either result.

LEVEL 1 AT-WILL PRAYERS

Bond of Pursuit — Avenger Attack 1

With your attack, you utter a promise to follow your enemy if it tries to escape.

At-Will ✦ Divine, Weapon
Standard Action — **Melee** weapon
Target: One creature
Attack: Wisdom vs. AC
Hit: 1[W] + Wisdom modifier damage. If the target doesn't end its next turn adjacent to you, you can shift a number of squares equal to 1 + your Dexterity modifier as a free action, and you must end that shift closer to the target.
Level 21: 2[W] + Wisdom modifier damage.

Bond of Retribution — Avenger Attack 1

Whirling divine energy promises swift retribution if one of your foe's companions attacks you.

At-Will ✦ Divine, Radiant, Weapon
Standard Action — **Melee** weapon
Target: One creature
Attack: Wisdom vs. AC
Hit: 1[W] + Wisdom modifier damage. The first time an enemy other than the target hits or misses you before the end of your next turn, the target takes radiant damage equal to your Intelligence modifier.
Level 21: 2[W] + Wisdom modifier damage.

Overwhelming Strike — Avenger Attack 1

As you attack, you maneuver around your foe, forcing it to move with you.

At-Will ✦ Divine, Weapon
Standard Action — **Melee** weapon
Target: One creature
Attack: Wisdom vs. AC
Hit: 1[W] + Wisdom modifier damage. You shift 1 square and slide the target 1 square into the space you occupied.
Level 21: 2[W] + Wisdom modifier damage.

Radiant Vengeance — Avenger Attack 1

Calling on the power of your deity, you transfer the pain of your wounds to a foe and regain some resilience.

At-Will ✦ Divine, Implement, Radiant
Standard Action — **Ranged** 10
Target: One creature
Attack: Wisdom vs. Reflex
Hit: 1d8 + Wisdom modifier radiant damage, and you gain temporary hit points equal to your Wisdom modifier.
Level 21: 2d8 + Wisdom modifier damage.

LEVEL 1 ENCOUNTER PRAYERS

Angelic Alacrity — Avenger Attack 1

You focus divine energy through your body to gain uncanny speed as you make your attack.

Encounter ✦ Divine, Weapon
Standard Action — **Melee** weapon
Effect: Before the attack, you shift 2 squares.
  Censure of Pursuit: The number of squares you shift equals 1 + your Dexterity modifier.
Target: One creature
Attack: Wisdom vs. AC
Hit: 2[W] + Wisdom modifier damage.

Avenging Echo — Avenger Attack 1

Your weapon sweeps in a deadly arc, leaving in its wake swirling radiant energy that keeps your foes at bay.

Encounter ✦ Divine, Radiant, Weapon
Standard Action — **Melee** weapon
Target: One creature
Attack: Wisdom vs. AC
Hit: 1[W] + Wisdom modifier damage. Until the end of your next turn, any enemy that ends its turn adjacent to you or that hits or misses you takes 5 radiant damage.
  Censure of Retribution: The radiant damage equals 5 + your Intelligence modifier.

Shared Madness — Avenger Attack 1

The wrath of your god sears the mind of one foe and echoes to assault another enemy as well.

Encounter ✦ Divine, Implement, Psychic
Standard Action — **Ranged** 10
Target: One creature
Attack: Wisdom vs. Will
Hit: 1d10 + Wisdom modifier psychic damage, and a second creature you can see takes the same damage.

Whirlwind Charge — Avenger Attack 1

As you charge your foe, divine light surrounds you in a protective nimbus, then erupts at your foe.

Encounter ✦ Divine, Weapon
Standard Action — **Melee** weapon
Target: One creature
Attack: Wisdom vs. AC
Hit: 2[W] + Wisdom modifier damage.
Special: When charging, you can use this power in place of a melee basic attack. If you charge, you gain a +4 bonus to AC against opportunity attacks you provoke while moving to the target.

LEVEL 1 DAILY PRAYERS

Aspect of Might — Avenger Attack 1

You strike a crippling blow against your foe, and divine power bolsters you.

Daily ✦ Divine, Weapon
Standard Action   **Melee** weapon
Target: One creature
Attack: Wisdom vs. AC
Hit: 3[W] + Wisdom modifier damage.
Miss: Half damage.
Effect: Until the end of the encounter, you gain a +5 power bonus to Athletics checks, a +2 power bonus to speed, and a +2 power bonus to the damage rolls of melee attacks.

Oath of the Final Duel — Avenger Attack 1

You swear an oath that you will slay the foe before you. As long as you work to fulfill this oath, that foe cannot escape.

Daily ✦ Divine, Teleportation, Weapon
Standard Action   **Melee** weapon
Target: One creature
Attack: Wisdom vs. AC
Hit: 2[W] + Wisdom modifier damage.
Miss: Half damage.
Effect: Until the end of the encounter, if the target is more than 3 squares away from you at the start of your turn, you can teleport to a space within 3 squares of it as a minor action. This effect ends if you end your turn more than 3 squares away from the target.

Renewing Strike — Avenger Attack 1

You draw on your deity's power to smite your foe with divine lightning and to heal your injuries.

Daily ✦ Divine, Healing, Implement, Lightning
Standard Action   **Ranged** 10
Target: One creature
Attack: Wisdom vs. Reflex
Hit: 2d10 + Wisdom modifier lightning damage.
Miss: Half damage.
Effect: You can spend a healing surge.

Temple of Light — Avenger Attack 1

Your weapon strike creates a field of searing energy around an enemy. The energy burns any foe you hit that is within the field.

Daily ✦ Divine, Radiant, Weapon, Zone
Standard Action   **Melee** weapon
Target: One creature
Attack: Wisdom vs. AC
Hit: 2[W] + Wisdom modifier radiant damage.
Effect: The attack creates a zone of radiant energy in a burst 2 centered on the target. The zone lasts until the end of the encounter. When the target moves, the zone moves with it, remaining centered on it. Whenever you hit a creature that is within the zone, that attack deals 1d6 extra radiant damage.

LEVEL 2 UTILITY PRAYERS

Blessing of Vengeance — Avenger Utility 2

With the death of your foe, your god grants you a boon.

Daily ✦ Divine
Free Action   **Personal**
Trigger: Your *oath of enmity* target drops to 0 hit points
Effect: You gain temporary hit points equal to your healing surge value.

Distracting Flare — Avenger Utility 2

Divine light surrounds you, providing a distraction while you slip away unseen.

Encounter ✦ Divine
Move Action   **Personal**
Effect: You become invisible and move your speed. You are invisible until the end of the movement.

Refocus Enmity — Avenger Utility 2

After searching your soul, you realize who your true foe is and swear an oath against it.

Encounter ✦ Divine
Minor Action   **Close** burst 10
Target: One creature you can see in burst
Effect: The target becomes the target of your *oath of enmity*, replacing the current target.

Resonant Escape — Avenger Utility 2

A quick prayer as you dodge calls forth divine power, which carries you a short distance away.

Encounter ✦ Divine, Teleportation
Immediate Reaction   **Personal**
Trigger: An enemy hits or misses you with a melee attack
Effect: You teleport 3 squares.

LEVEL 3 ENCOUNTER PRAYERS

Deflecting Thunder — Avenger Attack 3

A thunderclap batters your foe as your weapon connects, and another thunderclap deflects the next attack against you, turning the attack toward a nearby foe.

Encounter ✦ Divine, Thunder, Weapon
Standard Action   **Melee** weapon
Target: One creature
Attack: Wisdom vs. AC
Hit: 1[W] + Wisdom modifier thunder damage. Until the end of your next turn, the next melee or ranged attack against you instead targets an enemy adjacent to you other than the attacker.

Enmity's Reach — Avenger Attack 3

A crash of thunder behind your foe shoves it closer to your waiting weapon and slows that foe's escape.

Encounter ✦ Divine, Implement, Thunder
Standard Action   **Close** burst 5
Target: One creature in burst
Attack: Wisdom vs. Fortitude
Hit: 1d10 + Wisdom modifier thunder damage, and you pull the target 2 squares. The target is slowed until the end of your next turn.

Halo of Fire
Avenger Attack 3

A circle of flame erupts around your foe, harming any other enemy that moves near the creature.

Encounter ✦ Divine, Fire, Weapon
Standard Action   Melee weapon
Target: One creature
Attack: Wisdom vs. AC
Hit: 2[W] + Wisdom modifier fire damage. Until the end of your next turn, any enemy that ends its turn adjacent to the target takes 5 fire damage.
  Censure of Retribution: The fire damage equals 5 + your Intelligence modifier.

Sequestering Strike
Avenger Attack 3

Your attack slices into your foe and through the fabric of space, hurtling both you and that foe a short distance away.

Encounter ✦ Divine, Teleportation, Weapon
Standard Action   Melee weapon
Target: One creature
Attack: Wisdom vs. AC
Hit: 2[W] + Wisdom modifier damage, and you teleport the target 2 squares. You then teleport to a space adjacent to the target.
  Censure of Pursuit: The number of squares you teleport the target equals 1 + your Dexterity modifier.

LEVEL 5 DAILY PRAYERS

Bond of Foresight
Avenger Attack 5

A bond of fate links you to your enemy, giving you the ability to foresee its every move. Whenever it moves or attacks you, you're ready.

Daily ✦ Divine, Weapon
Standard Action   Melee weapon
Target: One creature
Attack: Wisdom vs. AC
Hit: 2[W] + Wisdom modifier damage.
Miss: Half damage.
Effect: When the target hits or misses you or shifts, the target provokes an opportunity attack from you (save ends).

Dawn Fire Sigil
Avenger Attack 5

A glowing mark of divine radiance prevents your foe from hiding from you and increases the accuracy of your attacks.

Daily ✦ Divine, Radiant, Weapon
Standard Action   Melee weapon
Target: One creature
Attack: Wisdom vs. AC
Hit: 2[W] + Wisdom modifier radiant damage.
Miss: Half damage.
Effect: The target doesn't benefit from cover or concealment against your attacks (save ends). The target can still benefit from superior cover or total concealment against your attacks. Until the end of the encounter, you gain a +1 bonus to attack rolls against the target.

Executioner's Cloak
Avenger Attack 5

With a stroke of your weapon, you cause shadows to flow over your foe's eyes, concealing you as you close in for the kill.

Daily ✦ Divine, Illusion, Weapon
Standard Action   Melee weapon
Target: One creature
Attack: Wisdom vs. AC
Hit: 2[W] + Wisdom modifier damage, and you are invisible to the target (save ends).
  Aftereffect: You are invisible to the target until the end of your next turn.
Miss: Half damage, and you are invisible to the target until the end of your next turn.

Oath of Consuming Light
Avenger Attack 5

You place a burning mark of divine radiance on your foe as you swear an oath to destroy this creature. With every wound you inflict on the creature, the burning mark erupts in searing light.

Daily ✦ Divine, Implement, Radiant
Standard Action   Ranged 10
Target: One creature
Attack: Wisdom vs. Reflex
Hit: 2d10 + Wisdom radiant damage. Whenever you hit the target with a divine power, the target takes 1d6 extra radiant damage (save ends).
  Aftereffect: Whenever you hit the target with a divine power, the target takes 1d4 extra radiant damage (save ends).
Miss: Half damage. Whenever you hit the target with a divine power, the target takes 1d4 extra radiant damage (save ends).

LEVEL 6 UTILITY PRAYERS

Aspect of Agility
Avenger Utility 6

You move with the speed of the west wind, leaving your foes with little chance of striking you.

Encounter ✦ Divine
Move Action   Personal
Effect: You shift 5 squares, and you gain a +2 bonus to AC and Reflex until the end of your next turn.

Oath of Enduring Wrath
Avenger Utility 6

You swear to defeat your enemies, and your god grants you the perseverance to overcome any hindrance.

Daily ✦ Divine
Minor Action   Personal
Effect: You gain a +2 power bonus to saving throws until the end of the encounter.

Oath of the Relentless Hunter
Avenger Utility 6

You touch an enemy and swear an oath to hunt it to the end of the world. With this oath, you can always find your foe.

Daily ✦ Divine
Minor Action   Melee touch
Target: One creature
Effect: Until you use this power on a different target, you can take a standard action to determine the distance and the direction to the target. The distance and the direction are based on a straight line between you and the target, ignoring any barriers. If the target is on a different plane from you, you know which plane but gain no other information.

Wrath of the Divine
Avenger Utility 6

Suffering a foe's lucky attack, you call on your god to visit your pain upon the one you have sworn to kill.

Daily ✦ Divine, Radiant
Immediate Reaction   Close burst 10
Trigger: An enemy scores a critical hit against you
Target: Your *oath of enmity* target in burst
Effect: The target takes radiant damage equal to the critical hit's damage.

LEVEL 7 ENCOUNTER PRAYERS

Avenging Winds
Avenger Attack 7

You whisper a prayer, calling a gust of wind that slams your foe and halts its movement if it tries to escape.

Encounter ✦ Divine, Implement
Standard Action   Ranged 10
Target: One creature
Attack: Wisdom vs. Reflex
Hit: 2d8 + Wisdom modifier damage. Until the end of your next turn, if the target moves, you can slide it 2 squares as an immediate reaction.

Blade Step
Avenger Attack 7

As you strike one foe, you teleport next to another.

Encounter ✦ Divine, Teleportation, Weapon
Standard Action   Melee weapon
Target: One creature
Attack: Wisdom vs. AC
Hit: 2[W] + Wisdom modifier damage, and you teleport 10 squares to a space that must be adjacent to an enemy.

Inexorable Pursuit
Avenger Attack 7

Shrouded in divine mist, you stride through any obstacle to reach your foe, then smite it with the wrath of your god.

Encounter ✦ Divine, Weapon
Standard Action   Melee weapon
Effect: Before the attack, you gain phasing until the end of your turn, and you shift 3 squares.
    Censure of Pursuit: The number of squares you shift equals 2 + your Dexterity modifier.
Target: One creature
Attack: Wisdom vs. AC
Hit: 2[W] + Wisdom modifier damage.

Splinter the Formation
Avenger Attack 7

You strike your foe and, with a wave of astral energy, you sweep away other enemies, isolating your prey.

Encounter ✦ Divine, Teleportation, Weapon
Standard Action   Melee weapon
Target: One creature
Attack: Wisdom vs. AC
Hit: 1[W] + Wisdom modifier damage, and you teleport each enemy within 2 squares of the target 2 squares.
    Censure of Retribution: The number of squares you teleport each enemy equals 1 + your Intelligence modifier.

LEVEL 9 DAILY PRAYERS

Aspect of Speed
Avenger Attack 9

You accelerate past your foes, making an attack and then darting away.

Daily ✦ Divine, Weapon
Standard Action   Melee weapon
Effect: Before and after the attack, you shift 5 squares.
Target: One creature
Attack: Wisdom vs. AC
Hit: 2[W] + Wisdom modifier damage.
Miss: Half damage.

Enduring Strike
Avenger Attack 9

As you strike at your foe, you call on your god to cast away an effect that plagues you.

Daily ✦ Divine, Weapon
Standard Action   Melee weapon
Target: One creature
Attack: Wisdom vs. AC
Hit: 3[W] + Wisdom modifier damage, and you make a saving throw with a +5 bonus.
Miss: Half damage, and you make a saving throw.

Oath of Pursuit
Avenger Attack 9

As you attack your foe, you swear an oath of relentless pursuit against it. Although your foe might try to escape, it can never evade you.

Daily ✦ Divine, Weapon
Standard Action   Melee weapon
Target: One creature
Attack: Wisdom vs. AC
Hit: 2[W] + Wisdom modifier damage.
Miss: Half damage.
Effect: Until the end of the encounter, if the target moves on its turn, you can shift 3 squares at the end of the target's turn as an opportunity action. You must end this movement closer to the target.

Temple of Shadow
Avenger Attack 9

You channel dark energy around your foe, creating a cloud of shadows that helps conceal you from your enemies.

Daily ✦ Divine, Weapon, Zone
Standard Action   Melee weapon
Target: One creature
Attack: Wisdom vs. AC
Hit: 2[W] + Wisdom modifier damage.
Miss: Half damage.
Effect: The attack creates a zone of swirling shadows in a burst 1 centered on the target. The zone lasts until the end of the encounter. When the target moves, the zone moves with it, remaining centered on it. While you are within the zone, you gain concealment and can make Stealth checks to become hidden. When you leave the zone, you have concealment until the end of your turn.

Level 10 Utility Prayers

Avenger's Readiness — Avenger Utility 10

As your opponents prepare to strike, you make a sudden move to spoil their plans.

Daily ✦ Divine
No Action — **Personal**
Trigger: You roll initiative at the beginning of an encounter
Effect: You gain a +5 power bonus to the initiative check. You shift 3 squares as a free action when the first creature in the initiative order starts its turn, even if you're surprised.

Channel Endurance — Avenger Utility 10

You focus your inner strength and tap into your god's power to forestall an injury.

Encounter ✦ Divine
Minor Action — **Personal**
Effect: You gain resist 5 to all damage until the end of your next turn.

Eye of Justice — Avenger Utility 10

Your eyes glow with divine energy, allowing you to spot foes no matter how well they hide.

Encounter ✦ Divine
Minor Action — **Personal**
Effect: Until the end of your next turn, you can see invisible creatures within 5 squares of you.

River of Life — Avenger Utility 10

Divine power flows through you, allowing you to shrug off injury after injury.

Daily ✦ Divine, Healing
Minor Action — **Personal**
Effect: You gain regeneration 5 until the end of the encounter.

Level 13 Encounter Prayers

Cloud of Souls — Avenger Attack 13

As you swing your weapon, you speak a prayer for your foe's innocent victims and summon them to torment your enemies.

Encounter ✦ Divine, Psychic, Weapon, Zone
Standard Action — **Melee** weapon
Target: One creature
Attack: Wisdom vs. Will
Hit: 2[W] + Wisdom modifier psychic damage. The attack creates a zone of shrieking souls in a close burst 1. The zone lasts until the end of your next turn or until you dismiss it as a minor action. Any enemy that enters the zone is dazed until the end of your next turn.
Censure of Retribution: Until the end of your next turn, you gain a bonus to attack rolls against the target equal to one-half your Intelligence modifier.

Light of the Avenging Sun — Avenger Attack 13

As your attack hits home, your become wrapped in blinding light, hindering a foe's ability to strike you.

Encounter ✦ Divine, Radiant, Weapon
Standard Action — **Melee** weapon
Target: One creature
Attack: Wisdom vs. AC
Hit: 2[W] + Wisdom modifier radiant damage, and the target takes a –4 penalty to attack rolls against you until the end of your next turn.

Sequestering Word — Avenger Attack 13

A word of divine power thunders from your mouth, smiting your foe and transporting it to a place where you can face it alone.

Encounter ✦ Divine, Implement, Teleportation, Thunder
Standard Action — **Ranged** 10
Target: One creature
Attack: Wisdom vs. Will
Hit: 2d8 + Wisdom modifier thunder damage, and you teleport the target 5 squares. You then teleport to a space adjacent to the target.
Censure of Pursuit: Until the end of your next turn, any enemy that ends its turn adjacent to you takes thunder damage equal to 5 + your Dexterity modifier.

Whirling Blades — Avenger Attack 13

When you have your foe alone, it becomes an easy target for your vicious cuts and lunges.

Encounter ✦ Divine, Weapon
Standard Action — **Melee** weapon
Target: One creature
Attack: Wisdom vs. AC. You gain a +2 bonus to the attack roll if no enemy is adjacent to the target.
Hit: 3[W] + Wisdom modifier damage. The attack deals 5 extra damage if no enemy is adjacent to the target.

Level 15 Daily Prayers

Aspect of Fury — Avenger Attack 15

You channel the anger of your god, creating a cloud of whirling death around you.

Daily ✦ Divine, Weapon
Standard Action — **Melee** weapon
Target: One creature
Attack: Wisdom vs. AC
Hit: 3[W] + Wisdom modifier damage.
Miss: Half damage.
Effect: Until the end of the encounter, any enemy that starts its turn adjacent to you or that hits or misses you with a melee attack takes 5 damage.

Bond of the Sacred Duel
Avenger Attack 15

In your single-minded devotion to destroying your chosen foe, you strike at that foe and form a psychic bond with it that causes it to suffer if its allies attack you.

Daily ✦ Divine, Psychic, Weapon
Standard Action   **Melee** weapon
Target: One creature
Attack: Wisdom vs. Will
Hit: 2[W] + Wisdom modifier psychic damage.
Miss: Half damage.
Effect: Until the end of the encounter or until you attack anyone other than the target, the target takes 5 psychic damage whenever another enemy hits you.

Oath of Divine Lightning
Avenger Attack 15

Lightning erupts around your weapon as you attack your foe, then lingers, promising punishment if your enemy remains in one place for too long.

Daily ✦ Divine, Lightning, Weapon
Standard Action   **Melee** weapon
Target: One creature
Attack: Wisdom vs. AC
Hit: 3[W] + Wisdom modifier lightning damage. The target takes 5 lightning damage at the end of its turn if it doesn't move at least 1 square during its turn (save ends). Shifting doesn't count toward this movement.
Miss: Half damage, and the target takes 5 lightning damage at the end of its next turn if it doesn't move at least 1 square during that turn. Shifting doesn't count toward this movement.

Sigil of Carceri
Avenger Attack 15

You mark your enemy with the baleful red sigil of Carceri, the prison realm of the gods. Spectral chains surround your foe, holding it in place and shielding your allies from its attacks.

Daily ✦ Divine, Force, Implement
Standard Action   **Ranged** 10
Target: One creature
Attack: Wisdom vs. Fortitude
Hit: 2d10 + Wisdom modifier force damage. The target is immobilized, and its attacks against creatures more than 5 squares away from it automatically miss (save ends both).
Miss: Half damage. Until the end of your next turn, the target is immobilized, and its attacks against creatures more than 5 squares away from it automatically miss.

LEVEL 16 UTILITY PRAYERS

Astral Cloak
Avenger Utility 16

With a glimmer of silvery mist, you fade from view for a brief time.

Encounter ✦ Divine, Illusion
Minor Action   **Personal**
Effect: You become invisible until the end of your turn.

Bulwark of Defiance
Avenger Utility 16

You push aside the pain of your foe's attacks, allowing you to act without hindrance for a moment.

Encounter ✦ Divine
No Action   **Personal**
Trigger: You fail a saving throw other than a death saving throw
Effect: Until the end of your next turn, the effect you failed the saving throw against doesn't affect you, but you make saving throws against it as normal.

Vengeful Revenant
Avenger Utility 16

Even the grip of death cannot keep you down. With hidden strength, you muster the energy to rise.

Daily ✦ Divine, Healing
No Action   **Personal**
Trigger: You fail a death saving throw
Effect: You succeed on the death saving throw and spend a healing surge. You gain a +5 power bonus to all defenses until the end of your next turn.

Winds of the Astral Sea
Avenger Utility 16

Silvery mist shimmers around you, and you disappear, then reappear a short distance away.

Encounter ✦ Divine, Teleportation
Move Action   **Personal**
Effect: You teleport 4 squares.

LEVEL 17 ENCOUNTER PRAYERS

Astral Fury
Avenger Attack 17

You send your foes tumbling through the Astral Sea, teleporting them a short distance and leaving them disoriented.

Encounter ✦ Divine, Implement, Psychic, Teleportation
Standard Action   **Ranged** 10
Target: One or two creatures
Attack: Wisdom vs. Will
Hit: 2d6 + Wisdom modifier psychic damage, and you teleport the target 3 squares. The target is immobilized until the end of your next turn.

Ready the Final Blow
Avenger Attack 17

Your attack leaves your foe frozen in place, less able to avoid your next assault.

Encounter ✦ Divine, Weapon
Standard Action   **Melee** weapon
Target: One creature
Attack: Wisdom vs. AC
Hit: 2[W] + Wisdom modifier damage, and the target is immobilized until the end of your next turn. You gain a +2 bonus to your next attack roll against the target before the end of your next turn.
     Censure of Pursuit: The bonus to the attack roll equals 2 + your Dexterity modifier.

Spectral Charge — Avenger Attack 17

As you move to engage your enemy, part of you leaves the physical world momentarily.

Encounter ✦ Divine, Weapon
Standard Action   Melee weapon
Effect: Before the attack, you become insubstantial until the end of your next turn.
Target: One creature
Attack: Wisdom vs. AC
Hit: 2[W] + Wisdom modifier damage.
Special: When charging, you can use this power in place of a melee basic attack. If you charge, you become insubstantial when you begin the charge.

Warding Blade — Avenger Attack 17

Your weapon cracks with thunder as it slams into your foe, knocking any nearby enemies away. If any other foes draw too close, your thunder-infused weapon is ready to punish them.

Encounter ✦ Divine, Thunder, Weapon
Standard Action   Melee weapon
Target: One creature
Attack: Wisdom vs. AC
Hit: 2[W] + Wisdom modifier thunder damage, and you push any enemy within 2 squares of you, other than the target, 2 squares. Until the end of your next turn, if any enemy other than the target enters a square adjacent to you or hits or misses you from a square within your reach, you can make a melee basic attack against that enemy as an opportunity action.
Censure of Retribution: You gain a power bonus to the attack roll of the melee basic attack equal to your Intelligence modifier.

LEVEL 19 DAILY PRAYERS

Aspect of Awe — Avenger Attack 19

Cloaking yourself in a divine glamor, you assault your foe's mind and compel the creature to approach you.

Daily ✦ Charm, Divine, Implement, Psychic
Standard Action   Close burst 5
Target: One creature in burst
Attack: Wisdom vs. Will
Hit: 4d8 + Wisdom modifier psychic damage, and you pull the target 3 squares. At the start of each of your turns, you pull the target 3 squares (save ends).
Miss: Half damage, and you pull the target 2 squares. At the start of your next turn, you pull the target 3 squares.

Oath of the Inevitable Blade — Avenger Attack 19

You swear that your blade shall taste your foe's blood, and even if your attack fails to draw blood, you are assured of a later success.

Daily ✦ Divine, Weapon
Standard Action   Melee weapon
Target: One creature
Attack: Wisdom vs. AC
Hit: 5[W] + Wisdom modifier damage.
Miss: Half damage. You gain a +5 power bonus to your next damage roll against the target before the end of the encounter, unless you attack another creature first.

Temple of Respite — Avenger Attack 19

Radiant power sears and slows your foe and forms a divine pattern that bolsters your defenses and hinders your enemies' movement.

Daily ✦ Divine, Radiant, Weapon, Zone
Standard Action   Melee weapon
Target: One creature
Attack: Wisdom vs. AC
Hit: 3[W] + Wisdom modifier radiant damage, and the target is slowed (save ends).
Miss: Half damage, and the target is slowed until the end of your next turn.
Effect: The attack creates a zone of radiance in a close burst 1. The zone lasts until the end of the encounter. While you are within the zone, you gain a +2 bonus to all defenses. The zone is difficult terrain to enemies.

Vengeful Recovery — Avenger Attack 19

You visit the pain of your wounds upon your foe as you draw strength and health from your god.

Daily ✦ Divine, Healing, Weapon
Standard Action   Melee weapon
Target: One creature
Attack: Wisdom vs. AC
Hit: 3[W] + Wisdom modifier damage, and the target is dazed (save ends). You regain hit points as if you had spent a healing surge.
Miss: Half damage, and the target is dazed until the end of your next turn. You can spend a healing surge.

LEVEL 22 UTILITY PRAYERS

Ghostly Vengeance — Avenger Utility 22

You slip between this world and the Astral Sea, allowing you to move through objects and protecting you from attacks.

Daily ✦ Divine
Minor Action   Personal
Effect: Until the end of the encounter, you gain phasing, and you take half damage from opportunity attacks.

Indomitable Resolve — Avenger Utility 22

The power of the gods sustains you, allowing you to ignore an injury.

Daily ✦ Divine
Immediate Interrupt   Personal
Trigger: You take damage
Effect: The damage is reduced to 0.

Oath of the Final Strike — Avenger Utility 22

Nothing can prevent you from completing the task set before you by the gods, not even death.

Daily ✦ Divine
Immediate Interrupt   Personal
Trigger: An attack reduces you to 0 hit points or fewer and doesn't kill you
Effect: You are dying but don't fall unconscious. Until the end of your next turn, you don't take any damage after the triggering attack, and you gain a +4 bonus to attack rolls. At the end of your next turn, you fall unconscious if you are still dying.

Twin Step
Avenger Utility 22

You appear next to a foe, launch a devastating assault, and then disappear beyond its reach.

Encounter ✦ Divine
Move Action   **Personal**
Effect: You teleport 8 squares. As the last action of your turn, you can teleport 8 squares as a free action.

Level 23 Encounter Prayers

Avenger's Shield
Avenger Attack 23

You create a sphere of radiance that burns your foe. The sphere also protects you, flaring brightly if that foe attacks you.

Encounter ✦ Divine, Implement, Radiant
Standard Action   **Ranged** 20
Target: One creature
Attack: Wisdom vs. Will
Hit: 4d6 + Wisdom modifier radiant damage. If the target hits or misses you before the end of your next turn, as an immediate reaction you cause the target to be blinded until the end of your next turn.

Bond of Justice
Avenger Attack 23

You strike your foe in an eruption of searing radiance, creating a bond between your spirits. If that foe moves away from you, you can teleport to its side and attack it.

Encounter ✦ Divine, Radiant, Teleportation, Weapon
Standard Action   **Melee** weapon
Target: One creature
Attack: Wisdom vs. AC
Hit: 4[W] + Wisdom modifier radiant damage. If the target is not adjacent to you at the start of your next turn, you gain a +4 bonus to attack rolls against it until the end of that turn, and during that turn, you can teleport to a space adjacent to the target as a move action.
  Censure of Pursuit: When you use this power to teleport adjacent to the target, it takes radiant damage equal to 5 + your Dexterity modifier.

Phase Duel
Avenger Attack 23

You knock your opponent out of phase with the world and join it in a solitary duel to the death. You both remain visible as hazy outlines in the world, but no other creature can touch either of you.

Encounter ✦ Divine, Weapon
Standard Action   **Melee** weapon
Target: One creature
Attack: Wisdom vs. AC
Hit: 3[W] + Wisdom modifier damage. Until the end of your next turn, you and the target are immobilized. In addition, no other creature has line of sight or line of effect to either of you, and the two of you have line of sight and line of effect only to each other. This effect ends if the immobilized condition ends on either of you before the end of your next turn.
  Censure of Retribution: Until the end of your next turn, you gain a bonus to all defenses against the target's attacks equal to your Intelligence modifier.

Level 25 Daily Prayers

Aspect of Death
Avenger Attack 25

You become a bearer of death. As long as you remain near your chosen foe, it suffers a foretaste of death.

Daily ✦ Divine, Weapon
Standard Action   **Melee** weapon
Target: One creature
Attack: Wisdom vs. Fortitude
Hit: 6[W] + Wisdom modifier damage, and the target takes 10 damage at the start of its turn if you are within 5 squares of it (save ends).
Miss: Half damage, and the target takes 5 damage at the start of its turn if you are within 5 squares of it (save ends).

Bond of Destiny
Avenger Attack 25

You insert a fragment of your spirit into your enemy's mind. Until that enemy ejects the fragment, you can transport yourself to the enemy's side.

Daily ✦ Divine, Implement, Psychic, Teleportation
Standard Action   **Ranged** 20
Target: One creature
Attack: Wisdom vs. Will
Hit: 6d8 + Wisdom modifier psychic damage.
Miss: Half damage.
Effect: The target suffers a bond of destiny (save ends). Until the bond ends, you can teleport to a space adjacent to the target as a minor action. You don't need line of sight to the destination space.
  Aftereffect: You can teleport to a space adjacent to the target as a free action once. You don't need line of sight to the destination space.

Executioner's Justice
Avenger Attack 25

Your attack sears your enemy's mind as much as its body, and sends it spiraling down a painful path toward annihilation.

Daily ✦ Divine, Psychic, Weapon
Standard Action   **Melee** weapon
Target: One creature
Attack: Wisdom vs. AC
Hit: 4[W] + Wisdom modifier psychic damage, and the target is dazed (save ends).
  First Failed Saving Throw: The target is stunned instead of dazed (save ends).
  Each Additional Failed Saving Throw: The target takes 20 psychic damage.
Miss: Half damage, and the target is dazed (save ends).

Sigil of Damnation
Avenger Attack 25

A horrid sigil appears on your enemy's head, marking the creature as damned.

Daily ✦ Divine, Weapon
Standard Action   **Melee** weapon
Target: One creature
Attack: Wisdom vs. AC
Hit: 4[W] + Wisdom modifier damage.
Miss: Half damage.
Effect: Until the end of the encounter, when you miss the target with an avenger encounter attack power, the attack deals half damage.

LEVEL 27 ENCOUNTER PRAYERS

Astral Charge
Avenger Attack 27

As you charge, energy from the Astral Sea empowers you, making your final attack stun your foe.

Encounter ✦ Divine, Weapon
Standard Action   **Melee** weapon
Target: One creature
Attack: Wisdom vs. AC
Hit: 1[W] + Wisdom modifier damage, and the target is stunned until the end of your next turn.
Special: When charging, you can use this power in place of a melee basic attack.

Death Stroke
Avenger Attack 27

When your foe's allies are distracted and distant, you deal a deadly attack.

Encounter ✦ Divine, Weapon
Standard Action   **Melee** weapon
Target: One creature
Attack: Wisdom vs. AC. You gain a +4 bonus to the attack roll if no enemy is adjacent to the target.
Hit: 4[W] + Wisdom modifier damage. The attack deals 2[W] extra damage if no enemy is adjacent to the target.

Inevitable End
Avenger Attack 27

Your devastating attack should be enough to exact vengeance for your god. If it is not, and your foe escapes you this time, then you can try the attack again.

Encounter ✦ Divine, Weapon
Standard Action   **Melee** weapon
Target: One creature
Attack: Wisdom vs. AC
    Censure of Pursuit: You gain a bonus to the attack roll equal to your Dexterity modifier.
Hit: 4[W] + Wisdom modifier damage.
Effect: If the target is still alive and not adjacent to you at the end of its next turn, you regain the use of this power. You can regain the use of this power in this manner once per encounter.

Scatter to the Astral Winds
Avenger Attack 27

As you strike your enemy, the winds of an astral tempest sweep over the area, carrying away your other foes.

Encounter ✦ Divine, Teleportation, Weapon
Standard Action   **Melee** weapon
Target: One creature
Attack: Wisdom vs. Will
Hit: 3[W] + Wisdom modifier damage, and you teleport each enemy within 5 squares of you, other than the target, 5 squares.
    Censure of Retribution: The number of squares you teleport each enemy equals 4 + your Intelligence modifier.

LEVEL 29 DAILY PRAYERS

Aspect of Terror
Avenger Attack 29

You take on a terrifying aspect, assaulting your enemies' minds and making them loath to attack you.

Daily ✦ Divine, Fear, Implement, Psychic
Standard Action   **Close** burst 5
Target: Each enemy in burst
Attack: Wisdom vs. Will
Hit: 5d6 + Wisdom modifier psychic damage, and you push the target 3 squares. If the target hits or misses you, it is stunned until the end of its next turn (save ends).
Miss: Half damage. If the target hits or misses you before the end of your next turn, the target is stunned until the end of its next turn.

Fiery Vengeance
Avenger Attack 29

With a fearsome cry, you transfer the pain of your wounds into an outburst of cleansing fire.

Daily ✦ Divine, Fire, Healing, Implement, Radiant
Standard Action   **Close** burst 3
Target: Each creature in burst
Attack: Wisdom vs. Reflex
Hit: 7d6 + Wisdom modifier fire and radiant damage.
Miss: Half damage.
Effect: You regain hit points as if you had spent a healing surge. Until the end of the encounter, any enemy that ends its turn adjacent to you takes 10 fire and radiant damage.

Final Oath
Avenger Attack 29

Delivering a wicked blow, you swear to your god that either you or your foe shall die this day.

Daily ✦ Divine, Weapon
Standard Action   **Melee** weapon
Target: One creature
Attack: Wisdom vs. AC
Hit: 9[W] + Wisdom modifier damage.
Miss: Half damage.
Effect: Until the end of the encounter, you and the target gain a +5 bonus to attack rolls against each other.

Temple of Resolution
Avenger Attack 29

As you strike, a prison of radiant blades appears around you and your foe, ensuring that no other enemies interfere with your battle.

Daily ✦ Divine, Radiant, Weapon, Zone
Standard Action   **Melee** weapon
Target: One creature
Attack: Wisdom vs. Reflex
Hit: 5[W] + Wisdom modifier radiant damage.
Miss: Half damage.
Effect: The attack creates a zone of radiant energy in a close burst 2. The zone lasts until the end of the encounter. The target takes 25 radiant damage whenever it leaves the zone. Any enemy other than the target takes 25 radiant damage when entering the zone or ending its turn there. An enemy that enters or leaves the zone as a result of forced movement does not take this damage.

HAMMER OF JUDGMENT

"The hammer of the smith must sometimes also be the hammer of the warrior."

Prerequisite: Avenger

As the blacksmith's hammer shapes metal according to the smith's will, so you have been sent to shape the world to your god's will. A tool and a weapon in your god's hand, you are called to shape the course of kingdoms and punish those who stand opposed to the ways of your god. Although the smith's hammer is a tool of building and creation, in time of need it can also be a weapon of destruction.

In following this path, you emphasize the control elements of many avenger powers, particularly pulling, pushing, sliding, and teleporting your foes. You gain abilities that let you push your foes even with powers that don't normally involve forced movement and that increase the distance you move your foes with your powers. Your new attack powers push your targets around or knock them to the ground.

True to the name of this path, you are most effective if you are wielding a hammer, such as a maul.

HAMMER OF JUDGMENT PATH FEATURES

Avalanche Action (11th level): When you spend an action point to make an attack and that attack hits, you push each target you hit with that attack a number of squares equal to your Intelligence modifier.

Bone Crusher (11th level): Whenever you hit a creature with a daily attack power, that creature takes a -2 penalty to AC until the end of your next turn.

Bloodthirsty Hammer (16th level): Whenever you pull, push, slide, or teleport a bloodied creature by using a power, you can move the creature an additional 2 squares.

HAMMER OF JUDGMENT PRAYERS

Thunder Hammer	Hammer of Judgment Attack 11

You slam your weapon into the ground, and the earth itself transmits your god's wrath, bludgeoning your enemies with the force of thunder and either knocking them to the ground or driving them back.

Encounter ✦ Divine, Thunder, Weapon
Standard Action   Close burst 3
Target: Each enemy in burst
Attack: Wisdom vs. Fortitude
Hit: 2[W] + Wisdom modifier thunder damage, and you either knock the target prone or push it 2 squares.
  Weapon: If you are wielding a hammer, the number of squares you can push the target equals 1 + your Intelligence modifier.

Resolve of Steel	Hammer of Judgment Utility 12

Like steel forged and tempered by a master smith, you resist the worst of your enemies' attacks.

Encounter ✦ Divine
Minor Action   Personal
Effect: You gain resist 10 to all damage until the end of your next turn.

Hammer of the Final Pronouncement	Hammer of Judgment Attack 20

Your god's judgment drives your foe back and roots it to the ground.

Daily ✦ Divine, Weapon
Standard Action   Melee weapon
Target: One creature
Attack: Wisdom vs. AC
Hit: 4[W] + Wisdom modifier damage. You push the target 3 squares, and it is immobilized (save ends).
Miss: Half damage. You push the target 3 squares, and it is immobilized until the end of your next turn.
Weapon: If you are wielding a hammer, the number of squares you can push the target equals 3 + your Intelligence modifier.

OATHSWORN

"Your words are nothing but wind. My words endure."

Prerequisite: Avenger, *oath of enmity* power

For certain avenger sects, the swearing of oaths is a central part of their religious observances and their rites of initiation. In the teachings of these sects, an oath sworn by an avenger is akin to the words of creation spoken by the gods to give lasting form to the world; when the avenger's will and the god's will are one, an avenger's oath has the power to make reality conform to the words of the oath.

As a member of one of these oathsworn sects, your *oath of enmity* power carries particular weight. When you swear your god's judgment against a foe, that creature's attacks are less likely to harm you. When your foe lies dead, you claim the reward of fulfilling your oath, drawing new vigor for the remaining battle. As you advance along the oathsworn path, you gain powers that are more effective against the target of your oath, weakening it or making it vulnerable to your later attacks. You can even grant the benefit of your *oath of enmity* to your allies for a short time, ensuring that they help you bring your foe to justice.

OATHSWORN PATH FEATURES

Blood Oath (11th level): You gain a +1 bonus to all defenses against attacks made by your *oath of enmity* target.

Sworn Action (11th level): When you spend an action point to make an attack, you make two attack rolls against each target of that attack and use either result.

Enduring Oath (16th level): When your *oath of enmity* target drops to 0 hit points, you can spend a healing surge as a free action.

OATHSWORN PRAYERS

Oath of Weakness — Oathsworn Attack 11

As you strike your sworn foe, the power of your oath saps its strength and will.

Encounter ✦ Divine, Weapon
Standard Action   Melee weapon
Target: Your *oath of enmity* target
Attack: Wisdom vs. AC
Hit: 2[W] + Wisdom modifier damage, and the target is weakened until the end of your next turn.

Sworn Crusade — Oathsworn Utility 12

The holy nimbus representing your oath against an enemy surrounds your allies too, endowing them with deadly accuracy.

Daily ✦ Divine
Minor Action   Close burst 5
Target: Each ally in burst
Effect: Until the end of your next turn, each target makes two attack rolls and uses the result he or she prefers when making a melee attack against your *oath of enmity* target.

Oath Bond — Oathsworn Attack 20

You bind a foe with your oath, consigning it to your god's punishment.

Daily ✦ Divine, Weapon
Standard Action   Melee weapon
Target: Your *oath of enmity* target
Attack: Wisdom vs. AC
Hit: 3[W] + Wisdom modifier damage.
Effect: The target gains vulnerable 5 to your attacks (save ends).

UNVEILED VISAGE

"Look upon my face and see the face of my god."

Prerequisite: Avenger

At the culmination of your rite of initiation years ago, one of the avengers in your secret temple pulled back the hood of a voluminous cloak to reveal a face that was not mortal, but fully divine. You saw the face of your god in that moment, and that sight transformed you. That knowledge of divine presence is what allows you to wield the power you have and what authorizes you to act in your god's name. Slowly—ever so slowly—you are growing into the image of your god, to the point where your face begins to reveal your deity's countenance as well.

To the initiated in your faith, the face of your god is a wondrous sight, capable of inspiring awe and increased devotion. To the enemies of your god, the face is a thing of fear, of searing and blinding radiance.

Your path is about your own physical and spiritual transformation. As you progress along the path of the unveiled visage, you become a more clear mirror of your god's face and a more faithful expression of the god's will. You can tap into the vigilance of the divine mind and transform yourself into a divine aspect not unlike an angel, flying on wings to better fight your god's foes.

UNVEILED VISAGE PATH FEATURES

Unveiled Action (11th level): When you spend an action point to take an extra action, you also gain an extra use of one of your Channel Divinity powers during this encounter.

Soaring Charge (11th level): When you charge, you can fly your speed as part of the charge. You also gain a +2 bonus to all defenses against opportunity attacks you provoke while moving during the charge.

Bloodied Might (16th level): The first time you become bloodied during an encounter, you regain the use of *radiant visage* if you have already used it during this encounter.

UNVEILED VISAGE PRAYERS

Radiant Visage	Unveiled Visage Attack 11

The light of your god's presence shines from your face, searing your foes.

Encounter ✦ Divine, Implement, Radiant
Standard Action   Close blast 5
Target: Each enemy in blast
Attack: Wisdom vs. Reflex
Hit: 3d6 + Wisdom modifier radiant damage.

Divine Vigilance	Unveiled Visage Utility 12

With senses heightened by your god's presence, you dash past your foes and deny them any opening to attack you.

Encounter ✦ Divine
Move Action   Personal
Effect: You shift your speed. You don't grant combat advantage to any enemy until the end of your next turn.

Divine Aspect	Unveiled Visage Attack 20

You become a more perfect expression of your god's presence, blistering your enemies with the light of your spirit and sprouting radiant wings to finish the battle.

Daily ✦ Divine, Implement, Polymorph, Radiant
Standard Action   Close burst 1
Target: Each enemy in burst
Attack: Wisdom vs. Reflex
Hit: 5d6 + Wisdom modifier radiant damage.
Effect: Until the end of the encounter, you gain a +2 power bonus to AC. In addition, you gain a fly speed equal to your speed, and you can hover.

MICHAEL BIEREK

ZEALOUS ASSASSIN

"It is the will of Sehanine that the servants of Lolth should die as they lived—in silence and in secret."

Prerequisite: Avenger, trained in Stealth

Every avenger is trained in the ruthless art of combat and skilled in the art of isolating a foe and dispatching it with a few swift blows. Some avenger sects also emphasize the art of stealth—particularly those dedicated to deities who favor stealth, shadows, and secrecy, including Sehanine, Lolth, Zehir, and Vecna. Among these avengers, the most dangerous follow the path of the zealous assassin.

As a follower of this path, you embody devotion and ruthlessness in equal measure, making you a deadly weapon aimed at your deity's foes. Your skills are focused on the ability to slip in and out of shadows at the edge of combat, dealing blows that quickly dispose of enemies. You pool shadows around yourself or hide in a nimbus of divine light, and you master techniques that take advantage of openings in combat, dealing greater damage when you have combat advantage or against bloodied foes. At the culmination of the path, you can make yourself invisible to your foe, then sear it with blinding radiance that leaves it more susceptible to your attacks.

EVA WIDERMANN

ZEALOUS ASSASSIN PATH FEATURES

Divine Shroud Action (11th level): When you spend an action point to take an extra action, you also gain concealment until the end of your next turn, and you can teleport 3 squares as a free action before or after the extra action.

Finishing Technique (11th level): When you hit a bloodied target that is granting combat advantage to you, the attack deals 1d6 extra damage against the target.

Zealot's Veil (16th level): When you charge, you can make a Stealth check opposed by the passive Perception check of the target of your charge attack. (You don't take a penalty to this check for moving during the charge.) If the check succeeds, you gain combat advantage for the attack.

ZEALOUS ASSASSIN PRAYERS

Strike from Empty Air — Zealous Assassin Attack 11

You teleport to the perfect position to deliver a deadly strike against your foe.

Encounter ✦ Divine, Teleportation, Weapon
Standard Action   Melee weapon
Target: One creature
Attack: Wisdom vs. AC
Hit: 3[W] + Wisdom modifier damage. If you have combat advantage against the target, the attack deals 1[W] extra damage.
Effect: Before or after the attack, you teleport 2 squares.

Avenging Shadow — Zealous Assassin Utility 12

You call upon your god to blot your image from your foe's mind.

Daily ✦ Divine, Illusion
Minor Action   Close burst 10
Target: One enemy in burst
Effect: You become invisible to the target until the end of your next turn. If the target is your *oath of enmity* target, you become invisible to it (save ends).

Blade of the Zealot — Zealous Assassin Attack 20

Your weapon sears your foe with radiant energy and leaves it vulnerable to your attacks.

Daily ✦ Divine, Radiant, Weapon
Standard Action   Melee weapon
Target: One creature
Attack: Wisdom vs. AC
Hit: 4[W] + Wisdom modifier radiant damage. The target takes ongoing 10 radiant damage and grants combat advantage to you (save ends both).
Miss: Half damage. The target takes ongoing 5 radiant damage and grants combat advantage to you (save ends both).

BARBARIAN

"My strength is the fury of the wild."

CLASS TRAITS

Role: Striker. You use powerful two-handed weapons to deal serious damage to your enemies. Your physical power and daunting presence can cause foes to cower before you, and you can temporarily increase your abilities by harnessing great bursts of terrifying rage. Depending on your choice of class features and powers, you lean toward either defender or leader as a secondary role.

Power Source: Primal. You are a primal champion, a warrior devoted to the natural world and an embodiment of your tribe's fierce traditions.

Key Abilities: Strength, Constitution, Charisma

Armor Proficiencies: Cloth, leather, hide
Weapon Proficiencies: Simple melee, military melee
Bonus to Defense: +2 Fortitude

Hit Points at 1st Level: 15 + Constitution score
Hit Points per Level Gained: 6
Healing Surges per Day: 8 + Constitution modifier

Trained Skills: From the class skills list below, choose three trained skills at 1st level.
Class Skills: Acrobatics (Dex), Athletics (Str), Endurance (Con), Heal (Wis), Intimidate (Cha), Nature (Wis), Perception (Wis)

Class Features: Barbarian Agility, Feral Might, *rage strike*, Rampage

Barbarians are savage warriors who deal out powerful blows from their mighty weapons. They charge from foe to foe and seldom feel the pain of an enemy's strike. For barbarians' foes, the moments of greatest terror come when barbarians call upon primal forces to lend power to their raging spirits. These rages, although temporary, give a barbarian incredible powers, a combination of skill, willpower, and a legacy of ancient tribal rituals.

As a barbarian, you have a link to powerful nature spirits and other primal forces bound to the warriors of your tribe by the songs and totems of your legacy. These spirits lend energy to your rages, transforming you into a devastating force on the battlefield. As you become more experienced, these rages transcend mortal limitations, manifesting directly as waves of elemental power or gifting you with supernatural recuperative powers.

When the heat of battle is upon you, will you respond with a sudden charge that fells with one mighty swing of your weapon, or with a prolonged rage that leaves destroyed foes in your wake?

BARBARIAN CLASS FEATURES

Barbarians have the following class features.

BARBARIAN AGILITY

While you are not wearing heavy armor, you gain a +1 bonus to AC and Reflex. The bonus increases to +2 at 11th level and +3 at 21st level.

FERAL MIGHT

Barbarians connect with the natural world in a variety of ways. Some barbarians grow so hardened to physical punishment that they find it easier to simply absorb, rather than avoid, attacks. Others are living examples of the power of one's will to shape one's fate.

Choose one of the following options. The choice you make gives you the benefit described below and also provides bonuses to certain barbarian powers, as detailed in those powers.

Rageblood Vigor: You gain the *swift charge* power. In addition, whenever your attack reduces an enemy to 0 hit points, you gain temporary hit points equal to your Constitution modifier. The number of temporary hit points equals 5 + your Constitution modifier at 11th level and 10 + your Constitution modifier at 21st level.

Thaneborn Triumph: You gain the *roar of triumph* power. In addition, whenever you bloody an enemy, the next attack by you or an ally against that enemy gains a bonus to the attack roll equal to your Charisma modifier.

RAGE STRIKE

Barbarian daily attack powers have the rage keyword (page 220). They allow you to unleash powerful bursts of emotion, willpower, and primal energy. Each rage power starts with a mighty attack, and then you enter a rage, which grants an ongoing benefit.

At 5th level, you gain the *rage strike* power, which lets you channel an unused rage power into a devastating attack while you're raging. Using *rage strike* is an alternative to using a second rage power in a climactic battle; it gives you the damage output of a daily power without forcing you to enter a different rage.

RAMPAGE

Once per round, when you score a critical hit with a barbarian attack power, you can immediately make a melee basic attack as a free action. You do not have to attack the same target that you scored a critical hit against.

CREATING A BARBARIAN

You can choose any barbarian powers you like for your character, though many barbarians favor one of two builds: the rageblood barbarian or the thaneborn barbarian. All barbarians rely on Strength. Barbarians also benefit from a high Constitution or Charisma, depending on which expression of the class they favor.

RAGEBLOOD BARBARIAN

You can withstand a great deal of physical punishment, especially when you are in the throes of rage. At higher levels, your powers, particularly your rages, visibly manifest the spirits sacred to your tribe. Strength should be your highest ability score, since you use it for your attacks, but make Constitution a close second. Charisma might be your third-best score, especially if you want to use some powers designed for the thaneborn barbarian build. Rageblood barbarians lean toward defender as a secondary role.

Suggested Class Feature: Rageblood Vigor
Suggested Feat: Weapon Expertise
Suggested Skills: Athletics, Endurance, Perception
Suggested At-Will Powers: *devastating strike, recuperating strike*
Suggested Encounter Power: *avalanche strike*
Suggested Daily Power: *bloodhunt rage*

BARBARIAN OVERVIEW

Characteristics: You combine powerful melee attacks with an excellent ability to absorb damage. You gain tremendous bursts of power through mighty rages. You have unusually high hit points for your role, making you more durable than other strikers.

Religion: Most barbarians revere the primal spirits of the natural world rather than calling on the gods of the Astral Sea. Some barbarians don't see conflict between the gods and the primal spirits and therefore honor deities of nature or warfare in addition to the primal spirits. These barbarians often revere Kord, Melora, Avandra, or the Raven Queen. Evil or chaotic evil barbarians turn to Gruumsh or, more rarely, Bane or Zehir.

Races: Goliaths are ideal rageblood barbarians. Dragonborn make excellent thaneborn barbarians. Half-orcs are often barbarians but don't favor either of the two types. Dwarf and shifter barbarians tend to be rageblood barbarians, while halfling and half-elf barbarians choose the thaneborn path.

THANEBORN BARBARIAN

You use primal power to fuel your mighty rages and lend power to your already imposing personal presence. Your combination of physical prowess and charismatic appeal draws allies to you as surely as it fills your foes with fear. Again, make Strength your highest ability score, followed by Charisma and then Constitution. Thaneborn barbarians lean toward leader as a secondary role.

Suggested Class Feature: Thaneborn Triumph
Suggested Feat: Rising Fury
Suggested Skills: Athletics, Intimidate, Perception
Suggested At-Will Powers: *howling strike, pressing strike*
Suggested Encounter Power: *vault the fallen*
Suggested Daily Power: *macetail's rage*

BARBARIAN POWERS

Your powers are evocations of primal strength. At lower levels, your powers rely partly on martial skill and personal presence, but even at the start of your career, the primal spirits of the world infuse your body with vigor. At higher levels, the primal spirits flow more freely through you and your weapons, creating effects that are more obviously supernatural.

Your barbarian daily attack powers have the rage keyword (page 220). While you are raging, your barbarian at-will attack powers gain certain benefits, as detailed in those powers.

CLASS FEATURES

Each barbarian gains the power *rage strike*, usable only during a rage, at 5th level.

Rage Strike	Barbarian Feature

You channel your primal rage into a devastating attack.

Daily (Special) ✦ Primal, Weapon
Standard Action — **Melee** weapon
Requirement: You must be raging and have at least one unused barbarian rage power.
Target: One creature
Attack: Strength vs. AC. To make this attack, you expend an unused barbarian rage power.
Hit: You deal damage based on the level of the rage power you expend:

1st level	3[W] + Strength modifier
5th level	4[W] + Strength modifier
9th level	5[W] + Strength modifier
15th level	6[W] + Strength modifier
19th level	7[W] + Strength modifier
25th level	8[W] + Strength modifier
29th level	9[W] + Strength modifier

Miss: Half damage.
Special: You can use this power twice per day.

The Feral Might class feature grants each barbarian one of the following powers.

Roar of Triumph	Barbarian Feature

Your howl of victory shakes your enemies to the core, as they know your blood thirst is not yet quenched.

Encounter ✦ Fear, Primal
Free Action — **Close** burst 5
Trigger: Your attack reduces an enemy to 0 hit points
Target: Each enemy in burst
Effect: Each target takes a -2 penalty to all defenses until the end of your next turn.

Swift Charge	Barbarian Feature

As your foe falls, you rush toward your next victim.

Encounter ✦ Primal
Free Action — **Personal**
Trigger: Your attack reduces an enemy to 0 hit points
Effect: You charge an enemy.

LEVEL 1 AT-WILL EVOCATIONS

Devastating Strike	Barbarian Attack 1

You strike with awesome power, more concerned with offensive strength than defensive posturing.

At-Will ✦ Primal, Weapon
Standard Action — **Melee** weapon
Requirement: You must be wielding a two-handed weapon.
Target: One creature
Attack: Strength vs. AC
Hit: 1[W] + 1d8 + Strength modifier damage.
  Level 11: 1[W] + 2d8 + Strength modifier damage.
  Level 21: 2[W] + 3d8 + Strength modifier damage.
Effect: Until the start of your next turn, any attacker gains a +2 bonus to attack rolls against you. If you are raging, attackers do not gain this bonus.

Howling Strike	Barbarian Attack 1

With a blood-freezing scream, you throw yourself into the fray.

At-Will ✦ Primal, Weapon
Standard Action — **Melee** weapon
Requirement: You must be wielding a two-handed weapon.
Target: One creature
Attack: Strength vs. AC
Hit: 1[W] + 1d6 + Strength modifier damage.
  Level 11: 1[W] + 2d6 + Strength modifier damage.
  Level 21: 2[W] + 3d6 + Strength modifier damage.
Special: When charging, you can use this power in place of a melee basic attack. If you are raging, you can move 2 extra squares as part of the charge.

Pressing Strike
Barbarian Attack 1

You push lesser foes from your path, moving through the lines of battle at will.

At-Will ✦ Primal, Weapon
Standard Action   Melee weapon
Effect: Before the attack, you shift 2 squares. You can move through an enemy's space during the shift, but you can't end there.
Target: One creature
Attack: Strength vs. AC
Hit: 1[W] + Strength modifier damage, and you push the target 1 square. If you are raging, the attack deals 1d6 extra damage.
Level 21: 2[W] + Strength modifier damage.

Recuperating Strike
Barbarian Attack 1

Nothing restores your will to fight more than slamming your weapon into a foe. Each crushing swing gives you more will to press on.

At-Will ✦ Primal, Weapon
Standard Action   Melee weapon
Requirement: You must be wielding a two-handed weapon.
Target: One creature
Attack: Strength vs. AC
Hit: 1[W] + Strength modifier damage, and you gain temporary hit points equal to your Constitution modifier. If you are raging, the number of temporary hit points you gain equals 5 + your Constitution modifier.
Level 11: 1[W] + 1d6 + Strength modifier damage.
Level 21: 2[W] + 2d6 + Strength modifier damage.

LEVEL 1 ENCOUNTER EVOCATIONS

Avalanche Strike
Barbarian Attack 1

You drop your guard and put all your strength into a devastating overhead swing.

Encounter ✦ Primal, Weapon
Standard Action   Melee weapon
Target: One creature
Attack: Strength vs. AC
Hit: 3[W] + Strength modifier damage.
Rageblood Vigor: The attack deals extra damage equal to your Constitution modifier.
Effect: Until the start of your next turn, any attacker gains a +4 bonus to attack rolls against you.

Bloodletting
Barbarian Attack 1

Your powerful attack is meant to finish off a wounded foe.

Encounter ✦ Primal, Weapon
Standard Action   Melee weapon
Target: One creature
Attack: Strength vs. AC
Hit: 2[W] + Strength modifier damage. If the target is bloodied, the attack deals extra damage equal to your Constitution modifier.

Great Cleave
Barbarian Attack 1

The numbers arrayed against you mean nothing. You swing your weapon in a great arc, stopped by nothing so trivial as flesh and bone.

Encounter ✦ Primal, Weapon
Standard Action   Close burst 1
Target: Each enemy in burst you can see
Attack: Strength vs. AC
Hit: 1[W] + Strength modifier damage + 1 damage for each enemy adjacent to you.

Vault the Fallen
Barbarian Attack 1

You leap from one foe to the next, leaving blood in your wake.

Encounter ✦ Primal, Weapon
Standard Action   Melee weapon
Target: One or two creatures
Attack: Strength vs. AC
Hit: 1[W] + 1d6 + Strength modifier damage.
Effect: If you target two creatures, you can shift 1 square after the first attack.
Thaneborn Triumph: The number of squares you can shift equals your Charisma modifier.

LEVEL 1 DAILY EVOCATIONS

Bloodhunt Rage
Barbarian Attack 1

Your rage surges up from the depths of your pain to bring pain to the wounded.

Daily ✦ Primal, Rage, Weapon
Standard Action   Melee weapon
Target: One creature
Attack: Strength vs. AC
Hit: 3[W] + Strength modifier damage.
Miss: Half damage.
Effect: You enter the rage of the bloodhunt. Until the rage ends, you gain a bonus to melee damage rolls equal to your Constitution modifier if either you or your target is bloodied.

Macetail's Rage
Barbarian Attack 1

You knock your enemy to the ground with a slam like the behemoth's heavy tail, and the rage of the macetail fills you, refreshing you with every blow of your weapon.

Daily ✦ Primal, Rage, Weapon
Standard Action   Close burst 1
Target: Each enemy in burst you can see
Attack: Strength vs. Reflex
Hit: 1[W] + Strength modifier damage, and you knock the target prone.
Miss: Half damage.
Effect: You enter the rage of the macetail behemoth. Until the rage ends, whenever you hit, you gain temporary hit points equal to your Strength modifier.

Rage Drake's Frenzy
Barbarian Attack 1

You slam your weapon into your wounded foe, and the rage drake's spirit fills you. You erupt in violence, swinging furiously at a new foe as soon as the last one falls.

Daily ✦ Primal, Rage, Weapon
Standard Action   Melee weapon
Target: One creature
Attack: Strength vs. AC. If the target is bloodied, you gain a +2 bonus to the attack roll.
Hit: 3[W] + Strength modifier damage.
Miss: Half damage.
Effect: You enter the rage of the rage drake. Until the rage ends, once per round when you reduce an enemy to 0 hit points, you can make a melee basic attack as a free action.

Swift Panther Rage
Barbarian Attack 1

You slash your foe with fury as the spirit of the swift panther grants you its speed and agility.

Daily ✦ Primal, Rage, Weapon
Standard Action   Melee weapon
Target: One creature
Attack: Strength vs. AC
Hit: 3[W] + Strength modifier damage.
Miss: Half damage.
Effect: You enter the rage of the swift panther. Until the rage ends, you gain a +2 bonus to speed and can shift 2 squares as a move action.

LEVEL 2 UTILITY EVOCATIONS

Combat Sprint
Barbarian Utility 2

Having saved a bit of strength for just this moment, you burst across the battlefield.

Encounter ✦ Primal
Move Action   Personal
Effect: You move your speed + 4. You gain a +4 bonus to all defenses against any opportunity attack you provoke with this movement.

Primal Vitality
Barbarian Utility 2

Drawing strength from the ground beneath your feet, you push away the pain of minor wounds.

Daily ✦ Primal
Minor Action   Personal
Effect: You gain temporary hit points equal to one-half your level + your Constitution modifier. If you are raging, the number of temporary hit points you gain equals one-half your level + twice your Constitution modifier.

Stonebreaker
Barbarian Utility 2

Without hesitation, you smash through the door.

Encounter ✦ Primal
Minor Action   Personal
Effect: Until the end of your next turn, you gain a +5 bonus to Strength checks to break objects, and you deal double damage against objects.

Tiger's Leap
Barbarian Utility 2

With a surge of strength and will, you leap a great distance without a running start.

Encounter ✦ Primal
Move Action   Personal
Prerequisite: You must be trained in Athletics.
Effect: You make an Athletics check to jump with a +5 power bonus. You are considered to have a running start and can move as far as the check allows.

LEVEL 3 ENCOUNTER EVOCATIONS

Blade Sweep
Barbarian Attack 3

Though the fury of your attack is directed at a single foe, no nearby enemy is spared your wrath.

Encounter ✦ Primal, Weapon
Standard Action   Melee weapon
Target: One creature
Attack: Strength vs. AC
Hit: 2[W] + Strength modifier damage, and each bloodied enemy adjacent to you takes damage equal to your Constitution modifier.
  Rageblood Vigor: Each enemy adjacent to you that is not bloodied also takes damage equal to your Constitution modifier.

Blood Strike
Barbarian Attack 3

Blood calls to blood. Your pain and your enemy's give strength to your assault.

Encounter ✦ Primal, Weapon
Standard Action   Melee weapon
Target: One creature
Attack: Strength vs. AC
Hit: 2[W] + Strength modifier damage. If you or the target is bloodied, the attack deals 1[W] extra damage.

Daring Charge
Barbarian Attack 3

You leap forward and charge your foes. Those who try to strike you as you charge ahead only embolden your attack.

Encounter ✦ Primal, Weapon
Standard Action   Melee weapon
Target: One creature
Attack: Strength vs. AC
Hit: 2[W] + Strength modifier damage.
Special: When charging, you can use this power in place of a melee basic attack. If you charge, you gain a +2 bonus to the attack roll and the damage roll for each opportunity attack made against you while you charge.
  Thaneborn Triumph: You gain a bonus to AC equal to your Charisma modifier against any opportunity attack you provoke during your charge.

Hammer Fall
Barbarian Attack 3

You swing your weapon in a great underhand arc, and the impact lifts your target off its feet and sends it crashing to the ground.

Encounter ✦ Primal, Weapon
Standard Action   Melee weapon
Target: One creature
Attack: Strength vs. Fortitude
Hit: 2[W] + Strength modifier damage, and you knock the target prone.

Shatterbone Strike
Barbarian Attack 3

The fury of your assault knocks your foe off balance, leaving a hole in its defenses.

Encounter ✦ Primal, Weapon
Standard Action   Melee weapon
Target: One creature
Attack: Strength vs. AC
Hit: 2[W] + Strength modifier damage, and the target takes a -2 penalty to AC until the end of your next turn.
    Thaneborn Triumph: The penalty to AC equals your Charisma modifier.

LEVEL 5 DAILY EVOCATIONS

Frost Wolf Rage
Barbarian Attack 5

Like the great spirit wolf whose breath is the cold north wind, you are wreathed in frost, chilling those who try to harm you.

Daily ✦ Cold, Primal, Rage, Weapon
Standard Action   Melee weapon
Target: One creature
Effect: Before the attack, the target can make a melee basic attack against you as a free action. If it does so, your attack deals 1[W] extra cold damage.
Attack: Strength vs. AC
Hit: 3[W] + Strength modifier cold damage.
Miss: Half damage.
Effect: You enter the rage of the frost wolf. Until the rage ends, any enemy that hits you with a melee attack takes cold damage equal to 3 + your Constitution modifier.

Silver Phoenix Rage
Barbarian Attack 5

Your mighty blow erupts in silver fire as the spirit of the phoenix enters you. As you rage, vitality surges through you to ward you from death.

Daily ✦ Fire, Healing, Primal, Rage, Weapon
Standard Action   Melee weapon
Target: One creature
Attack: Strength vs. AC
Hit: 2[W] + Strength modifier fire damage, and ongoing 5 fire damage (save ends).
Miss: Half damage.
Effect: You enter the rage of the silver phoenix. Until the rage ends, you gain regeneration 3. In addition, the first time you drop to 0 hit points or fewer, you can spend a healing surge as an immediate interrupt.

Thunder Hawk Rage
Barbarian Attack 5

Your thunderous attack dazes your foe as you channel the great spirit hawk whose wings rumble across the sky. Your screaming charge blasts your enemies with thunder.

Daily ✦ Primal, Rage, Thunder, Weapon
Standard Action   Melee weapon
Primary Target: One creature
Primary Attack: Strength vs. AC
Hit: 2[W] + Strength modifier thunder damage, and the primary target is dazed (save ends).
Miss: Half damage.
Effect: You enter the rage of the thunder hawk. Until the rage ends, you can make the following secondary attack once during each of your turns.
Free Action   Melee 1
Secondary Target: One creature
Secondary Attack: Strength vs. Fortitude
Hit: You knock the secondary target prone.

Vengeful Storm Rage
Barbarian Attack 5

Your whirlwind assault engulfs your enemies in lightning as you channel the storm's fury.

Daily ✦ Lightning, Primal, Rage, Weapon
Standard Action   Close burst 1
Target: Each enemy in burst
Attack: Strength vs. AC
Hit: 2[W] + Strength modifier lightning damage.
Miss: Half damage.
Effect: You enter the rage of the vengeful storm. Until the rage ends, at the start of each of your turns, each enemy adjacent to you takes 3 lightning damage.

THOMAS DENMARK

LEVEL 6 UTILITY EVOCATIONS

Combat Surge — Barbarian Utility 6

As your attack goes awry, you react from the heat of your rage, without pause or thought, reversing your weapon and striking again.

Daily ✦ Primal
Free Action   **Personal**
Trigger: You miss with an attack
Requirement: You must be raging.
Effect: You reroll the attack.

Indomitable Shift — Barbarian Utility 6

You pound across the battlefield, leaving no opening as you move and drawing strength from the numbers arrayed against you.

Daily ✦ Primal
Minor Action   **Personal**
Effect: You shift a number of squares equal to your Constitution modifier. You gain 1d10 temporary hit points plus 1 additional temporary hit point for each enemy within 2 squares of you.

Instinctive Charge — Barbarian Utility 6

Instinctively aware of danger, you are poised to fight as soon as the battle begins.

Daily ✦ Primal
No Action   **Personal**
Trigger: You roll initiative at the beginning of an encounter
Effect: You gain a +5 power bonus to your initiative. You also gain a +2 power bonus to your first attack roll during the encounter.

Loss of Will — Barbarian Utility 6

As you turn aside your foe's attack, you stare into its eyes. Your enemy now knows that the battle is in your favor.

Encounter ✦ Primal
Immediate Reaction   **Personal**
Trigger: An enemy misses you with you an attack
Target: The triggering enemy
Effect: Until the end of the target's next turn, the target takes a penalty to attack rolls against you equal to your Charisma modifier.

LEVEL 7 ENCOUNTER EVOCATIONS

Curtain of Steel — Barbarian Attack 7

You are the pacing lion, the circling predator. No attack will come toward you without being answered in kind.

Encounter ✦ Primal, Weapon
Immediate Reaction   **Melee 1**
Trigger: An enemy adjacent to you hits or misses you
Target: The triggering enemy
Attack: Strength vs. AC
    Thaneborn Triumph: You gain a bonus to the attack roll equal to your Charisma modifier.
Hit: 3[W] + Strength modifier damage.

Great Shout — Barbarian Attack 7

You slam your weapon into a foe, then give voice to the fury of your ancestors, cowing those who dare to stand against you.

Encounter ✦ Primal, Weapon
Standard Action   **Melee weapon**
Target: One creature
Attack: Strength vs. AC
Hit: 2[W] + Strength modifier damage, and each enemy within 5 squares of you takes a -2 penalty to attack rolls until the end of your next turn.

Feast of Violence — Barbarian Attack 7

You drop your guard as you come close for your attack, drawing primal strength from the violence directed at you.

Encounter ✦ Primal, Weapon
Standard Action   **Melee weapon**
Target: One creature
Attack: Strength vs. AC
Hit: 2[W] + Strength modifier damage.
Special: You can choose to provoke opportunity attacks when you make this attack. If you do so, you gain a +1 bonus to the attack roll for each creature that attacks you, and the attack deals 1[W] extra damage.

Tide of Blood — Barbarian Attack 7

Your anger sweeps over every nearby enemy, drawing blood to fuel the tide of your assault on one of them.

Encounter ✦ Primal, Weapon
Standard Action   **Melee weapon**
Target: One creature
Attack: Strength vs. AC
Hit: 2[W] + Strength modifier damage. The attack deals 1 extra damage for each enemy adjacent to you.
    Rageblood Vigor: The attack instead deals 1 extra damage for each enemy within a number of squares of you equal to your Constitution modifier.

LEVEL 9 DAILY EVOCATIONS

Black Dragon Rage — Barbarian Attack 9

Channeling the spirit of the black dragon's caustic heart, your attack erupts in searing acid. As you rage, acid sears the eyes of nearby foes.

Daily ✦ Acid, Primal, Rage, Weapon
Standard Action   **Melee weapon**
Target: One creature
Attack: Strength vs. AC
Hit: 2[W] + Strength modifier acid damage, and ongoing 5 acid damage (save ends).
Miss: Half damage.
Effect: You enter the rage of the black dragon. Until the rage ends, at the start of each of your turns, each enemy adjacent to you is blinded until the end of your turn.

Oak Hammer Rage
Barbarian Attack 9

The ancient spirit of the oak knocks your foe to the ground. As you rage, you knock foe after foe down to the earth, then strike them with the earth's fury.

Daily ✦ Primal, Rage, Weapon
Standard Action   **Melee** weapon
Target: One creature
Attack: Strength vs. AC
Hit: 3[W] + Strength modifier damage, and you knock the target prone.
Miss: Half damage.
Effect: You enter the rage of the oak hammer. Until the rage ends, whenever you hit a target with a melee attack, you knock that target prone. If that target is already prone, the attack instead deals extra damage equal to your Constitution modifier.

Stone Bear Rage
Barbarian Attack 9

The spirit of the stone bear that hunts at the mountains' roots courses through you, and its fury blunts the pain of your wounds.

Daily ✦ Primal, Rage, Weapon
Standard Action   **Melee** weapon
Target: One creature
Attack: Strength vs. AC
Hit: 3[W] + Strength modifier damage.
Miss: Half damage.
Effect: You enter the rage of the stone bear. Until the rage ends, you gain resistance to all damage equal to your Constitution modifier.

White Tiger Rage
Barbarian Attack 9

The spirit of the white tiger empowers your attack, freezing your enemy in place. As the tiger's rage fills you, winter's chill slows your foes.

Daily ✦ Cold, Primal, Rage, Weapon
Standard Action   **Melee** weapon
Target: One creature
Attack: Strength vs. AC
Hit: 2[W] + Strength modifier cold damage, and the target is immobilized (save ends).
Miss: Half damage, and the target is slowed (save ends).
Effect: You enter the rage of the white tiger. Until the rage ends, any enemy that starts its turn adjacent to you is slowed until the end of its turn.

LEVEL 10 UTILITY EVOCATIONS

Deny Death
Barbarian Utility 10

The darkness will not swallow you until you have finished what you set out to do.

Daily ✦ Primal
Immediate Interrupt   Personal
Trigger: You drop to 0 hit points or fewer and don't die
Effect: You are dying but don't fall unconscious because of that condition. At the end of your next turn, you fall unconscious if you are still dying.

CHRIS SEAMAN

Heart Strike
Barbarian Utility 10

You put the weight of your spirit behind every swing of your weapon.

Daily ✦ Primal, Stance
Minor Action   **Personal**
Effect: Until the stance ends, whenever you hit with an at-will attack power, the attack deals extra damage equal to your Charisma modifier.

Mountain Roots
Barbarian Utility 10

You sink your spirit into the earth to stand your ground.

Daily ✦ Primal, Stance
Immediate Interrupt   **Personal**
Trigger: You are pulled, pushed, or slid
Effect: You negate the forced movement. Until the stance ends, you can negate forced movement against you.

Wellspring of Renewal
Barbarian Utility 10

You draw on a fount of primal energy to renew your strength and your focus.

Encounter ✦ Primal
Minor Action   **Personal**
Effect: You gain temporary hit points equal to one-half your level + your Constitution modifier. In addition, if you are marked, that condition ends.

LEVEL 13 ENCOUNTER EVOCATIONS

Blade Whirlwind
Barbarian Attack 13

Driven by strength and will, your weapon sweeps in a mighty arc that cuts every foe around you and drives them back from your fury.

Encounter ✦ Primal, Weapon
Standard Action   **Close** burst 1
Target: Each enemy in burst you can see
Attack: Strength vs. AC
Hit: 2[W] + Strength modifier damage.
    Rageblood Vigor: You also push the target 1 square.

Crack the Skull
Barbarian Attack 13

You slam your weapon against the skull of your foe, leaving it disoriented.

Encounter ✦ Primal, Weapon
Standard Action   **Melee** weapon
Target: One creature
Attack: Strength vs. Fortitude
Hit: 3[W] + Strength modifier damage, and the target is dazed until the end of your next turn.

Storm of Blades
Barbarian Attack 13

You lift your weapon again and again, each blow's impact fueling the next swing.

Encounter ✦ Primal, Weapon
Standard Action   **Melee** weapon
Target: One creature
Attack: Strength vs. AC
Hit: 1[W] + Strength modifier damage. Then repeat the attack against the target or against another creature within reach. You can make the attack a number of times equal to your Constitution modifier.

Terror's Cry
Barbarian Attack 13

As you smite your foe, you utter a terrible howl that strikes terror into your enemies' hearts.

Encounter ✦ Fear, Primal, Weapon
Standard Action   **Melee** weapon
Primary Target: One creature
Primary Attack: Strength vs. Fortitude
Hit: 3[W] + Strength modifier damage. Make a secondary attack that is a close burst 1.
    Secondary Target: Each enemy in burst
    Secondary Attack: Charisma vs. Will
    Hit: The secondary target moves 2 squares away from you as a free action and takes a -2 penalty to attack rolls until the end of your next turn.
    Thaneborn Triumph: The penalty to attack rolls equals your Charisma modifier.

Thunderfall
Barbarian Attack 13

You lower your shoulder, dipping your weapon beneath your opponent's guard and driving it up into the foe's body to knock it off balance.

Encounter ✦ Primal, Weapon
Standard Action   **Melee** weapon
Target: One creature
Attack: Strength vs. AC
Hit: 3[W] + Strength modifier damage, and you push the target 1 square and knock it prone.
Special: When charging, you can use this power in place of a melee basic attack. If you charge and hit, the number of squares you push the target equals your Constitution modifier.

LEVEL 15 DAILY EVOCATIONS

Flameheart Rage
Barbarian Attack 15

The spirit of the red dragon imbues your attack with fiery wrath, scorching your foe. As you rage, the fire of the dragon's heart lashes out at those that strike you.

Daily ✦ Fire, Primal, Rage, Weapon
Standard Action   **Close** burst 1
Targets: Each enemy in burst
Attack: Strength vs. AC
Hit: 2[W] + Strength modifier fire damage, and ongoing 5 fire damage (save ends).
Miss: Half damage.
Effect: You enter the rage of the red dragon. Until the rage ends, any creature that hits you with a melee attack takes fire damage equal to 5 + your Constitution modifier.

Hunting Lion Rage
Barbarian Attack 15

You channel the spirit of the hunting lion into a mighty blow. As you rage, the lion's spirit makes the most of every advantage.

Daily ✦ Primal, Rage, Weapon
Standard Action   **Melee** weapon
Target: One creature
Attack: Strength vs. AC
Hit: 4[W] + Strength modifier damage.
Miss: Half damage.
Effect: You enter the rage of the hunting lion. Until the rage ends, you gain a +2 power bonus to attack rolls against any target that is granting combat advantage to you.

Iron Hammer Rage — Barbarian Attack 15

Even the iron that sleeps in the earth has its primal spirits, which fuel your mighty attacks to dash your foes against walls and large trees.

Daily ✦ Primal, Rage, Weapon
Standard Action   **Melee** weapon
Target: One creature
Attack: Strength vs. AC
Hit: 3[W] + Strength modifier damage, and you push the target a number of squares equal to your Strength modifier.
Miss: Half damage, and you push the target 1 square.
Effect: You enter the rage of the iron hammer. Until the rage ends, whenever you hit a creature with a melee attack, you push that creature 2 squares. If the creature is adjacent to blocking terrain at the end of the push, the creature takes damage equal to your Strength modifier.

Thunderfury Rage — Barbarian Attack 15

Charging at your foe and knocking it to the ground, you call on the spirit of the thunderfury boar to drive you into a frenzy. In your rage, you lash out at foes that attack you.

Daily ✦ Primal, Rage, Weapon
Standard Action   **Melee** weapon
Target: One creature
Attack: Strength vs. AC
Hit: 3[W] + Strength modifier damage, and you knock the target prone.
Miss: Half damage.
Effect: You enter the rage of the thunderfury boar. Until the rage ends, when any enemy adjacent to you hits or misses you, you can make a melee basic attack against that enemy as an immediate reaction.

LEVEL 16 UTILITY EVOCATIONS

Fuel the Fire — Barbarian Utility 16

You lower your weapon, allowing your opponent to score a glancing blow, but the pain only fuels your rage and adds strength to your own attacks.

Encounter ✦ Primal
Minor Action   **Personal**
Effect: Each enemy adjacent to you can make an opportunity attack against you. Until the end of your next turn, you gain a bonus to attack rolls equal to +2 for each enemy that makes the opportunity attack.

Great Stomp — Barbarian Utility 16

As you slam your foot into the ground, primal energy pours through you, buckling the ground beneath you with its power.

Daily ✦ Primal
Minor Action   **Close** burst 5
Effect: Each square in the burst becomes difficult terrain until the end of your next turn.

Primal Resistance — Barbarian Utility 16

You stand untouched by the magical energy of your foes.

Daily ✦ Primal, Stance
Minor Action   **Personal**
Effect: Until the stance ends, you gain resist 10 against a damage type of your choice: acid, cold, fire, lightning, or thunder.

Spur the Cycle — Barbarian Utility 16

Just as in the natural world, death leads to new life: killing your foe spurs you to further action.

Daily ✦ Primal
Free Action   **Personal**
Trigger: You reduce an enemy to 0 hit points during your turn
Effect: You take a standard action.

LEVEL 17 ENCOUNTER EVOCATIONS

Devastating Blow — Barbarian Attack 17

Your powerful blow shatters your target's defenses.

Encounter ✦ Primal, Weapon
Standard Action   **Melee** weapon
Target: One creature
Attack: Strength vs. AC
Hit: 4[W] + Strength modifier damage, and the target takes a -2 penalty to AC until the end of your next turn.
   Thaneborn Triumph: The penalty to AC equals your Charisma modifier.

Mountain Grasp — Barbarian Attack 17

You bring your weapon down in a great overhead arc, rooting your foe in place with the weight of your blow.

Encounter ✦ Primal, Weapon
Standard Action   **Melee** weapon
Target: One creature
Attack: Strength vs. AC
Hit: 2[W] + Strength modifier damage, and the target is immobilized and grants combat advantage to you until the end of your next turn.

Shoulder Slam — Barbarian Attack 17

You lower your shoulder into your foes, driving them across the ground.

Encounter ✦ Primal, Weapon
Standard Action   **Melee** weapon
Primary Target: One creature
Primary Attack: Strength vs. Fortitude
Hit: 2[W] + Strength modifier damage, and you push the target 1 square. You then shift 1 square and make a secondary attack.
   Secondary Target: One creature other than the primary target
   Secondary Attack: Strength vs. AC
   Hit: 1[W] + Strength modifier damage.
Special: When charging, you can use this power in place of a melee basic attack. If you charge, you gain a bonus to the primary attack roll equal to your Constitution modifier.

Threatening Fury
Barbarian Attack 17

Your fierce attack brings you into your opponent's reach, ensuring that it can't attack you or escape without reprisal.

Encounter ✦ Primal, Weapon
Standard Action   **Melee** weapon
Target: One creature
Attack: Strength vs. AC
Hit: 3[W] + Strength modifier damage.
Effect: Whenever the target shifts or makes an attack roll against you before the end of your next turn, you can make an opportunity attack against it.

Vigorous Strike
Barbarian Attack 17

You strike your foe with a mighty assault that bolsters you against attacks.

Encounter ✦ Primal, Weapon
Standard Action   **Melee** weapon
Target: One creature
Attack: Strength vs. AC
Hit: 3[W] + Strength modifier damage, and you gain temporary hit points equal to one-half your level.
     Rageblood Vigor: The number of temporary hit points you gain equals one-half your level + your Constitution modifier.

LEVEL 19 DAILY EVOCATIONS

Ghost Viper Rage
Barbarian Attack 19

The spirit of the ghost viper infuses you, sending venom coursing through the veins of your foe. As you rage, the viper's spirit throws nearby foes off guard.

Daily ✦ Poison, Primal, Rage, Weapon
Standard Action   **Melee** weapon
Target: One creature
Attack: Strength vs. AC
Hit: 3[W] + Strength modifier damage, and ongoing 10 poison damage (save ends).
Miss: Half damage.
Effect: You enter the rage of the ghost viper. Until the rage ends, any enemy that starts its turn next to you grants combat advantage to you and your allies until the end of its next turn.

Hydra Rage
Barbarian Attack 19

Your overwhelming attack leaves your target staggered, and the spirit of the hydra courses through you. As you rage, your weapon darts and bites like the hydra's many heads.

Daily ✦ Primal, Rage, Weapon
Standard Action   **Melee** weapon
Target: One creature
Attack: Strength vs. AC
Hit: 4[W] + Strength modifier damage, and the target is dazed (save ends).
Miss: Half damage.
Effect: You enter the rage of the hydra. Until the rage ends, once per round when you make an attack that misses, you can make a melee basic attack as a free action.

Storm Drake Rage
Barbarian Attack 19

Lightning cascades around you and flows into your enemy. As you rage, lightning lashes out at any foe that strikes you, knocking it to the ground.

Daily ✦ Lightning, Primal, Rage, Weapon
Standard Action   **Melee** weapon
Target: One creature
Attack: Strength vs. AC
Hit: 3[W] + Strength modifier lightning damage, and ongoing 10 lightning damage (save ends).
Miss: Half damage.
Effect: You enter the rage of the storm drake. Until the rage ends, any enemy that hits you with a melee attack takes 5 lightning damage and is knocked prone.

Winter Phoenix Rage
Barbarian Attack 19

Your blow erupts in grasping frost as the spirit of the winter phoenix enters you. As you rage, vitality surges through you to ward you from death.

Daily ✦ Cold, Healing, Primal, Rage, Weapon
Standard Action   **Melee** weapon
Target: One creature
Attack: Strength vs. AC
Hit: 3[W] + Strength modifier cold damage, and ongoing 10 cold damage (save ends).
Miss: Half damage.
Effect: You enter the rage of the winter phoenix. Until the rage ends, you gain regeneration 5 + your Constitution modifier. In addition, the first time you drop to 0 hit points or fewer, you can spend a healing surge as an immediate interrupt.

LEVEL 22 UTILITY EVOCATIONS

Last Stand
Barbarian Utility 22

As death looms before you, you push yourself to battle on.

Daily ✦ Primal
Immediate Interrupt   **Personal**
Trigger: You drop to 0 hit points or fewer and don't die
Effect: You are dying but don't fall unconscious because of that condition. At the end of your next turn, you fall unconscious if you are still dying.
Sustain Minor: You take 5 damage and don't fall unconscious.

Primal Instinct
Barbarian Utility 22

You close your eyes and strike, guided more by your instincts than by your senses.

Daily ✦ Primal
Minor Action   **Personal**
Effect: You gain blindsight 10 until the end of the encounter.

Primal Vigor
Barbarian Utility 22

Infused with primal energy, you draw on the power of your opponent's attack to spur your will to live.

Daily ✦ Primal
Immediate Interrupt   **Personal**
Trigger: You are hit by an attack
Effect: Until the end of your next turn, you gain resistance to all damage equal to one-half your level + your Constitution modifier.

Untouched
Barbarian Utility 22

Primal energy from the earth and the air courses through you, cleansing you of the dire effects of battle.

Daily ✦ Primal
Minor Action   **Personal**
Effect: You make a saving throw against each effect on you that a save can end. You gain a bonus to each saving throw equal to your Constitution modifier.

LEVEL 23 ENCOUNTER EVOCATIONS

Arcing Throw
Barbarian Attack 23

Spirits of wind and storm carry your weapon across the battlefield to smite your target, then linger around that foe to hinder its movement.

Encounter ✦ Primal, Weapon
Standard Action   **Ranged** 5/10
Target: One creature
Attack: Strength vs. AC
Hit: 5[W] + Strength modifier damage, and the target is slowed until the end of your next turn.
Special: When you use this power, you can make the attack with a melee weapon as if it were a heavy thrown weapon. If it is a magic weapon, it returns to your hand after the attack is resolved.

Berserker's Shout
Barbarian Attack 23

You shout your fury as you strike your foe, sending fear like daggers into the hearts of nearby enemies.

Encounter ✦ Fear, Primal, Weapon
Standard Action   **Melee** weapon
Target: One creature
Attack: Strength vs. AC
Hit: 5[W] + Strength modifier damage, and each enemy adjacent to you takes a -2 penalty to attack rolls until the end of your next turn.
Thaneborn Triumph: The penalty to attack rolls equals your Charisma modifier.

Crater Fall
Barbarian Attack 23

You swing your weapon in a great underhand arc and then drive it up into your opponent, sending the foe flying back through the air.

Encounter ✦ Primal, Weapon
Standard Action   **Melee** weapon
Target: One creature
Attack: Strength vs. AC
Hit: 3[W] + Strength modifier damage, and you push the target 3 squares and knock it prone. This forced movement ignores hindering terrain, such as a pit, between the target's starting square and its destination. If you push the target through squares occupied by other enemies, those enemies are knocked prone.
Special: When charging, you can use this power in place of a melee basic attack. If you charge, the number of squares you push the target equals your Strength modifier.

Fatal Strike
Barbarian Attack 23

Your powerful attack, like the coming of winter, puts an end to growth and healing.

Encounter ✦ Primal, Weapon
Standard Action   **Melee** weapon
Target: One creature
Attack: Strength vs. AC
Hit: 4[W] + Strength modifier damage, and the target cannot regain hit points until the start of your next turn.
Rageblood Vigor: The attack deals extra damage equal to your Constitution modifier.

Feral Scythe
Barbarian Attack 23

Your weapon is a swirling vortex of destruction, biting deep into every foe beside you.

Encounter ✦ Primal, Weapon
Standard Action   **Close** burst 1
Target: Each enemy in burst
Attack: Strength vs. AC
Hit: 3[W] + Strength modifier damage.

Staggering Strike
Barbarian Attack 23

With a quick, instinctive strike, you knock your opponent senseless.

Encounter ✦ Primal, Weapon
Standard Action   **Melee** weapon
Target: One creature
Attack: Strength vs. Fortitude
Hit: 2[W] + Strength modifier damage, and the target is stunned until the end of your next turn.

LEVEL 25 DAILY EVOCATIONS

Ash Hammer Rage
Barbarian Attack 25

You pull the unyielding might of the forest into your weapon and drive your foe back. As you rage, you draw vitality through your rooted connection to the ground.

Daily ✦ Primal, Rage, Weapon
Standard Action   **Melee** weapon
Target: One creature
Attack: Strength vs. AC
Hit: 7[W] + Strength modifier damage, and you push the target a number of squares equal to your Constitution modifier.
Miss: Half damage, and you push the target 1 square.
Effect: You enter the rage of the ash hammer. Until the rage ends, whenever you hit with an attack, you gain temporary hit points equal to 10 + your Charisma modifier. If that attack already grants temporary hit points to you, add your Charisma modifier to the number of temporary hit points you gain.

Blood Hunger Rage
Barbarian Attack 25

Your fierce attack leaves your target reeling. As you rage, the Primal Beast surges in your blood, drawing on the carnage around you to empower your attacks.

Daily ✦ Primal, Rage, Weapon
Standard Action   **Melee** weapon
Target: One creature
Attack: Strength vs. AC
Hit: 7[W] + Strength modifier, and the target is dazed (save ends).
Miss: Half damage.
Effect: You enter the blood hunger rage. Until the rage ends, you gain a bonus to attack rolls equal to the number of bloodied creatures within 3 squares of you.

Blue Dragon Rage
Barbarian Attack 25

Your weapon surges with lightning like the blue dragon's horn. As you rage, the spirit of the blue dragon courses through you, and your blows erupt in bursts of lightning.

Daily ✦ Lightning, Primal, Rage, Weapon
Standard Action   **Melee** weapon
Target: One creature
Attack: Strength vs. AC
Hit: 5[W] + Strength modifier damage, and ongoing 10 lightning damage (save ends).
Miss: Half damage.
Effect: You enter the rage of the blue dragon. Until the rage ends, once per round when you hit a target with a melee attack, each enemy adjacent to that target takes 10 lightning damage.

Stone Tempest Rage
Barbarian Attack 25

Like the mighty storms that shake the earth, your attack crashes into your foe and brings it to the ground. As you rage, your fury turns your attacks into devastating wounds.

Daily ✦ Primal, Rage, Thunder, Weapon
Standard Action   **Melee** weapon
Target: One creature
Attack: Strength vs. AC
Hit: 7[W] + Strength modifier thunder damage, and you knock the target prone.
Miss: Half damage.
Effect: You enter the rage of the stone tempest. Until the rage ends, you can score a critical hit on a roll of 18–20.

Level 27 Encounter Evocations

Blood Wrath
Barbarian Attack 27

The blood of your foes fills you with a thirst for more violence.

Encounter ✦ Primal, Weapon
Standard Action   **Melee** weapon
Target: One creature
Attack: Strength vs. AC. You gain a +2 bonus to the attack roll if the target is bloodied.
Hit: 5[W] + Strength modifier damage, and you gain a +2 bonus to attack rolls until the end of your next turn.
  Rageblood Vigor: The bonus to attack rolls equals your Constitution modifier.

Bonebreaker
Barbarian Attack 27

You twist and lean into your weapon just as your opponent tries to pull away, rending flesh and bone.

Encounter ✦ Primal, Weapon
Immediate Interrupt   **Melee** weapon
Trigger: An enemy leaves a square adjacent to you
Target: The triggering enemy
Attack: Strength vs. Fortitude
Hit: 4[W] + Strength modifier damage, and the target takes 10 damage if it moves more than 1 square during the movement that this attack interrupts.

Butcher's Feast
Barbarian Attack 27

No attack will come toward you without being answered in kind.

Encounter ✦ Primal, Weapon
Standard Action   **Melee** weapon
Target: One creature
Attack: Strength vs. AC
Hit: 6[W] + Strength modifier damage. Until the end of your next turn, you can make a melee basic attack as a free action against any enemy adjacent to you that hits or misses you.
  Thaneborn Triumph: Until the end of your next turn, you gain a power bonus to basic attack rolls equal to your Charisma modifier.

Hurricane of Blades
Barbarian Attack 27

You become a tempest of steel, ripping through your foes in a horrific display of carnage.

Encounter ✦ Primal, Weapon
Standard Action   **Melee** weapon
Target: One creature
Attack: Strength vs. AC
Hit: 1[W] + Strength modifier damage.
Effect: Make the attack five more times against the same target or different ones.

Rampaging Dragon Strike
Barbarian Attack 27

Like a terrible dragon, you dominate the battlefield, knocking aside the lesser foes to pit your strength against the strongest.

Encounter ✦ Primal, Weapon
Standard Action   **Melee** weapon
Primary Target: One or two creatures
Primary Attack: Strength vs. AC
Hit: 2[W] + Strength modifier damage, and you push the primary target 1 square.
Effect: You move your speed and then make a secondary attack.
  Secondary Target: One creature other than the primary target
  Secondary Attack: Strength + 1 vs. AC
  Hit: 3[W] + Strength modifier damage.

LEVEL 29 DAILY EVOCATIONS

Crimson Phoenix Rage — Barbarian Attack 29

Your mighty blow erupts in flame to engulf your nearby foes as the spirit of the crimson phoenix enters you. As you rage, fire bursts from your weapon with every strike, and vitality surges through you to ward you from death.

Daily ✦ Fire, Healing, Primal, Rage, Weapon
Standard Action   **Close** burst 1
Targets: Each creature in burst
Attack: Strength vs. AC
Hit: 3[W] + Strength modifier fire damage, and ongoing 10 fire damage (save ends).
Miss: Half damage.
Effect: You enter the rage of the crimson phoenix. Until the rage ends, your at-will attack powers deal 1[W] extra fire damage on a hit. In addition, whenever you drop to 0 hit points or fewer, you can spend a healing surge as an immediate interrupt.

Rage of the Primal Beast — Barbarian Attack 29

The Primal Beast awakens within you, and your attack leaves your foe bleeding. As you rage, you feed on the presence of your foes; overwhelming numbers only make you stronger.

Daily ✦ Primal, Rage, Weapon
Standard Action   **Melee** weapon
Target: One creature
Attack: Strength vs. AC
Hit: 5[W] + Strength modifier damage, and ongoing 10 damage (save ends).
Miss: Half damage.
Effect: You enter the rage of the Primal Beast. Until the rage ends, you gain a bonus to attack rolls equal to the number of enemies you can see.

Winter Ghost Rage — Barbarian Attack 29

The touch of your weapon is the wintry chill of death. As you rage, the spirit of winter fills you, causing you to become a ghost to your foes as you near death.

Daily ✦ Cold, Primal, Rage, Weapon
Standard Action   **Melee** weapon
Target: One creature
Attack: Strength vs. AC
Hit: 6[W] + Strength modifier cold damage, and ongoing 10 cold damage (save ends).
Miss: Half damage.
Effect: You enter the rage of the winter ghost. Until the rage ends, you are insubstantial while you are bloodied.

World Serpent Rage — Barbarian Attack 29

You smash your weapon into your foe with all your strength as the spirit of the World Serpent courses through you. As you rage, your spirit's coils keep your enemies close and empower your attacks against them.

Daily ✦ Primal, Rage, Weapon
Standard Action   **Melee** weapon
Target: One creature
Attack: Strength vs. AC
Hit: 7[W] + Strength modifier damage.
Miss: Half damage.
Effect: You enter the rage of the World Serpent. Until the rage ends, you can make a melee basic attack as a free action against any enemy adjacent to you that shifts. In addition, on your turn, you gain a +5 bonus to damage rolls against any enemy that was adjacent to you at the start of your turn.
Special: When charging, you can use this power in place of a melee basic attack.

BEAR WARRIOR

"The bear's power and strength are my guides. The bear's form is my weapon of choice."

Prerequisite: Barbarian

You revere the bear as a symbol of the warrior's strength and prowess. Through long and ancient rites, you have bound that symbol to your heart with more than just words and totems. In battle, you become the bear, shaping your form to its form and your strength to its strength.

Most bear warriors strive to emulate the bear beyond combat situations. You might catch fish with your bare hands, tear open beehives to feast on the honey inside, or roar in an aggressive territorial display. Like many barbarians, you're more at home in the wild places of the world than when surrounded by buildings.

BEAR WARRIOR PATH FEATURES

Bear's Toughness (11th level): When you spend an action point to take an extra action, you can also spend a healing surge.

Bear Form (11th level): As a bear warrior, you have the ability to channel the primal energy of beasts into your physical form. While you are raging, you take on a bearlike appearance. Your head becomes that of a bear, your body sprouts thick fur, and your hands become heavy claws. Until the rage ends, you gain a +1 bonus to AC and can use your second wind as a free action.

Wild Push (16th level): Whenever you score a critical hit with a melee attack while you are raging, you push the target a number of squares equal to your Strength modifier.

BEAR WARRIOR EVOCATIONS

Mauling Bear — Bear Warrior Attack 11

You channel the bear's strength into a powerful blow that knocks your opponent to the ground. Like an angry bear, you stand over your foe, waiting for its next move.

Encounter ✦ Primal, Weapon
Standard Action   **Melee** weapon
Target: One creature
Attack: Strength vs. AC
Hit: 2[W] + Strength modifier damage, and you knock the target prone.
Effect: Until the end of your next turn, if you are adjacent to the target when it stands up, you can make a melee basic attack against it as an immediate reaction.

Bestial Vigor — Bear Warrior Utility 12

Primal might wells within you, allowing you to shake off wounds and see the fight to its end.

Daily ✦ Primal
Minor Action   **Personal**
Effect: You gain temporary hit points equal to your healing surge value and can make a saving throw against each effect on you that a save can end.

Rampaging Bear — Bear Warrior Attack 20

With a mighty roar, you crash through the battle lines of your enemies.

Daily ✦ Primal, Rage, Weapon
Standard Action   **Melee** weapon
Primary Target: One creature
Primary Attack: Strength vs. AC
Hit: 3[W] + Strength modifier damage, and you push the target 1 square and knock it prone.
Effect: You shift a number of squares equal to your Strength modifier and then make a secondary attack.
  Secondary Target: One creature other than the primary target
  Secondary Attack: Strength vs. AC
Hit: 2[W] + Strength modifier damage, and you push the secondary target 1 square and knock it prone.
Effect: You shift a number of squares equal to your Strength modifier. You then enter the bear warrior's rage. Until the rage ends, you gain regeneration 5, and whenever you are pulled, pushed, or slid, you can reduce the distance of the forced movement by 1 square.

Fearbringer Thane

"You needn't wait until the bodies fall to know the victor. Simply find the eyes that first hold fear—those are the eyes that can never see victory."

Prerequisite: Barbarian

Many barbarians combine mastery of primal power with an imposing personal presence and natural leadership ability. The most dreaded warriors among them are fearbringer thanes, who harness those twin powers to strike terror into their enemies' hearts.

As a fearbringer thane, you shape battles with your will and your fearsome presence. Fear is a weapon you wield, turning your foes to quaking weaklings before you cut them down with your axe or sword. As your rages seize you and fill you with primal power, that power flows out from you to inspire your allies and fill your enemies with terror.

Many fearbringer thanes use their power to gather hordes of savage warriors under their banners. Others, including most player characters, lead smaller bands of adventurers on raids into dungeons and other adventure sites. In either case, a fearbringer thane is something like a hybrid of barbarian and warlord, as close to a leader as a barbarian comes.

Fearbringer Thane Path Features

Staggering Fury (11th level): When you spend an action point to make a melee attack while you are raging, each enemy that can see you takes a -2 penalty to attack rolls until the end of your next turn.

Inspire Ferocity (11th level): While you are raging, any ally within 5 squares of you who hits with a melee attack gains a +2 bonus to the damage roll.

Dominating Presence (16th level): Whenever you score a critical hit, your allies gain a +2 bonus to attack rolls against the target until the end of your next turn.

Fearbringer Thane Evocations

Screaming Hawk Strike	Fearbringer Thane Attack 11

Your terrifying attack leaves your foe hesitant, diminishing its defenses.

Encounter ✦ Fear, Primal, Weapon
Standard Action   Melee weapon
Target: One creature
Attack: Strength vs. AC
Hit: 2[W] + Strength modifier damage, and the target takes a -2 penalty to AC until the end of your next turn.
Special: If you use this power while you are raging, roll a d20. On a 10 or higher, you retain the use of this power.

Fearsome Presence	Fearbringer Thane Utility 12

You enemies quake before you, their attacks becoming weak because of their fear.

Daily ✦ Primal, Stance
Minor Action   Personal
Effect: Until the stance ends, you gain a +2 bonus to all defenses.

Tide of Battle	Fearbringer Thane Attack 20

Your allies take heart as you slam your weapon into your foes.

Daily ✦ Healing, Primal, Weapon
Standard Action   Melee weapon
Target: One, two, or three creatures
Attack: Strength vs. AC
Hit: 2[W] + Strength modifier damage.
Miss: Half damage.
Effect: An ally within 5 squares of you can spend a healing surge.

FRENZIED BERSERKER

"Caution? Discretion? No! Valor is to face your foe in battle and then stand over the broken corpse."

Prerequisite: Barbarian

The devastation of the thunderstorm howls in your soul, wild and untamed. You thrill in the chaos of battle, your wrath unquenched and uncontrollable. Battle, for you, is not a means to an end; it is an end in itself. The thrill of combat draws you on, and wounds only drive you to greater frenzy.

Caught in the tumult of your anger, you must attack–calculated maneuvers and intricate strategies are diversions. You attack with sweeping blows that cleave through your enemies or lock single foes in deadly exchanges that can end only in the death of one or the other of you. When the furor of battle seizes you, you ignore pain and keep fighting when others would fall, an unconquerable whirlwind of destruction.

FRENZIED BERSERKER PATH FEATURES

Frenzied Blood (11th level): If you spend an action point to make a melee attack and that attack misses, you deal half of that attack's damage on the miss. This benefit does not apply to attacks that already deal damage on a miss.

Warpath (11th level): Whenever you hit with a melee attack while raging, the attack deals 2 extra damage. In addition, whenever you start your turn adjacent to one or more enemies while you are raging and are able to take actions, you must make either a melee or a close attack against one of those enemies during your turn or be stunned until the end of your next turn.

Unfeeling Rage (16th level): You gain resist 5 to all damage while you are bloodied and raging.

FRENZIED BERSERKER EVOCATIONS

Persistent Frenzy	Frenzied Berserker Attack 11

Caught up in the madness of your wrath, you swing your weapon again and again.

Encounter ✦ Primal, Weapon
Standard Action   **Close** burst 1
Target: Each creature in burst you can see
Attack: Strength vs. AC
Hit: 1[W] + Strength modifier damage.
Special: If you use this power while you are raging, roll a d20. On a 10 or higher, you retain the use of this power.

Deathless Frenzy	Frenzied Berserker Utility 12

For a time, your anger can stave off even death.

Daily ✦ Primal
Immediate Interrupt   **Personal**
Trigger: You drop to 0 hit points or fewer and don't die
Effect: Until you regain hit points, you are dying but don't fall unconscious because of that condition. If you fail a death saving throw, you fall unconscious, and this effect ends.

Final Confrontation	Frenzied Berserker Attack 20

Your fury spills over to your foe, locking the two of you in a lethal duel.

Daily ✦ Primal, Weapon
Standard Action   **Melee** weapon
Target: One creature
Effect: Before the attack, if the target is marked, that condition ends on it. It can then make a melee basic attack against you as a free action.
Attack: Strength vs. AC
Hit: 7[W] + Strength modifier damage.
Miss: Half damage.
Effect: After the attack, you can allow the target to make a melee basic attack against you as a free action. If the target makes that attack, you can make a melee basic attack against it as a free action. You can repeat this effect until the target chooses not to make the attack.

WAYNE ENGLAND

WILDRUNNER

"The land gives wings to my feet and makes my spirit soar."

Prerequisite: Barbarian, trained in Nature

The wilderness is your home, and your connection to the primal spirits of the land grants you speed and ferocity. You move through the forest like a deer, and you charge into battle with the cheetah's speed and fury.

The powers of a wildrunner emphasize mobility, letting you shift and move quickly while striking your foes. You pounce from foe to foe, avoiding opportunity attacks while dealing all the damage your rage can muster.

Elf barbarians are frequently drawn to this paragon path, because its powers complement their natural mobility. Likewise, many rangers who nurture a connection to the primal forces of nature by taking barbarian multiclass feats find this path appealing.

WILDRUNNER PATH FEATURES

Hunter's Fury (11th level): When you spend an action point to make a melee attack, you can shift a number of squares equal to your Strength modifier after the attack.

Wildrunner's Swiftness (11th level): You gain a +1 bonus to your speed, or a +2 bonus while you are raging.

Wild Resilience (16th level): While you are raging, you gain a +2 bonus to saving throws.

WILDRUNNER EVOCATIONS

Shifting Wilds Strike — Wildrunner Attack 11

Like a predator in the wild, you shift to a better position after your attack.

Encounter ✦ Primal, Weapon
Standard Action Melee weapon
Target: One creature
Attack: Strength vs. AC
Hit: 2[W] + Strength modifier damage, and you shift 3 squares.
Special: If you use this power while you are raging, roll a d20. On a 10 or higher, you retain the use of this power.

Press the Kill — Wildrunner Utility 12

As one foe drops, you turn with lightning speed and prepare to attack your next target.

Encounter ✦ Primal
Free Action Personal
Trigger: You reduce an enemy to 0 hit points
Effect: You shift a number of squares equal to your Strength modifier.

Wildrunner's Rage — Wildrunner Attack 20

You dart among your enemies, hampering their movement with each well-placed attack.

Daily ✦ Primal, Rage, Weapon
Standard Action Melee weapon
Primary Target: One creature
Primary Attack: Strength vs. AC
Hit: 3[W] + Strength modifier damage, and the primary target is immobilized until the end of your next turn.
Miss: Half damage.
Effect: You shift a number of squares equal to your Strength modifier and then make a secondary attack.
  Secondary Target: One creature other than the primary target
  Secondary Attack: Strength vs. AC
  Hit: 2[W] + Strength modifier damage, and the secondary target is immobilized until the end of your next turn.
  Miss: Half damage.
Effect: You enter the wildrunner's rage. Until the rage ends, you gain a +2 bonus to AC and Reflex, and you ignore difficult terrain. In addition, you can shift 2 squares as a move action.

"The clash of blades, a note.
A battle fought, a verse.
The hero's war, a song."

CLASS TRAITS

Role: Leader. Your spells inspire and invigorate your allies. Your spells also include significant control elements, making controller a natural secondary role.

Power Source: Arcane. You channel magical power through words and music, studying long and hard to master the power contained in the lore and sagas of old.

Key Abilities: Charisma, Intelligence, Constitution

Armor Proficiencies: Cloth, leather, hide, chainmail; light shield

Weapon Proficiencies: Simple melee, longsword, scimitar, short sword, simple ranged, military ranged

Implements: Wands

Bonus to Defense: +1 Reflex, +1 Will

Hit Points at 1st Level: 12 + Constitution score

Hit Points per Level Gained: 5

Healing Surges per Day: 7 + Constitution modifier

Trained Skills: Arcana. From the class skills list below, choose four more trained skills at 1st level.

Class Skills: Acrobatics (Dex), Arcana (Int), Athletics (Str), Bluff (Cha), Diplomacy (Cha), Dungeoneering (Wis), Heal (Wis), History (Int), Insight (Wis), Intimidate (Cha), Nature (Wis), Perception (Wis), Religion (Int), Streetwise (Cha)

Class Features: Bardic Training, Bardic Virtue, *majestic word*, Multiclass Versatility, Skill Versatility, Song of Rest, *words of friendship*

Bards are artists first and foremost, and they practice magic just as they practice song, drama, or poetry. They have a clear sense of how people perceive reality, so they master charm magic and some illusions. Sagas of great heroes are part of a bard's repertoire, and most bards follow the example of many fables and become skilled in a variety of fields. A bard's artistic ability, knowledge of lore, and arcane might are widely respected, particularly among the world's rulers.

Art and magic share a sublime beauty, and, as a bard, you seek the place where the two meet. You might be a naturally talented wanderer who casts impressive spells almost instinctively, a student of a bardic college who learned ordered systems of magic and epic poetry, a warrior skald who mixes skill at arms with thundering music, a dashing performer known for putting on a good show even for your enemies, or a perfectionist who seeks the consummate formula that blends art and magic into a higher force.

A steady rhythm beats in the back of your mind as you brandish your sword. Your eyes and ears pick up the motion of the villains that surround you, and one glance tells you everything you need to know to defeat them. You whistle three staccato notes, letting your allies know the symphony of battle is about to begin.

BARD CLASS FEATURES

Bards have the following class features.

BARDIC TRAINING

You gain the Ritual Caster feat as a bonus feat, allowing you to use magical rituals. You own a ritual book, and it contains two rituals of your choice that you have mastered: one 1st-level ritual that has bard as a prerequisite (see Chapter 4) and another 1st-level ritual.

In addition, you can perform one bard ritual per day of your level or lower without expending components, although you must pay any other costs and use any focus required by the ritual. At 11th level, you can perform two bard rituals per day of your level or lower without expending components; at 21st level, you can perform three.

BARDIC VIRTUE

Bards praise many virtues in their stories, telling tales of people whose particular qualities set them above common folk. The valor of dauntless heroes and the cunning of great minds are among these virtues, and a bard can choose to emphasize either quality.

Choose one of the following options. The choice you make gives you the benefit described below and also provides bonuses to certain bard powers, as detailed in those powers.

Virtue of Cunning: Once per round, when an enemy attack misses an ally within a number of squares of you equal to 5 + your Intelligence modifier, you can slide that ally 1 square as a free action.

Virtue of Valor: Once per round, when any ally within 5 squares of you reduces an enemy to 0 hit points or bloodies an enemy, you can grant temporary hit points to that ally as a free action. The number of temporary hit points equals 1 + your Constitution modifier at 1st level, 3 + your Constitution modifier at 11th level, and 5 + your Constitution modifier at 21st level.

MAJESTIC WORD

The arcane power of a bard's voice can heal allies. You gain the *majestic word* power.

MULTICLASS VERSATILITY

You can choose class-specific multiclass feats from more than one class.

SKILL VERSATILITY

You gain a +1 bonus to untrained skill checks.

SONG OF REST

When you play an instrument or sing during a short rest, you and each ally who can hear you are affected by your Song of Rest. When an affected character spends healing surges at the end of the rest, that character regains additional hit points equal to your Charisma modifier with each healing surge. A character can be affected by only one Song of Rest at a time.

WORDS OF FRIENDSHIP

Bards use magic to honey their words and turn the simplest argument into a compelling oration. You gain the *words of friendship* power.

IMPLEMENTS

Bards use wands to direct and control their spells. When you wield a magic wand, you can add its enhancement bonus to the attack rolls and the damage rolls of bard powers and bard paragon path powers that have the implement keyword. Without a wand, you can still use these powers.

Songblades and some magic musical instruments (see Chapter 3) can be used as implements for bard powers and bard paragon path powers. Bards treasure these magic musical instruments not only for the power they offer, but for the wondrous melodies they produce in the hands of a skilled musician.

BARD OVERVIEW

Characteristics: Your powers are a mix of ranged, melee, and close attacks, giving you plenty of options whether you choose to lead from the front or the rear. Your attacks can provide bonuses and extra movement to you and your allies, or they can charm and deceive your enemies.

Religion: Many bards revere Corellon, patron of both artists and wielders of arcane magic. Cunning bards also honor Avandra and Sehanine, who are credited with inspiring trickery in the heroes of old. Valorous bards are more likely to revere Bahamut, Kord, or Moradin. Evil bards often worship Lolth, Tiamat, or Zehir.

Races: Half-elves are sometimes said to be the best bards, partly because their ability score bonuses favor the valorous bard and partly because their Dilettante racial trait complements the bard's Multiclass Versatility. Gnomes and tieflings both make excellent cunning bards.

Creating a Bard

Your choice of ability scores, class features, and powers suggests one of two builds based on the storied virtues of cunning and valor. All bards use Charisma for their attacks. Intelligence increases the effect of tricky attacks, and Constitution is best for powers that inspire allies.

Cunning Bard

The heroes of the past whom you hold as exemplars overcame adversity and escaped danger using their wits, by tricking their foes and concocting cunning stratagems. You seek to emulate those heroes, combining your winning personality with a keen intellect. You use Charisma for your attack powers, so make it your highest score, followed by Intelligence to improve the effects of your tricky powers. Constitution is a good third score. Look for powers that let you put your cunning to work. Most cunning bards focus on ranged attack powers, using a wand from a safe distance to orchestrate the flow of battle.

Suggested Class Feature: Virtue of Cunning
Suggested Feat: Advantage of Cunning
Suggested Skills: Arcana, Bluff, Intimidate, Perception, Streetwise
Suggested At-Will Powers: *misdirected mark, vicious mockery*
Suggested Encounter Power: *blunder*
Suggested Daily Power: *stirring shout*

Valorous Bard

To your mind, the ancient heroes most worthy of emulation are those whose courage in the face of overwhelming odds carried them to victory. Your own fortitude and forceful personality inspire similar valor in your allies. Your highest ability score should be Charisma, since you use it for attack powers, followed by Constitution to improve your powers of inspiration. It's a good idea to make Intelligence your third score. Choose powers that emphasize valor and endurance in the face of adversity. Most valorous bards focus on melee and close attack powers, wielding a sword in the thick of battle and leading by example.

Suggested Class Feature: Virtue of Valor
Suggested Feat: Strength of Valor
Suggested Skills: Arcana, Athletics, Diplomacy, Intimidate, Perception
Suggested At-Will Powers: *guiding strike, war song strike*
Suggested Encounter Power: *shout of triumph*
Suggested Daily Power: *slayer's song*

Bard Powers

Your powers are called spells, and you create them by gracefully mixing art, magic, and weapon skill.

Class Features

Each bard has the powers *majestic word* and *words of friendship*.

Majestic Word — Bard Feature

You utter words laden with preternatural inspiration, restoring your ally's stamina and making wounds seem insignificant.

Encounter (Special) ✦ Arcane, Healing
Minor Action   Close burst 5
         (10 at 11th level, 15 at 21st level)
Target: You or one ally in burst
Effect: The target can spend a healing surge and regain additional hit points equal to your Charisma modifier. You also slide the target 1 square.
  Level 6: 1d6 + Charisma modifier additional hit points.
  Level 11: 2d6 + Charisma modifier additional hit points.
  Level 16: 3d6 + Charisma modifier additional hit points.
  Level 21: 4d6 + Charisma modifier additional hit points.
  Level 26: 5d6 + Charisma modifier additional hit points.
Special: You can use this power twice per encounter, but only once per round. At 16th level, you can use this power three times per encounter, but only once per round.

Words of Friendship — Bard Feature

You infuse your words with arcane power, transforming even the simplest speech into compelling oratory.

Encounter ✦ Arcane
Minor Action   Personal
Effect: You gain a +5 power bonus to the next Diplomacy check you make before the end of your next turn.

Level 1 At-Will Spells

Guiding Strike — Bard Attack 1

Your weapon stroke guides your allies, showing them where to focus their attacks.

At-Will ✦ Arcane, Weapon
Standard Action   Melee weapon
Target: One creature
Attack: Charisma vs. AC
Hit: 1[W] + Charisma modifier damage, and the target takes a −2 penalty to the defense of your choice until the end of your next turn.
  Level 21: 2[W] + Charisma modifier damage.

Misdirected Mark — Bard Attack 1

You conceal your arcane attack, tricking your foe into thinking the attack came from one of your allies.

At-Will ✦ Arcane, Implement
Standard Action   Ranged 10
Target: One creature
Attack: Charisma vs. Reflex
Hit: 1d8 + Charisma modifier damage, and the target is marked by an ally within 5 squares of you until the end of your next turn.
  Level 21: 2d8 + Charisma modifier damage.

Vicious Mockery — Bard Attack 1

You unleash a string of insults at your foe, weaving them with bardic magic to send the creature into a blind rage.

At-Will ✦ Arcane, Charm, Implement, Psychic
Standard Action　　　　**Ranged** 10
Target: One creature
Attack: Charisma vs. Will
Hit: 1d6 + Charisma modifier psychic damage, and the target takes a -2 penalty to attack rolls until the end of your next turn.
　Level 21: 2d6 + Charisma modifier damage.

War Song Strike — Bard Attack 1

You sing a song of war and victory, invigorating your allies as they press the attack.

At-Will ✦ Arcane, Weapon
Standard Action　　　　**Melee** weapon
Target: One creature
Attack: Charisma vs. AC
Hit: 1[W] + Charisma modifier damage, and any ally who hits the target before the end of your next turn gains temporary hit points equal to your Constitution modifier.
　Level 21: 2[W] + Charisma modifier damage.

LEVEL 1 ENCOUNTER SPELLS

Blunder — Bard Attack 1

You fog your foe's mind, causing it to stumble past your allies.

Encounter ✦ Arcane, Charm, Implement
Standard Action　　　　**Ranged** 5
Target: One creature
Attack: Charisma vs. Will
Hit: 1d6 + Charisma modifier damage, and you slide the target 2 squares. During the slide, you or one of your allies can make a melee basic attack against the target as a free action, with a +2 power bonus to the attack roll.
Virtue of Cunning: The power bonus to the attack roll equals 1 + your Intelligence modifier.

Fast Friends — Bard Attack 1

You sing a tune of false friendship, leaving your foe in a reverie.

Encounter ✦ Arcane, Charm, Implement
Standard Action　　　　**Ranged** 5
Target: One creature
Attack: Charisma vs. Will
Hit: Choose yourself or an ally. The target cannot attack that character until the end of your next turn or until you or one of your allies attacks the target.

Inspiring Refrain — Bard Attack 1

Your weapon hums with an arcane song that helps guide nearby allies to glory.

Encounter ✦ Arcane, Weapon
Standard Action　　　　**Melee** weapon
Target: One creature
Attack: Charisma vs. AC
Hit: 2[W] + Charisma modifier damage, and each ally within 5 squares of you gains a +1 power bonus to attack rolls until the end of your next turn.

Shout of Triumph — Bard Attack 1

You unleash a mighty call of battle, scattering your enemies while urging your allies forward.

Encounter ✦ Arcane, Implement, Thunder
Standard Action　　　　**Close** blast 3
Target: Each enemy in blast
Attack: Charisma vs. Fortitude
Hit: 1d6 + Charisma modifier thunder damage, and you push the target 1 square.
Effect: You slide each ally in the blast 1 square.
Virtue of Valor: The number of squares you push the target and slide the allies equals your Constitution modifier.

LEVEL 1 DAILY SPELLS

Echoes of the Guardian — Bard Attack 1

You recite a verse from the saga of a great warrior, confounding your enemy so that one of your companions can more easily protect the others.

Daily ✦ Arcane, Weapon
Standard Action　　　　**Melee** weapon
Target: One creature
Attack: Charisma vs. AC
Hit: 2[W] + Charisma modifier damage, and until the end of your next turn, the target is marked by an ally within 5 squares of you.
Miss: Half damage.
Effect: Until the end of the encounter, once during each of your turns, choose an ally within 5 squares of you when you hit an enemy. Until the end of your next turn, that enemy is marked by that ally.

Slayer's Song — Bard Attack 1

You sing a tune of war that diminishes your foes' defenses with each blow you strike.

Daily ✦ Arcane, Weapon
Standard Action　　　　**Melee** weapon
Target: One creature
Attack: Charisma vs. AC
Hit: 2[W] + Charisma modifier damage, and the target grants combat advantage to you and your allies (save ends).
Miss: Half damage.
Effect: Until the end of the encounter, whenever you hit an enemy, that enemy grants combat advantage to you and your allies until the end of your next turn.

Stirring Shout — Bard Attack 1

Your shout of wrath stabs into your foe's mind. Each time your allies hit that foe, they draw strength from its weakness.

Daily ✦ Arcane, Healing, Implement, Psychic
Standard Action　　　　**Ranged** 10
Target: One creature
Attack: Charisma vs. Will
Hit: 2d6 + Charisma modifier psychic damage.
Effect: Until the end of the encounter, whenever an ally hits the target, that ally regains hit points equal to your Charisma modifier.

Verse of Triumph
Bard Attack 1

Your voice crescendos as you sing of victory. Your inspirational words drive allies forward to attack.

Daily ✦ Arcane, Charm, Weapon
Standard Action   Melee weapon
Target: One creature
Attack: Charisma vs. AC
Hit: 2[W] + Charisma modifier damage.
Miss: Half damage.
Effect: Until the end of the encounter, you and any ally within 5 squares of you gain a +1 power bonus to damage rolls and saving throws. In addition, whenever you or an ally reduces an enemy to 0 hit points with an attack, you and any ally within 5 squares of the enemy can shift 1 square as a free action.

LEVEL 2 UTILITY SPELLS

Hunter's Tune
Bard Utility 2

You shape the flow of sound, containing it and creating an area of silence.

Daily ✦ Arcane
Minor Action   Ranged 10
Target: One ally
Effect: Until the end of your next turn, the target gains a +5 power bonus to Stealth checks and doesn't take a penalty to Stealth checks for moving more than 2 squares or running.
Sustain Minor: The effect persists if the target is within range.

Inspire Competence
Bard Utility 2

Your magic channels the skill of ancient experts to help with the task at hand.

Encounter ✦ Arcane
Minor Action   Close burst 5
Target: You and each ally in burst
Effect: Choose a skill. Until the end of the encounter, each target gains a +2 power bonus to his or her next check using that skill.

Song of Courage
Bard Utility 2

Your magic creates shouts of encouragement, making it seem as though an entire army were cheering on your allies.

Daily ✦ Arcane, Zone
Minor Action   Close burst 5
Effect: The burst creates a zone of inspirational shouts that lasts until the end of your next turn. When you move, the zone moves with you, remaining centered on you. While within the zone, any ally gains a +1 power bonus to attack rolls.
Sustain Minor: The zone persists.

Song of Defense
Bard Utility 2

You intone a few notes from a battle hymn, and your magic bolsters your allies' ability to parry attacks.

Daily ✦ Arcane, Zone
Minor Action   Close burst 5
Effect: The burst creates a zone of bolstering song that lasts until the end of your next turn. When you move, the zone moves with you, remaining centered on you. While within the zone, any ally gains a +1 power bonus to AC.
Sustain Minor: The zone persists.

LEVEL 3 ENCOUNTER SPELLS

Charger's Call
Bard Attack 3

You weave a song of fearless knights and mighty chargers, encouraging your allies to throw themselves into the fray.

Encounter ✦ Arcane, Weapon
Standard Action   Melee weapon
Target: One creature
Attack: Charisma vs. AC
Hit: 2[W] + Charisma modifier damage, and each ally within 5 squares of you gains a +2 bonus to attack rolls while charging until the end of your next turn.
  Virtue of Valor: The bonus to attack rolls equals 1 + your Constitution modifier.

Cunning Ferocity
Bard Attack 3

The mark of your weapon on your target's hide gives strength to your allies' attacks against the same foe.

Encounter ✦ Arcane, Weapon
Standard Action   Melee weapon
Target: One creature
Attack: Charisma vs. Reflex
Hit: 1[W] + Charisma modifier damage, and each ally within 5 squares of you gains a +2 bonus to damage rolls against the target until the end of your next turn.
  Virtue of Cunning: The bonus to damage rolls equals 1 + your Intelligence modifier.

Dissonant Strain
Bard Attack 3

You sing in two pitches at once, creating a song that harms your foe while helping your ally.

Encounter ✦ Arcane, Implement, Psychic
Standard Action   Ranged 5
Target: One creature
Attack: Charisma vs. Will
Hit: 2d6 + Charisma modifier psychic damage, and the target takes a –2 penalty to attack rolls until the end of your next turn. In addition, an ally within 5 squares of you can make a saving throw.

Impelling Force
Bard Attack 3

A bolt of force shoves your foe next to one of your allies.

Encounter ✦ Arcane, Force, Implement
Standard Action   Ranged 10
Target: One creature
Attack: Charisma vs. Fortitude
Hit: 1d10 + Charisma modifier force damage, and you slide the target 5 squares to a space adjacent to one of your allies.

LEVEL 5 DAILY SPELLS

Satire of Bravery — Bard Attack 5

Your verse mocks your foes' courage, forcing them to become the cowards you describe.

Daily ✦ Arcane, Implement, Psychic
Standard Action   **Close** blast 3
Target: Each enemy in blast
Attack: Charisma vs. Will
Hit: 2d6 + Charisma modifier psychic damage, and the target is affected by your satire of bravery (save ends). While the target is affected by the satire, if the target ends its turn closer to you than where it started its turn, the target takes 1d6 + Charisma modifier psychic damage and is dazed until the end of its next turn.
Miss: Half damage.
Effect: You push the target 3 squares.

Song of Discord — Bard Attack 5

You foster distrust in one of your foes, causing it to strike out at its allies.

Daily ✦ Arcane, Charm, Implement
Standard Action   **Ranged** 10
Target: One creature
Attack: Charisma vs. Will
Hit: The target is dominated until the end of your next turn.
Effect: The target makes a basic attack against an enemy of your choice as a free action.

Tune of Ice and Wind — Bard Attack 5

You hum a discordant tune, slowing your enemies with ice and moving your allies with wind.

Daily ✦ Arcane, Cold, Implement
Standard Action   **Area** burst 1 within 10 squares
Target: Each enemy in burst
Attack: Charisma vs. Will
Hit: 2d6 + Charisma modifier cold damage, and the target is slowed (save ends).
Miss: Half damage, and the target is slowed until the end of your next turn.
Effect: You slide each ally in the burst 3 squares.

Word of Mystic Warding — Bard Attack 5

A word of power assaults your foe's mind, establishing a ward that harms it further if it draws closer to the ally you name.

Daily ✦ Arcane, Psychic, Weapon
Standard Action   **Melee** weapon
Target: One creature
Attack: Charisma vs. AC
Hit: 3[W] + Charisma modifier psychic damage. Choose an ally within 5 squares of you. If the target moves closer to that ally during the target's turn, the target takes psychic damage equal to your Charisma modifier (save ends).
Miss: Half damage.

LEVEL 6 UTILITY SPELLS

Allegro — Bard Utility 6

You drum out a hasty rhythm that infuses you and your comrades with magical speed.

Daily ✦ Arcane
Minor Action   **Close** burst 10
Target: You and each ally in burst
Effect: You slide each target 2 squares.

Ode to Sacrifice — Bard Utility 6

Like many heroes who prove their worth by shouldering the burdens of others, you take a harmful effect from an ally.

Encounter ✦ Arcane
Minor Action   **Close** burst 5
Target: One ally in burst
Effect: You transfer one effect on the target that a save can end to yourself or to another ally in the burst. The new subject of the effect gains a power bonus to saving throws against that effect equal to your Constitution modifier.

Song of Conquest — Bard Utility 6

Your arcane song bolsters your allies, so they fight your foes with renewed vigor.

Encounter ✦ Arcane
Minor Action   **Personal**
Effect: Until the end of your next turn, any ally within 5 squares of you who hits an enemy gains temporary hit points equal to 3 + your Constitution modifier.

Trickster's Healing — Bard Utility 6

Your magic turns an enemy's blunder into an opportunity for your allies to overcome their wounds.

Daily ✦ Arcane, Healing
Immediate Reaction   **Close** burst 10
Trigger: An attack misses an ally within 10 squares of you
Target: Each ally in burst missed by the triggering attack
Effect: Each target regains hit points equal to one-half your level + your Intelligence modifier.

LEVEL 7 ENCOUNTER SPELLS

Deflect Attention — Bard Attack 7

You focus a foe's violent determination elsewhere, making you or an ally invisible to it for a moment.

Encounter ✦ Arcane, Implement, Psychic
Standard Action   **Ranged** 10
Target: One creature
Attack: Charisma vs. Will
Hit: 2d6 + Charisma modifier psychic damage, and you or an ally within 10 squares of you becomes invisible to the target until the end of your next turn.

Distracting Shout
Bard Attack 7

Your shout draws the enemy's attention so that your allies can maneuver around the foe, letting them get in close or get away.

Encounter ✦ Arcane, Implement, Thunder
Standard Action   **Ranged** 10
Target: One creature
Attack: Charisma vs. Will
Hit: 2d8 + Charisma modifier thunder damage, and the
target takes a -5 penalty to opportunity attack rolls until
the end of your next turn.
   Virtue of Cunning: The penalty to opportunity attack rolls
equals 4 + your Intelligence modifier.

Scorpion's Claw Strike
Bard Attack 7

Your distraction allows one of your allies to slip around a foe.

Encounter ✦ Arcane, Weapon
Standard Action   **Melee** weapon
Target: One creature
Attack: Charisma vs. AC
Hit: 2[W] + Charisma modifier damage, and you slide an
ally who is adjacent to the target to another space adjacent to it.
   Virtue of Valor: Until the end of your next turn, the ally
also gains a power bonus to AC equal to your Constitution
modifier.

Unluck
Bard Attack 7

You manipulate what was once an ode to fate, speaking it in reverse and warping the weave of fortune.

Encounter ✦ Arcane, Implement, Necrotic
Standard Action   **Ranged** 5
Target: One creature
Attack: Charisma vs. Reflex
Hit: 1d8 + Charisma modifier necrotic damage. The next
time the target makes an attack roll before the end of
your next turn, you roll a d20 and can replace the target's roll with yours. In addition, choose an ally within
5 squares of you. The next time that ally attacks the
target before the end of your next turn, you roll a d20
and can replace the ally's roll with yours.

LEVEL 9 DAILY SPELLS

Forceful Conduit
Bard Attack 9

A jolt of pain establishes an arcane link between your foe and one of your allies. Your ally can see through the foe's eyes and channel his or her own powers through its body.

Daily ✦ Arcane, Implement, Psychic
Standard Action   **Ranged** 10
Target: One creature
Attack: Charisma vs. Will
Hit: 2d8 + Charisma modifier psychic damage, and the
target is affected by a forceful conduit (save ends).
Choose an ally within 10 squares of you. While the
target is affected by this forceful conduit, that ally can
make implement attacks during his or her turn as if occupying the target's space.
   Miss: Half damage. Until the end of your next turn, an ally
within 10 squares of you can make implement attacks
during his or her turn as if occupying the target's space.

Hideous Laughter
Bard Attack 9

Horrible convulsions seize your foe in a terrible mockery of laughter.

Daily ✦ Arcane, Charm, Implement, Psychic
Standard Action   **Ranged** 10
Target: One creature
Attack: Charisma vs. Will
Hit: 3d8 + Charisma modifier psychic damage, and the
target can't take opportunity actions and takes a -2
penalty to attack rolls (save ends both).
   Aftereffect: The target can't take opportunity actions (save
ends).
   Miss: Half damage, and the target can't take opportunity
actions until the end of your next turn.

Hymn of the Daring Rescue
Bard Attack 9

Your attack resonates in an arcane song that allows an ally to teleport to your side.

Daily ✦ Arcane, Teleportation, Weapon
Standard Action   **Melee** weapon
Target: One creature
Attack: Charisma vs. Reflex
Hit: 3[W] + Charisma modifier damage.
Effect: Choose an ally within 5 squares of you. Until the end
of the encounter, that ally can teleport to a space adjacent
to you as a move action.

Thunder Blade
Bard Attack 9

Your weapon resonates with thunder, smiting your foe and enabling you to move enemies into locations where your allies can more easily reach them.

Daily ✦ Arcane, Thunder, Weapon
Standard Action   **Melee** weapon
Target: One creature
Attack: Charisma vs. AC
Hit: 3[W] + Charisma modifier thunder damage, and you
slide the target 2 squares.
Effect: Until the end of the encounter, whenever you hit a
target with an at-will attack power, you slide the target 2
squares to a space that must be adjacent to at least one of
your allies.

LEVEL 10 UTILITY SPELLS

Illusory Erasure
Bard Utility 10

Your magic song makes an ally abruptly disappear, giving him or her a chance to sneak up on foes.

Encounter ✦ Arcane, Illusion
Minor Action   **Ranged** 10
Target: One ally
Effect: The target becomes invisible until the end of your
next turn, and you slide the target 2 squares.

Song of Recovery
Bard Utility 10

You instill a sense of perseverance in your allies with an inspiring song.

Encounter ✦ Arcane
Minor Action   **Personal**
Effect: Until the end of your next turn, any ally within 5
squares of you gains a +2 power bonus to saving throws.

Veil
Bard Utility 10

You mask the appearance of your party, sculpting an illusory disguise.

Daily ✦ Arcane, Illusion
Minor Action   **Close** burst 10
Target: You and each ally in burst
Effect: You transform the auditory, tactile, and visual qualities of the targets' bodies and equipment. Each target assumes the appearance of a humanoid of the same size, even the appearance of a specific individual you have seen. The illusion lasts for 1 hour, or you can end it as a minor action. A creature can recognize a target's form as illusory with an Insight check opposed by that target's Bluff check with a +5 power bonus.

Word of Life
Bard Utility 10

A single word is sufficient to save an ally from death's grasp while punishing the foe who dealt the deadly blow.

Daily ✦ Arcane, Healing
Immediate Reaction   **Close** burst 20
Trigger: An enemy attack reduces an ally within 20 squares of you to 0 hit points or fewer
Target: The triggering ally in burst
Effect: The target can spend a healing surge. In addition, the attacking enemy takes a –5 penalty to all defenses until the end of your next turn.

LEVEL 13 ENCOUNTER SPELLS

Earthquake Strike
Bard Attack 13

The rhythm of your attack makes the earth quake beneath your and your allies' targets.

Encounter ✦ Arcane, Weapon
Standard Action   **Melee** weapon
Target: One creature
Attack: Charisma vs. AC
Hit: 2[W] + Charisma modifier damage, and you knock the target prone. Until the end of your next turn, each ally within 10 squares of you can knock prone any creature he or she hits.
    Virtue of Valor: Until the end of your next turn, the allies gain a bonus to damage rolls equal to your Constitution modifier.

Foolhardy Fighting
Bard Attack 13

Your attack inspires recklessness in your foe, causing it to act without caution.

Encounter ✦ Arcane, Charm, Implement, Psychic
Standard Action   **Ranged** 10
Target: One creature
Attack: Charisma vs. Will
Hit: 1d10 + Charisma modifier psychic damage. Until the end of your next turn, any attack the target makes provokes opportunity attacks.
    Virtue of Cunning: Until the end of your next turn, the target takes a penalty to attack rolls equal to your Intelligence modifier.

Harmony of the Two
Bard Attack 13

As you strike your foe, a nearby ally lashes out with an attack in harmony with yours.

Encounter ✦ Arcane, Weapon
Standard Action   **Melee** weapon
Target: One creature
Attack: Charisma vs. AC
Hit: 2[W] + Charisma modifier damage. An ally within 2 squares of you can make a basic attack against the target as a free action.

Song of Storms
Bard Attack 13

With a sonorous hum, you summon lightning, blasting your foes with it and imbuing your allies' attacks with its power.

Encounter ✦ Arcane, Implement, Lightning
Standard Action   **Close** blast 5
Target: Each enemy in blast
Attack: Charisma vs. Reflex
Hit: 2d6 + Charisma modifier lightning damage. Each ally in the blast deals 1d6 extra lightning damage on a hit until the end of your next turn.

LEVEL 15 DAILY SPELLS

Confusing Chorus
Bard Attack 15

Hundreds of voices jeer and threaten your foe from all sides. Lashing out blindly, the foe might hit anyone.

Daily ✦ Arcane, Charm, Implement, Psychic
Standard Action   **Ranged** 10
Target: One creature
Attack: Charisma vs. Will
Hit: 3d6 + Charisma modifier psychic damage. As the first action of each of the target's turns, the target makes a melee basic attack against a creature of your choice as a free action (save ends).
Miss: Half damage. As the first action of the target's next turn, the target makes a melee basic attack against a creature of your choice as a free action.

Dance of Biting Wind
Bard Attack 15

Your attack impedes your foe's attacks. Its echoes carry you and your allies in a combat dance, letting you move away from clumsy attackers.

Daily ✦ Arcane, Weapon
Standard Action   **Melee** weapon
Target: One creature
Attack: Charisma vs. AC
Hit: 2[W] + Charisma modifier damage, and the target takes a –2 penalty to attack rolls (save ends).
Effect: Until the end of the encounter, whenever an enemy's attack misses you or an ally within 5 squares of you, the target of the attack can shift 1 square as a free action.

Menacing Thunder — Bard Attack 15

The echoes of your blow resound as the fight continues, guiding the attacks of your allies to bring your foes to a quick end.

Daily ✦ Arcane, Implement, Thunder, Zone
Standard Action   **Close** burst 2
Target: Each enemy in burst
Attack: Charisma vs. Fortitude
Hit: 2d8 + Charisma modifier thunder damage.
Effect: The burst creates a zone of resonating thunder that lasts until the end of the encounter. While within the zone, any ally gains a +2 power bonus to attack rolls.

Quick Steel Dance — Bard Attack 15

You land a mighty blow that befuddles your foe, redirecting its attention to an ally near you. The echoes of that strike quicken your allies, allowing them to react to a foe's movement.

Daily ✦ Arcane, Weapon
Standard Action   **Melee** weapon
Target: One creature
Attack: Charisma vs. AC
Hit: 3[W] + Charisma modifier damage, and until the end of your next turn, the target is marked by an ally within 10 squares of you.
Miss: Half damage.
Effect: Until the end of the encounter, whenever an enemy that is adjacent to any of your allies shifts, those allies can each shift 1 square as an opportunity action.

Level 16 Utility Spells

Blink Zone — Bard Utility 16

You warp the boundaries between worlds, causing the boundaries to fade and mingle.

Daily ✦ Arcane, Teleportation, Zone
Standard Action   **Area** burst 2 within 10 squares
Effect: The burst creates a zone of planar instability that lasts until the end of your next turn. While within the zone, you and any ally gain a +2 power bonus to AC and Reflex and can teleport 2 squares as a move action.
Sustain Minor: The zone persists.

Chorus of Recovery — Bard Utility 16

You whisper a quiet song of peace and health, fortifying your allies against the ills that plague them.

Daily ✦ Arcane
Minor Action   **Close** burst 3
Effect: The burst creates a zone of rejuvenation that lasts until the end of your next turn. When you move, the zone moves with you, remaining centered on you. Any ally who starts his or her turn within the zone can make a saving throw.
Sustain Minor: The zone persists.

Elegy of the Undefeated — Bard Utility 16

This ancient lament returns an ally from the brink of death.

Daily ✦ Arcane, Healing
Standard Action   **Close** burst 5
Target: One dying ally in burst
Effect: The target regains hit points as if he or she had spent two healing surges. The target can then stand up as a free action.

Song of Sublime Snowfall — Bard Utility 16

Your song causes gleaming white motes to fall from above, healing your allies and pulling at your foes as they try to move in the area.

Daily ✦ Arcane, Healing, Zone
Standard Action   **Area** burst 2 within 10 squares
Target: Each ally in burst
Effect: Each target regains hit points equal to your Charisma modifier. The burst creates a zone of difficult terrain for enemies that lasts until the end of your next turn. This difficult terrain also affects flying enemies.
Sustain Minor: The zone persists, and each target within the zone regains hit points equal to your Charisma modifier.

Level 17 Encounter Spells

Masks of Menace — Bard Attack 17

You warp your enemy's perception so that it perceives your allies as frightful beasts. Only one ally retains a normal appearance.

Encounter ✦ Arcane, Fear, Implement, Psychic
Standard Action   **Ranged** 10
Target: One creature
Attack: Charisma vs. Will
Hit: 3d6 + Charisma modifier psychic damage. Choose an ally within 5 squares of you. Until the end of your next turn, the target takes a -5 penalty to attack rolls for any attack that doesn't include that ally as a target.

Shout of Evasion — Bard Attack 17

Your shout batters your foe with arcane thunder and spurs you and your allies into motion.

Encounter ✦ Arcane, Implement, Thunder
Standard Action   **Ranged** 10
Target: One creature
Attack: Charisma vs. Reflex
Hit: 2d8 + Charisma modifier thunder damage, and you and each ally within 10 squares of you can shift 2 squares as a free action.
  Virtue of Cunning: The number of squares you and your allies can shift equals 1 + your Intelligence modifier.

Song of Summons — Bard Attack 17

As you strike your foe with your weapon, you call an ally to lend aid to your attack.

Encounter ✦ Arcane, Teleportation, Weapon
Standard Action   **Melee** weapon
Target: One creature
Attack: Charisma vs. AC
Hit: 2[W] + Charisma modifier damage, and you teleport an ally within 10 squares of you to a space adjacent to you.
  Virtue of Valor: Until the end of your next turn, the ally also gains a power bonus to attack rolls against the target equal to your Constitution modifier.

Word of Vulnerability — Bard Attack 17

You speak a word of power as you strike your foe, and the foe becomes vulnerable to your allies' attacks.

Encounter ✦ Arcane, Weapon
Standard Action   **Melee** weapon
Target: One creature
Attack: Charisma vs. AC
Hit: 3[W] + Charisma modifier damage. Until the end of your next turn, each ally who hits the target and has combat advantage against it deals extra damage equal to your Charisma modifier.

LEVEL 19 DAILY SPELLS

Encircling Dance — Bard Attack 19

As dazzling light bursts around your foes, you and your allies can move to better positions.

Daily ✦ Arcane, Implement, Radiant
Standard Action   **Ranged** 10
Target: One or two creatures
Attack: Charisma vs. Reflex
Hit: 3d8 + Charisma modifier radiant damage.
Miss: Half damage.
Effect: You and each ally within 10 squares of you can shift 5 squares as a free action.

Increasing the Tempo — Bard Attack 19

Your ally attacks with incredible speed, becoming a blur of motion.

Daily ✦ Arcane
Standard Action   **Ranged** 10
Target: One ally
Effect: The target makes four basic attacks as a free action.

Irresistible Dance — Bard Attack 19

An eerie piping fills an area, forcing the creatures there into an idiot dance that sends them careening around at your command.

Daily ✦ Arcane, Charm, Implement, Psychic
Standard Action   **Area** burst 1 within 10 squares
Target: Each creature in burst
Attack: Charisma vs. Will
Hit: 3d6 + Charisma modifier psychic damage, and the target grants combat advantage to you and your allies (save ends).
Miss: Half damage.
Effect: You slide each target a number of squares equal to your Charisma modifier.

Satire of Prowess — Bard Attack 19

Your verse mocks your foe's attacks and forces it to conform to your description of its ineptitude.

Daily ✦ Arcane, Charm, Implement, Psychic
Standard Action   **Ranged** 10
Target: One creature
Attack: Charisma vs. Will
Hit: 4d6 + Charisma modifier psychic damage, and the target is affected by your satire of prowess (save ends). While the target is affected by the satire, the target rolls twice when it makes an attack roll and must use the lower roll, and any attacker rolls twice when it makes an attack roll against the target and must use the higher roll.
Miss: Half damage. Until the end of your next turn, the target rolls twice when it makes an attack roll and must use the lower roll, and any attacker rolls twice when it makes an attack roll against the target and must use the higher roll.

LEVEL 22 UTILITY SPELLS

Elegy Unwritten — Bard Utility 22

Your quick word staves off death before it can grasp your friend.

Daily ✦ Arcane, Healing
Immediate Interrupt   **Close** burst 5
Trigger: An ally within 5 squares of you dies
Target: The triggering ally in burst
Effect: The target regains hit points as if he or she had spent a healing surge. In addition, the target can stand up and shift 2 squares as a free action.

Invisible Troupe — Bard Utility 22

As you whisper a word, you and your allies fade from view.

Encounter ✦ Arcane, Illusion
Minor Action   **Close** burst 3
Target: You and each ally in burst
Effect: Each target becomes invisible until the end of your next turn.

Mirrored Entourage — Bard Utility 22

You weave a song of illusion, causing duplicates to appear next to your allies. The duplicates try to intercept enemy attacks and disappear when they succeed.

Daily ✦ Arcane, Illusion
Minor Action   Close burst 20
Target: Each ally in burst
Effect: Each target gains two illusory duplicates of him- or herself that last until the end of the encounter. Until the duplicates disappear, the duplicates share the target's space and move with him or her. In addition, the target gains a +4 power bonus to AC. When an attack against AC misses the target, one of that target's duplicates disappears, and the power bonus to AC decreases by 2.

Song of Transition — Bard Utility 22

Your song swells and bends planar boundaries, allowing allies to make jaunts through space.

Daily ✦ Arcane, Teleportation, Zone
Minor Action   Area burst 1 within 10 squares
Effect: You create a zone of music that lasts until the end of your next turn. While within the zone, you and any ally can teleport to any space within 10 squares of you as a move action.
Sustain Minor: The zone persists.

LEVEL 23 ENCOUNTER SPELLS

Echoes in Time — Bard Attack 23

As arcane force tears into your foe, the force rends the fabric of time. For a moment, your allies can move about and attack before teleporting back to the place they now stand.

Encounter ✦ Arcane, Force, Implement, Teleportation
Standard Action   Ranged 10
Target: One creature
Attack: Charisma vs. Reflex
Hit: 3d8 + Charisma modifier force damage. Each ally within 10 squares of you, as the last action of his or her next turn, can teleport as a free action back to the space where he or she started that turn.
  Virtue of Cunning: Until the start of your next turn, any ally who teleports using this power gains a power bonus to all defenses equal to your Intelligence modifier.

Rhythm of Disorientation — Bard Attack 23

A clatter of sounds surrounds your foes, causing them to lose their balance and creating opportunities for your allies to attack.

Encounter ✦ Arcane, Implement, Thunder
Standard Action   Area burst 2 within 10 squares
Target: Each enemy in burst
Attack: Charisma vs. Will
Hit: 1d6 + Charisma modifier thunder damage, and you knock the target prone. In addition, an ally of yours adjacent to the target can make a melee basic attack against it as a free action.

Song of Liberation — Bard Attack 23

A burst of arcane music erupts from your weapon and washes over your allies, loosing them from bonds that restrain their movement.

Encounter ✦ Arcane, Weapon
Standard Action   Melee weapon
Target: One creature
Attack: Charisma vs. Reflex
Hit: 4[W] + Charisma modifier damage, and the immobilized, restrained, and slowed conditions end on each ally within 5 squares of you, provided a save can end the condition.

Weal and Woe — Bard Attack 23

Your attack brings doom to your foe and glory to your ally.

Encounter ✦ Arcane, Weapon
Standard Action   Melee weapon
Target: One creature
Attack: Charisma vs. AC
Hit: 3[W] + Charisma modifier damage, and one ally adjacent to the target makes a saving throw with a +5 power bonus.
  Virtue of Valor: The ally gains a power bonus to his or her next attack roll against the target equal to your Constitution modifier.

LEVEL 25 DAILY SPELLS

Adversarial Song — Bard Attack 25

Your song erupts in your foe's mind, weakening its attacks against any creature but the ally you name. At the same time, it bolsters that ally so that he or she can fight the foe to the bitter end.

Daily ✦ Arcane, Charm, Implement, Psychic
Standard Action   Ranged 10
Target: One creature
Attack: Charisma vs. Will
Hit: 3d10 + Charisma modifier psychic damage.
Miss: Half damage.
Effect: Choose an ally within 10 squares of you. The target deals half damage to any of your allies except the chosen ally (save ends). In addition, that ally deals 1d10 extra damage on a hit against the target until the end of the encounter.

Fraught with Failure — Bard Attack 25

Your mocking song saps your foe's will and breaks its confidence, leaving it immobile and ineffectual.

Daily ✦ Arcane, Charm, Psychic, Weapon
Standard Action   Melee weapon
Target: One creature
Attack: Charisma vs. AC
Hit: 2[W] + Charisma modifier psychic damage, and the target is immobilized (save ends) and weakened (save ends).
Miss: Half damage, and the target is immobilized and weakened until the end of your next turn.

Frenzied Rhythm
Bard Attack 25

The wild rhythm of your chant drives your enemies into senseless violence upon each other.

Daily ✦ Arcane, Charm, Implement
Standard Action   **Close** burst 5
Target: Each enemy in burst
Attack: Charisma vs. Will
Hit: You slide the target 5 squares. The target makes a basic attack as a free action against a creature of your choice. The target is then stunned until the end of your next turn.
Miss: The target is dazed until the end of your next turn.

Vision Distortion
Bard Attack 25

A burst of blinding light skews the vision of your enemies.

Daily ✦ Arcane, Illusion, Implement, Radiant
Standard Action   **Area** burst 2 within 20 squares
Target: Each creature in burst
Attack: Charisma vs. Will
Hit: 3d8 + Charisma modifier radiant damage. The target's vision is distorted (save ends). While the target's vision is distorted, you are invisible to the target, and whenever an ally hits it, that ally becomes invisible to the target until the end of the ally's next turn.
Miss: Half damage, and you are invisible to the target until the end of your next turn.

LEVEL 27 ENCOUNTER SPELLS

Bond of Malediction
Bard Attack 27

You intone a dread curse upon your foe, linking its fate to the safety of your ally. If your friend is hurt, your foe will be hurt as well.

Encounter ✦ Arcane, Implement, Psychic
Standard Action   **Ranged** 10
Target: One creature
Attack: Charisma vs. Reflex
Hit: 3d10 + Charisma modifier psychic damage. Choose an ally within 10 squares of you. Until the end of your next turn, the target takes 10 psychic damage whenever that ally takes damage.
   Virtue of Cunning: Whenever the ally takes damage, the target takes psychic damage equal to 10 + your Intelligence modifier.

Kaleidoscopic Burst
Bard Attack 27

You sculpt prismatic colors that dazzle your enemies and allow allies to escape.

Encounter ✦ Arcane, Implement, Radiant
Standard Action   **Area** burst 2 within 10 squares
Target: Each enemy in burst
Attack: Charisma vs. Will
Hit: 3d8 + Charisma modifier radiant damage.
Effect: Each ally in the burst can shift 2 squares as a free action.

Surge of Valor
Bard Attack 27

Inspired and empowered by the example of your fierce blow, your allies surge forward to attack.

Encounter ✦ Arcane, Weapon
Standard Action   **Melee** weapon
Target: One creature
Attack: Charisma vs. AC
Hit: 2[W] + Charisma modifier damage, and each ally within 10 squares of you can shift 2 squares and make a melee basic attack as a free action.
   Virtue of Valor: The allies gain a bonus to the attack roll and the damage roll equal to 1 + your Constitution modifier.

LEVEL 29 DAILY SPELLS

Hero's Beacon
Bard Attack 29

Your weapon erupts in blazing light that ignites your foe in radiant flames. The light of those flames persists, healing your allies and searing your enemies.

Daily ✦ Arcane, Healing, Radiant, Weapon, Zone
Standard Action   **Melee** weapon
Target: One creature
Attack: Charisma vs. AC
Hit: 4[W] + Charisma modifier radiant damage.
Effect: The attack creates a zone of bright light in a burst 2 centered on the target. The zone lasts until the end of the encounter. When the target moves, the zone moves with it, remaining centered on it. Any ally who starts his or her turn within the zone regains hit points equal to your Charisma modifier. Any enemy that starts its turn within the zone takes 10 radiant damage.

Satire of Leadership
Bard Attack 29

Your verse mocks your foe's leadership and bends reality to conform with your words; any enemy near your foe is more vulnerable to attack.

Daily ✦ Arcane, Implement, Psychic
Standard Action   **Ranged** 10
Target: One creature
Attack: Charisma vs. Will
Hit: 5d10 + Charisma modifier psychic damage.
Effect: The target and each enemy within 3 squares of it take a -2 penalty to all defenses and gain vulnerable 5 to all damage (save ends both).

Spellbind
Bard Attack 29

Your unrivaled charm, combined with cunning magic, convinces an enemy to obey you.

Daily ✦ Arcane, Charm, Implement
Standard Action   **Ranged** 10
Target: One creature
Attack: Charisma vs. Will
Hit: The target is dominated (save ends).
   Aftereffect: 2d10 + Charisma modifier damage, and the target is dazed until the end of your next turn.
Miss: The target is dazed (save ends).
   Aftereffect: 2d10 + Charisma modifier damage.

PARAGON PATHS

STUDENT OF THE SEVEN

"Why hitch your cart to just one horse?"

Prerequisite: Bard, any multiclass feat

Among the many legends told by bards, a few mythic figures appear with some regularity, including the mysterious Seven. The Seven are sisters, or sometimes brothers, whose names vary from tale to tale. They're not gods, but they're not mortals either; sometimes they're exarchs of Corellon or some other god, and sometimes they're angels who come from seven different dominions. But most often, they're simply the Seven. Some tales describe them as patrons of the arts, inventors or sponsors of dance, poetry, singing, instrumental music, painting, drama, and the like. Other tales describe them as patrons of every mortal activity, or even as sponsors of different power sources. The Seven are never exactly the same in any two tales, or even in the same tale told twice. And as their student, neither are you.

Following the promptings of the Seven, your interests accept no limitations. No narrow field of study can contain your wide-ranging curiosity. You excel as an arcane leader, but what's to prevent you from learning a few tricks from a martial defender or a primal controller? No knowledge is off limits, and nothing is impossible.

By taking multiclass feats and learning powers from a variety of classes, you always have the right tool for the job. In addition, you learn spells that have enormous versatility, ensuring that you can provide help anytime you or an ally needs a bonus in a specific area. You dabble in a little bit of everything, and you manage not only to improve yourself but also to make others a little better at what they do best.

STUDENT OF THE SEVEN PATH FEATURES

Daily Mastery (11th level): At the end of an extended rest, you can replace a daily attack power granted through a multiclass feat with another daily attack power of the same level or lower from the same class.

Versatile Action (11th level): When you spend an action point to take an extra action, you regain the use of an encounter utility power or an encounter attack power that you gained through a multiclass feat and that you have used during this encounter.

Compensatory Insight (16th level): When you use an attack power granted through a multiclass feat, you gain a bonus to the attack's damage roll equal to your Intelligence modifier.

STUDENT OF THE SEVEN SPELLS

Anyspell	Student of the Seven Attack 11

Drawing on the raw arcane power around you, you shape your spell to the form and purpose you need. As a side effect, you grant momentary protection or a surge of aggressive inspiration to a nearby ally.

Encounter ✦ Arcane, Implement
Standard Action   Close burst 5
Target: One creature in burst
Attack: Charisma vs. Fortitude, Reflex, or Will (choose one)
Hit: 3d8 + Charisma modifier damage.
Effect: Until the end of your next turn, one ally in the burst gains a +2 power bonus to all defenses or a +1 power bonus to attack rolls.

Versatile Glamor	Student of the Seven Utility 12

You have the perfect spell for any situation.

Daily ✦ Arcane
Minor Action   Ranged 5
Target: You or one ally
Effect: The target gains one of the following benefits until the end of the encounter:
- ✦ +2 power bonus to speed
- ✦ +2 power bonus to attack rolls and damage rolls with opportunity attacks
- ✦ +4 bonus, instead of +2, to attack rolls with combat advantage
- ✦ Concealment
- ✦ Resist 10 to a damage type of your choice

Voice of the Seven	Student of the Seven Attack 20

You speak one word with seven supernatural voices, and your target is driven back and rooted to the ground.

Daily ✦ Arcane, Implement
Standard Action   Ranged 5
Target: One creature
Attack: Charisma vs. Fortitude, Reflex, or Will (choose one)
Hit: 3d10 + Charisma modifier damage. Either the target is dazed (save ends), or you push the target 3 squares and it is immobilized (save ends).
Miss: Half damage, and the target is either dazed or immobilized until the end of your next turn.

SUMMER RHYMER

"Ancient rhythms, endlessly refreshed. This blade cuts like a poem."

Prerequisite: Bard, Virtue of Cunning class feature

Among the most powerful residents of the Feywild is Tiandra, the Summer Queen (see *Manual of the Planes*). Her court is a reflection of her unearthly beauty, hung with flower garlands and alive with bustling activity. Her smile can ripen crops, and her favor bestowed on a mortal can quicken the gifts of song and poetry.

Whether the Summer Queen has actually smiled on you or you merely aspire to seek her blessing, you claim some association with the Summer Fey and study their musical magic. In your feytouched presence, you and your allies teleport freely, and you can call on the Summer Queen's powers of growth to aid your own healing powers.

If you serve the Summer Queen well, you might hope to receive some favor from her. Great heroes of the past have sometimes received noble titles, magic instruments, access to powerful enchantments, and other gifts from her hand. As the fey go, the Summer Queen is relatively trustworthy, but be warned: No fey gift is truly free.

SUMMER RHYMER PATH FEATURES

Feypath (11th level): When you spend an action point to take an extra action, you teleport yourself or an ally adjacent to you 5 squares as a free action before or after the extra action.

The Queen's Grace (11th level): Whenever you grant healing with a bard healing power, add your Charisma modifier to the hit points regained by each target.

Judgment of the Summer Court (16th level): Whenever an enemy's missed attack triggers your Virtue of Cunning class feature, you gain a +2 bonus to attack rolls against that enemy until the end of your next turn.

SUMMER RHYMER SPELLS

Song of the Queen's Protection	Summer Rhymer Attack 11

You sing a melody of eldritch quality that assaults your foe's senses while causing wisps of light to blur the outlines of your allies.

Encounter ✦ Arcane, Implement, Psychic
Standard Action   **Ranged** 10
Target: One creature
Attack: Charisma vs. Will
Hit: 2d10 + Charisma modifier psychic damage, and until the end of your next turn, any ally within 10 squares of you gains concealment until the end of his or her next turn.

Song of Spiral Paths	Summer Rhymer Utility 12

This song weaves qualities of the Feywild into the air, causing space to bend around you and your allies.

Daily ✦ Arcane, Teleportation, Zone
Minor Action   **Close** burst 10
Effect: The burst creates a zone of fey magic that lasts until the end of your next turn. While within the zone, you and any ally can teleport 2 squares as a move action.
Sustain Minor: The zone persists.

Song of the High Court	Summer Rhymer Attack 20

Bright leaves of radiant power flare around you and your allies as you sing an ode lauding the durability of nature.

Daily ✦ Arcane, Implement, Radiant, Zone
Standard Action   **Close** burst 5
Target: Each enemy in burst
Attack: Charisma vs. Will
Hit: 3d10 + Charisma modifier radiant damage.
Effect: The burst creates a zone of song that lasts until the end of your next turn. While within the zone, you and any ally gain resist 5 to all damage.
Sustain Minor: The zone persists.

Voice of Thunder

"When thunder speaks, all nature feels a twinge of fear."

Prerequisite: Bard

Your voice is your power, and as you study and practice ancient bardic traditions, your power grows stronger. The rumble of thunder in a stormy sky, the tremor of the earth that topples buildings, the rhythm of waves crashing against the shore, the explosive detonation of fire—your voice is the raw elemental power of sound, booming and concussive.

Variations of this path appear in the bardic traditions of many races and cultures. Eladrin often associate their magical traditions with forces of nature, and like a bralani of autumn winds or a tulani of summer sun, you might be a noble eladrin of the thunderstorm. Dwarf and goliath bards are more inclined to think of the rumble of stone. Drow bards speak of the voice of fury or of madness that empowers their harshly beautiful music. Tieflings wield explosive force with their mighty voices.

The features and powers of this path increase the range and effectiveness of your thunder powers. Your thunderous songs and shouts echo to repeat their assault on your foes, and your *song of thunder* gives your allies the ability to conjure echoes of your booming voice.

Voice of Thunder Path Features

Voice of Thunder (11th level): When you spend an action point to take an extra action, the size of any close burst attack you make during that action increases by 1, and the size of any close blast attack you make during that action increases by 2.

Voice to Wake the Dead (11th level): As a free action, you can grant a dying ally within 10 squares of you a +2 power bonus to death saving throws. The bonus lasts until that ally is no longer dying.

Booming Words (16th level): You gain a +2 bonus to damage rolls when using a thunder power.

Voice of Thunder Spells

Rolling Echo	Voice of Thunder Attack 11

You send two successive waves of thunder rolling from you.

Encounter ✦ Arcane, Implement, Thunder
Standard Action   Close burst 2
Target: Each enemy in burst
Attack: Charisma vs. Fortitude
Hit: 2d6 + Charisma modifier thunder damage, and you push the target 1 square. Before you take any actions during your next turn, you can repeat the attack as a free action.

Doom Echo	Voice of Thunder Utility 12

You call upon the distant echoes of your magic to create an echo of a spell that you have already unleashed upon the world.

Daily ✦ Arcane
Minor Action   Personal
Effect: You regain the use of a bard encounter attack power that has the thunder keyword and that you have used during this encounter.

Song of Thunder	Voice of Thunder Attack 20

You initiate a song of pealing thunder that echoes between you and your allies, battering your enemies into submission.

Daily ✦ Arcane, Implement, Thunder
Standard Action   Close blast 5
Target: Each enemy in blast
Attack: Charisma vs. Fortitude
Hit: 3d6 + Charisma modifier thunder damage, and you knock the target prone.
Miss: Half damage.
Effect: At the start of the next turn of each ally in the blast, the ally deals 5 thunder damage to each enemy within 2 squares of him or her.

WAR CHANTER

"Together we take our place among the greatest heroes the world has ever known!"

Prerequisite: Bard, Virtue of Valor class feature

Bards look to the tales of past heroes for inspiration and use those tales to spur their allies. As a war chanter, you embrace those tales as a pattern for your own life, leading your companions into battle with songs and cadences that extol the virtues of bravery, endurance, and strength of arms. The roar of battle, the clash of steel on steel, the warrior's cry, the tramp of marching feet–these are all notes you weave into the symphony of war, which flows across the field like a raging torrent, catching up your friends and foes alike.

Your music and oratory inspire your allies to greater deeds of valor. Your Virtue of Valor grants temporary hit points to you as well as to your allies, and your own battle prowess can bolster your allies against injury. Your powers are similar in some ways to those of a warlord, granting your allies movement and attacks against the foes you strike with your own weapon.

WAR CHANTER PATH FEATURES

Inspire by Example (11th level): When you spend an action point to take an extra action, each ally within 5 squares of you gains a bonus to attack rolls and damage rolls equal to your Constitution modifier until the end of your next turn.

Inspire by Word (11th level): When an ally gains temporary hit points from your Virtue of Valor, you gain the same number of temporary hit points. In addition, when you reduce an enemy to 0 hit points or bloody an enemy, one ally within 10 squares of you gains temporary hit points equal to 5 + your Constitution modifier. The number of temporary hit points equals 8 + your Constitution modifier at 21st level.

Inspire by Deed (16th level): You can spend 2 action points during an encounter, instead of only 1.

WAR CHANTER SPELLS

Victorious Smite	War Chanter Attack 11

Striking your foe, you call an ally to your side to attack the same target.

Encounter ✦ Arcane, Weapon
Standard Action   Melee weapon
Target: One creature
Attack: Charisma vs. AC
Hit: 1[W] + Charisma modifier damage.
Effect: As a free action, an ally within 5 squares of you can shift 3 squares and make a basic attack against the target with a bonus to the attack roll and the damage roll equal to your Constitution modifier.

Battle Chant	War Chanter Utility 12

You inspire your allies with visions of glory, focusing their attacks on a particular foe.

Encounter ✦ Arcane
Minor Action   Close burst 10
Target: You and each ally in burst
Effect: Choose an enemy in the burst. Each target gains a +2 power bonus to attack rolls against that enemy until the end of your next turn.

Visions of Victory	War Chanter Attack 20

Inspired by visions of a glorious victory, your ally unleashes a powerful attack on the foe that you just hit.

Daily ✦ Arcane, Weapon
Standard Action   Melee weapon
Target: One creature
Attack: Charisma vs. AC
Hit: 1[W] + Charisma modifier damage. As a free action, an ally of yours adjacent to the target can use an encounter melee attack power against the target, hitting it automatically.
Miss: As a free action, an ally of yours adjacent to the target can use an at-will melee attack power against the target, hitting it automatically.

ERIC DESCHAMPS

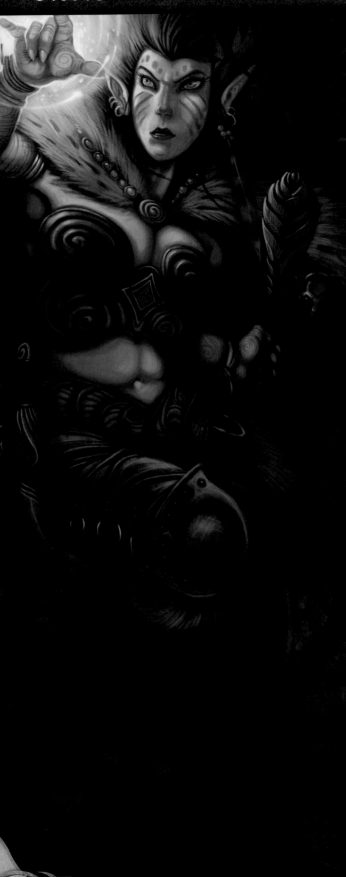

"I am the seeker. I am the stalker. I am the storm."

CLASS TRAITS

Role: Controller. Your beast form gives you access to powers that provide control at close range, while your humanoid form allows you to hinder your opponents from a distance. Depending on your choice of class features and powers, you might lean toward either leader or striker as a secondary role.

Power Source: Primal. You have gained your powers through a careful study of and communion with the natural world.

Key Abilities: Wisdom, Dexterity, Constitution

Armor Proficiencies: Cloth, leather, hide
Weapon Proficiencies: Simple melee, simple ranged
Implements: Staffs, totems
Bonus to Defense: +1 Reflex, +1 Will

Hit Points at 1st Level: 12 + Constitution score
Hit Points per Level Gained: 5
Healing Surges per Day: 7 + Constitution modifier

Trained Skills: Nature. From the class skills list below, choose three more trained skills at 1st level.
Class Skills: Arcana (Int), Athletics (Str), Diplomacy (Cha), Endurance (Con), Heal (Wis), History (Int), Insight (Wis), Nature (Wis), Perception (Wis)

Class Features: Balance of Nature, Primal Aspect, Ritual Casting, *wild shape*

Secretive and enigmatic, druids call the wilderness their home. They are capable of running with a wolf pack, speaking with the most ancient trees, and watching thunderstorms from atop the clouds themselves. They regard challenges as tests, both of their fitness and of their connection with the wild places of the world. And though many druids project an outward calm, they have the cunning of the beast and the fury of the storm.

Whether you were born to the wilds or retreated from civilization, whether you chose your path or answered a call that whispered in your heart, you share a bond with the primal spirits of nature. You are neither their servant nor their master, but winds, trees, and beasts heed your words, for they recognize you as kin.

Call to the spirits, and they will entangle your foes or smite your enemies with the storm. Unleash your own spirit, and you will become the Primal Beast, uncaged and untamed.

WILLIAM O'CONNOR

DRUID CLASS FEATURES

Druids have the following class features.

BALANCE OF NATURE

Some druids favor being in beast form, while others prefer being in humanoid form. However, just as druids seek balance in the world between divine and primordial forces, druids pursue balance within their own minds and bodies.

You begin with three at-will attack powers. Throughout your career, at least one of those powers, and no more than two, must have the beast form keyword. By this means, you have access to useful attacks in either beast form or humanoid form.

PRIMAL ASPECT

Druidic lore speaks of the Primal Beast, the first spirit of the world's noble predators. A formless thing of shadows, fur, feathers, and claws, this creature appears in many druids' visions, and they speak of channeling the Primal Beast when using their *wild shape* and beast form powers. As a druid, you choose which aspect of the Primal Beast you most strongly manifest with your powers.

Choose one of these options. Your choice provides bonuses to certain druid powers, as detailed in those powers.

Primal Guardian: While you are not wearing heavy armor, you can use your Constitution modifier in place of your Dexterity or Intelligence modifier to determine your AC.

Primal Predator: While you are not wearing heavy armor, you gain a +1 bonus to your speed.

RITUAL CASTING

You gain the Ritual Caster feat as a bonus feat, allowing you to use magical rituals. You own a ritual book, and it contains two rituals of your choice that you have mastered: Animal Messenger (*Player's Handbook*, page 300) and another 1st-level ritual.

Once per day, you can use Animal Messenger without expending components.

WILD SHAPE

As a druid, you have the ability to channel the primal energy of beasts into your physical form and transform into a beast. You have an at-will power, *wild shape*, that allows you to assume the form of a beast, and many druid powers have the beast form keyword (page 219) and therefore can be used only while you are in beast form.

The *wild shape* power lets you assume a form of your size that resembles a natural or a fey beast, usually a four-legged mammalian predator such as a bear, a boar, a panther, a wolf, or a wolverine. Your beast form might also be an indistinct shape

of shadowy fur and claws, an incarnation of the Primal Beast of which all earthly beasts are fractured images. You choose a specific form whenever you use *wild shape*, and that form has no effect on your game statistics or movement modes.

Your choice of Primal Aspect might suggest a specific form you prefer to assume, and certain beast form powers specify changes to your form when you use them. You might also resemble a more exotic beast when you're in beast form: a reptile such as a rage drake or a crocodile, or a fantastic beast such as an owlbear or a bulette.

IMPLEMENTS

Druids employ staffs and totems as a means of focusing their primal energy. When you wield a magic staff or a magic totem, you can add its enhancement bonus to the attack rolls and the damage rolls of druid powers and druid paragon path powers that have the implement keyword. Without an implement, you can still use these powers.

CREATING A DRUID

Druids rely on Wisdom, Dexterity, and Constitution for their powers. You can choose any powers you like, but many druids choose powers that complement their choice of Primal Aspect.

GUARDIAN DRUID

As a guardian druid, you are a protector of the land and those who rely on it. Yours is the magic of earth, forest, and sky, the enduring aspects of nature that outlive any mortal tyrant. Your powers incline you toward leader as a secondary role. Wisdom should be your highest ability score, since your attack powers rely on it, but make Constitution your second-best

---

DRUID OVERVIEW

Characteristics: You combine a number of potent ranged and area powers with the ability to take beast form and bring the fight directly to your foes. Depending on the powers you choose, you can spend more combat time in beast form or more in your humanoid form.

Religion: Most druids do not worship the gods of the Astral Sea, instead orienting their lives and beliefs around the primal spirits of nature. It might be misleading to call their relationship with these spirits worship, but druids invoke the spirits in times of passage, implore them for aid, and appease them with offerings of burned food or spilled blood.

Races: Elves and razorclaw shifters make excellent predator druids, combining native insight and attunement to nature with grace and agility. Dwarves excel as guardian druids; goliath and human druids often follow that path as well.

score to heighten your endurance and your guardian powers.

Suggested Class Feature: Primal Guardian
Suggested Feat: Primal Instinct
Suggested Skills: Arcana, Heal, Insight, Nature
Suggested At-Will Powers: *call of the beast, chill wind, grasping claws*
Suggested Encounter Power: *frost flash*
Suggested Daily Power: *fires of life*

PREDATOR DRUID

As a predator druid, you hunt down and destroy those who despoil the natural world. Yours is the magic of the bared fang, the stalking wolf pack, and the blood-red moon. Your powers make striker your secondary role, with a focus on dealing significant damage along with your control effects. Make Wisdom your highest ability score to get the most out of your attacks, followed by Dexterity to enhance your predator powers.

Suggested Class Feature: Primal Predator
Suggested Feat: Primal Fury
Suggested Skills: Arcana, Athletics, Nature, Perception
Suggested At-Will Powers: *flame seed, pounce, savage rend*
Suggested Encounter Power: *darting bite*
Suggested Daily Power: *savage frenzy*

CHOOSING DRUID POWERS

As you choose druid powers, you have two factors to consider. One is how the powers fit into your character concept—whether you imagine your character as more of a guardian or more of a predator. The other is how much time you envision spending in beast form. This factor is independent of your choice of build; both guardian druids and predator druids can choose powers that are mostly used in beast form or mostly used in humanoid form. But it's important for how your druid feels during play.

The easiest strategy is to choose the power at each level that appeals to you most. If most of those powers are beast form powers, then you'll spend a lot of time in beast form, using powers that you enjoy. If most of those powers are ranged and area powers you use in humanoid form, that will change the way you play your character. As long as you enjoy the powers you're using, that's fine.

If you need more guidance, choose beast form powers for about half of your powers. At 1st level, choose one or two beast form at-will attack powers, then choose either a beast form encounter power or a beast form daily power. As you advance in levels, continue trying to balance your power selections between beast form powers and other powers.

Remember that you can use retraining (*Player's Handbook*, page 28) to change your power selections if you find your choices unsatisfying.

DRUID POWERS

Your powers are evocations that call on primal spirits to alter your physical form and hamper your enemies. You call up roots and vines from the ground, summon lightning from the sky, engulf your enemies in fire, or transform yourself into a fierce predator whose howl can shake your foes with fear.

CLASS FEATURES

Each druid has the power *wild shape*.

Wild Shape	Druid Feature

You assume an aspect of the Primal Beast or return to your humanoid form.

At-Will ✦ Polymorph, Primal
Minor Action (Special)   Personal
Effect: You change from your humanoid form to beast form or vice versa. When you change from beast form back to your humanoid form, you shift 1 square. While you are in beast form, you can't use attack, utility, or feat powers that lack the beast form keyword, although you can sustain such powers.

You choose a specific form whenever you use *wild shape* to change into beast form. The beast form is your size, resembles a natural beast or a fey beast, and normally doesn't change your game statistics or movement modes. Your equipment becomes part of your beast form, but you drop anything you are holding, except implements you can use. You continue to gain the benefits of the equipment you wear.

You can use the properties and the powers of implements as well as magic items that you wear, but not the properties or the powers of weapons or the powers of wondrous items. While equipment is part of your beast form, it cannot be removed, and anything in a container that is part of your beast form is inaccessible.

Special: You can use this power once per round.

LEVEL 1 AT-WILL EVOCATIONS

Call of the Beast	Druid Attack 1

You draw forth the savagery that dwells in every creature, compelling your enemies to fight without forethought or plan.

At-Will ✦ Charm, Implement, Primal, Psychic
Standard Action   Area burst 1 within 10 squares
Target: Each creature in burst
Attack: Wisdom vs. Will
Hit: The target can't gain combat advantage until the end of your next turn. In addition, on its next turn the target takes psychic damage equal to 5 + your Wisdom modifier when it makes any attack that doesn't include your ally nearest to it as a target.
Level 21: 10 + Wisdom modifier psychic damage.

Chill Wind	Druid Attack 1

A howling gust of icy wind savages your enemies, scattering them.

At-Will ✦ Cold, Implement, Primal
Standard Action   Area burst 1 within 10 squares
Target: Each creature in burst
Attack: Wisdom vs. Fortitude
Hit: 1d6 cold damage, and you slide the target 1 square.
Level 21: 2d6 cold damage.

DRUID

Flame Seed — Druid Attack 1

You hurl a seed infused with primal energy at your foes. When it strikes the ground, the seed explodes in a fiery burst.

At-Will ✦ Fire, Implement, Primal, Zone
Standard Action   **Ranged** 10
Target: One creature
Attack: Wisdom vs. Reflex
Hit: 1d6 fire damage, and the squares adjacent to the target become a fiery zone that lasts until the end of your next turn. Any enemy that enters the zone or starts its turn there takes fire damage equal to your Wisdom modifier.
    Level 21: 2d6 fire damage.

Grasping Claws — Druid Attack 1

You rend and tear your foe with your claws, leaving it unable to escape your next assault.

At-Will ✦ Beast Form, Implement, Primal
Standard Action   **Melee** touch
Target: One creature
Attack: Wisdom vs. Reflex
Hit: 1d8 + Wisdom modifier damage, and the target is slowed until the end of your next turn.
    Level 21: 2d8 + Wisdom modifier damage.
Special: This power can be used as a melee basic attack.

Pounce — Druid Attack 1

You leap at your foe, catching it off guard.

At-Will ✦ Beast Form, Implement, Primal
Standard Action   **Melee** touch
Target: One creature
Attack: Wisdom vs. Reflex
Hit: 1d8 + Wisdom modifier damage. The target grants combat advantage to the next creature that attacks it before the end of your next turn.
    Level 21: 2d8 + Wisdom modifier damage.
Special: When charging, you can use this power in place of a melee basic attack.

Savage Rend — Druid Attack 1

You rake your foe with your claws, setting it up for the kill.

At-Will ✦ Beast Form, Implement, Primal
Standard Action   **Melee** touch
Target: One creature
Attack: Wisdom vs. Reflex
Hit: 1d8 + Wisdom modifier damage, and you slide the target 1 square.
    Level 21: 2d8 + Wisdom modifier damage.
Special: This power can be used as a melee basic attack.

Storm Spike — Druid Attack 1

A bolt of lightning spears your foe and charges the air around it. If your enemy doesn't move away, a second spark will erupt around it.

At-Will ✦ Implement, Lightning, Primal
Standard Action   **Ranged** 10
Target: One creature
Attack: Wisdom vs. Reflex
Hit: 1d8 + Wisdom modifier lightning damage. If the target doesn't move at least 2 squares on its next turn, it takes lightning damage equal to your Wisdom modifier.
    Level 21: 2d8 + Wisdom modifier damage.

Thorn Whip — Druid Attack 1

Barbed vines whip out from the wood of your staff or totem to lash and ensnare your prey.

At-Will ✦ Implement, Primal
Standard Action   **Ranged** 10
Target: One creature
Attack: Wisdom vs. Fortitude
Hit: 1d8 + Wisdom modifier damage, and you pull the target 2 squares.
    Level 21: 2d8 + Wisdom modifier damage.

LEVEL 1 ENCOUNTER EVOCATIONS

Cull the Herd — Druid Attack 1

Your feral glare rends your foe's mind with a sense of doom and drags that foe toward your claws.

Encounter ✦ Beast Form, Charm, Implement, Primal, Psychic
Standard Action   **Ranged** 5
Target: One creature
Attack: Wisdom vs. Will
Hit: 2d8 + Wisdom modifier psychic damage, and you pull the target 3 squares.

Darting Bite — Druid Attack 1

With quickness and cunning, you bite your enemies and dodge to avoid a counterattack.

Encounter ✦ Beast Form, Implement, Primal
Standard Action   **Melee** touch
Target: One or two creatures
Attack: Wisdom vs. Reflex
Hit: 1d10 + Wisdom modifier damage. If at least one of the attacks hits, you can shift 2 squares.
    Primal Predator: The number of squares you can shift equals your Dexterity modifier.

Frost Flash — Druid Attack 1

You blast your enemy with cold that leaves it frozen in place.

Encounter ✦ Cold, Implement, Primal
Standard Action   **Ranged** 10
Target: One creature
Attack: Wisdom vs. Fortitude
Hit: 1d6 + Wisdom modifier cold damage, and the target is immobilized until the end of your next turn.
    Primal Guardian: The attack deals extra damage equal to your Constitution modifier.

Twisting Vines — Druid Attack 1

Vines and roots erupt from the ground around nearby creatures.

Encounter ✦ Implement, Primal
Standard Action   **Area** burst 1 within 10 squares
Target: Each creature in burst
Attack: Wisdom vs. Reflex
Hit: 1d8 + Wisdom modifier damage, and each square adjacent to the target becomes difficult terrain until the end of your next turn.

LEVEL 1 DAILY EVOCATIONS

Faerie Fire — Druid Attack 1

A burst of colorful light envelops your foes, distracting and slowing them. As each creature breaks free of the effect, the light flares one last time, searing the flesh and dazzling the eyes.

Daily ✦ Implement, Primal, Radiant
Standard Action   Area burst 1 within 10 squares
Target: Each creature in burst
Attack: Wisdom vs. Will
Hit: The target is slowed and grants combat advantage (save ends both).
    Aftereffect: 3d6 + Wisdom modifier radiant damage, and the target grants combat advantage until the end of your next turn.
Miss: 1d6 + Wisdom modifier radiant damage, and the target grants combat advantage until the end of your next turn.

Fires of Life — Druid Attack 1

Searing flame engulfs your foes and burns them for a time. As each creature extinguishes the flames that burn it, healing fire leaps to one of your allies.

Daily ✦ Fire, Healing, Implement, Primal
Standard Action   Area burst 1 within 10 squares
Target: Each enemy in burst
Attack: Wisdom vs. Reflex
Hit: 1d6 + Wisdom modifier fire damage, and ongoing 5 fire damage (save ends). If the target drops to 0 hit points before it saves against the ongoing damage, one creature of your choice within 5 squares of the target regains hit points equal to 5 + your Constitution modifier.
    Aftereffect: One creature of your choice within 5 squares of the target regains hit points equal to your Constitution modifier.
Miss: Half damage.

Savage Frenzy — Druid Attack 1

In a blur of claw and fang, you strike out at nearby enemies.

Daily ✦ Beast Form, Implement, Primal
Standard Action   Close burst 1
Target: Each enemy in burst you can see
Attack: Wisdom vs. Reflex
Hit: 1d6 + Wisdom modifier damage, and the target is dazed and slowed (save ends both).
Miss: Half damage, and the target is slowed until the end of your next turn.

Wind Prison — Druid Attack 1

Gusting winds batter your foe, and when the foe moves, the winds blast outward and knock your enemies to the ground.

Daily ✦ Implement, Primal
Standard Action   Ranged 10
Target: One creature
Attack: Wisdom vs. Reflex
Hit: 2d10 + Wisdom modifier damage.
Effect: The target grants combat advantage until it moves or until the end of the encounter. When the target first moves before the end of the encounter, each enemy within 5 squares of the target is knocked prone.

LEVEL 2 UTILITY EVOCATIONS

Barkskin — Druid Utility 2

A protective layer of tree bark covers your body and armor.

Encounter ✦ Primal
Minor Action   Ranged 5
Target: You or one ally
Effect: Until the end of your next turn, the target gains a power bonus to AC equal to your Constitution modifier.

Fleet Pursuit — Druid Utility 2

Your limbs propel you forward with the speed of a cheetah.

Daily ✦ Beast Form, Primal
Minor Action   Personal
Effect: Until the end of the encounter, you gain a power bonus to your speed while you are in beast form equal to your Dexterity modifier.

Obscuring Mist — Druid Utility 2

A thick fog coalesces from nowhere, hiding your allies.

Daily ✦ Primal, Zone
Standard Action   Area burst 1 within 10 squares
Effect: The burst creates a zone of lightly obscured squares that lasts until the end of your next turn.
Sustain Minor: The zone persists, and you can increase its size by 1 to a maximum of burst 5.

Skittering Sneak — Druid Utility 2

You can adopt the form of a mouse, a large spider, or another animal that wouldn't draw a second glance from most observers.

Daily ✦ Primal
Free Action   Personal
Prerequisite: You must have the *wild shape* power.
Effect: Until the end of the encounter, you can use *wild shape* to assume the form of a Tiny natural beast or fey beast, such as a mouse, a house cat, or a large spider. In this form, you gain a +5 bonus to Stealth checks. You can't attack, pick up anything, or manipulate objects.
    Until this power ends, you can use *wild shape* to change among this form, another beast form, and your humanoid form.

LEVEL 3 ENCOUNTER EVOCATIONS

Battering Claws — Druid Attack 3

You fall upon your foes like a thunderbolt, hurling them aside with a series of ferocious attacks.

Encounter ✦ Beast Form, Implement, Primal
Standard Action   Melee touch
Target: One or two creatures
Attack: Wisdom vs. Reflex
Hit: 1d8 + Wisdom modifier damage, and you slide the target 2 squares.

Call Lightning

Druid Attack 3

Bolts of lightning spear your foes as thunder rumbles around them, distracting them and threatening to blast them if they move away.

Encounter ✦ Implement, Lightning, Primal, Thunder, Zone
Standard Action   Area burst 1 within 10 squares
Target: Each creature in burst
Attack: Wisdom vs. Reflex
Hit: 1d8 + Wisdom modifier lightning damage.
Effect: The burst creates a zone of rumbling thunder that lasts until the end of your next turn. While within the zone, any enemy takes a –2 penalty to attack rolls, and any enemy that leaves the zone takes 5 thunder damage.

Predator's Flurry

Druid Attack 3

You dart across the battlefield, attacking your foes as you slip through their ranks.

Encounter ✦ Beast Form, Implement, Primal
Standard Action   Melee touch
Primary Target: One creature
Primary Attack: Wisdom vs. Reflex
Hit: 1d6 + Wisdom modifier damage, and the primary target is dazed until the end of your next turn.
Effect: You shift 2 squares and then make a secondary attack.
  Primal Predator: The number of squares you shift equals your Dexterity modifier.
  Secondary Target: One creature other than the primary target
  Secondary Attack: Wisdom vs. Reflex
  Hit: 1d6 + Wisdom modifier damage, and the secondary target is dazed until the end of your next turn.

Tundra Wind

Druid Attack 3

A roaring wind batters your foes, encrusting them with ice and knocking them to the ground.

Encounter ✦ Cold, Implement, Primal
Standard Action   Close blast 3
Target: Each creature in blast
Attack: Wisdom vs. Fortitude
Hit: 2d6 + Wisdom modifier cold damage, and you knock the target prone.
  Primal Guardian: You also push the target a number of squares equal to your Constitution modifier.

Level 5 Daily Evocations

Hobbling Rend

Druid Attack 5

You rip into your foes' legs, leaving them hobbled and bleeding.

Daily ✦ Beast Form, Implement, Primal
Standard Action   Melee touch
Target: One or two creatures
Attack: Wisdom vs. Reflex
Hit: 2d8 + Wisdom modifier damage, and the target is slowed (save ends).
Miss: Half damage, and the target is slowed until the end of your next turn.

Primal Wolverine

Druid Attack 5

You transform into a dire wolverine, snapping and biting at any foe foolish enough to attack you. Your fierce attack on a nearby foe rips muscle and tendon, slowing its movement.

Daily ✦ Beast Form, Implement, Primal
Standard Action   Melee touch
Target: One creature
Attack: Wisdom vs. Reflex
Hit: 1d8 + Wisdom modifier damage, and ongoing 5 damage (save ends).
Miss: Half damage.
Effect: Until the end of the encounter, while you are in beast form and are able to take actions, any enemy that makes a melee attack against you takes damage equal to your Constitution modifier.

Roar of Terror

Druid Attack 5

Your roar is the voice of the Great Bear, striking terror into every heart.

Daily ✦ Beast Form, Fear, Implement, Primal, Psychic
Standard Action   Close blast 5
Target: Each creature in blast
Attack: Wisdom vs. Will
Hit: 2d6 + Wisdom modifier psychic damage, and the target is dazed (save ends).
Miss: Half damage, and the target is dazed until the end of your next turn.

VINCENT DUTRAIT

Wall of Thorns
Druid Attack 5

A thicket of briars confounds and traps your enemies.

Daily ✦ Conjuration, Implement, Primal
Standard Action   Area wall 8 within 10 squares

Effect: You conjure a wall of thorny, writhing vines. The wall can be up to 4 squares high and must be on a solid surface, and it lasts until the end of your next turn. The wall provides cover. A creature's line of sight through a wall square is blocked unless the creature is adjacent to that square.

Entering a wall square costs 3 extra squares of movement. If a creature enters the wall's space or starts its turn there, that creature takes 1d10 + your Wisdom modifier damage and ongoing 5 damage (save ends).

Sustain Minor: The wall persists.

LEVEL 6 UTILITY EVOCATIONS

Black Harbinger
Druid Utility 6

You can turn into a raven and take wing, no longer earthbound.

Daily ✦ Primal
Free Action   Personal

Prerequisite: You must have the *wild shape* power.

Effect: Until the end of the encounter, you can use *wild shape* to assume the form of a Tiny raven. In this form, you gain a fly speed equal to your speed, and your walking speed becomes 2. You can't attack, pick up anything, or manipulate objects.

Until this power ends, you can use *wild shape* to change among this form, another beast form, and your humanoid form.

Camouflage Cloak
Druid Utility 6

Your target takes on the appearance of the surrounding terrain, fading from view.

Encounter ✦ Primal
Minor Action   Ranged 5

Target: You or one ally

Effect: The target becomes invisible until he or she moves or until the end of your next turn.

Chant of Sustenance
Druid Utility 6

You intone a brief petition to primal spirits, who funnel power on your behalf to sustain effects you have created.

Daily ✦ Primal
Minor Action   Close burst 10

Target: Each of your zones in burst

Effect: You move each target 5 squares. If any of those targets will end at the end of your current turn, you can make those targets last until the end of your next turn.

Stalker's Eyes
Druid Utility 6

Your eyesight, hearing, and sense of smell grow as strong as those of a predator.

Daily ✦ Primal
Minor Action   Personal

Effect: You gain low-light vision and a +4 bonus to Perception checks until the end of the encounter.

LEVEL 7 ENCOUNTER EVOCATIONS

Feast of Fury
Druid Attack 7

You are a flurry of fangs and claws, carving a bloody swath through your foes.

Encounter ✦ Beast Form, Implement, Primal
Standard Action   Melee touch

Primary Target: One creature
Primary Attack: Wisdom vs. Reflex

Hit: 2d8 + Wisdom modifier damage.

Effect: Make a secondary attack.

Secondary Target: One creature other than the primary target

Secondary Attack: Wisdom vs. Reflex

Hit: 1d10 + Wisdom modifier damage. The secondary attack deals 5 extra damage if the primary attack hit.

Latch On
Druid Attack 7

You sink your teeth and claws into your prey, preventing it from escaping.

Encounter ✦ Beast Form, Implement, Primal
Standard Action   Melee touch

Target: One creature
Attack: Wisdom vs. Reflex

Hit: 2d10 + Wisdom modifier damage, and you grab the target.

Primal Predator: The target takes a penalty to checks to escape the grab equal to your Dexterity modifier.

Swirling Winds
Druid Attack 7

A cone of turbulent air forms around your foe, battering it and blowing other creatures toward you.

Encounter ✦ Implement, Primal
Standard Action   Ranged 10

Target: One creature
Attack: Wisdom vs. Reflex

Hit: 1d10 + Wisdom modifier damage, and you pull each creature within 3 squares of the target 1 square.

Primal Guardian: If you pull one or more creatures that are adjacent to the target, the target takes extra damage equal to your Constitution modifier.

Tremor
Druid Attack 7

The ground shakes under your enemies' feet.

Encounter ✦ Implement, Primal
Standard Action   Ranged 10

Target: One creature
Attack: Wisdom vs. Fortitude

Hit: 2d8 + Wisdom modifier damage, and you knock the target and each enemy adjacent to it prone.

Feral Mauling   Druid Attack 9

Your savage assault leaves your enemy too weak to make effective attacks.

Daily ✦ Beast Form, Implement, Primal
Standard Action   **Melee** touch
Target: One creature
Attack: Wisdom vs. Reflex
Hit: 2d10 + Wisdom modifier damage, and the target takes a –2 penalty to attack rolls (save ends).
Miss: Half damage, and the target takes a –2 penalty to attack rolls until the end of your next turn.

Primal Wolf   Druid Attack 9

You transform into a dire wolf, knocking your enemy prone and savagely tearing into any others where they lie.

Daily ✦ Beast Form, Implement, Primal
Standard Action   **Melee** touch
Target: One creature
Attack: Wisdom vs. Reflex
Hit: 2d8 + Wisdom modifier damage. You knock the target prone, and it can't stand up (save ends).
Miss: Half damage, and you knock the target prone.
Effect: Until the end of the encounter, you gain a +2 bonus to attack rolls against prone targets. In addition, whenever you hit an enemy with a melee attack while you are in beast form, you can knock that enemy prone.

Sunbeam   Druid Attack 9

Brilliant rays of light dazzle your enemies' eyes.

Daily ✦ Implement, Primal, Radiant
Standard Action   **Area** burst 1 within 10 squares
Target: Each enemy in burst
Attack: Wisdom vs. Will
Hit: The target is blinded (save ends).
    Aftereffect: 1d10 + Wisdom modifier radiant damage.
Miss: 1d10 + Wisdom modifier radiant damage.

LEVEL 10 UTILITY EVOCATIONS

Armor of the Wild   Druid Utility 10

Your hide hardens into armored plates. Your enemies can hurt you, but not as badly as they would like.

Daily ✦ Beast Form, Primal
Minor Action   **Personal**
Effect: Until the end of the encounter, while you are in beast form, you gain resistance to all damage equal to your Constitution modifier.

Feywild Sojourn   Druid Utility 10

You take a jaunt to the Feywild, returning to the world when you have healed and changed form.

Encounter ✦ Primal, Teleportation
Move Action   **Personal**
Effect: You teleport to a safe place in the Feywild. While you are there, you can't take any actions other than using your second wind and *wild shape*. At the end of your next turn or as a move action before then, you reappear in an unoccupied space within 10 squares of the space you left.

LEVEL 9 DAILY EVOCATIONS

Entangle   Druid Attack 9

Roots and vines reach up from the earth to clutch at any creature nearby. As the plants slow enemies, your fangs and claws gain savage power against those foes.

Daily ✦ Implement, Primal, Zone
Standard Action   **Area** burst 2 within 10 squares
Target: Each creature in burst
Attack: Wisdom vs. Reflex
Hit: 1d6 + Wisdom modifier damage, and the target is immobilized (save ends).
Effect: The burst creates a zone of grasping roots and vines that lasts until the end of the encounter. Any enemy that starts its turn within the zone is slowed until the end of your next turn. While you are in beast form, your melee attacks against enemies within the zone can score critical hits on rolls of 18–20.

Roots of Rescue
Druid Utility 10

Roots erupt from the ground and hold your ally in place.

Encounter ✦ Primal
Immediate Interrupt   **Ranged** 10
Trigger: You or an ally within 10 squares of you is pulled, pushed, or slid
Target: The character affected by the forced movement
Effect: The target is unaffected by the forced movement.

Winter Storm
Druid Utility 10

Ice covers the ground, and biting wind makes your foes more vulnerable to your cold attacks.

Daily ✦ Primal, Zone
Standard Action   **Area** burst 2 within 10 squares
Effect: The burst creates a zone of difficult terrain that lasts until the end of your next turn. While within the zone, any enemy gains vulnerable 5 cold. You can end the zone as a minor action.
Sustain Minor: The zone persists, and you can increase its size by 1 to a maximum of burst 5.

LEVEL 13 ENCOUNTER EVOCATIONS

Claws of Retribution
Druid Attack 13

Wet with your enemy's blood, your claws lash out at any foe adjacent to you that dares to attack.

Encounter ✦ Beast Form, Implement, Primal
Standard Action   **Melee** touch
Target: One creature
Attack: Wisdom vs. Reflex
Hit: 2d6 + Wisdom modifier damage. Until the end of your next turn, you can make a melee basic attack as an opportunity action against any enemy adjacent to you that hits or misses with an attack.
    Primal Predator: You gain a bonus to the attack rolls of the melee basic attacks equal to your Dexterity modifier.

Expose Weakness
Druid Attack 13

You expose a hole in your prey's defenses, creating an opening for another strike.

Encounter ✦ Beast Form, Implement, Primal
Standard Action   **Melee** touch
Target: One creature
Attack: Wisdom vs. Reflex
Hit: 2d8 + Wisdom modifier damage. The next attack against the target before the end of your next turn is made against the target's lowest defense.
    Primal Guardian: If the next attack hits the target, the attack deals extra damage equal to your Constitution modifier.

Thunder Crash
Druid Attack 13

A crash of thunder leaves your target stunned.

Encounter ✦ Implement, Primal
Standard Action   **Ranged** 5
Target: One creature
Attack: Wisdom vs. Fortitude
Hit: The target is stunned until the end of your next turn.

Tidal Surge
Druid Attack 13

A wave of water rises up, moving creatures where you want them.

Encounter ✦ Implement, Primal
Standard Action   **Close** blast 5
Target: Each creature in blast
Attack: Wisdom vs. Fortitude
Hit: 2d6 + Wisdom modifier damage, and you slide the target 3 squares.

LEVEL 15 DAILY EVOCATIONS

Baleful Polymorph
Druid Attack 15

Transformed into a harmless animal, your enemy can do nothing but struggle against its useless new form.

Daily ✦ Implement, Polymorph, Primal
Standard Action   **Ranged** 10
Target: One creature
Attack: Wisdom vs. Will
Hit: The target is stunned and assumes the form of a harmless, Tiny natural beast or fey beast such as a newt, a turtle, or a mouse (save ends both). As a minor action, you can end the effect, which makes the target subject to the aftereffect.
    Aftereffect: 1d10 + Wisdom modifier damage.
Miss: 1d10 + Wisdom modifier damage, and the target is dazed (save ends).

Call Lightning Storm
Druid Attack 15

Lightning strikes from dark clouds overhead.

Daily ✦ Implement, Lightning, Primal, Zone
Standard Action   **Area** burst 1 within 10 squares
Target: Each creature in burst
Attack: Wisdom vs. Reflex
Hit: 2d6 + Wisdom modifier lightning damage.
Effect: The burst creates a zone of wind and lightning that lasts until the end of your next turn. Any creature that enters the zone or starts its turn there is slowed until the end of your next turn. As a move action, you can move the zone 5 squares.
Sustain Minor: The zone persists, and each creature within it takes 5 lightning damage.

Devouring Ice
Druid Attack 15

A coating of ice forms over your enemy, rooting it to the ground and freezing its flesh. The ice cuts the enemy when it breaks free.

Daily ✦ Cold, Implement, Primal, Reliable
Standard Action   **Ranged** 10
Target: One creature
Attack: Wisdom vs. Fortitude
Hit: The target is immobilized and takes ongoing 5 cold damage (save ends both).
    Aftereffect: 2d10 + Wisdom modifier cold damage.

Revitalizing Pounce — Druid Attack 15

As you leap at your prey, you are energized by the hunt.

Daily ✦ Beast Form, Implement, Primal
Standard Action   Melee touch
Target: One creature
Attack: Wisdom vs. Reflex
Hit: 3d8 + Wisdom modifier damage, and you remove from yourself every effect that a save can end.
Miss: Half damage, and you make a saving throw against each effect that a save can end.

Slashing Claws — Druid Attack 15

Your claws leave bleeding wounds that refuse to close.

Daily ✦ Beast Form, Implement, Primal
Standard Action   Melee touch
Target: One creature
Attack: Wisdom vs. Fortitude
Hit: 2d10 + Wisdom modifier damage, and ongoing 10 damage (save ends).
  Aftereffect: Ongoing 5 damage (save ends).
Miss: Half damage, and ongoing 5 damage (save ends).

LEVEL 16 UTILITY EVOCATIONS

Howl of the Wild — Druid Utility 16

Your eerie howl channels primal power into your allies.

Daily ✦ Beast Form, Healing, Primal
Minor Action   Close burst 5
Target: You and each ally in burst
Effect: You spend a healing surge, and each target regains 2d6 hit points.
  Level 21: Each target regains 3d6 hit points.
  Level 26: Each target regains 4d6 hit points.

Insect Plague — Druid Utility 16

You turn into a swarm of scurrying insects, held together by the power of your consciousness.

Daily ✦ Primal
Free Action   Personal
Prerequisite: You must have the *wild shape* power.
Effect: Until the end of the encounter, you can use *wild shape* to assume the form of a cloud of insects. In this form, you gain a fly speed equal to your speed, and you can hover. You also become insubstantial. When you squeeze, you can move at full speed instead of half speed and can fit through any opening large enough to accommodate even a single insect. You can't attack, pick up anything, or manipulate objects.
  Until this power ends, you can use *wild shape* to change among this form, another beast form, and your humanoid form.

Primal Restoration — Druid Utility 16

A green glow surrounds your nearby allies, purging them of various afflictions.

Daily ✦ Healing, Primal
Standard Action   Close burst 2
Target: You and each ally in burst
Effect: Each target can spend a healing surge either to regain hit points or to remove one effect that a save can end.

Wall of Stone — Druid Utility 16

A granite wall emerges from the ground as you direct.

Daily ✦ Conjuration, Primal
Standard Action   Area wall 12 within 10 squares
Effect: You conjure a wall of rough stone. The wall can be up to 6 squares high and must be on a solid surface. The wall is a solid obstacle. Each square of the wall has 100 hit points and crumbles into difficult terrain if it is destroyed. The whole wall crumbles into difficult terrain at the end of the encounter.

LEVEL 17 ENCOUNTER EVOCATIONS

Windstorm — Druid Attack 17

A brief but mighty cyclone batters creatures and carries them away.

Encounter ✦ Implement, Primal
Standard Action   Area burst 1 within 10 squares
Target: Each creature in burst
Attack: Wisdom vs. Fortitude
Hit: 3d6 + Wisdom modifier damage, and you slide the target 2 squares.
  Primal Guardian: The number of squares you slide the target equals 1 + your Constitution modifier.

Lightning Cascade — Druid Attack 17

Lightning shoots from your fingertips to electrify one enemy and then a second.

Encounter ✦ Implement, Lightning, Primal
Standard Action   Ranged 10
Primary Target: One creature
Primary Attack: Wisdom vs. Reflex
Hit: 2d8 + Wisdom modifier lightning damage, and the primary target is slowed until the end of your next turn.
Effect: Make a secondary attack that is an area burst 5 centered on the primary target.
  Secondary Target: One creature other than the primary target in burst
  Secondary Attack: Wisdom vs. Reflex
  Hit: 1d8 + Wisdom modifier lightning damage to the primary and secondary targets, and the secondary target is slowed until the end of your next turn.

Scavenger's Prize — Druid Attack 17

Your foe is trapped in your grasp as you drag it off.

Encounter ✦ Beast Form, Implement, Primal
Standard Action   Melee touch
Target: One creature
Attack: Wisdom vs. Fortitude
Hit: 3d10 + Wisdom modifier damage, and you grab the target.
  Primal Predator: You can also shift a number of squares equal to your Dexterity modifier and pull the target with you.

Shifting Rake
Druid Attack 17

You easily duck under your foe's defenses to deliver a crippling attack.

Encounter ✦ Beast Form, Implement, Primal
Standard Action   Melee touch
Effect: Before and after the attack, you shift 2 squares.
Target: One creature
Attack: Wisdom vs. Reflex
Hit: 2d10 + Wisdom modifier damage, and the target cannot shift until the end of your next turn.

LEVEL 19 DAILY EVOCATIONS

Entangling Thorns
Druid Attack 19

Thorny vines burst from the ground to entangle creatures. Ripping free of the thorns causes even greater pain.

Daily ✦ Implement, Primal
Standard Action   Area burst 2 within 10 squares
Target: Each creature in burst
Attack: Wisdom vs. Reflex
Hit: The target is immobilized and takes ongoing 5 damage (save ends both).
     Aftereffect: 2d6 + Wisdom modifier damage.
Miss: 1d6 + Wisdom modifier damage, and the target is immobilized until the end of your next turn.

Lunge and Vanish
Druid Attack 19

You disappear after mauling your enemy.

Daily ✦ Beast Form, Implement, Primal
Standard Action   Melee touch
Target: One creature
Attack: Wisdom vs. Reflex
Hit: 4d10 + Wisdom modifier damage.
Effect: You become invisible and then shift 5 squares. You remain invisible until the end of your next turn.

Primal Bear
Druid Attack 19

You transform into a dire bear, grabbing your foes and squeezing the life from their bodies.

Daily ✦ Beast Form, Healing, Implement, Primal
Standard Action   Melee touch
Target: One creature
Attack: Wisdom vs. Fortitude
Hit: 3d10 + Wisdom modifier damage, and you grab the target. Until the grab ends, the target takes 10 damage at the start of your turn.
Miss: Half damage, and you grab the target.
Effect: Until the end of the encounter, while you are in beast form, you gain a +2 bonus to AC and Fortitude.

Winter Hailstorm
Druid Attack 19

A blizzard appears, growing to encompass an ever-wider area.

Daily ✦ Cold, Implement, Primal, Zone
Standard Action   Area burst 2 within 20 squares
Target: Each creature in burst
Attack: Wisdom vs. Fortitude
Hit: 4d6 + Wisdom modifier cold damage.
Miss: Half damage.
Effect: The burst creates a zone of wind and hail that lasts until the end of your next turn. Any creature that enters the zone or starts its turn there is slowed until the end of your next turn and takes 5 cold damage. You can end the zone as a minor action.
Sustain Minor: The zone persists, and you can increase its size by 1 to a maximum of burst 5.

LEVEL 22 UTILITY EVOCATIONS

Phantom Beast
Druid Utility 22

Your beast form takes on properties of the primal spirits that hunt like ghosts through the world.

Daily ✦ Beast Form, Primal
Minor Action   Personal
Effect: Until the end of the encounter, whenever you use *wild shape* to change into beast form, you become insubstantial and gain phasing until the end of your turn.

Sky Talon
Druid Utility 22

You can take the form of a majestic eagle, soaring above the fray and swooping down to claw at your foes.

Daily ✦ Primal
Free Action   Personal
Prerequisite: You must have the *wild shape* power.
Effect: Until the end of the encounter, you can use *wild shape* to assume the form of an eagle that is your size. In this form, you gain a fly speed equal to 2 + your speed, and you can hover. You can't use daily attack powers or manipulate objects.
     Until this power ends, you can use *wild shape* to change among this form, another beast form, and your humanoid form.

Unseen Beast
Druid Utility 22

You vanish and then emerge where your enemies least expect it.

Daily ✦ Primal
Minor Action   Personal
Effect: Until the end of the encounter, whenever you use *wild shape* to change into beast form, you become invisible until the end of your turn.

Unyielding Roots
Druid Utility 22

Your allies sprout roots from their legs and feet, which draw healing power from the earth and plant them firmly in place.

Daily ✦ Healing, Primal
Standard Action   Close burst 5
Target: You and each ally in burst
Effect: Until the end of your next turn, each target can negate being pulled, pushed, or slid. In addition, if a target is bloodied at the start of his or her turn, he or she regains hit points equal to your Constitution modifier.
Sustain Minor: The effect persists.

LEVEL 23 ENCOUNTER EVOCATIONS

Grasping Earth — Druid Attack 23

The earth itself grabs at your enemies, holding them in place for your claws to tear at them.

Encounter ✦ Implement, Primal
Standard Action   **Area** burst 2 within 20 squares
Target: Each creature in burst
Attack: Wisdom vs. Will
Hit: 2d6 + Wisdom modifier damage, and the target is immobilized until the end of your next turn.
  Primal Predator: Until the end of your next turn, while you are in beast form you gain a bonus to attack rolls against the target equal to your Dexterity modifier.

Primal Roar — Druid Attack 23

Your earthshaking roar blasts your enemies' ears and minds, sending them sprawling.

Encounter ✦ Beast Form, Implement, Primal, Psychic
Standard Action   **Close** blast 5
Target: Each enemy in blast
Attack: Wisdom vs. Will
Hit: 2d8 + Wisdom modifier psychic damage, and the target is knocked prone and deafened until the end of your next turn.

Stormburst — Druid Attack 23

A thundercloud appears overhead, and lightning crackles down onto the heads of your enemies.

Encounter ✦ Implement, Lightning, Primal
Standard Action   **Area** burst 2 within 20 squares
Target: Each creature in burst
Attack: Wisdom vs. Reflex
Hit: 2d6 + Wisdom modifier lightning damage, and the target is slowed until the end of your next turn.
Effect: Until the end of your next turn, any creature that enters the area of the burst or starts its turn there takes 5 lightning damage.

Strength of the Hunt — Druid Attack 23

You slash at your foe, drawing strength and health from the same primal spirits that empower your attack.

Encounter ✦ Beast Form, Healing, Implement, Primal
Standard Action   **Melee** touch
Target: One creature
Attack: Wisdom vs. Reflex
Hit: 3d10 + Wisdom modifier damage, and you can spend a healing surge.
  Primal Guardian: An ally within 5 squares of you can also spend a healing surge.

LEVEL 25 DAILY EVOCATIONS

Ferocious Maul — Druid Attack 25

In a flurry of bestial savagery, you tear into your foe, knocking it prone, sapping its strength, and tossing it away.

Daily ✦ Beast Form, Implement, Primal
Standard Action   **Melee** touch
Target: One creature
Primary Attack: Wisdom vs. Reflex
Hit: You knock the target prone.
Effect: Make a secondary attack against the target.
  Secondary Attack: Wisdom vs. Will
  Hit: The target is weakened (save ends).
Effect: Make a tertiary attack against the target.
  Tertiary Attack: Wisdom vs. Fortitude
  Hit: You push the target a number of squares equal to your Constitution modifier, and the target is dazed (save ends).
Effect: The target takes 2d10 + your Wisdom modifier damage. If all three attacks hit, the target takes extra damage equal to your Dexterity modifier.

Primal Storm — Druid Attack 25

The sky churns with storm clouds as fire and lightning batter your foes.

Daily ✦ Fire, Implement, Lightning, Primal, Zone
Standard Action   Area burst 4 within 20 squares
Primary Target: Each enemy in burst
Primary Attack: Wisdom vs. Fortitude
Hit: 4d6 + Wisdom modifier fire and lightning damage, and the primary target is knocked prone.
Miss: Half damage.
Effect: The burst creates a zone of raging wind that lasts until the end of your next turn. While the zone persists, you can make the following secondary attack, using a square within the zone as the attack's origin square.
  Opportunity Action   Close burst 1
  Trigger: A prone enemy within the zone stands up
  Secondary Target: The triggering enemy in burst
  Secondary Attack: Wisdom vs. Reflex
  Hit: The secondary target cannot stand up during its current turn.
Sustain Minor: The zone persists.

Primal Tiger — Druid Attack 25

You transform into a dire tiger, lashing out at foes that dare draw near.

Daily ✦ Beast Form, Implement, Primal
Standard Action   Close burst 1
Target: Each enemy in burst you can see
Attack: Wisdom vs. Reflex
Hit: 6d6 + Wisdom modifier damage. If the attack hits at least once, you shift a number of squares equal to your Dexterity modifier.
Effect: Until the end of the encounter, while you are in beast form you can make a melee basic attack as an opportunity action against any enemy that enters a square adjacent to you.

Level 27 Encounter Evocations

Explosive Wind — Druid Attack 27

A sudden eruption of howling, swirling wind scatters creatures in all directions.

Encounter ✦ Implement, Primal
Standard Action   Area burst 2 within 20 squares
Target: Each creature in burst
Attack: Wisdom vs. Fortitude
Hit: 4d6 + Wisdom modifier damage, and you slide the target 5 squares.

Feral Whirlwind — Druid Attack 27

You claw and bite every enemy within reach.

Encounter ✦ Beast Form, Implement, Primal
Standard Action   Close burst 1
Target: Each enemy in burst you can see
Attack: Wisdom vs. Reflex
Hit: 4d6 + Wisdom modifier damage.

Fey Lure — Druid Attack 25

Glittering motes of eldritch light both sear and enchant your foes, who follow the motes.

Daily ✦ Charm, Implement, Primal, Radiant, Zone
Standard Action   Area burst 3 within 20 squares
Target: Each enemy in burst
Attack: Wisdom vs. Will
Hit: 3d6 + Wisdom modifier radiant damage.
Miss: Half damage.
Effect: The burst creates a zone of eldritch lights that lasts until the end of your next turn. While the zone persists, you slide each enemy within it 3 squares at the end of your turn.
Sustain Minor: The zone persists.

Leaping Rake — Druid Attack 27

You jump at your enemy, maul it with your claws, and then leap to the next foe.

Encounter ✦ Beast Form, Implement, Primal
Standard Action   **Melee** touch
Effect: Before the attack, you shift 3 squares.
   Primal Predator: The number of squares you shift equals 1 + your Dexterity modifier.
Target: Each enemy within reach during the shift
Attack: Wisdom vs. Reflex
Hit: 1d10 + Wisdom modifier damage, and the target is dazed until the end of your next turn.

Polar Blast — Druid Attack 27

You channel the force of the northern wastes into a blast of freezing wind.

Encounter ✦ Cold, Implement, Primal
Standard Action   **Close** blast 5
Target: Each creature in blast
Attack: Wisdom vs. Reflex
Hit: 3d8 + Wisdom modifier cold damage, and the target is immobilized until the end of your next turn.
   Primal Guardian: Until the end of your next turn, the target also gains vulnerability to all damage equal to your Constitution modifier.

LEVEL 29 DAILY EVOCATIONS

Blinding Blizzard — Druid Attack 29

Polar winds and snow move across the battlefield as you direct.

Daily ✦ Cold, Implement, Primal, Zone
Standard Action   **Area** burst 2 within 20 squares
Primary Target: Each creature in burst
Primary Attack: Wisdom vs. Fortitude
Hit: 4d6 + Wisdom modifier cold damage, and the primary target is blinded (save ends).
Miss: Half damage.
Effect: The burst creates a zone of snow that lasts until the end of your next turn. While the zone persists, you can make the following secondary attack, using a square within the zone as the attack's origin square.
   Opportunity Action   **Close** burst 1
   Trigger: A creature enters the zone or starts its turn there
   Secondary Target: The triggering creature in burst
   Secondary Attack: Wisdom vs. Reflex
   Hit: The secondary target is restrained until the end of your next turn.
Sustain Minor: The zone persists.

Gaze of the Beast — Druid Attack 29

As your foe catches your gaze, you call up the beast inside it and take control.

Daily ✦ Beast Form, Charm, Implement, Primal, Psychic
Standard Action   **Ranged** 10
Target: One creature
Attack: Wisdom vs. Will
Hit: The target is dominated (save ends).
   Aftereffect: 3d10 + Wisdom modifier psychic damage.
Miss: The target is dazed (save ends).
   Aftereffect: 2d10 + Wisdom modifier psychic damage.

Lifeleech Thorns — Druid Attack 29

Your enemies struggle to free themselves from the roots that trap them, even as you draw the life from them to heal your own wounds.

Daily ✦ Healing, Implement, Primal
Standard Action   **Area** burst 2 within 20 squares
Target: Each creature in burst
Attack: Wisdom vs. Reflex
Hit: The target is immobilized and weakened and takes ongoing 10 damage (save ends all). You regain hit points equal to your Constitution modifier for each target you hit with this power.
   Aftereffect: 3d8 + Wisdom modifier damage.
Miss: 1d10 + Wisdom modifier damage, and the target is weakened (save ends).

Primal Archetype — Druid Attack 29

No longer an imperfect reflection of the Primal Beast, your beast form becomes a true expression of the first predator.

Daily ✦ Beast Form, Implement, Primal
Standard Action   **Melee** touch
Target: One or two creatures
Attack: Wisdom vs. Reflex. You gain a +2 bonus to the attack roll against a bloodied target.
Hit: 2d6 + Wisdom modifier damage, and the target is stunned (save ends).
Miss: Half damage, and the target is stunned until the end of your next turn.
Effect: Until the end of the encounter, while you are in beast form you gain a +4 bonus to speed and a +2 bonus to attack rolls against bloodied targets, and you can shift 2 squares as a move action.

BLOOD MOON STALKER

"Tonight, the full moon rises red over the mountains. This is the night of the blood moon—my night."

Prerequisite: Druid, *wild shape* power

Several legends tell of the blood moon, a night or sometimes a season when the Primal Beast stalks the wilderness of the world in physical form. During the blood moon, the predators of the world are said to be more dangerous and to have an insatiable hunger. According to some legends, the blood moon is a perversion of the world's natural state, brought about by the gods or by the fierce response of the primal spirits to some violation of their precepts. Whatever the cause and exact effects of the blood moon, some druids use these legends as a symbol for their own ferocious zeal in protecting the natural balance of the world.

You are a blood moon stalker, favoring your beast form and choosing powers that make you more

dangerous in that form. As your body transforms into beast form, so too your mind embraces your bestial side. You take pride and pleasure in fighting without conscious thought, drawing on bestial instinct and wisdom to guide your attacks upon your prey. You are a fierce hunter, a silent stalker of the wilds, but you are also a crusader for the primal spirits, ensuring that neither gods nor primordials overstep the bounds set for them at the dawn of time.

Through the power of the blood moon, you and your spirit brothers, sisters, and ancestors are the custodians of the world.

BLOOD MOON STALKER PATH FEATURES

Blood Moon Action (11th level): When you spend an action point to take an extra action while you are in beast form, you can also make a melee basic attack as a free action.

Blood Moon Hunger (11th level): When you reduce an enemy to 0 hit points with a melee or a close attack, you can use your second wind as a free action.

Frenzied Claws (16th level): While you are in beast form, you can score a critical hit on a roll of 19–20.

BLOOD MOON STALKER EVOCATIONS

Blood Moon Frenzy	Blood Moon Stalker Attack 11

With a fearsome roar, you claw at the enemies around you, dealing harsher wounds to those near death.

Encounter ✦ Beast Form, Implement, Primal
Standard Action   **Close** burst 1
Target: Each enemy in burst you can see
Attack: Wisdom vs. Reflex
Hit: 2d6 + Wisdom modifier damage. The attack deals 1d6 extra damage against a target that is already bloodied.

Feral Accuracy	Blood Moon Stalker Utility 12

Your claws and eyes glow red, as the blood moon heightens the accuracy of your attacks.

Daily ✦ Beast Form, Primal
Minor Action   **Personal**
Effect: Until the end of your next turn, you can reroll any melee or close attack that misses, and you must use the second roll.

Nature's Grave	Blood Moon Stalker Attack 20

You leap at the enemy in a furious attack. One of you will not walk away from this fight.

Daily ✦ Beast Form, Implement, Primal
Standard Action   **Melee** touch
Requirement: You or the target must be bloodied.
Target: One creature
Attack: Wisdom vs. Reflex
Hit: 6d10 + Wisdom modifier damage.
Miss: Half damage.

ERIC BELISLE

GUARDIAN OF THE LIVING GATE

"There are creatures from beyond this world that seek to destroy all that we have built. My task is to destroy them first."

Prerequisite: Druid

Ancient compacts and edicts protect the natural world from too much interference by gods and primordials. As much as primordials, as well as demons, might like to tear the world apart and draw it back into the Elemental Chaos from which it was made, their power is limited. To many druids' eyes, the greatest threat that now faces the world is not god or primordial, but alien creatures from the Far Realm that are not bound by the ancient laws. These creatures don't necessarily want to destroy the world, but whether or not they mean to, they corrupt it simply by being in it.

As a guardian of the Living Gate, you have sworn to seek out and kill aberrant creatures that have ties to the Far Realm and to seal any portals between that plane and the world. You might have joined an order of like-minded druids (the organization known as the Circle of the True is the largest such order), or you might have found your own way into the esoteric knowledge of the Living Gate. The mystical powers you learn on this path, starting with the *first ward of the Living Gate*, are generally useful for protecting your allies and bringing ruin to your enemies, but your charge is to use them to defend the natural world from forces that would corrupt and destroy it.

GUARDIAN OF THE LIVING GATE PATH FEATURES

Guardian Action (11th level): When you spend an action point to take an extra action, you or an ally within 5 squares of you can make a saving throw with a +5 bonus.

Entwining Evocation (11th level): When you make an area attack, you gain combat advantage against each target that has no creatures adjacent to it.

Enduring Spirit (16th level): Once per round, when you fail a saving throw, an ally within 5 squares of you can make a saving throw.

GUARDIAN OF THE LIVING GATE EVOCATIONS

First Ward of the Living Gate
Guardian of the Living Gate Attack 11

You evoke a curse that wracks your foe with pain and marks it and its companions as enemies of the primal spirits.

Encounter ✦ Implement, Primal
Standard Action   **Ranged** 10
Attack: Wisdom vs. Reflex
Target: One creature
Hit: 3d10 + Wisdom modifier damage. Until the end of your next turn, you gain a +2 bonus to the attack rolls of any primal attack powers you use against the target and any enemy within 5 squares of it.

Second Ward of the Living Gate
Guardian of the Living Gate Utility 12

You expunge the corrupting influence of your enemy from the world.

Daily ✦ Primal
Minor Action   **Close** burst 5
Target: One enemy in burst
Effect: Until the end of the encounter, you and your allies gain a +4 bonus to saving throws against effects caused by the target.

Third Ward of the Living Gate
Guardian of the Living Gate Attack 20

Your foe begins to dissipate as the primal spirits tear it apart.

Daily ✦ Implement, Primal
Standard Action   **Ranged** 20
Target: One creature
Attack: Wisdom vs. Will
Hit: 4d10 + Wisdom modifier damage, and ongoing 10 damage (save ends). Whenever the target takes the ongoing damage, it is knocked prone and each enemy within 5 squares of it takes 5 damage.
Miss: Half damage, and ongoing 5 damage (save ends).

KEEPER OF THE HIDDEN FLAME

"The Hidden Flame burns within us all. Draw on it for your fury, or I will call it out for your doom."

Prerequisite: Druid

According to druidic legend, the Hidden Flame is a spark of vigor and vitality that exists within every creature. Beasts, especially predatory mammals, are said to live in harmony with the Hidden Flame within them, calling upon it to fuel their hunting fury. When a creature lets the Hidden Flame burn out of control, the result is a mad savagery that is no more in harmony with the natural way of things than the behavior of those civilized folk who act as if no flame burns within them at all.

You are a keeper of the Hidden Flame, able to tap into this wellspring of strength and bestial fury. By calling to the Hidden Flame in a creature, you can spur that creature into a frenzy that leaves no room for strategic or tactical thinking. You draw on the Hidden Flame in yourself and your allies to perfect your predatory instinct, helping you fight with terrible ferocity.

KEEPER OF THE HIDDEN FLAME PATH FEATURES

Keeper's Action (11th level): When you spend an action point to take an extra action, you can also reroll the next attack you make that misses before the end of your turn, and you must use the second roll.

Fury of the Hidden Flame (11th level): You gain a +1 bonus to ranged, area, and close attack rolls against the enemy nearest to you.

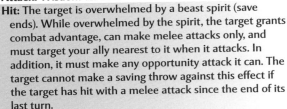

Leap to the Fray (16th level): Whenever an ally within 5 squares of you charges, you and each other ally within 5 squares of you can shift 1 square as a free action.

KEEPER OF THE HIDDEN FLAME EVOCATIONS

Summon the Beast	Keeper of the Hidden Flame Attack 11

Your foe howls with bestial rage, throwing itself into the fight and right into your trap.

Encounter ✦ Implement, Primal
Standard Action　　　　**Ranged** 5
Target: One creature
Attack: Wisdom vs. Will
Hit: You pull the target 5 squares and knock it prone. In addition, the target is dazed until the end of your next turn.

Spark of Fury	Keeper of the Hidden Flame Utility 12

You call on the wellspring of wrath that burns within you and your allies. For a critical moment, all of you fight with the ferocity of cornered beasts.

Encounter ✦ Primal
Minor Action　　　　**Close** burst 5
Target: You and each ally in burst
Effect: Until the end of your next turn, each target gains a +1 power bonus to attack rolls and a +2 power bonus to damage rolls.

Spirit of the Beast	Keeper of the Hidden Flame Attack 20

The spirit of the beast overwhelms your foe, driving it into a reckless rampage.

Daily ✦ Implement, Primal
Standard Action　　　　**Ranged** 20
Target: One creature
Attack: Wisdom vs. Will
Hit: The target is overwhelmed by a beast spirit (save ends). While overwhelmed by the spirit, the target grants combat advantage, can make melee attacks only, and must target your ally nearest to it when it attacks. In addition, it must make any opportunity attack it can. The target cannot make a saving throw against this effect if the target has hit with a melee attack since the end of its last turn.
Miss: The target grants combat advantage and must target your ally nearest to it when it attacks (save ends both). The target cannot make a saving throw against this effect if the target has hit with a melee attack since the end of its last turn.

SKY HUNTER

"The eagle is the perfect predator. Not bound to earth, it hunts like a primal spirit in the world."

Prerequisite: Druid, *wild shape* power

Although the Primal Beast usually appears as a mammalian predator, some aspects of the Primal Beast soar through the sky on feathered wings, hunting prey from the air. Eagles, hawks, and falcons are no less fierce predators than panthers and wolves, and some druids assume their forms to fly after their own prey.

You are such a druid, a sky hunter who emulates birds of prey in your beast form. Your beast form can't always fly, but it can take to the air from time to time. Some sky hunters assume a beast form a little like a cockatrice–a stalking predator with primitive wings that allow it to fly in short bursts. Others retain their normal beast form but change momentarily into a bird form when they use their sky hunter powers.

SKY HUNTER PATH FEATURES

Sky Hunter's Action (11th level): When you spend an action point to take an extra action, you can fly your speed before taking that action.

Master of Wings (11th level): You gain a +2 bonus to attack rolls against flying creatures.

Beast Senses (16th level): Whenever you use a beast form daily power, you gain a +5 power bonus to Perception checks until the end of the encounter.

SKY HUNTER EVOCATIONS

Blinding Talons	Sky Hunter Attack 11

Changing into a flying raptor's form, you swoop at your enemy's eyes.

Encounter ✦ Beast Form, Implement, Primal
Standard Action   Personal
Effect: You assume the form of an eagle that is your size, fly twice your speed, and make the following melee touch attack at any point during the movement. You don't provoke an opportunity attack for moving away from the attack's target. After the attack, you return to your normal beast form.
Target: One creature
Attack: Wisdom vs. Reflex
Hit: 1d10 + Wisdom modifier damage, and the target is blinded until the end of your next turn.

Soaring Falcon	Sky Hunter Utility 12

You can take the form of a swift bird of prey to soar above your foes.

Daily ✦ Primal
Free Action   Personal
Prerequisite: You must have the *wild shape* power.
Effect: Until the end of the encounter, you can use *wild shape* to assume the form of a Tiny falcon. In this form, you gain a fly speed equal to your speed. You also gain a +5 bonus to Perception checks and a +4 bonus to AC against opportunity attacks. You can't attack, pick up anything, or manipulate objects.

Until this power ends, you can use *wild shape* to change among this form, another beast form, and your humanoid form.

Primal Eagle	Sky Hunter Attack 20

You transform into a dire eagle, swooping from the air to batter your foes with the thunder of your wings.

Daily ✦ Beast Form, Implement, Primal, Thunder
Standard Action   Personal
Effect: You assume the form of an eagle that is your size, fly your speed, and then make the following attack, which is a close burst 5. You then return to your normal beast form. Until the end of the encounter, while you are in beast form you can assume this eagle form and fly your speed as a move action. At the end of that action, you must land, and you return to your normal beast form.
Target: Each enemy in burst
Attack: Wisdom vs. Fortitude
Hit: 4d6 + Wisdom modifier thunder damage, and the target is slowed (save ends).
Miss: Half damage, and the target is slowed until the end of your next turn.

INVOKER

"The only thing stronger than my faith is the fire I use to burn away those who stand against the will of the gods."

CLASS TRAITS

Role: Controller. You invoke the power of a god to blast your foes from a distance, leave them unable to defend themselves, and scatter them to the four winds. Depending on your choice of class features and powers, you lean toward either leader or striker as a secondary role.

Power Source: Divine. You practice an ancient form of divine magic, wielding the power that the gods themselves used in their battle against the primordials.

Key Abilities: Wisdom, Constitution, Intelligence

Armor Proficiencies: Cloth, leather, hide, chainmail
Weapon Proficiencies: Simple melee, simple ranged
Implements: Rods, staffs
Bonus to Defense: +1 Fortitude, +1 Reflex, +1 Will

Hit Points at 1st Level: 10 + Constitution score
Hit Points per Level Gained: 4
Healing Surges per Day: 6 + Constitution modifier

Trained Skills: Religion. From the class skills list below, choose three more trained skills at 1st level.
Class Skills: Arcana (Int), Diplomacy (Cha), Endurance (Con), History (Int), Insight (Wis), Intimidate (Cha), Religion (Int)

Class Features: Channel Divinity, Divine Covenant, Ritual Casting

At the dawn of time, the gods who inhabited the Astral Sea warred with the primordials of the Elemental Chaos, the mighty beings who shaped the world out of formless void. The greatest of the gods' mortal agents in that war were invokers, imbued with a fragment of the gods' own might to fight alongside them. No other mortal servant of the gods can claim the same kind of power. Through rites of investiture, avengers, clerics, and paladins gain the ability to manifest echoes of that power, uttering careful prayers and channeling divine energy through their holy symbols. You, however, channel your god's power directly. No mere symbol can contain it, for you speak the words of creation, shaping the universe to your and your god's will.

Perhaps you were trained in a secret monastery, or you studied in a library where the universe's oldest lore was preserved. Or perhaps you experienced the presence of your god firsthand and took a shard of divine power into yourself. You might even be an immortal born into flesh, slowly awakening to the awesome divine power that is your birthright. Whatever your past, you are among the gods' most trusted servants, bound to a covenant in which you swore to use divine power with great care. To what end will you wield that might?

INVOKER CLASS FEATURES

Invokers have the following class features.

CHANNEL DIVINITY

Once per encounter, you can use a Channel Divinity power. You start with two Channel Divinity powers: *rebuke undead* and a power determined by your Divine Covenant. You can gain additional Channel Divinity powers by taking divinity feats.

DIVINE COVENANT

Invokers wield ancient divine power that is not accessible to most mortals—only to those who enter into a personal covenant with a god. Invokers undergo long years of study and testing. Only after that time are they allowed to enter into the final covenant that grants them access to this class's powers. Some say that, in the final swearing of the covenant, the invoker's god briefly manifests, but the details of an invoker's initiation are a closely held secret.

Choose one of the options described below. The Divine Covenant you choose provides you with a Channel Divinity power and a covenant manifestation that takes effect whenever you use a divine encounter or daily attack power. Your choice also provides bonuses to certain invoker powers, as detailed in those powers.

COVENANT OF PRESERVATION

The gods have charged you to defend the faithful and to ally with those who seek to defeat the gods' enemies.

Channel Divinity: You gain the Channel Divinity power *preserver's rebuke*.

Covenant Manifestation: When you use a divine encounter or daily attack power on your turn, you can slide an ally within 10 squares of you 1 square.

COVENANT OF WRATH

You have sworn to seek out and destroy those that oppose the gods. Primordials, demons, and devils fall before your magic like wheat before a scythe.

Channel Divinity: You gain the Channel Divinity power *armor of wrath*.

Covenant Manifestation: When you use a divine encounter or daily attack power on your turn, you gain a bonus to the damage roll equal to 1 for each enemy you attack with the power.

RITUAL CASTING

You gain the Ritual Caster feat as a bonus feat, allowing you to use magical rituals (see Chapter 10 of the *Player's Handbook*). You own a ritual book, and it contains two rituals of your choice that you have mastered: Hand of Fate and one 1st-level ritual.

Once per day, you can use Hand of Fate without expending components.

IMPLEMENTS

Invokers do not make use of holy symbols, since they believe that their magic predates and transcends such representations of divine power. Instead, invokers make use of rods and staffs as representations of the gods' dominion over the world. When you wield a magic rod or a magic staff, you can add its enhancement bonus to the attack rolls and the damage rolls of invoker powers and invoker paragon path powers that have the implement keyword. Without an implement, you can still use these powers.

INVOKERS AND DEITIES

Choice of Deity: Like other divine characters, invokers are dedicated servants of one or more deities. Most invokers devote themselves to a single deity, but all invokers recognize the entire pantheon as worthy of respect (see "Deities," *Player's Handbook*, page 20). Whereas a cleric might revere Corellon and despise Lolth as a rival and enemy, an invoker dedicated to Corellon recognizes Lolth and her servants

---

INVOKER OVERVIEW

Characteristics: Your powers are aimed at controlling your foes: slowing, stopping, or compelling their movement; weakening their attacks; or hedging them in zones of divine fire. You summon angelic beings to face your enemies, and you empower your allies to fight with divine fervor.

Religion: Like clerics, invokers can worship any deity, but few invokers serve gods who are newer arrivals to the pantheon, such as the Raven Queen and Vecna. Invokers dedicated to Bahamut often revere Tiamat as well, worshiping those two gods as the two halves of the slain dragon-god Io. More than most other divine characters, invokers offer prayers to and call on favors from the entire pantheon, for all the gods, whatever their alignments, fought together against the primordials.

Races: Dwarves and devas make particularly good invokers; both the dwarven devotion to the gods and the devas' heritage lend themselves to the invoker's worldview. Ancient and long-lived, eladrin and elves have a racial memory that keeps alive the legends of the first wars between the gods and the primordials, and the two races often follow in the paths of the first invokers. Invokers can be found among all races, however.

as comrades in arms against the forces that seek to destroy the world and the gods. That's not to say that you can't oppose the evil schemes of Lolth's followers if you're dedicated to Corellon, only that you shouldn't lose sight of the grander scheme of things.

Choice of Alignment: Invokers don't gain their power through rites of investiture or ordination, as avengers, clerics, and paladins do. You bear the touch of your god's own hand on your soul, a direct channel through which divine power can flow into the world, shaped by your will. Because you strive to bring your will into perfect accordance with your deity's, your alignment must match your deity's. For instance, an invoker of Moradin must be lawful good, an invoker of Pelor must be good, and an invoker of Ioun must be unaligned.

CREATING AN INVOKER

Invokers rely on Wisdom—as an expression of their link to the divine will—for the accuracy and potency of their attacks. Each invoker enters into a covenant with a god, a sworn pact in which the invoker agrees to fulfill certain duties in exchange for the divine power he or she will use to carry out those duties. The two most common covenants—the Covenant of Preservation and the Covenant of Wrath—lend themselves to two common invoker builds. Even though you must choose a covenant, you can choose any powers you like to help you fulfill it.

PRESERVING INVOKER

You defend your allies, combining defensive magic with prayers that hinder or prevent your enemies' attacks. Wisdom should be your highest ability score, followed by Intelligence, since you need foresight and cunning to protect your allies. Choose powers that grant defensive benefits to your allies or penalties to your enemies. The preserving invoker leans toward leader as a secondary role.

Suggested Class Feature: Covenant of Preservation

Suggested Feat: Insightful Preservation

Suggested Skills: Arcana, Diplomacy, History, Religion

Suggested At-Will Powers: *sun strike, vanguard's lightning*

Suggested Encounter Power: *blades of astral fire*

Suggested Daily Power: *binding invocation of chains*

WRATHFUL INVOKER

You are an instrument of divine wrath, smiting those who have the temerity to doubt the reach of your god's power. Make Wisdom your highest ability score, followed by Constitution, since your physical durability allows you to withstand and channel divine wrath. Focus on powers that bring ruin to your foes. The wrathful invoker leans toward striker as a secondary role.

Suggested Class Feature: Covenant of Wrath

Suggested Feat: Invoker Defense

Suggested Skills: Endurance, Insight, Intimidate, Religion

Suggested At-Will Powers: *avenging light, grasping shards*

Suggested Encounter Power: *thunder of judgment*

Suggested Daily Power: *purging flame*

INVOKER POWERS

Your invoker powers are called prayers, but they are not as much supplications to the gods as direct manifestations of divine power.

CLASS FEATURES

Each invoker has the Channel Divinity power *rebuke undead*. Your choice of Divine Covenant determines the other Channel Divinity power you start with.

Channel Divinity: Invoker Feature
Armor of Wrath

As your foe strikes, you invoke the gods' power to encase yourself in a burning aura of radiant energy.

Encounter ✦ Divine, Radiant
Immediate Reaction   Close burst 5
Trigger: An enemy within 5 squares of you hits you
Target: The triggering enemy in burst
Effect: The target takes radiant damage equal to your Constitution modifier, and you push the target 2 squares.
    Level 11: 1d6 + Constitution modifier radiant damage.
    Level 21: 2d6 + Constitution modifier radiant damage.

Channel Divinity: Invoker Feature
Preserver's Rebuke

You call upon the gods to punish the enemy that dares harm those entrusted to your care.

Encounter ✦ Divine
Immediate Reaction   Personal
Trigger: An enemy within 10 squares of you hits your ally
Effect: Before the end of your next turn, you gain a bonus to your next attack roll against the triggering enemy equal to your Intelligence modifier.

Channel Divinity: Rebuke Undead
Invoker Feature

Undead flee and then cower in your presence, their bodies seared by divine light.

Encounter ✦ Divine, Implement, Radiant
Standard Action   **Close** blast 5
Target: Each undead creature in blast
Attack: Wisdom vs. Will
Hit: 1d10 + Wisdom modifier radiant damage. You push the target 2 squares, and it is dazed until the end of your next turn.
  Level 5: 2d10 + Wisdom modifier radiant damage.
  Level 11: 3d10 + Wisdom modifier radiant damage.
  Level 15: 4d10 + Wisdom modifier radiant damage.
  Level 21: 5d10 + Wisdom modifier radiant damage.
  Level 25: 6d10 + Wisdom modifier radiant damage.
Miss: Half damage.

LEVEL 1 AT-WILL PRAYERS

Avenging Light
Invoker Attack 1

You smite your foe with a searing orb of light, which burns with the fire of vengeance if your allies have been harmed.

At-Will ✦ Divine, Implement, Radiant
Standard Action   **Ranged** 10
Target: One creature
Attack: Wisdom vs. Fortitude
Hit: 1d10 + Wisdom modifier radiant damage. If a bloodied ally is adjacent to the target, the attack deals extra radiant damage equal to your Constitution modifier.
  Level 21: 2d10 + Wisdom modifier radiant damage.
Special: You can use this power as a ranged basic attack.

Divine Bolts
Invoker Attack 1

You hurl bolts of divine lightning at your enemies.

At-Will ✦ Divine, Implement, Lightning
Standard Action   **Ranged** 10
Target: One or two creatures
Attack: Wisdom vs. Reflex
Hit: 1d6 + Wisdom modifier lightning damage.
  Level 21: 2d6 + Wisdom modifier lightning damage.

Grasping Shards
Invoker Attack 1

You hurl a crystalline sphere of magic at your foes. On impact, it splinters into hundreds of tiny, radiant blades, which slice into your enemies and slow their movement.

At-Will ✦ Divine, Implement, Radiant
Standard Action   **Area** burst 1 within 10 squares
Target: Each creature in burst
Attack: Wisdom vs. Fortitude
Hit: Wisdom modifier radiant damage, and the target is slowed until the end of your next turn.
  Level 21: 1d10 + Wisdom modifier radiant damage.

Sun Strike
Invoker Attack 1

A beam of radiant energy extends from your hands to bathe a foe in searing light and force it to move.

At-Will ✦ Divine, Implement, Radiant
Standard Action   **Ranged** 10
Target: One creature
Attack: Wisdom vs. Reflex
Hit: 1d8 + Wisdom modifier radiant damage, and you slide the target 1 square.
  Level 21: 2d8 + Wisdom modifier radiant damage.
Special: You can use this power as a ranged basic attack.

Vanguard's Lightning
Invoker Attack 1

Bolts of divine lightning arc from your hands to scorch the area before you. The bolts linger, ready to avenge any attacks made by your foes.

At-Will ✦ Divine, Implement, Lightning
Standard Action   **Area** burst 1 within 10 squares
Target: Each creature in burst
Attack: Wisdom vs. Reflex
Hit: 1d6 + Wisdom modifier lightning damage. Whenever the target makes an opportunity attack before the end of your next turn, the target takes lightning damage equal to your Intelligence modifier.
  Level 21: 2d6 + Wisdom modifier lightning damage.

LEVEL 1 ENCOUNTER PRAYERS

Astral Terror
Invoker Attack 1

Astral energy surges through you, transforming you into a beacon of divine terror that sends your foes reeling.

Encounter ✦ Divine, Fear, Implement, Psychic
Standard Action   **Close** burst 3
Target: Each enemy in burst
Attack: Wisdom vs. Will
Hit: 1d6 + Wisdom modifier psychic damage, and you push the target 2 squares.

Blades of Astral Fire
Invoker Attack 1

Gleaming blades of radiant energy appear and strike your foes. The blades then transform into spectral shields that protect your allies.

Encounter ✦ Divine, Implement, Radiant
Standard Action   **Area** burst 1 within 10 squares
Target: Each enemy in burst
Attack: Wisdom vs. Reflex
Hit: 1d6 + Wisdom modifier radiant damage.
Effect: Each ally in the burst gains a +2 power bonus to AC until the end of your next turn.
  Covenant of Preservation: The bonus to AC equals 1 + your Intelligence modifier.

Spear of the Inquisitor
Invoker Attack 1

A lance of gleaming energy slices through the air and into your foe, burning it with the power of the gods and rooting it in place.

Encounter ✦ Divine, Implement, Radiant
Standard Action   **Ranged** 10
Target: One creature
Attack: Wisdom vs. Reflex
Hit: 1d10 + Wisdom modifier radiant damage, and the target is immobilized until the end of your next turn.

Thunder of Judgment
Invoker Attack 1

Blasts of thunder rock the air around your foes each time you strike your staff on the ground, leaving them battered and senseless.

Encounter ✦ Divine, Implement, Thunder
Standard Action   **Ranged** 10
Target: One, two, or three creatures
Attack: Wisdom vs. Fortitude
Hit: 1d6 + Wisdom modifier thunder damage, or 2d6 + Wisdom modifier thunder damage if you target only one creature. In addition, the target is dazed until the end of your next turn.
  Covenant of Wrath: You also push the target a number of squares equal to your Constitution modifier.

LEVEL 1 DAILY PRAYERS

Angelic Echelon
Invoker Attack 1

Spectral angels swoop down to attack the foes around you and then linger briefly, threatening to inflict further damage.

Daily ✦ Divine, Implement, Radiant
Standard Action   **Close** burst 3
Target: Each enemy in burst
Attack: Wisdom vs. Will
Hit: 1d6 + Wisdom modifier radiant damage. Whenever the target attacks before the end of your next turn, the target takes 5 radiant damage.
Miss: Half damage.

Binding Invocation of Chains
Invoker Attack 1

You whisper ancient words of binding, invoking the power of the gods to hinder your foes' movement with spectral chains.

Daily ✦ Divine, Implement
Standard Action   **Close** burst 10
Target: Each enemy in burst
Attack: Wisdom vs. Reflex
Hit: The target is slowed (save ends).
Miss: The target is slowed until the end of your next turn.

Purging Flame
Invoker Attack 1

Divine fire washes over your foe, burning not only its physical form but the very stuff of its soul.

Daily ✦ Divine, Fire, Implement
Standard Action   **Ranged** 10
Target: One creature
Attack: Wisdom vs. Reflex
Hit: 1d10 + Wisdom modifier fire damage, and ongoing 10 fire damage (save ends).
Miss: Half damage, and ongoing 5 fire damage (save ends).

Summon Angel of Fire
Invoker Attack 1

A mote of light appears before you, and from it steps an angelic figure wreathed in fire.

Daily ✦ Divine, Fire, Implement, Summoning
Minor Action   **Ranged** 5
Effect: You summon a Medium angel of fire in an unoccupied square within range. The angel has speed 6 and fly 6 (hover). You can give the angel the following special commands.
  Standard Action: Close burst 1; targets each creature in burst; Wisdom vs. Reflex; 1d8 + Wisdom modifier fire damage.
  Opportunity Attack: Melee 1; targets one creature; Wisdom vs. Reflex; 1d8 + Wisdom modifier fire damage.

LEVEL 2 UTILITY PRAYERS

Divine Call
Invoker Utility 2

You intone a word of power to rally your allies to your side.

Encounter ✦ Divine
Minor Action   **Ranged** 10
Target: One or two allies
Effect: You pull each target 3 squares.

Emissary of the Gods
Invoker Utility 2

You speak with the voice of the gods, compelling others to heed your words.

Daily ✦ Divine
Minor Action   **Personal**
Effect: You gain a +5 power bonus to your next Diplomacy check or Intimidate check during this encounter. If you make this check as part of a skill challenge, you gain 2 successes if the check is successful and don't gain a failure if the check fails.

Shroud of Awe
Invoker Utility 2

Your voice resonates with thunder, and you are shrouded in divine majesty that strikes awe and respect in your listeners' hearts.

Encounter ✦ Divine
Minor Action   **Personal**
Effect: You can speak with a thunderous voice that allows creatures within 500 feet of you to hear you clearly. Before the end of your turn, you gain a power bonus to your next Intimidate check equal to your Constitution modifier.

Shroud of Warning
Invoker Utility 2

You invoke the gods' protection, allowing you and your allies to act a moment sooner when combat erupts.

Daily ✦ Divine
No Action   **Close** burst 10
Trigger: You and your allies roll initiative at the beginning of an encounter
Target: You and each ally in burst
Effect: Each target gains a bonus to the initiative check equal to 2 + your Intelligence modifier.

Wall of Light · Invoker Utility 2

You transform divine energy into the form of a long, glowing wall.

Daily ✦ Conjuration, Divine
Minor Action   **Area** wall 5 within 10 squares
Effect: You conjure a wall of divine energy. The wall is 1
   square high, and it lasts until the end of your next turn.
   While within the wall, any ally gains a +1 power bonus
   to AC, and each ally who starts his or her turn in the wall
   gains 5 temporary hit points.
Sustain Minor: The wall persists.

LEVEL 3 ENCOUNTER PRAYERS

Chains of Carceri · Invoker Attack 3

*You invoke the power of the prison of Carceri, causing
red chains to appear around your enemies to hinder their
movement.*

Encounter ✦ Divine, Implement
Standard Action   **Area** burst 1 within 10 squares
Target: Each creature in burst
Attack: Wisdom vs. Reflex
Hit: 2d8 + Wisdom modifier damage, and the target is
   slowed until the end of your next turn.

Glyph of Imprisonment · Invoker Attack 3

*A divine glyph of censure forms around your foes, searing
them and glowing with radiant power. If they move from their
positions, the glyph flares with searing light.*

Encounter ✦ Divine, Implement, Radiant
Standard Action   **Area** burst 1 within 10 squares
Target: Each creature in burst
Attack: Wisdom vs. Will
Hit: 1d8 + Wisdom modifier radiant damage. If the target
   moves before the end of its next turn, the target takes 5
   radiant damage.

Offering of Justice · Invoker Attack 3

*You call out to the gods, demanding retribution against a foe
who dares to strike at you or your allies and mercy for a foe who
refrains from attacking.*

Encounter ✦ Divine, Implement, Radiant
Standard Action   **Ranged** 10
Target: One creature
Effect: If the target attacks you or your allies before
   the end of its next turn, the target takes 2d10 + your
   Wisdom modifier radiant damage at the end of that turn.
   If the target doesn't attack you or your allies before the
   end of its next turn, the target instead gains 5 temporary
   hit points at the end of that turn.

Sun Hammer · Invoker Attack 3

*Forged from the light of the Bright City of Hestavar, the sun
hammer glows brighter the more your allies suffer. You invoke
the hammer to call down a radiant burst upon your foes.*

Encounter ✦ Divine, Implement, Radiant
Standard Action   **Area** burst 1 within 10 squares
Target: Each enemy in burst
Attack: Wisdom vs. Fortitude
Hit: 1d10 + Wisdom modifier radiant damage. If any
   bloodied allies are in the burst, the attack deals 2 extra
   radiant damage.

FRANZ VOHWINKEL

LEVEL 5 DAILY PRAYERS

Blade of Vengeance
Invoker Attack 5

A spectral form like a shining angel appears amid your foes. Though the angel is indistinct and incorporeal, its curving blade seems solid and poised to attack an enemy that threatens your allies.

Daily ✦ Conjuration, Divine, Implement
Standard Action   Ranged 10
Effect: You conjure a blade of vengeance in an unoccupied square within range. The blade lasts until the end of your next turn. The blade occupies 1 square. Enemies cannot move through its space, but allies can. The blade can flank enemies with you and your allies. In addition, you can make the following attack with the blade.
  Immediate Interrupt   Melee 1
  Trigger: An enemy within 10 squares of the blade hits your ally
  Effect: Before the attack, you move the blade to a square adjacent to the triggering enemy.
  Target: The triggering enemy
  Attack: Wisdom vs. Reflex
  Hit: 1d8 + Wisdom modifier damage.
Sustain Minor: The blade persists, and you can move it 5 squares.

Grasping Chains of the Justiciar
Invoker Attack 5

You invoke the chains of Rathos, an exarch of the gods charged with capturing renegade angels. These glowing blue chains erupt from the ground to tether your foes in place.

Daily ✦ Divine, Force, Implement
Standard Action   Area burst 2 within 10 squares
Target: Each enemy in burst
Attack: Wisdom vs. Reflex
Hit: 1d6 + Wisdom modifier force damage, and the target is immobilized (save ends).
Miss: Half damage, and the target is slowed until the end of your next turn.

Icon of Terror
Invoker Attack 5

You invoke the Icon of Terror, an image that was once used to drive the beings of the Far Realm from this reality. You drive nearby creatures back in fear as the icon assaults their minds.

Daily ✦ Divine, Fear, Implement, Psychic
Standard Action   Close blast 5
Target: Each creature in blast
Attack: Wisdom vs. Will
Hit: 2d6 + Wisdom modifier psychic damage, and you push the target 2 squares.
  Covenant of Wrath: The number of squares you push the target equals your Constitution modifier.
Miss: Half damage, and you push the target 1 square.

Searing Orb
Invoker Attack 5

A miniature sun appears amid your foes, blinding them with divine radiance.

Daily ✦ Divine, Implement, Radiant
Standard Action   Area burst 1 within 10 squares
Target: Each creature in burst
Attack: Wisdom vs. Fortitude
Hit: 1d8 + Wisdom modifier radiant damage, and the target is blinded (save ends).
  Covenant of Preservation: The target is also dazed until the end of your next turn.
Miss: Half damage, and the target is blinded until the end of your next turn.

LEVEL 6 UTILITY PRAYERS

Astral Step
Invoker Utility 6

You create momentary doorways through the Astral Sea, teleporting yourself and your companions a short distance.

Daily ✦ Divine, Teleportation
Move Action   Close burst 5
Target: You and each ally in burst
Effect: You teleport each target 3 squares.
  Covenant of Preservation: The number of squares you teleport each target equals 3 + your Intelligence modifier.

Demand Justice
Invoker Utility 6

Whether an ally labors under a deadly effect or a foe seeks to escape the just end wrought by your magic, you tilt fate in your favor.

Encounter ✦ Divine
Immediate Interrupt   Ranged 10
Trigger: A creature within 10 squares of you makes a saving throw
Target: The triggering creature
Effect: The target rerolls the saving throw and must use the new result.

Shared Endurance
Invoker Utility 6

During the ancient war, the gods stood as one against their primordial foes. Your magic can help you and your allies stand as one as well, taking wounds on one another's behalf.

Daily ✦ Divine
Immediate Interrupt   Ranged 10
Trigger: An ally within 10 squares of you takes damage from an attack
Target: The triggering ally
Effect: You or an ally within 10 squares of you takes the damage from the triggering attack instead of the target, but the target takes any other effect caused by the attack.

Shield of Light — Invoker Utility 6

A flash of light flares in your enemy's eyes, disrupting its attack against your ally.

Encounter ✦ Divine
Immediate Interrupt   Ranged 10
Trigger: An enemy within 10 squares of you makes an attack roll against your ally
Target: The triggering enemy
Effect: The target takes a -3 penalty to the triggering attack roll. If the attack hits and deals damage, you slide the ally 1 square after the damage is dealt.

Symbol of Hope — Invoker Utility 6

You conjure a glowing symbol of hope, which renews your allies' efforts against the enemy.

Daily ✦ Conjuration, Divine
Minor Action   Ranged 10
Effect: You conjure a symbol of hope in an unoccupied square within range. The symbol lasts until the end of your next turn. Any ally within 5 squares of the symbol gains a +2 power bonus to saving throws, and any ally who starts his or her turn within 5 squares of the symbol gains 5 temporary hit points.
Sustain Minor: The symbol persists.

LEVEL 7 ENCOUNTER PRAYERS

Baleful Eye of Judgment — Invoker Attack 7

You fix your wrathful glare upon a group of enemies, filling them with awe and terror.

Encounter ✦ Divine, Fear, Implement, Psychic
Standard Action   Area burst 1 within 10 squares
Target: Each creature in burst
Attack: Wisdom vs. Will
Hit: 2d8 + Wisdom modifier psychic damage, and the target takes a -2 penalty to attack rolls until the end of its next turn.

Bolt of the Rising Sun — Invoker Attack 7

A soft ray of light dances across your foe. The light increases in radiance until it chars the foe's flesh and impairs its vision.

Encounter ✦ Divine, Implement, Radiant
Standard Action   Ranged 10
Target: One creature
Attack: Wisdom vs. Reflex
Hit: 1d10 + Wisdom modifier radiant damage. Until the end of your next turn, the target doesn't have line of sight to any creature more than 3 squares away from it.

Invoke Obedience — Invoker Attack 7

As you are filled with glory, your enemies know they must either bow before you or suffer your wrath.

Encounter ✦ Divine, Implement, Psychic
Standard Action   Area burst 1 within 10 squares
Target: Each creature in burst
Effect: Before the attack, each target can fall prone as a free action. The attack automatically misses a prone target.
　　Covenant of Wrath: Each prone target takes 1d6 psychic damage.
Attack: Wisdom + 5 vs. Will
Hit: 2d6 + Wisdom modifier psychic damage.

Thunderbolt of the Heavens — Invoker Attack 7

A crackling bolt of blue energy leaps from your staff, knocking your enemies away from you.

Encounter ✦ Divine, Implement, Thunder
Standard Action   Area burst 1 within 10 squares
Target: Each creature in burst
Attack: Wisdom vs. Fortitude
Hit: 2d8 + Wisdom modifier thunder damage, and you push the target 1 square.
　　Covenant of Preservation: The number of squares you push the target equals 1 + your Intelligence modifier.

LEVEL 9 DAILY PRAYERS

Cerulean Flames — Invoker Attack 9

Ancient texts speak of the Cerulean Sign, a powerful sigil used to hold creatures from beyond the cosmos at bay. You invoke this sign, creating a pool of radiance that blinds those that leave its grasp.

Daily ✦ Divine, Implement, Radiant, Zone
Standard Action   Area burst 1 within 10 squares
Target: Each creature in burst
Attack: Wisdom vs. Reflex
Hit: 3d6 + Wisdom modifier radiant damage.
Miss: Half damage.
Effect: The burst creates a zone of cerulean light that lasts until the end of your next turn. Any creature that starts its turn within the zone and leaves it is blinded (save ends).
Sustain Minor: The zone persists.

Fourfold Invocation of Doom — Invoker Attack 9

As you speak the four verses of doom, your foes wilt in fear, their enthusiasm for the battle doused.

Daily ✦ Divine, Fear, Implement, Psychic
Standard Action   Close burst 10
Target: Each enemy in burst
Attack: Wisdom vs. Will
Hit: The target is dazed (save ends).
Miss: The target is dazed until the end of your next turn.
Effect: Until the end of the encounter, any creature that hits or misses you takes 5 psychic damage.

Summon Blade Angel — Invoker Attack 9

You trace a shimmering sigil in the air, and an angelic figure steps from it, bearing the twin swords of vengeance and pain.

Daily ✦ Divine, Implement, Summoning
Minor Action   Ranged 5
Effect: You summon a Medium blade angel in an unoccupied square within range. The angel has speed 6 and fly 6 (hover). It has a +4 bonus to AC. You can give the angel the following special commands.
　　Minor Action: Melee 1; targets one creature; Wisdom vs. Fortitude; 1d8 + Wisdom modifier damage.
　　Opportunity Attack: Melee 1; targets one creature; Wisdom vs. Reflex; 1d8 + Wisdom modifier damage, and the target is slowed until the end of its turn.

Visions of Paradise — Invoker Attack 9

You speak the seven words of peace, sending your foe into a dreamlike state as visions of paradise cloud its mind.

Daily ✦ Charm, Divine, Implement
Standard Action   **Ranged** 10
Target: One creature
Attack: Wisdom vs. Will
Hit: The target is unable to make attacks (save ends). Whenever the target is attacked, it can make a saving throw against this effect.
Miss: The target is unable to make attacks until the end of its next turn. If the target is attacked before the end of its next turn, this effect ends.

LEVEL 10 UTILITY PRAYERS

Angelic Visage — Invoker Utility 10

As your foe attacks, you transform into the image of a death angel. Filled with terror, the foe backs away.

Encounter ✦ Divine, Fear
Immediate Interrupt   **Close** burst 5
Trigger: An enemy within 5 squares of you makes an attack roll against you
Target: The triggering enemy
Effect: The target takes a -2 penalty to the triggering attack roll. After the attack is resolved, you push the target 3 squares.

Covenant of Endurance — Invoker Utility 10

You offer your life energy on your friends' behalf.

Daily ✦ Divine
Minor Action   **Personal**
Effect: Until the end of the encounter, whenever an ally within 10 squares of you has an opportunity to spend a healing surge, you can spend a healing surge on that ally's behalf as a free action. You spend the healing surge but regain no hit points, and the ally regains hit points as if he or she had spent a healing surge.

Divine Renewal — Invoker Utility 10

You fortify your allies with life-sustaining power.

Daily ✦ Divine
Standard Action   **Ranged** 10
Target: One or two allies who each have two healing surges or fewer
Effect: Each target regains a healing surge.

Martyr's Ward — Invoker Utility 10

You unleash a shield of divine energy that deflects an attack from your friend to yourself.

Daily ✦ Divine
Immediate Interrupt   **Close** burst 10
Trigger: An ally within 10 squares of you is hit by an area or a close attack
Effect: The triggering attack hits you instead of the ally.

LEVEL 13 ENCOUNTER PRAYERS

Compel Attention — Invoker Attack 13

You speak with the voice of divine authority, forcing an enemy to pause.

Encounter ✦ Divine, Implement, Psychic
Standard Action   **Ranged** 10
Target: One creature
Attack: Wisdom vs. Will
Hit: 3d8 + Wisdom modifier psychic damage, and the target is dazed until the end of your next turn.
Effect: You gain a +5 bonus to Diplomacy checks and Intimidate checks against the target until the end of your next turn.

Pillar of Guardian Flame — Invoker Attack 13

You whisper a divine word that rumbles like distant thunder as a pillar of flame erupts around your enemies.

Encounter ✦ Divine, Fire, Implement, Zone
Standard Action   **Area** burst 1 within 10 squares
Target: Each creature in burst
Attack: Wisdom vs. Reflex
Hit: 3d6 + Wisdom modifier fire damage.
Effect: The burst creates a zone of divine fire that lasts until the end of your next turn. When any enemy within the zone leaves it or hits or misses you or your allies outside it, that enemy takes 5 fire damage.

Seal of the Heretic | Invoker Attack 13

You mark your foes with a divine brand, bringing the wrathful eyes of the gods upon them.

Encounter ✦ Divine, Implement
Standard Action   **Ranged** 10
Target: One, two, or three creatures
Attack: Wisdom vs. Will
Hit: 2d8 + Wisdom modifier damage, or 3d8 + Wisdom modifier damage if you target only one creature. The target takes a -5 penalty to a saving throw of your choice before the end of your next turn.
     Covenant of Wrath: The target takes the -5 penalty to all saving throws before the end of your next turn.

Winds of Celestia | Invoker Attack 13

You call the winds that buffet the upper reaches of Celestia to scatter your foes.

Encounter ✦ Divine, Implement
Standard Action   **Area** burst 1 within 10 squares
Target: Each enemy in burst
Attack: Wisdom vs. Fortitude
Hit: 3d6 + Wisdom modifier damage, and you either slide the target 2 squares or knock it prone.
     Covenant of Preservation: Either the number of squares you slide the target equals 1 + your Intelligence modifier, or you slide the target 1 square before knocking it prone.

Level 15 Daily Prayers

God Hammer | Invoker Attack 15

A gleaming, spectral warhammer appears above your foes and slams down in their midst, creating a crash of thunder. The hammer is an image of Guldarak, which the gods shaped out of pure thunder to drive primordials out of the earth's depths.

Daily ✦ Divine, Implement, Thunder, Zone
Standard Action   **Area** burst 2 within 10 squares
Target: Each creature in burst
Attack: Wisdom vs. Reflex
Hit: 4d6 + Wisdom modifier thunder damage.
Miss: Half damage.
Effect: Each target drops prone. In addition, the burst creates a zone of resounding thunder that lasts until the end of your next turn. At the start of your next turn, any creature within the zone drops prone.
Sustain Minor: The zone persists.

Mark of Anathema | Invoker Attack 15

You place a mark of anathema on your foe, a shining brand that sears the flesh and harms those who ally with your enemy.

Daily ✦ Divine, Implement, Radiant
Standard Action   **Ranged** 10
Target: One creature
Attack: Wisdom vs. Fortitude
Hit: 2d10 + Wisdom modifier radiant damage, and ongoing 10 radiant damage (save ends).
     First Failed Saving Throw: Ongoing 15 radiant damage (save ends).
Miss: Half damage, and ongoing 5 radiant damage (save ends).
Effect: Whenever the target fails a saving throw against the ongoing damage, each enemy within 5 squares of the target takes 5 radiant damage.

Three Beacons of Twilight | Invoker Attack 15

In the darkest days of the war against the primordials, the gods used three gleaming beacons to guide them across the Astral Sea. Today, those lights still burn, misleading your enemies while guiding your allies to safety.

Daily ✦ Divine, Implement, Radiant, Zone
Standard Action   **Area** burst 2 within 10 squares
Target: Each enemy in burst
Attack: Wisdom vs. Will
Hit: 4d6 + Wisdom modifier radiant damage.
Miss: Half damage.
Effect: The burst creates a zone of glimmering light that lasts until the end of the encounter. As a minor action, you can teleport a creature within the zone 5 squares.

Wall of Blades | Invoker Attack 15

You draw shards of astral steel into the world and arrange them into a deadly wall of spinning blades. You then command parts of the wall to fly at your enemies.

Daily ✦ Conjuration, Divine, Implement, Radiant
Standard Action   **Area** wall 8 within 20 squares
Effect: You conjure a wall in unoccupied squares that consists of radiant blades. The wall can be up to 4 squares high, and it lasts until the end of your next turn. The wall provides cover to you and your allies. Any creature that enters the wall or starts its turn there takes 2d10 + your Wisdom modifier radiant damage.
     While you are within 5 squares of the wall, you can make the following attack.
Standard Action   **Ranged** 10
Effect: Before the attack, remove a square of the wall.
Target: One creature
Attack: Wisdom vs. Reflex
Hit: 2d10 + Wisdom modifier radiant damage.
Sustain Minor: The wall persists.

Level 16 Utility Prayers

Covenant of Life | Invoker Utility 16

You create a divine pact with one of your allies, offering your strength, and the strength of your friends, if your ally needs it.

Daily ✦ Divine
Minor Action   **Close** burst 10
Target: You or one ally in burst
Effect: Until the end of the encounter, you and your allies can use second wind either to gain the normal benefits or to grant the benefits to the target. A donor character uses his or her second wind but neither regains hit points nor gains a bonus to all defenses, and the target regains hit points as if he or she had spent a healing surge and gains a +2 bonus to all defenses until the start of the donor's next turn.

Icon of Life
Invoker Utility 16

You invoke the symbol of life, a gleaming icon of gold that pulls your allies' spirits back to their mortal shells, even as death tries to draw them away.

Daily ✦ Divine, Zone
Minor Action   Area burst 5 within 20 squares
Effect: The burst creates a zone of golden light that lasts until the end of the encounter. While within the zone, any ally gains a +5 bonus to death saving throws, and if the ally rolls a natural 20 on a death saving throw, that ally can spend two healing surges rather than one.

Shield of Justice
Invoker Utility 16

You invoke the justice of the gods, shielding your ally while calling doom upon your foe.

Encounter ✦ Divine
Immediate Interrupt   Ranged 10
Trigger: An enemy within 10 squares of you makes an attack roll against your ally
Target: The triggering enemy
Effect: The target takes a -4 penalty to the triggering attack roll. Until the end of your next turn, any attacker gains a +2 power bonus to attack rolls against the target.

Walk Between Worlds
Invoker Utility 16

The gods built many strange passages through time and space to help them in their battles against the primordials. You know of many such paths.

Daily ✦ Divine
Minor Action   Ranged 10
Target: You or one ally
Effect: The target gains phasing until the end of your next turn.
Sustain Minor: The effect persists.

LEVEL 17 ENCOUNTER PRAYERS

Blood Debt
Invoker Attack 17

Each wound your foe deals adds to its mounting debt of blood and invites your allies' retribution.

Encounter ✦ Divine, Implement, Radiant
Standard Action   Ranged 10
Target: One creature
Attack: Wisdom vs. Will
Hit: 3d10 + Wisdom radiant damage. Until the end of your next turn, each creature that the target attacks gains a +2 bonus to its next attack roll against the target.
Covenant of Wrath: The bonus to the attack roll equals 1 + your Constitution modifier.

Curse of Haemnathuun
Invoker Attack 17

You invoke a faint echo of the curse that transformed the fearsome primordial Haemnathuun into a statue, partially encasing your foes in stone for a moment.

Encounter ✦ Divine, Implement
Standard Action   Close blast 5
Target: Each creature in blast
Attack: Wisdom vs. Fortitude
Hit: 2d8 + Wisdom modifier damage, and the target is dazed and immobilized until the end of your next turn.

Glyph of Radiance
Invoker Attack 17

You invoke a glyph of radiance, a tool used by the gods both to illuminate the darkest realms and to blind their enemies with the glyph's unyielding light.

Encounter ✦ Divine, Implement, Radiant
Standard Action   Area burst 1 within 10 squares
Target: Each creature in burst
Attack: Wisdom vs. Will
Hit: 2d6 + Wisdom modifier radiant damage, and the target is blinded until the end of your next turn.

Glyph of Three Blades
Invoker Attack 17

In ages past, the gods forged three sacred blades that could surround and trap the mightiest primordials. You invoke these weapons to trap your foes in a ring of spectral blades.

Encounter ✦ Divine, Implement
Standard Action   Area burst 1 within 10 squares
Target: Each creature in burst
Attack: Wisdom vs. Reflex
Hit: 2d8 + Wisdom modifier damage. If the target moves more than 1 square before the end of your next turn, the target takes 5 damage.
Covenant of Preservation: The damage the target takes from moving more than 1 square equals 5 + your Intelligence modifier.

LEVEL 19 DAILY PRAYERS

Astral Tempest
Invoker Attack 19

You breach the wall between this world and an astral dominion, causing a storm of divine energy to rip through your foes, scattering them, before it dissipates.

Daily ✦ Divine, Implement
Standard Action   Area burst 2 within 10 squares
Target: Each creature in burst
Attack: Wisdom vs. Fortitude
Hit: 7d6 + Wisdom modifier damage, and you slide the target 5 squares and knock it prone.
Miss: Half damage, and you slide the target 3 squares and knock it prone.

Malediction of Gartak
Invoker Attack 19

The exarch Gartak betrayed the gods. He was cursed so that the next killing blow he landed on a foe caused him to die with the same wound.

Daily ✦ Divine, Implement
Standard Action   Ranged 10
Target: One creature
Attack: Wisdom vs. Will
Hit: 5d6 + Wisdom modifier damage.
Effect: Whenever the target hits with an attack, the target takes 10 damage. This effect ends at the end of the target's turn if it has not attacked since the end of its last turn.

Summon Angel of Light | Invoker Attack 19

A mote of light appears before you, and an angel clad in glowing silver armor steps forth from it. The angel wields a flail that ends in an orb of pure radiance.

Daily ✦ Divine, Implement, Radiant, Summoning
Minor Action　　　　　**Ranged** 10

Effect: You summon a Medium angel of light in an unoccupied square within range. The angel has speed 6 and fly 8 (hover). It has a +4 bonus to AC and a +2 bonus to its other defenses. Any enemy that starts its turn adjacent to the angel is marked by the angel until the end of your next turn. You can give the angel the following special commands.

　　Minor Action: Melee 1; targets one creature; Wisdom vs. Reflex; 1d10 + Wisdom modifier radiant damage, and until the end of your next turn, the target doesn't have line of sight to creatures more than 5 squares away from it.

　　Opportunity Attack: Melee 1; targets one creature; Wisdom vs. Reflex; 1d10 + Wisdom modifier radiant damage.

Tomb of Magrym | Invoker Attack 19

You invoke the name of Magrym—an exarch of stone and darkness who helped build the prison Carceri—to entomb your foes.

Daily ✦ Conjuration, Divine, Implement
Standard Action　　　　　**Area** burst 1 within 10 squares

Effect: The burst conjures a tomb of white stone. The tomb fills the burst and must be on a solid surface. The tomb is a solid obstacle, and it can be attacked as an object: AC 6, Fortitude 10, Reflex 5, and 60 hit points. When the tomb is destroyed, it crumbles into difficult terrain.

　　As the tomb appears, make the following attack.

Target: Each creature in burst
Attack: Wisdom vs. Reflex
Hit: 3d6 + Wisdom modifier damage, and the target disappears into the tomb. While inside the tomb, the target is dazed and doesn't have line of sight or line of effect to anything other than the tomb. The target can make melee and close attacks only against the tomb. When the tomb is destroyed, the target reappears in the space it last occupied or in the nearest unoccupied space.
Miss: Half damage, and you slide the target to the nearest space outside the burst.

LEVEL 22 UTILITY PRAYERS

Covenant of Vengeance | Invoker Utility 22

You forge a covenant with your ally. Anyone foolish enough to attack that ally will suffer your wrath.

Daily ✦ Divine
Minor Action　　　　　**Close** burst 10

Target: You or one ally in burst
Effect: All of the target's marks end. Until the end of the encounter or until the target marks a creature, if a creature attacks the target, you and your allies gain a +4 power bonus to attack rolls against that creature until the end of your next turn.

Invoke Angelic Form | Invoker Utility 22

Your ally partially transforms into an angel and can now fly on divine wings.

Daily ✦ Divine, Polymorph
Minor Action　　　　　**Ranged** 10

Target: You or one ally
Effect: Until the end of the encounter, the target gains a fly speed of 8 and can hover.

Invoke Heroism | Invoker Utility 22

The greatest heroes of the gods fought with the fury of two. You grant an ally such might.

Daily ✦ Divine
Minor Action　　　　　**Ranged** 20

Target: One ally
Effect: The target can take an extra standard action during his or her next turn.

Ward of Divine Light | Invoker Utility 22

You shroud yourself in a column of blinding light that sustains your life and shields you from harm.

Daily ✦ Divine, Healing
Standard Action　　　　　**Personal**

Effect: You can spend two healing surges, and you are immune to all damage until the start of your next turn. If you willingly attack before the end of your next turn, you take damage equal to your bloodied value.

LEVEL 23 ENCOUNTER PRAYERS

Cascade of Five Suns | Invoker Attack 23

You invoke the power of the five suns—a group of stars the gods used to navigate the Astral Sea when the primordials threatened to extinguish all light—to sear your enemies with radiant energy.

Encounter ✦ Divine, Implement, Radiant
Standard Action　　　　　**Area** burst 2 within 10 squares

Target: Each creature in burst
Attack: Wisdom vs. Reflex. Make a number of attack rolls equal to the number of targets, and then assign each roll to a target.
Hit: 4d8 + Wisdom modifier radiant damage.

Storm of Celestia | Invoker Attack 23

You invoke the storms that sometimes rumble over Celestia's slopes, using their winds and thunder to scatter the enemy.

Encounter ✦ Divine, Implement, Thunder
Standard Action　　　　　**Area** burst 2 within 10 squares

Target: Each enemy in burst
Attack: Wisdom vs. Fortitude
Hit: 5d6 + Wisdom modifier thunder damage, and you slide the target to any unoccupied space in the burst.

Vindicating Flames — Invoker Attack 23

A barrage of fiery orbs fills an area with lingering flames, which surround your foes.

Encounter ✦ Divine, Fire, Implement
Standard Action   **Area** burst 2 within 10 squares
Target: Each creature in burst
Attack: Wisdom vs. Reflex
Hit: 2d6 + Wisdom modifier fire damage, and if the target moves before the end of your next turn, it takes 10 fire damage.
     Covenant of Wrath: If the target moves before the end of your next turn, the fire damage equals 10 + your Constitution modifier.

Word of Rebuke — Invoker Attack 23

You speak a word of divine rebuke, disrupting your foe's mind and hindering its attacks.

Encounter ✦ Divine, Implement
Standard Action   **Ranged** 10
Target: One creature
Attack: Wisdom vs. Will
Hit: 5d6 + Wisdom modifier damage, and the target is dazed until the end of your next turn.
     Covenant of Preservation: Until the end of your next turn, the target also takes a penalty to attack rolls equal to your Intelligence modifier.

LEVEL 25 DAILY PRAYERS

Anthem of the First Dawn — Invoker Attack 25

When the gods struck their final blow against those who would destroy the cosmos, the dawning of the first day brought death to their enemies and life to their surviving friends.

Daily ✦ Divine, Healing, Implement, Radiant
Standard Action   **Close** burst 10
Target: Each enemy in burst
Attack: Wisdom vs. Will
Hit: 6d6 + Wisdom modifier radiant damage.
Miss: Half damage.
Effect: Each ally in the burst can spend a healing surge.

Invoke the Fallen — Invoker Attack 25

In their final battles, the gods used their fallen as terrible weapons. The ashes of dead gods choked, blinded, and killed their enemies. You invoke these remains and turn them against your foes.

Daily ✦ Divine, Implement, Zone
Standard Action   **Area** burst 2 within 10 squares
Target: Each creature in burst
Attack: Wisdom vs. Fortitude
Hit: 2d8 + Wisdom modifier damage, and the target takes ongoing 10 damage and is blinded (save ends both).
Miss: Half damage, and the target is blinded until the end of your next turn.
Effect: The burst creates a zone of lightly obscured terrain until the end of the encounter. While within the zone, you and your allies gain a +2 bonus to attack rolls with divine powers.

Racking Invocation of Pain — Invoker Attack 25

You invoke the divine word of pain to send agony coursing through your enemies. The slightest touch causes them to double over in pain.

Daily ✦ Divine, Implement
Standard Action   **Area** burst 2 within 20 squares
Target: Each creature in burst
Attack: Wisdom vs. Fortitude
Hit: 4d8 + Wisdom modifier damage, and the target is dazed and takes 10 extra damage whenever it is hit by a melee attack (save ends both).
Miss: Half damage, and the target is dazed (save ends).

Rain of Colorless Fire — Invoker Attack 25

Ancient legends tell of fire without color that fell from the sky for a year to annihilate a nation of wizards who sought to overthrow the gods.

Daily ✦ Divine, Fire, Implement, Zone
Standard Action   **Area** burst 2 within 10 squares
Target: Each creature in burst
Attack: Wisdom vs. Reflex
Hit: 3d10 + Wisdom modifier fire damage.
Miss: Half damage.
Effect: The burst creates a zone of colorless fire that lasts until the end of your next turn. At the start of your turn, each creature within the zone takes 3d10 + your Wisdom modifier fire damage.
Sustain Minor: The zone persists.

LEVEL 27 ENCOUNTER PRAYERS

Invoke Terror — Invoker Attack 27

You invoke the words of fear that the gods once cast at the primordials to drive them into the prisons that hold them to this day.

Encounter ✦ Divine, Fear, Implement, Psychic
Standard Action   **Area** burst 2 within 10 squares
Target: Each creature in burst
Attack: Wisdom vs. Will
Hit: 3d8 + Wisdom modifier psychic damage, and the target moves half its speed away from you, avoiding unsafe squares and difficult terrain if it can.
     Covenant of Wrath: Until the start of your next turn, opportunity attacks that hit the target deal extra damage equal to your Constitution modifier.

Offering of Peace — Invoker Attack 27

You invoke the word of the gods, offering a foe a moment of respite. If either your foe or your allies break this bond, the gods impose their judgment.

Encounter ✦ Divine, Implement, Radiant
Standard Action   **Ranged** 10
Target: One enemy
Effect: If the target attacks before the end of your next turn, it takes 4d10 + your Wisdom modifier radiant damage. If you or an ally attacks the target before the end of your next turn, the target gains 10 temporary hit points and a +5 bonus to its next attack roll.
     Covenant of Preservation: You and your allies gain a +2 power bonus to all defenses until the end of your next turn.

Swarm of Astral Steel — Invoker Attack 27

You call on the gods to send a swarm of astral blades to attack your foes. The blades follow your command, slicing at enemies that advance or forcing them to disperse.

Encounter ✦ Divine, Implement, Zone
Standard Action **Area** burst 2 within 10 squares
Target: Each enemy in burst
Attack: Wisdom vs. Reflex
Hit: 2d6 + Wisdom modifier damage.
Effect: The burst creates a zone of blades that lasts until the end of your next turn. Choose the zone's effect: Each target hit by the attack either takes 10 damage if it ends its next turn within the zone or takes 10 damage if it ends its next turn outside the zone.

Word of Annihilation — Invoker Attack 27

You whisper a word of annihilation, threatening your enemies with oblivion.

Encounter ✦ Divine, Implement
Standard Action **Close** blast 3
Target: Each creature in blast
Attack: Wisdom vs. Will
Hit: 4d10 + Wisdom modifier damage.

Level 29 Daily Prayers

Fires of the Silver Gate — Invoker Attack 29

You invoke the power of the Silver Gate, a prison that holds a primordial whose name is long forgotten. The gate's radiance pours forth, consuming your foe and marking it as anathema. Only a fool lingers near it as you consign its soul to the gods.

Daily ✦ Divine, Implement, Radiant
Standard Action **Ranged** 20
Target: One creature
Attack: Wisdom vs. Will
Hit: 7d6 + Wisdom modifier radiant damage.
Miss: Half damage.
Effect: The target takes ongoing 10 radiant damage (save ends). Until the target saves against this ongoing damage, any enemy takes 10 radiant damage when it ends its turn within 5 squares of the target.

Invoke the Absolute Dark — Invoker Attack 29

A sphere of absolute darkness appears amid your foes as you create a gate to the dead space between the planes. The sphere rips at your foes as it draws them near.

Daily ✦ Divine, Implement, Zone
Standard Action **Area** burst 2 within 20 squares
Target: Each creature in burst
Attack: Wisdom vs. Fortitude
Hit: 6d6 + Wisdom modifier damage.
Miss: Half damage.
Effect: The burst creates a zone of darkness that lasts until the end of your next turn. The zone is totally obscured. In addition, any creature that starts its turn within the zone takes 10 damage, slides 1 square toward the zone's center, and is slowed until the end of its turn. You can dismiss the zone as a minor action.
Sustain Minor: The zone persists, and you can increase its size by 1 to a maximum of burst 5.

Summon Angel of Victory — Invoker Attack 29

With a great shout, you call to the gods for aid against your foes. An angel of victory, a member of the angelic host that defeated the primordials, answers your call.

Daily ✦ Divine, Implement, Summoning
Minor Action **Ranged** 20
Effect: You summon a Medium angel of victory in an unoccupied square within range. The angel has speed 6 and fly 8 (hover). It has a +4 bonus to AC and a +2 bonus to its other defenses. You can give the angel the following special commands.
  Minor Action: Melee 1; targets one creature; Wisdom vs. Will; 2d10 + Wisdom modifier damage, and the target takes a –2 penalty to all defenses until the end of your next turn.
  Standard Action: Close burst 2; targets each enemy in burst; Wisdom vs. Reflex; the angel pulls the target 1 square, and the target is slowed until the end of your next turn.
  Opportunity Attack: Melee 1; targets one creature; Wisdom vs. Will; 2d10 + Wisdom modifier damage.

Word of the Gods — Invoker Attack 29

Speaking with the authority of the gods, you utter a word of command. Those who hear it must obey or suffer.

Daily ✦ Charm, Divine, Implement, Psychic
Standard Action **Close** blast 5
Target: Each enemy in blast
Attack: Wisdom vs. Will
Hit: The target is dominated (save ends).
  Aftereffect: 3d6 + Wisdom modifier psychic damage.
Miss: 6d6 + Wisdom modifier psychic damage.

ANGELIC ASPECT

"I am one with the angels that serve my god."

Prerequisite: Invoker

During the gods' ancient war against the primordials, invokers were their most trusted mortal servants, allowed to wield the raw divine power typically reserved for the gods' immortal agents, the angels. Over time, the distinction between the most favored mortal invokers and the angels themselves became hard to define. Some invokers drew so much divine energy into themselves that they took on angelic aspects. Some angels, conversely, emptied themselves of divine essence and clothed themselves in mortal flesh as invokers, voluntarily limiting their own power in order to serve as more effective divine agents in the world.

One of those paths is yours, and it has led you to this point: You are neither fully mortal nor fully angel, but some of both. As an angelic aspect, you can channel divine energy through your mortal body to take on angelic characteristics: resistance to the forces of dark and light, an awesome presence that strikes fear into the hearts of those who try to strike you, wings to fly across the field of battle, and mighty attacks akin to those of angels.

If you were born mortal, your transformation is beginning; you are on the threshold of becoming something more, and immortality awaits. If you have always been an angelic being veiled in flesh, the veil is beginning to part and your true nature is being revealed. Either way, your enemies have much to fear.

ANGELIC ASPECT PATH FEATURES

Wings of Action (11th level): When you spend an action point to take an extra action, you can fly 8 squares as a free action, and you gain a +2 bonus to AC until the start of your next turn.

Angelic Resistance (11th level): You gain resist 10 necrotic and resist 10 radiant. If you already have either resistance, that resistance increases by 5.

Angelic Emanation (16th level): While you aren't bloodied, attackers take a –2 penalty to attack rolls against you.

ANGELIC ASPECT PRAYERS

Angelic Blades	Angelic Aspect Attack 11

The metallic wings of an angel of battle sprout from your back and shower your foes with razor-sharp blades.

Encounter ✦ Divine, Implement
Standard Action   Close burst 2
Target: Each enemy in burst
Attack: Wisdom vs. Reflex
Hit: 2d6 + Wisdom modifier damage, and the target is slowed until the end of your next turn.
Effect: You gain a fly speed of 8 until the end of your next turn.

Shielding Nimbus	Angelic Aspect Utility 12

Divine power surges through you, giving you an angelic visage and shielding you from damage.

Daily ✦ Divine
Minor Action   Personal
Effect: Choose a damage type: acid, cold, fire, force, lightning, necrotic, poison, psychic, radiant, or thunder. You gain resist 10 to that damage type until the end of the encounter. If you already have resistance to that damage type, the resistance increases by 5 until the end of the encounter.

Coldfire Pillar	Angelic Aspect Attack 20

You bond with an angel of vengeance, transforming yourself into a raging pillar of cold fire.

Daily ✦ Cold, Divine, Fire, Implement
Standard Action   Close burst 3
Target: Each enemy in burst
Attack: Wisdom vs. Reflex
Hit: 4d8 + Wisdom modifier cold and fire damage.
Miss: Half damage.
Effect: You are immune to cold damage and fire damage until the start of your next turn.

VINCENT DUTRAIT

BLIGHTSPEAKER

"Pelor is compassionate, but the wicked deserve the punishment I bring to them in his name."

Prerequisite: Invoker

Divine wrath can manifest as punishing blasts of radiant light, as fire from the heavens, or as thunder and lightning that smite the gods' foes. Sometimes, though, the gods' anger is manifested in plagues and curses upon the wicked. Even good deities can resort to extreme methods to purge the world of corruption.

As a blightspeaker, you wield such extreme methods in your god's name. Like an angel of death, you wield the scythe of necrotic power and harvest life from your enemies to fuel your own strength. To the common folk, you are a frightful presence, a grim reminder of your god's darker side. To your enemies, you are a terror, a manifestation of the judgment that has been pronounced upon them and of the punishment that awaits.

BLIGHTSPEAKER PATH FEATURES

Blighting Action (11th level): When you spend an action point to take an extra action, each enemy within 5 squares of you gains vulnerable 5 necrotic until the end of your next turn. In addition, all damage you deal during this turn is necrotic in addition to its other damage types.

Dissolution's Call (11th level): Whenever you score a critical hit with a divine attack power, you regain a number of hit points equal to 5 + your Wisdom modifier.

Echoed Malediction (16th level): When a creature saves against an effect caused by you, that creature takes 10 necrotic damage.

BLIGHTSPEAKER PRAYERS

Chains of Death	Blightspeaker Attack 11

Deadly necrotic energy binds your foe where it stands.

Encounter ✦ Divine, Implement, Necrotic
Standard Action   Ranged 10
Target: One creature
Attack: Wisdom vs. Will
Hit: 2d6 + Wisdom modifier necrotic damage, and the target is restrained until the end of your next turn.

False Life	Blightspeaker Utility 12

You draw the life force from your opponent, gathering it to yourself and gaining a temporary boost of vitality.

Daily ✦ Divine
Minor Action   Personal
Effect: You gain temporary hit points equal to one-half your level + your Wisdom modifier. If you have hit an enemy since the end of your last turn, you instead gain temporary hit points equal to your level + your Wisdom modifier.

Endbringer	Blightspeaker Attack 20

Writhing dark energy, the precursor of an apocalypse, tears at your foe.

Daily ✦ Divine, Implement, Necrotic
Standard Action   Ranged 10
Target: One creature
Attack: Wisdom vs. Will
Hit: 2d6 + Wisdom modifier damage, and the target takes ongoing 15 necrotic damage and is blinded (save ends both).
Miss: Half damage, and the target takes ongoing 10 necrotic damage (save ends).

FLAME OF HOPE

"I do not aspire to greatness. I hope instead that my actions can kindle the flame of greatness in others."

Prerequisite: Invoker

When the gods warred with the primordials at the dawn of time, the gods fought to bring hope to the world they had helped to create. If the world had been left to the primordials, it would have been a fearsome place, dominated by tyrants who might destroy and remake any part of the world without warning. All the mortal inhabitants of the world might have been slaves, as the dwarves were enslaved by the titan servitors of the primordials. At best, they might have been terrified fugitives, hiding in despair from the wanton destruction of the world's elemental rulers.

Because the gods fought the primordials and freed the world from their dominion, the mortal races can live in hope. It is your sacred trust to nurture the embers of hope in the world and stir them into great bonfires that shed light into the world's darkest places. As a flame of hope, you wield powers of fiery radiance that heal and inspire your allies while burning and blinding your foes.

FLAME OF HOPE PATH FEATURES

Inspiring Attack Action (11th level): When you spend an action point to make an attack, you and each ally within 5 squares of you gain a bonus to attack rolls against each target of that attack until the start of your next turn. The bonus equals your Intelligence modifier.

Enduring Hope (11th level): While you aren't bloodied, each ally within 5 squares of you gains a +1 bonus to saving throws.

Righteous Resurgence (16th level): When you use your second wind, each enemy within 5 squares of you takes 1d6 + your Intelligence modifier fire and radiant damage, and each ally within 5 squares of you gains temporary hit points equal to that damage.

FLAME OF HOPE PRAYERS

Numinous Cascade — Flame of Hope Attack 11

Brilliant fire streams from you to burn your foe, and cascades past that foe to sear another. Radiance dances across both targets, guiding the attacks of your allies against them.

Encounter ✦ Divine, Fire, Implement, Radiant
Standard Action   **Ranged** 10
Primary Target: One creature
Primary Attack: Wisdom vs. Reflex
Hit: 2d10 + Wisdom modifier fire and radiant damage. Until the end of your next turn, your allies gain a +2 bonus to attack rolls against the primary target.
Effect: Make a secondary attack.
  Secondary Target: One creature within 5 squares of the primary target
  Secondary Attack: Wisdom vs. Reflex
  Hit: 1d10 + Wisdom modifier fire and radiant damage. Until the end of your next turn, your allies gain a +2 bonus to attack rolls against the secondary target.

Blinding Ward — Flame of Hope Utility 12

Brilliant fire erupts from your ally at your word, blinding the enemy who sought to harm your friend.

Daily ✦ Divine
Immediate Interrupt   **Ranged** 10
Trigger: An enemy within 10 squares of you makes an attack roll against you or your ally
Target: The triggering enemy
Effect: The target is blinded until the start of your next turn.

Sunburst Bulwark — Flame of Hope Attack 20

Radiant fire erupts from you, bringing respite to your allies and searing your foes, rooting your enemies in place.

Daily ✦ Divine, Fire, Healing, Implement, Radiant
Standard Action   **Close** burst 3
Target: Each enemy in burst
Attack: Wisdom vs. Fortitude
Hit: 2d8 + Wisdom modifier fire and radiant damage, and the target is immobilized until the end of your next turn.
Effect: Each ally in the burst can spend a healing surge and regains additional hit points equal to your Intelligence modifier.

HECTOR ORTIZ

Hammer of Vengeance

"By the hammer Guldarak, Moradin will have vengeance against his foes. And I will deliver it."

Prerequisite: Invoker

During the war against the primordials, Moradin and Kord worked together to forge Guldarak, "the God Hammer." They crafted the hammer out of raw thunder and bound its handle with rings of lightning. Moradin was the first to wield the hammer, taking it into the Great Dismal Delve in the heart of the Elemental Chaos. Moradin used the God Hammer to shatter the stone that protected the primordial Zurtharak, who was called the Vein of Iron for the way he burrowed and twisted through solid stone. With Kord and Bahamut at his side, Moradin then used the hammer to shatter the primordial's body.

Several other gods wielded Guldarak during the war, and the hammer became a symbol of divine vengeance. Each time the primordials scored a victory against the gods, a god lay a hand on Guldarak, swore an oath of vengeance, and then took up the hammer and carried out that oath.

Like Guldarak, you are an instrument of divine vengeance, wielding thunder to smite your god's foes. Thunder wards your allies and dazes your enemies, and can even teleport your allies to your side.

Hammer of Vengeance Path Features

Lingering Rebuke (11th level): When you spend an action point to take an extra action, each enemy that hits or misses you or an ally within 5 squares of you before the end of your next turn takes 1d6 + your Constitution modifier thunder damage.

Enduring Castigation (11th level): While you're not bloodied, each enemy within 5 squares of you takes a -2 penalty to saving throws.

Penance (16th level): Whenever you score a critical hit with a divine attack power, the target is dazed until the end of your next turn.

Hammer of Vengeance Prayers

Mark of Castigation	Hammer of Vengeance Attack 11

You batter your foe with thunder and promise it explosive retribution if it attacks.

Encounter ✦ Divine, Implement, Thunder
Standard Action　　　**Ranged** 10
Target: One creature
Attack: Wisdom vs. Will
Hit: 1d10 + Wisdom modifier thunder damage. If the target hits or misses you or your ally before the end of your next turn, the target takes 3d10 + your Wisdom modifier thunder damage.

Thundering Summons	Hammer of Vengeance Utility 12

With a thundering word, you call your allies to your side. They arrive like echoes rolling across the sky.

Encounter ✦ Divine, Teleportation
Move Action　　　**Close** burst 10
Target: One or two allies in burst
Effect: You teleport each target to a space adjacent to you.

Warding Thunder	Hammer of Vengeance Attack 20

You surround yourself and your allies with a ward of thunder, which batters your enemies. One of your allies carries your mark of protection, so if your foes attack that ally, the ward erupts in thunder again.

Daily ✦ Divine, Implement, Thunder, Zone
Standard Action　　　**Area** burst 2 within 10 squares
Target: Each enemy in burst
Attack: Wisdom vs. Fortitude
Hit: 5d6 + Wisdom modifier thunder damage.
Effect: The burst creates a zone of warding thunder that lasts until the end of your next turn. Choose an ally when the zone is created. If any enemy attacks that ally, you can repeat the attack against each enemy within the zone as a free action.
Sustain Minor: The zone persists.

"The spirits surround us, guide us, and hold all the knowledge of the world."

CLASS TRAITS

Role: Leader. Your spirit companion bolsters and heals your nearby allies, and you can evoke other spirits to aid your allies and harm your foes. Depending on your choice of class features and powers, you lean toward either defender or striker as a secondary role.

Power Source: Primal. The spirits of the natural world give you power and manifest on your behalf.

Key Abilities: Wisdom, Constitution, Intelligence

Armor Proficiencies: Cloth, leather
Weapon Proficiencies: Simple melee, longspear
Implements: Totems
Bonus to Defense: +1 Fortitude, +1 Will

Hit Points at 1st Level: 12 + Constitution score
Hit Points per Level Gained: 5
Healing Surges per Day: 7 + Constitution modifier

Trained Skills: Nature. From the class skills list below, choose three more trained skills at 1st level.
Class Skills: Arcana (Int), Athletics (Str), Endurance (Con), Heal (Wis), History (Int), Insight (Wis), Nature (Wis), Perception (Wis), Religion (Int)

Class Features: Companion Spirit, *healing spirit, speak with spirits*

Shamans are inspiring and dangerous battle leaders. They command powerful spirit guides, and through them lead their allies. These nature spirits bolster their allies' attacks and offer protection and healing when needed.

In a rite of passage or initiation, you pledged yourself to the spirits, to be their voice and hands in the world. Through ancient song and sacred ceremony, you have called a powerful spirit companion to your side. The primal spirits of nature affirm your will, guide the actions of your allies, and deal mighty attacks against your foes. You might be a venerable advisor to a tribal leader, a young traveler seeking to bring tales of a wider world back to your people, or a scholar devoted to the pursuit of nearly forgotten lore.

The spirits and voices of nature guide your every step. Their power flows through you, calling you to lead, to fight, and to triumph.

SHAMAN CLASS FEATURES

Shamans have the following class features.

COMPANION SPIRIT

As part of your initiation as a shaman, you acquired a spirit companion, an animal spirit that accompanies and assists you. Many shaman powers have the spirit keyword (page 220). Your spirit companion must be present when you use such a power.

You gain the *call spirit companion* power, which allows you to call your spirit companion to your side. In addition, choose one of the following Companion Spirit options. Your choice provides you with a Spirit Boon as well as a special attack made through your spirit companion, and your choice determines one of your at-will attack powers. Your choice also provides bonuses to certain shaman powers, as detailed in those powers.

PROTECTOR SPIRIT

You draw on the strength of the bear or a similar protective spirit to defend and bolster your allies.

Spirit Boon: Any ally adjacent to your spirit companion regains additional hit points equal to your Constitution modifier when he or she uses second wind or when you use a healing power on him or her.

Spirit's Shield: You gain the *spirit's shield* power, an attack you make through your spirit companion as an opportunity action.

At-Will Attack Power: You gain the *protecting strike* power. You choose a second at-will attack power as normal.

STALKER SPIRIT

You call on the stealth and cunning of the panther or a similar stalking spirit to empower and position your allies.

Spirit Boon: Any ally adjacent to your spirit companion gains a bonus to damage rolls against bloodied enemies equal to your Intelligence modifier.

Spirit's Fangs: You gain the *spirit's fangs* power, an attack you make through your spirit companion as an opportunity action.

At-Will Attack Power: You gain the *stalker's strike* power. You choose a second at-will attack power as normal.

CUSTOM SPIRIT COMPANIONS

Whichever type of spirit companion you choose, it can have any appearance you like. If your character's culture reveres the basilisk as the embodiment of the stalker spirit, your spirit companion might resemble a basilisk. Or you could decide that your dragonborn shaman's protector spirit looks like a rage drake. A drow shaman's spirit companion might look like a spider or a lizard.

HEALING SPIRIT

You gain the *healing spirit* power. Through this power, you grant your allies additional resilience with a short evocation of primal power.

SPEAK WITH SPIRITS

You gain the *speak with spirits* power. You are aware of the constant presence of spirits that float at the edges of reality. You can focus your inner energy and open your mind to these spirits, letting them guide your actions or fill you with insights.

IMPLEMENTS

Shamans use totems carved to resemble the spirits they most commonly call upon, particularly their spirit companions. When you wield a magic totem, you can add its enhancement bonus to the attack rolls and the damage rolls of shaman powers and shaman paragon path powers that have the implement keyword. Without an implement, you can still use these powers.

CREATING A SHAMAN

All shamans rely on Wisdom, and they also benefit from a high Constitution or Intelligence. You can choose any shaman powers you like for your character, though many shamans favor one of two different builds, letting their power choices be shaped by the form of their spirit companions.

BEAR SHAMAN

You excel at protecting your allies and preserving life. Make Wisdom your highest ability score, followed by Constitution so that you can better lend health to

SHAMAN OVERVIEW

Characteristics: You lead your adventuring party from a position of relative safety, sending your spirit companion to the front of the battle while you linger behind. Your powers fall into two broad categories: melee attacks your spirit companion makes, and ranged attacks. Your daily powers include a number of conjurations and zones, representing your ability to call on additional spirits for aid.

Religion: Shamans draw their power from the primal power source and therefore don't usually worship gods. They view themselves as agents—not servants or masters—of the spirits of nature and instruct others how to live their lives in harmony with those spirits. Like druids, shamans call on the spirits to witness significant events but don't worship them.

Races: Elves, humans, and shifters are the most common shamans, putting their high Wisdom and innate connection to nature to good use in this class. Dwarves make excellent bear shamans, and devas excel as panther shamans.

your allies. You'll want a good Intelligence score to improve your AC as well. Choose powers that help guard your allies against attacks, restore hit points, or provide temporary hit points. Your secondary role is defender.

Suggested Class Feature: Protector Spirit
Suggested Feat: Shared Healing Spirit
Suggested Skills: Endurance, Heal, Nature, Perception
Suggested At-Will Powers: *defending strike, protecting strike*
Suggested Encounter Power: *thunder bear's warding*
Suggested Daily Power: *spirit of the healing flood*

PANTHER SHAMAN

You wield the spirits' power to see events before they unfold and to shape them as you like, guiding your allies' actions in battle. Wisdom should be your best ability score, then Intelligence so that you can increase your allies' tactical advantage. A high Constitution will improve your hit points and Fortitude. Choose powers that support your allies in melee, particularly allies who seek combat advantage and who relish quick movement. Your secondary role is striker.

Suggested Class Feature: Stalker Spirit
Suggested Feat: Stalker Spirit Adept
Suggested Skills: Athletics, Heal, Nature, Perception
Suggested At-Will Powers: *stalker's strike, watcher's strike*
Suggested Encounter Power: *twin panthers*
Suggested Daily Power: *wrath of the spirit world*

SHAMAN POWERS

Your powers evoke primal spirits that you view as partners and revered elders. Many of your powers channel primal energy through your spirit companion and have the spirit keyword (page 220), including powers that have "spirit" as part of the range. Those powers treat your spirit companion's space as the origin square for the power, so "melee spirit 1" means you can target a creature adjacent to your spirit.

Other shaman powers call on other spirits to intervene in the course of battle on your behalf, and many of those spirits then channel their energy through your spirit companion either to benefit allies or to harm enemies.

CLASS FEATURES

Each shaman has the powers *call spirit companion, healing spirit,* and *speak with spirits.* Your choice of Companion Spirit determines whether you have the power *spirit's fangs* or *spirit's shield.*

Call Spirit Companion — Shaman Feature

Your soul reaches out to your spirit friend, which faithfully appears at your side.

At-Will ✦ Conjuration, Primal
Minor Action   **Close** burst 20
Effect: You conjure your spirit companion in an unoccupied square in the burst. The spirit lasts until you fall unconscious or until you dismiss it as a minor action. The spirit occupies 1 square. Enemies cannot move through its space, but allies can. When you take a move action, you can also move the spirit a number of squares equal to your speed.

The spirit can be targeted by melee or ranged attacks, although it lacks hit points. If a single melee or ranged attack deals damage to the spirit equal to 10 + one-half your level or higher, the spirit disappears, and you take damage equal to 5 + one-half your level. Otherwise, the spirit is unaffected by the attack.

Healing Spirit — Shaman Feature

You call to the spirits on behalf of a wounded ally, closing wounds and filling your ally with vigor.

Encounter (Special) ✦ Healing, Primal
Minor Action   **Close** burst 5
Target: You or one ally in burst
Effect: The target can spend a healing surge. If the target does so, one ally adjacent to your spirit companion, other than the target, regains 1d6 hit points.
Level 6: 2d6 hit points.
Level 11: 3d6 hit points.
Level 16: 4d6 hit points.
Level 21: 5d6 hit points.
Level 26: 6d6 hit points.
Special: You can use this power twice per encounter, but only once per round. At 16th level, you can use this power three times per encounter, but only once per round.

Speak with Spirits — Shaman Feature

You commune with the spirits, letting them guide your words and actions.

Encounter ✦ Primal
Minor Action   **Personal**
Effect: During this turn, you gain a bonus to your next skill check equal to your Wisdom modifier.

Spirit's Fangs — Shaman Feature

When an enemy drops its guard, your spirit companion leaps on it, claws and fangs bared.

At-Will ✦ Implement, Primal, Spirit
Opportunity Action   **Melee** spirit 1
Trigger: An enemy leaves a square adjacent to your spirit companion without shifting
Target: The triggering enemy
Attack: Wisdom vs. Reflex
Hit: 1d10 + Wisdom modifier damage.
Level 21: 2d10 + Wisdom modifier damage.

Spirit's Shield
Shaman Feature

Your spirit companion bats at a foe that drops its guard, and a nearby ally draws healing energy from the spirit.

At-Will ✦ Healing, Implement, Primal, Spirit
Opportunity Action   **Melee** spirit 1
Trigger: An enemy leaves a square adjacent to your spirit companion without shifting
Target: The triggering enemy
Attack: Wisdom vs. Reflex
Hit: Wisdom modifier damage.
Effect: One ally within 5 squares of your spirit companion regains hit points equal to your Wisdom modifier.

LEVEL 1 AT-WILL EVOCATIONS

Defending Strike
Shaman Attack 1

Your spirit companion strikes a foe, drawing energy from the enemy and turning that energy into a protective shield.

At-Will ✦ Implement, Primal, Spirit
Standard Action   **Melee** spirit 1
Target: One creature
Attack: Wisdom vs. Reflex
Hit: 1d8 + Wisdom modifier damage. Until the end of your next turn, you and your allies gain a +1 power bonus to AC while adjacent to your spirit companion.
    Level 21: 2d8 + Wisdom modifier damage.

Haunting Spirits
Shaman Attack 1

Howling spirits appear around your foe, distracting it from your ally's attack.

At-Will ✦ Implement, Primal, Psychic
Standard Action   **Ranged** 5
Target: One creature
Attack: Wisdom vs. Will
Hit: 1d6 + Wisdom modifier psychic damage. Until the end of your next turn, the target grants combat advantage to an ally of your choice.
    Level 21: 2d6 + Wisdom modifier psychic damage.

Protecting Strike
Shaman Attack 1

Roaring echoes from ancient caves and hollows accompany your spirit companion's attack, infusing your allies with vitality.

At-Will ✦ Implement, Primal, Spirit
Standard Action   **Melee** spirit 1
Target: One creature
Attack: Wisdom vs. Will
Hit: 1d8 + Wisdom modifier damage, and each ally adjacent to your spirit companion gains temporary hit points equal to your Constitution modifier.
    Level 21: 2d8 + Wisdom modifier damage.

Stalker's Strike
Shaman Attack 1

As your spirit companion claws at your foe, the spirit is filled with predatory fury, becoming a greater threat to your enemies.

At-Will ✦ Implement, Primal, Spirit
Standard Action   **Melee** spirit 1
Target: One creature
Attack: Wisdom vs. Fortitude. If the target is bloodied, you gain a bonus to the attack roll equal to one-half your Intelligence modifier.
Hit: 1d10 + Wisdom modifier damage. Until the end of your next turn, your spirit companion can flank with you and your allies.
    Level 21: 2d10 + Wisdom modifier damage.

Watcher's Strike
Shaman Attack 1

Your spirit companion harries your enemies, distracting them and giving you openings for your attacks. You and your allies can also draw on the spirit's heightened senses for a moment.

At-Will ✦ Implement, Primal, Spirit
Standard Action   **Melee** spirit 1
Target: One creature
Attack: Wisdom vs. Reflex
Hit: 1d8 + Wisdom modifier damage. Until the end of your next turn, you and your allies gain a +1 bonus to attack rolls and a +5 bonus to Perception checks while adjacent to your spirit companion.
    Level 21: 2d8 + Wisdom modifier damage.

Wrath of Winter
Shaman Attack 1

Winter spirits surround your enemy, ripping into it with spectral fangs and claws and calling your spirit companion to join the fray.

At-Will ✦ Cold, Implement, Primal, Teleportation
Standard Action　　　**Ranged** 5
Target: One creature
Attack: Wisdom vs. Fortitude
Hit: 1d10 + Wisdom modifier cold damage. You can teleport your spirit companion to a space adjacent to the target.
　Level 21: 2d10 + Wisdom modifier cold damage.

LEVEL 1 ENCOUNTER EVOCATIONS

Call to the Ancestral Warrior
Shaman Attack 1

Your spirit companion channels a mighty ancestor spirit as it attacks your foe and bolsters your allies' defenses.

Encounter ✦ Implement, Primal, Spirit
Standard Action　　　**Melee** spirit 1
Target: One creature
Attack: Wisdom vs. Reflex
Hit: 1d10 + Wisdom modifier damage. Until the end of your next turn, you and your allies gain a +2 power bonus to all defenses while adjacent to your spirit companion.

Call to the Ancient Defender
Shaman Attack 1

Your spirit companion channels the spirit of an ancestral warrior, which helps your spirit companion cover your allies' retreat.

Encounter ✦ Implement, Primal, Spirit
Standard Action　　　**Melee** spirit 1
Target: One creature
Attack: Wisdom vs. Fortitude
Hit: 2d8 + Wisdom modifier damage. Until the end of your next turn, you and your allies gain a +5 bonus to all defenses against opportunity attacks while adjacent to your spirit companion.

Thunder Bear's Warding
Shaman Attack 1

An ancient bear spirit roars with thunder and channels its strength through your spirit companion to bolster your allies.

Encounter ✦ Implement, Primal, Thunder
Standard Action　　　**Ranged** 5
Target: One creature
Attack: Wisdom vs. Fortitude
Hit: 1d6 + Wisdom modifier thunder damage. Until the end of your next turn, you and your allies gain resistance to all damage equal to your Constitution modifier while adjacent to your spirit companion.
　Protector Spirit: You or an ally within 5 squares of you gains temporary hit points equal to your Constitution modifier.

Twin Panthers
Shaman Attack 1

Two panther spirits leap on your foes, and the panthers channel their predatory instincts through your spirit companion so that it menaces nearby enemies.

Encounter ✦ Implement, Primal
Standard Action　　　**Ranged** 5
Target: One creature
Attack: Wisdom vs. Reflex
　Stalker Spirit: If the target is bloodied, you gain a bonus to the attack roll equal to your Intelligence modifier.
Hit: 1d8 + Wisdom modifier damage. Until the end of your next turn, you and your allies have combat advantage when making melee attacks against any enemy adjacent to your spirit companion.
Effect: Make the attack one more time against the same target or a different one.

LEVEL 1 DAILY EVOCATIONS

Blessing of the Seven Winds
Shaman Attack 1

You call on the spirits of the seven winds. They roar over the battlefield, knocking aside a foe and sending other enemies sprawling.

Daily ✦ Implement, Primal, Zone
Standard Action　　　**Ranged** 5
Target: One creature
Attack: Wisdom vs. Fortitude
Hit: 2d10 + Wisdom modifier damage, and you slide the target 2 squares.
Miss: Half damage.
Effect: The attack creates a zone of swirling winds in a burst 1 centered on the target. The zone lasts until the end of the encounter. As a move action, you can move the zone 5 squares. As a minor action, you can slide each creature within the zone 1 square.

Cleansing Wind of the North
Shaman Attack 1

You call on the spirits of the frigid north to bite into your enemies and to carry away your allies' ills.

Daily ✦ Cold, Implement, Primal
Standard Action　　　**Close** blast 5
Target: Each enemy in blast
Attack: Wisdom vs. Fortitude
Hit: 1d10 + Wisdom modifier cold damage.
Miss: Half damage.
Effect: Each ally in the blast makes a saving throw with a +5 power bonus.

Spirit of the Healing Flood
Shaman Attack 1

The spirit of the great flood appears, a being of storm-tossed water. Its essence sustains your allies and drowns your foes.

Daily ✦ Healing, Implement, Primal
Standard Action　　　**Close** burst 5
Target: Each enemy in burst
Attack: Wisdom vs. Fortitude
Hit: 1d8 + Wisdom modifier damage.
Miss: Half damage.
Effect: Until the end of the encounter, you and each ally in the burst gain regeneration 2 while bloodied. As a minor action, a character can end this effect on himself or herself to regain 10 hit points.

Wrath of the Spirit World — Shaman Attack 1

Angry spirits lash out at the minds of your foes all around you and your spirit companion.

Daily ✦ Implement, Primal, Psychic
Standard Action   **Close** burst 2
Target: Each enemy in burst and each enemy adjacent to your spirit companion
Attack: Wisdom vs. Will
Hit: 3d6 + Wisdom modifier psychic damage, and you knock the target prone.
Miss: Half damage.

LEVEL 2 UTILITY EVOCATIONS

Bonds of the Clan — Shaman Utility 2

You take on a portion of your ally's injury.

Encounter ✦ Primal
Immediate Interrupt   **Ranged** 10
Trigger: An ally within 10 squares of you takes damage
Target: The triggering ally
Effect: You and the target each take half of the damage.

Spirit Call — Shaman Utility 2

You whisper words of ancient power, causing your guardian spirits to move as you command.

Encounter ✦ Primal
Minor Action   **Close** burst 10
Target: Each of your shaman conjurations and zones in burst
Effect: You move each target 5 squares.

Spirit of Life — Shaman Utility 2

The spirit of a golden owl alights on your ally's shoulder and flutters off, carrying with it that friend's aches and wounds.

Daily ✦ Healing, Primal
Standard Action   **Close** burst 10
Target: One ally in burst
Effect: The target regains hit points as if he or she had spent a healing surge.

Spirits of Battle — Shaman Utility 2

You invoke ancestral spirits of battle. Under their shadow, your allies fight with greater might.

Daily ✦ Primal, Zone
Minor Action   **Area** burst 5 within 10 squares
Effect: The burst creates a zone filled with ancestral spirits that lasts until the end of the encounter. While within the zone, your allies gain a +1 bonus to attack rolls.

LEVEL 3 ENCOUNTER EVOCATIONS

Call to the Savage Elder — Shaman Attack 3

Your spirit companion lashes out in a savage attack, filling your allies with ferocity.

Encounter ✦ Implement, Primal, Spirit
Standard Action   **Melee** spirit 1
Target: One creature
Attack: Wisdom vs. Reflex
Hit: 2d8 + Wisdom modifier damage. Until the end of your next turn, any ally adjacent to your spirit companion gains a power bonus to the damage rolls of melee attacks equal to your Wisdom modifier.

Lightning Panther Spirit — Shaman Attack 3

With a rumbling growl, a panther spirit appears and strikes your foe with lightning before it vanishes. Your spirit companion channels the panther's swiftness to your allies.

Encounter ✦ Implement, Lightning, Primal
Standard Action   **Ranged** 5
Target: One creature
Attack: Wisdom vs. Reflex
Hit: 1d10 + Wisdom modifier lightning damage. Until the end of your next turn, any ally adjacent to your spirit companion can shift as a minor action.
    Stalker Spirit: Until the end of your next turn, any ally ignores difficult terrain in your spirit companion's space and in squares adjacent to it.

Rimefire Spirit — Shaman Attack 3

A spirit of ice and flame freezes and burns your foe, and the spirit's energies emanate from your spirit companion, making nearby enemies vulnerable to further attacks.

Encounter ✦ Cold, Fire, Implement, Primal
Standard Action   **Ranged** 5
Target: One creature
Attack: Wisdom vs. Will
Hit: 2d6 + Wisdom modifier cold and fire damage. Until the end of your next turn, any enemy adjacent to your spirit companion gains vulnerable 5 cold and vulnerable 5 fire.

Spring Renewal Strike — Shaman Attack 3

As your spirit companion attacks your foe, the spirit channels healing power into a nearby ally.

Encounter ✦ Healing, Implement, Primal, Spirit
Standard Action   **Melee** spirit 1
Target: One creature
Attack: Wisdom vs. Fortitude
Hit: 2d8 + Wisdom modifier damage, and one ally adjacent to your spirit companion can spend a healing surge.
    Protector Spirit: The ally regains additional hit points equal to your Constitution modifier.

Level 5 Daily Evocations

Earthrage Spirit
Shaman Attack 5

The spirit of the great earth serpent rages beneath your enemies, knocking them to the ground and sending minor tremors to topple them for the rest of the battle.

Daily ✦ Implement, Primal
Standard Action   Close blast 5
Target: Each enemy in blast
Attack: Wisdom vs. Reflex
Hit: 2d6 + Wisdom modifier damage, and you knock the target prone.
Miss: Half damage.
Effect: Each target drops prone whenever it is hit by an attack (save ends).

Spirit of the Hawk's Wind
Shaman Attack 5

A wind sweeps over the area as a shining hawk spirit swoops down on your foe. As the spirit beats its wings, it creates gusts that lift your allies aloft, allowing them to move in safety.

Daily ✦ Implement, Primal, Radiant, Zone
Standard Action   Ranged 5
Target: One creature
Attack: Wisdom vs. Reflex
Hit: 2d8 + Wisdom modifier radiant damage, and the target is blinded until the end of your next turn.
Miss: Half damage.
Effect: The attack creates a zone of uplifting winds in a burst 3 centered on the target. The zone lasts until the end of the encounter. While within the zone, any ally can use a move action to shift 4 squares and ignore difficult terrain during the shift. As a move action, you can move the zone 5 squares.

Spirit of the Shielding Fire
Shaman Attack 5

A spirit of flame shields your ally from harm, lashing out at your command when the ally comes under attack.

Daily ✦ Fire, Implement, Primal
Standard Action   Close burst 5
Primary Target: One ally in burst
Effect: The primary target gains 10 temporary hit points. Until the end of the encounter, the primary target gains resist 5 fire, and you can make the following attack.
  Immediate Interrupt   Ranged 5
  Trigger: An enemy hits the primary target with a melee attack
  Secondary Target: The triggering enemy
  Attack: Wisdom vs. Reflex
  Hit: 2d6 + Wisdom modifier fire damage.

War Chieftain's Blessing
Shaman Attack 5

The spirit of a regal warrior clad in a chieftain's robes utters a great battle cry and hews at your foe with an axe. Your allies, heartened by the chieftain's efforts, redouble their attacks.

Daily ✦ Implement, Primal
Standard Action   Ranged 10
Target: One creature
Attack: Wisdom vs. Will
Hit: 2d10 + Wisdom modifier damage.
Miss: Half damage.
Effect: Until the end of the encounter, you and your allies gain a +2 bonus to attack rolls against the target.

Level 6 Utility Evocations

Blessing of the Iron Tree
Shaman Utility 6

You invoke the spirit of the legendary tree of iron to grant your ally the endurance needed to survive.

Daily ✦ Primal
Minor Action   Close burst 5
Target: One bloodied ally in burst
Effect: The target gains resist 5 to all damage until the end of the encounter.

Spirit of Dawn
Shaman Utility 6

A spirit of the sun appears before you, casting a light on your foes that makes it nearly impossible for them to hide from you.

Daily ✦ Primal, Zone
Minor Action   Area burst 5 within 10 squares
Effect: The burst creates a zone of bright light that lasts until the end of your next turn. You and your allies ignore cover, superior cover, concealment, and total concealment when attacking any enemy that is within the zone. While within the zone, any enemy takes a –5 penalty to Stealth checks.

Spirit of the Keeper
Shaman Utility 6

A protective ancestor spirit appears and lays a healing hand on your ally. The spirit's warding power flows into your spirit companion, helping it defend your allies from attack.

Daily ✦ Healing, Primal
Minor Action   Close burst 5
Target: One creature in burst
Effect: The target can spend a healing surge and regain 1d6 additional hit points. Until the end of the encounter, any ally adjacent to your spirit companion doesn't grant combat advantage.

Sudden Restoration
Shaman Utility 6

Primal energy surges into your allies to drive away harmful effects.

Encounter ✦ Primal
Minor Action   Ranged 10
Target: One or two allies
Effect: Each target makes a saving throw.

Level 7 Encounter Evocations

Call to the Blood Dancer
Shaman Attack 7

A vicious spirit of blood and wrath infuses your spirit companion, which howls in fury as it slashes your foe with claws and fangs.

Encounter ✦ Implement, Primal, Spirit
Standard Action   Melee spirit 1
Target: One creature
Attack: Wisdom vs. Will
Hit: 2d10 + Wisdom modifier damage. Until the end of your next turn, any ally can score a critical hit on a roll of 18–20 while adjacent to your spirit companion.
  Stalker Spirit: Until the end of your next turn, any ally gains a bonus to damage rolls equal to your Intelligence modifier while adjacent to your spirit companion.

Call to the Howling Storm — Shaman Attack 7

Your spirit companion takes on an aspect of howling winds and lightning to strike at your enemy while whirling a nearby ally into a better position.

Encounter ✦ Implement, Lightning, Primal, Spirit, Thunder
Standard Action   Melee spirit 1
Target: One creature
Attack: Wisdom vs. Reflex
Hit: 2d8 + Wisdom modifier lightning and thunder damage, and one ally adjacent to your spirit companion can shift 5 squares as a free action.

Thunderstorm Spirit — Shaman Attack 7

A storm spirit lashes out at your enemy and then focuses its power around your spirit companion.

Encounter ✦ Implement, Lightning, Primal, Thunder
Standard Action   Ranged 5
Target: One creature
Attack: Wisdom vs. Reflex
Hit: 1d12 + Wisdom modifier lightning and thunder damage. Until the end of your next turn, when you and your allies hit any enemy adjacent to your spirit companion, that enemy takes 1d6 extra lightning and thunder damage.

Winter Wind Spirit — Shaman Attack 7

A whirling spirit of biting winds and driving snow lashes your enemy. Its power funnels through your spirit companion to shield your ally from harm.

Encounter ✦ Cold, Implement, Primal
Standard Action   Ranged 5
Target: One creature
Attack: Wisdom vs. Fortitude
Hit: 1d10 + Wisdom modifier cold damage. Before the end of your next turn, as an immediate interrupt, you can grant an ally adjacent to your spirit companion a +4 bonus to AC against an attack that hits.
    Protector Spirit: The bonus to AC equals 3 + your Constitution modifier.

LEVEL 9 DAILY EVOCATIONS

Ancient Warlord's Inspiration — Shaman Attack 9

A spectral figure clad in elaborate hide armor appears beside your foe, accompanied by the booming of a distant war horn. The figure swings its club at your enemy and remains to give inspiration to your allies.

Daily ✦ Conjuration, Implement, Primal
Standard Action   Ranged 5
Target: One creature
Attack: Wisdom vs. Reflex
Hit: 1d10 + Wisdom modifier damage.
Effect: You conjure an ancient warlord spirit in an unoccupied square adjacent to the target. The spirit lasts until the end of the encounter. If an ally starts his or her turn adjacent to the spirit or in its space, as an immediate reaction you can allow that ally to make a basic attack as a free action. As a move action, you can move the spirit 5 squares.

Clever Trickster Spirit — Shaman Attack 9

An ephemeral creature of stealth, cunning, and deception leaps on your foe, attacking that enemy and keeping it off balance. When your enemy finally shakes the spirit off, the spirit moves on to bedevil another foe.

Daily ✦ Implement, Primal, Psychic
Standard Action   Ranged 10
Target: One creature
Attack: Wisdom vs. Will
Hit: 2d8 + Wisdom modifier psychic damage.
Miss: Half damage.
Effect: The target is slowed and grants combat advantage (save ends both).
    Aftereffect: The enemy nearest to the target is slowed and grants combat advantage (save ends both).

Raging Storm Spirit — Shaman Attack 9

With a peal of thunder, a storm cloud laden with dancing bolts of lightning appears and lashes out at your foe, then lingers to empower the attacks of your allies.

Daily ✦ Implement, Lightning, Primal, Thunder, Zone
Standard Action   Area burst 5 within 10 squares
Target: One creature in burst
Attack: Wisdom vs. Reflex
Hit: 3d6 + Wisdom modifier lightning damage.
Effect: The burst creates a zone of thunder that lasts until the end of the encounter. Any ally deals 1d6 extra thunder damage when he or she hits an enemy that is within the zone.

Spirit of Autumn's Reaping — Shaman Attack 9

A spirit of a robed figure swings its scythe to harvest the enemy's life, using that energy to heal you and your allies.

Daily ✦ Healing, Implement, Necrotic, Primal
Standard Action **Ranged 10**
Target: One creature
Attack: Wisdom vs. Fortitude
Hit: 3d6 + Wisdom modifier necrotic damage, and the target gains vulnerable 5 to all damage (save ends).
Miss: Half damage, and the target gains vulnerable 2 to all damage (save ends).
Effect: You and each ally within 10 squares of you regain 5 hit points.

LEVEL 10 UTILITY EVOCATIONS

Primal Gust — Shaman Utility 10

A gust moves an ally or an enemy into position.

Encounter ✦ Primal
Minor Action **Ranged 10**
Target: One creature
Effect: You slide the target 3 squares.

Rock Shield Spirits — Shaman Utility 10

Spirits of earth rise up to protect your allies.

Daily ✦ Primal, Zone
Minor Action **Area burst 1 within 5 squares**
Effect: The burst creates a zone filled with rock spirits that lasts until the end of the encounter. While within the zone, any ally gains a +2 power bonus to AC and Fortitude. As a move action, you can move the zone 5 squares.

Spirits of the Shadowed Moon — Shaman Utility 10

A spirit of the moon—a creature of mist and shadow—conceals your allies.

Daily ✦ Primal, Zone
Minor Action **Close burst 3**
Effect: The burst creates a zone of glimmering lights and shadows that lasts until the end of the encounter. While within the zone, you and your allies gain concealment and can make Stealth checks to become hidden. As a move action, you can move the zone 5 squares.

Spirit Summons — Shaman Utility 10

You send forth a call into the spirit world and summon a second companion to guide your way.

Daily ✦ Primal
Free Action **Personal**
Effect: Until the end of the encounter, you can use your *call spirit companion* power to conjure a second spirit companion. When you attack with a spirit power, you choose which spirit companion to use for the attack. When an effect applies to creatures adjacent to your spirit companion, that effect applies to creatures adjacent to both spirit companions. The second spirit companion disappears at the end of the encounter.

LEVEL 13 ENCOUNTER EVOCATIONS

Call to the Indomitable Defender — Shaman Attack 13

Slamming into your opponent, your spirit companion channels a spirit of iron and earth. That spirit's invulnerability flows through your spirit companion to protect you and your allies.

Encounter ✦ Implement, Primal, Spirit
Standard Action **Melee spirit 1**
Target: One creature
Attack: Wisdom vs. Fortitude
Hit: 2d6 + Wisdom modifier damage. Until the end of your next turn, you and your allies gain resist 5 to all damage while adjacent to your spirit companion.
  Protector Spirit: The resistance equals 4 + your Constitution modifier.

Call to the Laughing Fortune — Shaman Attack 13

Your spirit companion channels a spirit of good fortune as it attacks your foe. For a moment, your spirit companion shares the blessing of that spirit with your nearby allies.

Encounter ✦ Implement, Primal, Spirit
Standard Action **Melee spirit 1**
Target: One creature
Attack: Wisdom vs. Reflex
Hit: 2d10 + Wisdom modifier damage. Until the start of your next turn, if an ally adjacent to your spirit companion misses with an attack, you can use an immediate interrupt to allow that ally to reroll the attack.
  Stalker Spirit: The ally gains a bonus to the new attack roll equal to your Intelligence modifier.

Howling Gust — Shaman Attack 13

A howling spirit of wind appears next to your foe and batters it with a gale, then channels its essence through your spirit companion to whisk a nearby ally across the battlefield.

Encounter ✦ Implement, Primal, Teleportation
Standard Action **Ranged 5**
Target: One creature
Attack: Wisdom vs. Reflex
Hit: 2d8 + Wisdom modifier damage, and you slide the target 2 squares. You teleport one ally adjacent to your spirit companion 5 squares.

Spirit of Cleansing Light — Shaman Attack 13

A swirling mote of shining light sears your foes, then channels healing power through your spirit companion, driving ill effects from one of your allies.

Encounter ✦ Implement, Primal, Radiant
Standard Action **Ranged 5**
Target: One or two creatures
Attack: Wisdom vs. Will
Hit: 3d6 + Wisdom modifier radiant damage, and one ally adjacent to your spirit companion makes a saving throw with a +2 bonus.

LEVEL 15 DAILY EVOCATIONS

Guardian of the Primal Copse — Shaman Attack 15

A spirit of the forest smashes your enemy with its mighty branches. For the moment, your foe's defenses are only as strong as the weakest.

Daily ✦ Implement, Primal
Standard Action   **Ranged** 5
Target: One creature
Attack: Wisdom vs. Fortitude
Hit: 4d8 + Wisdom modifier damage.
Miss: Half damage.
Effect: After the attack, the target's defenses all equal the lowest of its defenses (save ends).

Searing Wind of the South — Shaman Attack 15

The first wind of the south blew through a trackless desert, scattering sand and gusting with bone-charring heat. Its spirit still races across the world, and you call it forth to aid you in battle.

Daily ✦ Fire, Implement, Primal
Standard Action   **Close** blast 5
Target: Each enemy in blast
Attack: Wisdom vs. Fortitude
Hit: 4d6 + Wisdom modifier fire damage.
Miss: Half damage.
Effect: You slide each ally in the blast to another space in or adjacent to the blast.

Spirit of the Wolf Pack — Shaman Attack 15

A great howl sweeps over the battle as a pack of spectral wolves bound from the spirit world to attack your foes.

Daily ✦ Implement, Primal
Standard Action   **Close** blast 5
Target: Each enemy in blast
Attack: Wisdom vs. Will
Hit: 3d6 + Wisdom modifier damage.
Miss: Half damage.
Effect: The target grants combat advantage, and an attack deals 1d6 extra damage to the target on a hit if the attacker is flanking the target (save ends both).

Storm Guardian Spirit — Shaman Attack 15

Thunder crashes over your foe as the storm guardian spirit appears. This spectral creature of dark storm clouds then surrounds your ally and avenges attacks against that ally.

Daily ✦ Implement, Primal, Thunder
Standard Action   **Ranged** 5
Target: One creature
Attack: Wisdom vs. Reflex
Hit: 3d10 + Wisdom modifier thunder damage.
Miss: Half damage.
Effect: Choose an ally within 5 squares of the target. Until the end of the encounter, when any enemy hits that ally, that enemy takes 5 thunder damage and is pushed 1 square from the ally.

LEVEL 16 UTILITY EVOCATIONS

Fate Weaver's Shield — Shaman Utility 16

You call on the spirit of the great spider known as the Fate Weaver to craft a web of protection around an ally.

Encounter ✦ Primal
Minor Action   **Close** burst 5
Target: One ally in burst
Effect: The target gains a +5 bonus to all defenses until the end of your next turn or until it attacks.

Forge the Chains of Life — Shaman Utility 16

As you feel an ally's spirit begin to slip away, you shout a word of command that fills that ally with new life.

Daily ✦ Healing, Primal
Immediate Interrupt   **Close** burst 10
Trigger: An ally within 10 squares of you fails a death saving throw
Target: The triggering ally in burst
Effect: The target regains hit points equal to his or her bloodied value.

Spirit Binding — Shaman Utility 16

You weave primal forces to strengthen the bond between your spirit companion and another spirit it is channeling, allowing the connection to linger for a moment longer.

Encounter ✦ Primal
Minor Action   **Personal**
Effect: If your spirit companion is granting any benefits until the end of this turn to allies adjacent to it, the benefits instead last until the end of your next turn.

Spirits of the Dancing Zephyr — Shaman Utility 16

Gentle winds fill the area, giving your allies the agility to spring to a better position after being attacked.

Daily ✦ Primal, Zone
Minor Action   **Area** burst 5 within 10 squares
Effect: The burst creates a zone of wind that lasts until the end of the encounter. Whenever you or an ally is hit or missed while within the zone, that character can shift 1 square as an immediate reaction. As a move action, you can move the zone 5 squares.

Level 17 Encounter Evocations

Call to the Lashing Behemoth — Shaman Attack 17

Your spirit companion channels the spirit of a behemoth with a lashing tail and knocks your foe to the ground. The behemoth spirit then empowers your nearby allies.

Encounter ✦ Implement, Primal, Spirit
Standard Action   Melee spirit 1
Target: One creature
Attack: Wisdom vs. Fortitude
Hit: 2d10 + Wisdom modifier damage, and the target falls prone. Until the end of your next turn, while adjacent to your spirit companion, any ally can knock a target prone that he or she hits. If the target is already prone, it takes 1d8 extra damage.

Shackles of the Mountain — Shaman Attack 17

Two spirits—humanoid forms of granite—appear and batter your foes. They then channel power through your spirit companion to weaken the defenses of nearby enemies.

Encounter ✦ Implement, Primal
Standard Action   Ranged 10
Target: One or two creatures
Attack: Wisdom vs. Reflex
Hit: 2d10 + Wisdom modifier damage. Until the end of your next turn, any enemy uses the lower of its AC and Reflex as its AC while adjacent to your spirit companion.
Stalker Spirit: The enemy instead uses the lowest of its AC, Fortitude, and Reflex as its AC.

Spirit Bond of Vengeance — Shaman Attack 17

Your spirit companion channels a vengeful spirit as it lashes out at a foe. For a short time, the pain of other enemies flows through your companion to wrack that enemy.

Encounter ✦ Implement, Primal, Spirit
Standard Action   Melee spirit 1
Target: One creature
Attack: Wisdom vs. Reflex
Hit: 2d6 + Wisdom modifier damage. Until the end of your next turn, the target takes 1d6 damage when any ally hits an enemy, other than the target, that is adjacent to your spirit companion.

Spirit of Spring's Renewal — Shaman Attack 17

A humanoid spirit formed of bark, vines, and roots appears and slams your enemy. Channeling power through your spirit companion, the spirit renews your allies' strength.

Encounter ✦ Healing, Implement, Primal
Standard Action   Ranged 10
Target: One creature
Attack: Wisdom vs. Will
Hit: 3d6 + Wisdom modifier damage, and each ally adjacent to your spirit companion can spend a healing surge.
Protector Spirit: Each of the allies who spends a healing surge regains additional hit points equal to twice your Constitution modifier.

Level 19 Daily Evocations

Great Bear Guardian — Shaman Attack 19

A bear spirit appears amid your foes. It knocks one enemy aside and stands alert, ready to protect you and your allies with its vicious claws.

Daily ✦ Conjuration, Implement, Primal
Standard Action   Ranged 10
Target: One creature
Attack: Wisdom vs. Fortitude
Hit: 2d10 + Wisdom modifier damage, and you push the target 2 squares and knock it prone.
Miss: Half damage, and you push the target 1 square.
Effect: You conjure a bear spirit in an unoccupied square adjacent to the target. The spirit lasts until the end of the encounter. The spirit occupies 1 square. Enemies cannot move through its space, but allies can. As a move action, you can move the spirit 5 squares.
　　The spirit can flank enemies with you and your allies, and it can make opportunity attacks against your enemies: Wisdom vs. Reflex; 2d10 + your Wisdom modifier damage.

Horns of the Undefeated Khan — Shaman Attack 19

Horns sound as the great khan—a champion of the primal forest who has never been defeated in battle—strides from the spirit world to lead your allies into the fray.

Daily ✦ Implement, Primal
Standard Action   Ranged 20
Target: One creature
Attack: Wisdom vs. Reflex
Hit: 4d8 + Wisdom modifier damage.
Miss: Half damage.
Effect: Until the end of your next turn, you and your allies gain a +2 bonus to attack rolls and a +5 bonus to damage rolls against the target. As a free action before your next turn, each ally within 20 squares of the target can make a saving throw and shift 3 squares as the first action of his or her turn.

Spirit of the Shield Breaker — Shaman Attack 19

A howling warrior bearing a greataxe leaps on your foe, shattering its defenses and urging your allies to greater glory.

Daily ✦ Conjuration, Implement, Primal
Standard Action   Ranged 10
Target: One creature
Attack: Wisdom vs. Will
Hit: 3d12 + Wisdom modifier damage, and the target takes a -4 penalty to AC (save ends).
Aftereffect: The target takes a -2 penalty to AC (save ends).
Miss: Half damage, and the target takes a -2 penalty to AC (save ends).
Effect: You conjure the spirit of the shield breaker in a square adjacent to the target. The spirit lasts until the end of the encounter. As a move action, you can move the spirit 5 squares. While adjacent to the spirit or in its space, you and your allies gain a +5 power bonus to damage rolls.

Tendrils of the Fate Weaver
Shaman Attack 19

You call on the spirit of the Fate Weaver, a great spider said to have created the bindings between the planes, to wrap your foe in rock-hard spiderwebs and to protect your friend.

Daily ✦ Implement, Primal
Standard Action   **Ranged** 10
Target: One creature
Attack: Wisdom vs. Will
Hit: 4d10 + Wisdom modifier damage, and the target is slowed and can't gain combat advantage against any target (save ends both). The target takes a -5 penalty to saving throws against this effect.
Miss: Half damage.
Effect: Choose an ally within 10 squares of you. Until the end of the encounter, if any enemy hits that ally, that enemy is immobilized until the end of its next turn.

LEVEL 22 UTILITY EVOCATIONS

Bounty of Life
Shaman Utility 22

You tap into the flow of primal energy and send vigor into your allies, allowing even the most grievous injury to knit in an instant.

Daily ✦ Healing, Primal
Minor Action   **Close** burst 10
Target: Each ally in burst
Effect: Each target gains regeneration 5 until the end of the encounter. The regeneration increases to 10 while a target is bloodied.

Call the Dead
Shaman Utility 22

You reach into the spirit world and grasp your allies' fleeing souls, returning them to their bodies so that they can fight on.

Daily ✦ Healing, Primal
Standard Action   **Close** burst 5
Target: Each dead ally in burst
Effect: Each target returns to life and spends a healing surge. Each target is also considered to have failed no death saving throws during this encounter.

Doorway to the Spirit World
Shaman Utility 22

The boundaries between the spiritual and the physical waver as you open a doorway to the spirit world to protect your allies from harm.

Daily ✦ Primal, Zone
Minor Action   **Area** burst 1 within 10 squares
Effect: The burst creates a zone of primal energy that lasts until the end of the encounter. While within the zone, you and your allies are insubstantial.

Spirit of the World Healer
Shaman Utility 22

You call on the spirit of the World Healer—the force that mended the world after the great war between the gods and the primordials—to tend to a wounded comrade.

Daily ✦ Healing, Primal
Minor Action   **Close** burst 10
Target: One ally in burst
Effect: The target regains all its hit points.

LEVEL 23 ENCOUNTER EVOCATIONS

Call to the Primal Protector
Shaman Attack 23

Your spirit companion briefly appears as a monstrous bear as it mauls your foe. The spirit's protective power wards your allies from your enemies' attacks.

Encounter ✦ Implement, Primal, Spirit
Standard Action   **Melee** spirit 1
Target: One creature
Attack: Wisdom vs. Reflex
Hit: 2d10 + Wisdom modifier damage. Until the end of your next turn, any ally takes half damage from any source while adjacent to your spirit companion.
Protector Spirit: Each ally adjacent to your spirit companion gains temporary hit points equal to 5 + your Constitution modifier.

Call to the Relentless Hunter
Shaman Attack 23

Your spirit companion is filled with the spirit of the relentless hunter as it ferociously rakes your enemy. For a short time, your allies are filled with a similar ferocity.

Encounter ✦ Implement, Primal, Spirit
Standard Action   **Melee** spirit 1
Target: One creature
Attack: Wisdom vs. Fortitude
Hit: 4d6 + Wisdom modifier damage. Until the end of your next turn, when any ally adjacent to your spirit companion misses with an at-will or an encounter attack power, that attack deals 1d10 damage.
Stalker Spirit: The damage on an ally's miss equals 1d10 + your Intelligence modifier.

Spirit of the Death Raven
Shaman Attack 23

A black bird swoops over your foe—a sign of ill omen, signifying that your enemy's death is at hand.

Encounter ✦ Implement, Primal, Psychic
Standard Action   **Ranged** 10
Target: One creature
Attack: Wisdom vs. Will
Hit: 4d8 + Wisdom modifier psychic damage. Before the end of your next turn, you roll a d20 the next time the target is hit by an attack that isn't a critical hit. If you roll 15 or higher, that attack becomes a critical hit.

Twin Tempest Spirits
Shaman Attack 23

Shrieking bird spirits of thunder and lightning descend on your foes, battering them as the planar winds from the spirits' wings flow through your spirit companion, allowing your allies to teleport.

Encounter ✦ Implement, Lightning, Primal, Teleportation, Thunder
Standard Action   **Ranged** 10
Target: One or two creatures
Attack: Wisdom vs. Reflex
Hit: 3d10 + Wisdom modifier lightning and thunder damage. If either attack hits, you can teleport each ally adjacent to your spirit companion 10 squares.

LEVEL 25 DAILY EVOCATIONS

Ironborn Spirit
Shaman Attack 25

A spirit of iron impales your foe with an iron spike, then creates an area where your allies can stand fast.

Daily ✦ Implement, Primal, Zone
Standard Action   Ranged 10
Target: One creature
Attack: Wisdom vs. Fortitude
Hit: 3d10 + Wisdom modifier damage, and the target is immobilized (save ends).
Miss: Half damage, and the target is immobilized until the end of your next turn.
Effect: The attack creates a zone that is a burst 5 centered on the target. The zone lasts until the end of the encounter. While within the zone, any ally gains a +2 power bonus to AC and can negate being pulled, pushed, or slid.

Spirit of the Laughing Wanderer
Shaman Attack 25

A spirit like a hyena appears and savages your foe's mind, barking its eerie cackle. Its laugh continues to dumbfound your enemy as it moves to a different foe.

Daily ✦ Implement, Primal, Psychic
Standard Action   Ranged 10
Target: One creature
Attack: Wisdom vs. Will
Hit: 3d10 + Wisdom modifier psychic damage, and the target is stunned (save ends).
  Aftereffect: The enemy nearest to the target is stunned (save ends).
Miss: Half damage, and the target is dazed and slowed (save ends both).
  Aftereffect: The enemy nearest to the target is dazed and slowed (save ends both).

Spirit of the World Serpent
Shaman Attack 25

The spirit of the World Serpent emerges from the ground to pierce your foe with its fangs, pinning the foe to the ground. Tremors from the spirit's movement shake the ground.

Daily ✦ Implement, Primal
Standard Action   Ranged 10
Target: One creature
Attack: Wisdom vs. Reflex
Hit: 5d8 + Wisdom modifier damage, and you knock the target prone. Whenever the target stands up, it takes 15 damage (save ends).
  Aftereffect: Whenever the target stands up, it takes 10 damage (save ends).
  Aftereffect: Whenever the target stands up, it takes 5 damage (save ends).
Miss: Half damage. Whenever the target stands up, it takes 10 damage (save ends).
Effect: At the start of the target's turn, it and any enemy within 3 squares of it are knocked prone (save ends).

Western Wind of Storms
Shaman Attack 25

You call on the spirit of the stormy western wind to hurl your enemies away, spinning them through the planar firmament and whisking your allies to safety.

Daily ✦ Implement, Lightning, Primal, Teleportation
Standard Action   Close blast 5
Target: Each enemy in blast
Attack: Wisdom vs. Reflex
Hit: 3d6 + Wisdom modifier lightning damage, and you teleport the target 10 squares.
Miss: Half damage, and you teleport the target 5 squares.
Effect: You teleport each ally in the blast 10 squares.

LEVEL 27 ENCOUNTER EVOCATIONS

Blood Reaper Spirits
Shaman Attack 27

Shrieking falcons with red feathers circle your foes, slashing at them with knifelike talons. Once the falcons have tasted blood, they channel their strength through your spirit companion to your allies.

Encounter ✦ Implement, Primal
Standard Action   Ranged 10
Target: One creature
Attack: Wisdom vs. Fortitude
Hit: 4d6 + Wisdom modifier damage. Until the end of your next turn, any ally gains a +2 bonus to damage rolls while adjacent to your spirit companion.
Effect: Make the attack two more times against the same target or different ones. The bonus to your allies' damage rolls increases to +4 if the attack hits twice and +6 if it hits three times.
  Stalker Spirit: Your Intelligence modifier is added to the bonus to damage rolls.

Call to the Cleansing Fire
Shaman Attack 27

A mote of white fire emerges from your spirit companion. Its radiance burns an enemy and sweeps away your allies' ills.

Encounter ✦ Fire, Implement, Primal, Radiant, Spirit
Standard Action   Melee spirit 1
Target: One creature
Attack: Wisdom vs. Reflex
Hit: 4d8 + Wisdom modifier fire and radiant damage. Until the end of your next turn, each ally gains a +5 bonus to saving throws while adjacent to your spirit companion.
  Protector Spirit: The bonus to saving throws equals 3 + your Constitution modifier.

Call to the Great Hunter
Shaman Attack 27

Your spirit companion is filled with the battle wisdom of the great hunter spirit as it rends your foe and then lends that wisdom to a nearby ally.

Encounter ✦ Implement, Primal, Spirit
Standard Action   Melee spirit 1
Target: One creature
Attack: Wisdom vs. Reflex
Hit: 4d8 + Wisdom modifier damage. One ally adjacent to your spirit companion gains a +5 bonus to attack rolls until the end of your next turn.

Spirit of Elder Wisdom — Shaman Attack 27

A spirit elder clad in robes and bearing a staff appears next to your foe. Lightning arcs from the spirit's hands to shock that foe. The spirit lends counsel to your allies, ensuring that their efforts are not wasted.

Encounter ✦ Implement, Lightning, Primal
Standard Action   Ranged 10
Target: One creature
Attack: Wisdom vs. Will
Hit: 3d8 + Wisdom modifier lightning damage, and the target is dazed until the end of your next turn. Any ally adjacent to your spirit companion who misses with an encounter attack power before the end of your next turn does not expend the use of that power.

LEVEL 29 DAILY EVOCATIONS

Death Spirit — Shaman Attack 29

Time seems to freeze for a moment as everything goes quiet. Death itself, the ender of all things, has entered the fray, wracking your foe with pain that only intensifies as others fall.

Daily ✦ Implement, Necrotic, Primal
Standard Action   Ranged 10
Target: One creature
Attack: Wisdom vs. Fortitude
Hit: 7d10 + Wisdom modifier necrotic damage.
Miss: Half damage.
Effect: When any creature drops to 0 hit points or fewer within 10 squares of the target, the target takes 3d10 necrotic damage (save ends).
  Aftereffect: When any creature drops to 0 hit points or fewer within 10 squares of the target, the target takes 2d10 necrotic damage (save ends).

Sea of Serpents — Shaman Attack 29

A wave of snake spirits surges forth to devour your foes and aid your allies in battle. The serpents impart their agility to your allies, allowing them to attack with lightning speed.

Daily ✦ Implement, Primal, Zone
Standard Action   Close blast 5
Target: Each enemy in blast
Attack: Wisdom vs. Reflex
Hit: 5d6 + Wisdom modifier damage.
Miss: Half damage.

Effect: The blast creates a zone of serpent spirits that lasts until the end of the encounter. Any ally that starts his or her turn within the zone gains three benefits until the start of his or her next turn: The ally can shift 3 squares as a minor action, gains combat advantage against each enemy, and can use an opportunity action to make a melee basic attack against any enemy adjacent to him or her that shifts.

Spirits of Mist — Shaman Attack 29

You call to the spirits that linger at the edge of the world and maintain the barriers of the planes. The spirits heed your call, smiting your enemies and guarding your allies from attack.

Daily ✦ Implement, Primal, Zone
Standard Action   Area burst 3 within 10 squares
Target: One creature in burst
Attack: Wisdom vs. Fortitude
Hit: 4d10 + Wisdom modifier damage.
Miss: Half damage.
Effect: The burst creates a zone of mist that lasts until the end of the encounter. While within the zone, you and your allies are insubstantial. As a move action, you can move the zone 3 squares.

Spirit of the Unbroken Vow — Shaman Attack 29

At the end of the war between the gods and the primordials, the primal forces forged a sacred compact that established the laws of nature. As you call on the power of that compact to ravage your foe, your ally swears an oath to slay your enemy.

Daily ✦ Implement, Primal, Psychic
Standard Action   Ranged 10
Target: One creature
Attack: Wisdom vs. Will
Hit: 7d6 + Wisdom modifier psychic damage.
Miss: Half damage.
Effect: Choose an ally within 10 squares of you. Until the end of the encounter, that ally gains a +2 bonus to attack rolls against the target. Whenever the ally damages the target, this bonus increases by 1 to a maximum of +10. If the ally doesn't attack the target during his or her turn, the bonus decreases by 2 to a minimum of +0.

PARAGON PATHS

DISCIPLE OF THE WORLD SERPENT

"The whole world rests in the coils of the great serpent. You would be wise to learn its ways."

Prerequisite: Shaman, *call spirit companion* power

The World Serpent, legend says, is among the greatest of the primal spirits that established the natural laws of the world and is one of the staunchest defenders of those laws. When a divine exarch and the servant of a primordial joined forces in an attempt to tamper with the natural order, the World Serpent simultaneously crushed the life from them both. The earth is said to rest in this mighty serpent's coils, the motion of which shakes the ground.

As a disciple of the World Serpent, you are charged with maintaining the balance of the natural order and ensuring that creatures from beyond the mortal realm keep to their place. You wield the World Serpent's power, using it to pierce your foes with its fangs or crush them in its coils. Your spirit companion hinders the movement of your enemies as the World Serpent's coils echo through the space around it. The World Serpent's venom empowers your evocations, poisoning creatures that break free of your power.

DISCIPLE OF THE WORLD SERPENT PATH FEATURES

Grasping Spirit (11th level): Enemies treat squares adjacent to your spirit companion as difficult terrain.

Spirit Shaman's Bounty (11th level): When you spend an action point to take an extra action, one ally adjacent to your spirit companion can spend a healing surge.

Spirit Venom (16th level): Whenever an enemy saves against your shaman daily attack powers, that enemy takes 10 poison damage.

DISCIPLE OF THE WORLD SERPENT EVOCATIONS

Serpent's Rebuke — Disciple of the World Serpent Attack 11

The jaws of the World Serpent bite at your foe, stabbing through its mind and rooting it in place. Enemies that draw too close to the transfixed foe feel the echoes of its pain.

Encounter ✦ Implement, Primal, Psychic
Standard Action   **Ranged** 10
Target: One creature
Attack: Wisdom vs. Will
Hit: 2d8 + Wisdom modifier psychic damage. Until the end of your next turn, the target is immobilized, and any enemy that enters a square adjacent to the target takes 5 psychic damage. An enemy takes this damage only once for each use of this power.

Seal of the Serpent — Disciple of the World Serpent Utility 12

A twisting mark like a glowing green serpent appears on your enemy's skin, drawing the attacks of your ally to unerringly strike the foe.

Encounter ✦ Primal
Minor Action   **Ranged** 5
Target: One creature
Effect: Choose yourself or one ally within 5 squares of you. Until the end of your next turn, that character ignores cover, superior cover, concealment, and total concealment when attacking the target. In addition, the character can make ranged attacks against the target without having line of sight or line of effect to it.

Crush of the Serpent — Disciple of the World Serpent Attack 20

You call on the spirit of the World Serpent to crush your enemy in its emerald coils.

Daily ✦ Implement, Primal
Standard Action   **Ranged** 10
Target: One creature
Attack: Wisdom vs. Fortitude
Hit: The target is immobilized and takes ongoing 15 damage (save ends both).
  Aftereffect: The target is immobilized and takes ongoing 5 damage (save ends both).
Miss: The target is slowed and takes ongoing 5 damage (save ends both).

Ghost Panther

"Do not trouble us again, or you will feed the panther spirits that stalk between the worlds."

Prerequisite: Shaman, *call spirit companion* power

The mystery of the primal stalker is that death is a constant presence in the midst of life; the death of the prey brings life to the predator. And when death comes to the predator, it brings life to scavengers and carrion feeders. Death is part of the great wheel of mortal existence, and an important part of the shaman's communion with the spirit world.

As a shaman, you have always walked close to death. Now you have set out on the path of the ghost panther, where life and death twine together still closer. You stalk the wild, hiding from your prey, leaping and climbing like the most agile of cats. You call on panther spirits to attack your foes, weaken your prey, help you leap away from enemy attacks, and lead you through the spirit world to teleport adjacent to your foes.

Ghost Panther Path Features

Ghost Panther's Wisdom (11th level): You and your allies gain a +5 power bonus to Stealth checks while adjacent to your spirit companion.

Ghost Panther Action (11th level): When you spend an action point to take an extra action, each enemy adjacent to your spirit companion grants combat advantage to you and your allies until the end of your next turn.

Panther Ancestors (16th level): You gain a bonus to Acrobatics, Athletics, and Stealth checks equal to your Wisdom modifier.

Ghost Panther Evocations

Predator Spirit	Ghost Panther Attack 11

A panther spirit appears and rends your foe; then its bloodthirstiness flows through your spirit companion to weaken your enemies.

Encounter ✦ Implement, Primal
Standard Action　　　　**Ranged** 10
Target: One creature
Attack: Wisdom vs. Reflex
Hit: 2d6 + Wisdom modifier damage. Until the end of your next turn, bloodied enemies are weakened while adjacent to your spirit companion.

Great Cat's Dodge	Ghost Panther Utility 12

Your eyes shine yellow like those of a great cat as you leap away from an enemy attack.

Encounter ✦ Primal
Immediate Interrupt　　　**Personal**
Trigger: An attack misses you
Effect: You shift 3 squares.

Ghost Panther Spiral	Ghost Panther Attack 20

A stream of frenzied panther spirits flows around you, savaging your enemies. The wind of the spirits' passage lets you and your allies slip through the spirit world to attack your foes.

Daily ✦ Implement, Primal, Teleportation, Zone
Standard Action　　　　**Close** burst 5
Target: Each enemy in burst
Attack: Wisdom vs. Will
Hit: 5d6 + Wisdom modifier damage.
Miss: Half damage.
Effect: The burst creates a zone of rushing spirits that lasts until the end of the encounter. You or any ally who is within the zone can use a minor action to teleport to a space adjacent to an enemy that is within the zone.

Great Bear Shaman

"Foulspawn cannot match the ancient powers of our land."

Prerequisite: Shaman, *call spirit companion* power

Many shaman traditions revere the Great Bear as the perfect example of the protector spirit. As a mother bear furiously guards her cubs against danger, so the Great Bear stands guard over the world, protecting it from those who would destroy or corrupt it, and so too do you, as a Great Bear shaman, protect your adventuring companions. Your spirit companion is your link to the Great Bear, channeling its strength and endurance to you through your evocations.

Your main purpose is to stand alongside other warriors and make them stronger. When you can, protect the weak. When you cannot, strengthen the strong to make them better protectors. As you pursue the path of the Great Bear shaman, your spirit companion channels the power of the Great Bear to harry your enemies, punishing them when they attack your friends. Your companion roars with the ferocious strength of the Great Bear, galvanizing your allies

into action. You give your allies additional attacks whenever you spur yourself to greater action, and you empower the attacks they make when enemies drop their guard.

You are the world's protector, and the Great Bear's roar echoes in every word you speak.

Great Bear Shaman Path Features

Great Protector's Prowess (11th level): You and your allies gain a +2 bonus to damage rolls against marked enemies adjacent to your spirit companion.

Great Bear's Action (11th level): When you spend an action point to take an extra action, one ally of your choice within 10 squares of you can make a melee basic attack as a free action, before or after the extra action.

Looming Presence (16th level): While adjacent to your spirit companion, your allies gain a +5 power bonus to attack rolls when making opportunity attacks.

Great Bear Shaman Evocations

Bear Fang Defense — Great Bear Shaman Attack 11

Your spirit companion lets out the terrible roar of the Great Bear and smashes its heavy paw into your foe. The presence of the bear spirit is impossible to ignore.

Encounter ✦ Implement, Primal, Spirit
Standard Action   **Melee** spirit 1
Target: One creature
Attack: Wisdom vs. Fortitude
Hit: 3d10 + Wisdom modifier damage, and the target is marked until the end of your next turn. Until the mark ends, whenever the target makes an attack while adjacent to your spirit companion, the target takes 1d10 damage and is knocked prone after the attack is resolved.

Galvanizing Bellow — Great Bear Shaman Utility 12

The roar of your spirit companion spurs your allies to move.

Encounter ✦ Primal
Minor Action   **Close** burst 5
Target: Each ally in burst
Effect: Each target can shift 2 squares as a free action.

Call to the Great Bear — Great Bear Shaman Attack 20

Your spirit companion mauls your enemy with its claws and teeth. The spirit of the Great Bear lingers around your foe, punishing it for harming your allies.

Daily ✦ Implement, Primal, Spirit
Standard Action   **Melee** spirit 1
Target: One creature
Attack: Wisdom vs. Reflex
Hit: 4d10 + Wisdom modifier damage.
Miss: Half damage.
Effect: The target takes a -2 penalty to attack rolls, and whenever it hits with an attack, the target takes 1d10 + your Wisdom modifier damage (save ends both).

Spirit Tempest

"The spirit wind is always blowing through the world. You need but feel it to draw on its power."

Prerequisite: Shaman, *call spirit companion* power

What is a spirit but an exhalation of the world, a distillation of life lived in the drawing and releasing of breath? The spirits of the world are alive, and that means they are in motion. They are a wind that blows through the world, even in the solid rock of the earth's deepest reaches.

As a spirit tempest, you tap into the movement of the spirit world, the wind that blows through all things. You draw on that movement to bring motion to the field of battle: You call spirit winds to transport yourself and your allies in the blink of an eye, to carry your healing power and the power of your attacks into larger areas, and to empower the attacks of your allies.

The spirits are the breath of the world. Breathe deeply, and let them move and guide you.

Spirit Tempest Path Features

Spirit Wind Action (11th level): When you spend an action point to take an extra action, each ally adjacent to your spirit companion can teleport 2 squares as a free action.

Healing Guides (11th level): When you restore hit points with your *healing spirit* power, any ally adjacent to or within a conjuration or a zone that you created with a shaman power or a shaman paragon path power also regains hit points as if he or she were adjacent to your spirit companion.

Spirit Combatant (16th level): When you use a shaman at-will attack power that has the spirit keyword, you gain combat advantage for that attack.

Spirit Tempest Evocations

Spirit Tide — Spirit Tempest Attack 11

Your spirit companion lashes out at an enemy, sending a swirling storm of spirits to batter other nearby foes.

Encounter ✦ Implement, Primal, Spirit
Standard Action   **Melee** spirit 1
Target: One creature
Attack: Wisdom vs. Will
Hit: 2d10 + Wisdom modifier damage, and each enemy within 5 squares of the target takes 1d10 damage.

Spirit Flow — Spirit Tempest Utility 12

Spirits swirl around your ally and your spirit companion as the two disappear, and then each reappears where the other just stood.

Encounter ✦ Primal, Teleportation
Minor Action   **Close** burst 20
Target: One ally in burst
Effect: You teleport the target and your spirit companion, swapping their positions.

Spirit Storm — Spirit Tempest Attack 20

A wind howls around your enemy as dozens of minor storm spirits appear and attack it. Your allies can trade positions inside the storm with a thought.

Daily ✦ Implement, Primal, Teleportation, Zone
Standard Action   **Area** burst 2 within 10 squares
Target: One creature in burst
Attack: Wisdom vs. Will
Hit: 4d8 + Wisdom modifier damage.
Miss: Half damage.
Effect: The burst creates a zone of storm spirits that lasts until the end of the encounter. While within the zone, any ally gains a +1 bonus to attack rolls and damage rolls against the target. In addition, any ally within the zone can teleport as a move action, swapping positions with another ally within the zone.

CHAPTER 2 | *Character Classes*

135

SORCERER

"I am in the arcane, and the arcane is in me."

CLASS TRAITS

Role: Striker. You channel powerful magical energy through your body, exerting control over wild arcane magic to blast foes. You lean toward controller as a secondary role.

Power Source: Arcane. Arcane magic is in your blood, as a touch of either ancient draconic power or untamed chaos energy, and you unleash it through sheer force of will and physical discipline.

Key Abilities: Charisma, Dexterity, Strength

Armor Proficiencies: Cloth
Weapon Proficiencies: Simple melee, simple ranged
Implements: Daggers, staffs
Bonus to Defense: +2 Will

Hit Points at 1st Level: 12 + Constitution score
Hit Points per Level Gained: 5
Healing Surges per Day: 6 + Constitution modifier

Trained Skills: Arcana. From the class skills list below, choose three more trained skills at 1st level.
Class Skills: Arcana (Int), Athletics (Str), Bluff (Cha), Diplomacy (Cha), Dungeoneering (Wis), Endurance (Con), History (Int), Insight (Wis), Intimidate (Cha), Nature (Wis)

Class Features: Spell Source

The sorcerer is the arcane antithesis of the wizard. Wielding raw, barely contained magical power, sorcerers channel bursts and blasts of arcane energy through their bodies. They gain their power not through rigorous study of esoteric tomes, but by harnessing magic in their blood, waiting to be tapped and shaped. If wizards wield magic as fighters wield swords, a sorcerer's magic is the arcing greataxe of a raging barbarian.

You might be a proud dragonborn scion of ancient Arkhosia, calling on the draconic power of your heritage, or perhaps you were bathed in dragon blood as an infant to fill you with that power. You might have been born in a place where planar forces converged in strange eddies, infusing you with chaos, or perhaps you survived implantation of a slaad embryo, which left the taint of chaos upon you.

Magic pulses through your veins, calling on you to give it expression. As it grows ever stronger, will it consume you or transform you into magic incarnate?

SORCERER CLASS FEATURES

Sorcerers have the following class features.

SPELL SOURCE

As a sorcerer, you gain power through an instinctive or inborn connection to an ancient arcane source. Choose either Dragon Magic or Wild Magic. The choice you make grants you specific features and also provides bonuses to certain sorcerer powers, as detailed in those powers.

DRAGON MAGIC

The elemental power of dragons flows through you, infusing your spells with draconic strength. Through force of will, you tap into the arcane might of dragons.

Draconic Power: You gain a bonus to the damage rolls of arcane powers equal to your Strength modifier. The bonus increases to your Strength modifier + 2 at 11th level and your Strength modifier + 4 at 21st level.

Draconic Resilience: While you are not wearing heavy armor, you can use your Strength modifier in place of your Dexterity or Intelligence modifier to determine your AC.

Dragon Soul: Choose a damage type: acid, cold, fire, lightning, poison, or thunder. You gain resist 5 to that damage type. The resistance increases to 10 at 11th level and 15 at 21st level.

Your arcane powers ignore any target's resistance to that damage type up to the value of your resistance.

Scales of the Dragon: The first time you become bloodied during an encounter, you gain a +2 bonus to AC until the end of the encounter.

WILD MAGIC

You draw your spells from the entropic forces of the Elemental Chaos. Whether tapping into the power of primordial beings or drawing strength directly from that plane, you unleash magic in wild surges.

Chaos Burst: Your first attack roll during each of your turns determines a benefit you gain in that round. If you roll an even number, you gain a +1 bonus to AC until the start of your next turn. If you roll an odd number, you make a saving throw.

Chaos Power: You gain a bonus to the damage rolls of arcane powers equal to your Dexterity modifier. The bonus increases to your Dexterity modifier + 2 at 11th level and your Dexterity modifier + 4 at 21st level.

Unfettered Power: When you roll a natural 20 on an attack roll for an arcane power, you slide the target 1 square and knock it prone after applying the attack's other effects.

When you roll a natural 1 on an attack roll for an arcane power, you must push each creature within 5 squares of you 1 square.

Wild Soul: When you finish an extended rest, roll a d10 to determine a damage type.

d10	Damage Type
1	Acid
2	Cold
3	Fire
4	Force
5	Lightning
6	Necrotic
7	Poison
8	Psychic
9	Radiant
10	Thunder

You gain resist 5 to that damage type until the end of your next extended rest. The resistance increases to 10 at 11th level and 15 at 21st level.

While you have resistance to that damage type, your arcane powers ignore any target's resistance to that damage type up to the value of your resistance.

IMPLEMENTS

Sorcerers wield daggers and staffs to channel their wild arcane power. When you wield a magic dagger or a magic staff, you can add its enhancement bonus to the attack rolls and the damage rolls of sorcerer powers and sorcerer paragon path powers that have the implement keyword. Without an implement, you can still use these powers.

Any dagger can function as a sorcerer implement. However, you don't gain a dagger's proficiency bonus when using the dagger as an implement.

CREATING A SORCERER

Charisma, Dexterity, and Strength are the most important ability scores for a sorcerer. You can choose any powers you like, but many sorcerers choose feats, skills, and powers to complement their Spell Source choice.

CHAOS SORCERER

Like the arcane power you wield, you can be reckless and hard to control. Charisma should be your highest ability score, followed by Dexterity. Select powers that use your high Dexterity to move your enemies, deal extra damage, or impose penalties on your foes.

    Suggested Class Feature: Wild Magic
    Suggested Feat: Arcane Spellfury
    Suggested Skills: Arcana, Bluff, Endurance, Insight
    Suggested At-Will Powers: *chaos bolt, storm walk*
    Suggested Encounter Power: *bedeviling burst*
    Suggested Daily Power: *dazzling ray*

DRAGON SORCERER

You command the ancient arcane power that flows through dragons. Make Charisma your highest ability score, followed by Strength. Select powers that use your high Strength to deal extra damage, grant yourself a bonus, or hinder your enemies.

    Suggested Class Feature: Dragon Magic
    Suggested Feat: Implement Expertise
    Suggested Skills: Arcana, Athletics, History, Intimidate
    Suggested At-Will Powers: *burning spray, dragonfrost*
    Suggested Encounter Power: *tempest breath*
    Suggested Daily Power: *lightning breath*

SORCERER POWERS

Like other arcane classes' powers, your powers are called spells. A sorcerer's arsenal is an eclectic mixture of deadly spells drawn from enigmatic or reckless traditions of magic. More studious arcane practitioners sometimes regard sorcerers as novices who play with dangerous power beyond their control, but the proof of their worth is in the havoc they wreak on their foes.

LEVEL 1 AT-WILL SPELLS

Acid Orb	Sorcerer Attack 1

You hurl a globe of acid at a distant enemy.

At-Will ✦ Acid, Arcane, Implement
Standard Action   **Ranged** 20
Target: One creature
Attack: Charisma vs. Reflex
Hit: 1d10 + Charisma modifier acid damage.
    Level 21: 2d10 + Charisma modifier acid damage.
Special: This power can be used as a ranged basic attack.

Burning Spray	Sorcerer Attack 1

You fling your arm in a wide arc, casting liquid fire at your foes.

At-Will ✦ Arcane, Fire, Implement
Standard Action   **Close** blast 3
Target: Each creature in blast
Attack: Charisma vs. Reflex
Hit: 1d8 + Charisma modifier fire damage.
    Level 21: 2d8 + Charisma modifier fire damage.
    Dragon Magic: The next enemy that hits you with a melee attack before the end of your next turn takes fire damage equal to your Strength modifier.

Chaos Bolt	Sorcerer Attack 1

A bolt of many-colored light leaps from your hand and screams toward an enemy's head.

At-Will ✦ Arcane, Implement, Psychic
Standard Action   **Ranged** 10
Primary Target: One creature
Primary Attack: Charisma vs. Will
Hit: 1d10 + Charisma modifier psychic damage.
    Level 21: 2d10 + Charisma modifier psychic damage.
    Wild Magic: If you rolled an even number for the primary attack roll, make a secondary attack.
Secondary Target: One creature within 5 squares of the target last hit by this power
Secondary Attack: Charisma vs. Will
Hit: 1d6 psychic damage. If you rolled an even number for the secondary attack roll, repeat the secondary attack. You can attack a creature only once with a single use of this power.

Dragonfrost — Sorcerer Attack 1

A gust of frost hammers your foe and knocks it back.

At-Will ✦ Arcane, Cold, Implement
Standard Action   **Ranged** 10
Target: One creature
Attack: Charisma vs. Fortitude
Hit: 1d8 + Charisma modifier cold damage, and you push the target 1 square.
  Level 21: 2d8 + Charisma modifier cold damage.
Special: This power can be used as a ranged basic attack.

Storm Walk — Sorcerer Attack 1

The thunder of your steps batters your foe.

At-Will ✦ Arcane, Implement, Thunder
Standard Action   **Ranged** 10
Target: One creature
Attack: Charisma vs. Fortitude
Hit: 1d8 + Charisma modifier thunder damage.
  Level 21: 2d8 + Charisma modifier thunder damage.
Effect: Before or after the attack, you shift 1 square.

LEVEL 1 ENCOUNTER SPELLS

Bedeviling Burst — Sorcerer Attack 1

An eruption of psychic energy assaults your enemies' minds, sending them staggering.

Encounter ✦ Arcane, Implement, Psychic
Standard Action   **Close** burst 3
Target: One or two creatures in burst
Attack: Charisma vs. Will
Hit: 1d10 + Charisma modifier psychic damage, and you push the target a number of squares equal to your Dexterity modifier.
  Wild Magic: If you rolled an even number on the attack roll, you slide the target instead of pushing it.

Explosive Pyre — Sorcerer Attack 1

Your foe stands at the center of a conflagration of your design.

Encounter ✦ Arcane, Fire, Implement
Standard Action   **Ranged** 10
Target: One creature
Attack: Charisma vs. Reflex
Hit: 2d8 + Charisma modifier fire damage. Until the start of your next turn, any enemy that enters a square adjacent to the target or starts its turn there takes 1d6 fire damage.

Frostbind — Sorcerer Attack 1

Creaking ice envelops and hinders your enemy.

Encounter ✦ Arcane, Cold, Implement
Standard Action   **Ranged** 10
Target: One creature
Attack: Charisma vs. Fortitude
Hit: 3d6 + Charisma modifier cold damage, and the target takes a –2 penalty to Reflex until the end of your next turn.

Tempest Breath — Sorcerer Attack 1

You exhale mist that burns and disorients your foes, and a lingering fog obscures you.

Encounter ✦ Acid, Arcane, Implement
Standard Action   **Close** blast 3
Target: Each creature in blast
Attack: Charisma vs. Reflex
Hit: 2d6 + Charisma modifier acid damage, and the target can't gain combat advantage against any creature until the end of your next turn.
  Dragon Magic: You gain concealment until the end of your next turn.

Thunder Slam — Sorcerer Attack 1

A shock wave of sound slams into the enemy.

Encounter ✦ Arcane, Implement, Thunder
Standard Action   **Ranged** 10
Target: One creature
Attack: Charisma vs. Fortitude
Hit: 2d10 + Charisma modifier thunder damage, and you push the target 3 squares.

LEVEL 1 DAILY SPELLS

Chromatic Orb — Sorcerer Attack 1

An orb of arcane energy shifts colors as it hurtles toward your enemy. On impact, it erupts with damaging force, releasing the energy that was dominant at the time of impact.

Daily ✦ Arcane, Implement; Varies
Standard Action   **Ranged** 10
Target: One creature
Attack: Charisma vs. Reflex
Hit: 3d10 + Charisma modifier damage. Roll a d6 to determine the attack's damage type and effect.
  1. **Yellow:** Radiant damage, and the target is dazed (save ends).
  2. **Red:** Fire damage, and each creature adjacent to the target takes fire damage equal to your Dexterity modifier.
  3. **Green:** Poison damage, and ongoing 5 poison damage (save ends).
  4. **Turquoise:** Lightning damage, and you slide the target a number of squares equal to your Dexterity modifier.
  5. **Blue:** Cold damage, and the target is immobilized (save ends).
  6. **Violet:** Psychic damage, and the target takes a –2 penalty to AC (save ends).
Miss: 1d10 damage. Roll a d6 to determine the attack's damage type and effect, as above.

Dazzling Ray — Sorcerer Attack 1

A brilliant beam lances out to strike your foe and befuddle it.

Daily ✦ Arcane, Implement, Radiant
Standard Action   **Ranged** 10
Target: One creature
Attack: Charisma vs. Will
Hit: 6d6 + Charisma modifier radiant damage.
  Wild Magic: If you rolled an even number on the attack roll, the target takes a penalty to attack rolls against you equal to your Dexterity modifier (save ends).
Miss: Half damage.

Dragonfang Bolt — Sorcerer Attack 1

Venomous fangs hurtle toward your foes, piercing their flesh and then poisoning them.

Daily ✦ Arcane, Implement, Poison
Standard Action   Ranged 10
Target: One or two creatures
Attack: Charisma vs. Fortitude
Hit: 2d8 + Charisma modifier damage, and ongoing 5 poison damage (save ends).
Miss: 2d8 + Charisma modifier damage.

Lightning Breath — Sorcerer Attack 1

You exhale a blast of lightning at your foes. The lightning then forms a ring around you, repelling nearby attackers.

Daily ✦ Arcane, Implement, Lightning
Standard Action   Close blast 3
Target: Each creature in blast
Attack: Charisma vs. Reflex
Hit: 3d8 + Charisma modifier lightning damage.
Miss: Half damage.
Effect: Until the end of your next turn, whenever an enemy hits you with a melee attack, you push that enemy 1 square.
  Dragon Magic: The enemy also takes 5 lightning damage.
Sustain Minor: The effect persists.

LEVEL 2 UTILITY SPELLS

Dragonflame Mantle — Sorcerer Utility 2

You ward yourself with a mantle of flame.

Encounter ✦ Arcane, Fire
Immediate Interrupt   Personal
Trigger: You are hit by an attack
Effect: Until the end of your next turn, you gain a +1 power bonus to all defenses, and any creature that hits you with a melee attack takes 1d6 fire damage.

Elemental Shift — Sorcerer Utility 2

The alignment of elements within you changes at your command.

Daily ✦ Arcane
Minor Action   Personal
Effect: You can change the resistance granted by your Dragon Soul or Wild Soul to one of the other damage types for the rest of the encounter. In addition, one ally adjacent to you gains resist 5 to the damage type that you resist until the end of the encounter.
  Level 11: Resist 10.
  Level 21: Resist 15.

Stretch Spell — Sorcerer Utility 2

You bend space to increase the extent of your spell.

Encounter ✦ Arcane
Minor Action   Personal
Effect: Until the end of your turn, add your Dexterity modifier to the range of your ranged arcane powers.

Unseen Aid — Sorcerer Utility 2

Invisible forces aid you in mysterious ways.

Encounter ✦ Arcane
Minor Action   Personal
Effect: You gain a +2 bonus to a skill check you make this turn.

LEVEL 3 ENCOUNTER SPELLS

Dancing Lightning — Sorcerer Attack 3

As lightning strikes your foe, thunder batters creatures around it.

Encounter ✦ Arcane, Implement, Lightning, Thunder
Standard Action   Ranged 10
Target: One creature
Attack: Charisma vs. Reflex
Hit: 2d10 + Charisma modifier lightning damage, and each creature adjacent to the target takes thunder damage equal to your Charisma modifier.

Flame Spiral — Sorcerer Attack 3

You surround yourself in a vortex of fire, which lashes out at nearby foes.

Encounter ✦ Arcane, Fire, Implement
Standard Action   Close burst 2
Target: One, two, or three creatures in burst
Attack: Charisma vs. Reflex
Hit: 1d10 + Charisma modifier fire damage.
Effect: Until the start of your next turn, any enemy that enters a square adjacent to you or starts its turn there takes 1d6 fire damage.

Ice Dragon's Teeth — Sorcerer Attack 3

Shards of ice like the teeth of a dragon explode among your foes, chilling and slowing them.

Encounter ✦ Arcane, Cold, Implement
Standard Action   Area burst 1 within 10 squares
Target: Each creature in burst
Attack: Charisma vs. Reflex
Hit: 2d8 + Charisma modifier cold damage, and the target is slowed until the end of your next turn.

Poisonous Exhalation — Sorcerer Attack 3

A cloud of poisonous vapor billows from your mouth to sap your enemies' endurance.

Encounter ✦ Arcane, Implement, Poison
Standard Action   Close blast 3
Target: Each creature in blast
Attack: Charisma vs. Fortitude
Hit: 2d8 + Charisma modifier poison damage, and the target takes a -2 penalty to Fortitude until the end of your next turn.
  Dragon Magic: The penalty to Fortitude equals 1 + your Strength modifier.

Spectral Claw
Sorcerer Attack 3

A claw of force crushes your foe in its grip.

Encounter ✦ Arcane, Force, Implement
Standard Action   **Ranged** 10
Target: One creature
Attack: Charisma vs. Fortitude
Hit: 1d8 + Charisma modifier force damage, and the target is immobilized until the end of your next turn.
    Wild Magic: If you rolled an even number on the attack roll, you slide the target a number of squares equal to your Dexterity modifier.

LEVEL 5 DAILY SPELLS

Acidic Implantation
Sorcerer Attack 5

You implant a bubble of acid in a foe and hurl the foe into its allies. The bubble then explodes.

Daily ✦ Acid, Arcane, Implement
Standard Action   **Ranged** 10
Primary Target: One creature
Primary Attack: Charisma vs. Fortitude
Hit: You slide the primary target 3 squares.
Effect: The primary target takes 2d6 acid damage. Make a secondary attack that is an area burst 1 centered on the primary target.
    Secondary Target: Each creature in burst
    Secondary Attack: Charisma vs. Reflex
    Hit: 2d6 acid damage.

Palest Flames
Sorcerer Attack 5

The blue flames that engulf your foe make it more susceptible to the ravages of cold.

Daily ✦ Arcane, Fire, Implement
Standard Action   **Ranged** 10
Target: One creature
Attack: Charisma vs. Reflex
Hit: 1d10 + Charisma modifier fire damage, and the target gains vulnerable 10 cold (save ends).
Miss: Half damage, and the target gains vulnerable 5 cold until the end of your next turn.

Reeling Torment
Sorcerer Attack 5

Your hold on your enemy's mind lets you move your foe, tormented by spasms, around the battlefield.

Daily ✦ Arcane, Charm, Implement, Psychic
Standard Action   **Ranged** 10
Target: One creature
Attack: Charisma vs. Will
Hit: 3d8 + Charisma modifier psychic damage. At the start of each of the target's turns, you can slide the target 3 squares as a free action (save ends).
Miss: Half damage. At the start of each of the target's turns, you can slide the target 1 square as a free action (save ends).

Serpentine Blast
Sorcerer Attack 5

A bolt of lightning leaps from your fingers to strike at your foe, twisting past obstacles.

Daily ✦ Arcane, Implement, Lightning
Standard Action   **Ranged** 10
Target: One creature
Attack: Charisma vs. Reflex. The attack ignores cover and concealment, but not superior cover or total concealment.
Hit: 3d10 + Charisma modifier lightning damage.
Miss: Half damage.

Thunder Leap
Sorcerer Attack 5

A thunderclap propels you into the air, and you land with a deafening crack, pushing your foes away.

Daily ✦ Arcane, Implement, Thunder
Standard Action   **Close** burst 1
Primary Target: Each creature in burst
Primary Attack: Charisma vs. Fortitude
Hit: 2d6 + Charisma modifier thunder damage.
Effect: You jump a number of squares equal to your speed + your Charisma modifier. This movement does not provoke opportunity attacks. Then make a secondary attack.
Secondary Target: Each creature in burst
Secondary Attack: Charisma vs. Fortitude
Hit: 2d6 thunder damage, and you push the secondary target 1 square.

LEVEL 6 UTILITY SPELLS

Arcane Empowerment
Sorcerer Utility 6

You force additional energy into your spells.

Daily ✦ Arcane
Minor Action   **Personal**
Effect: Until the end of your turn, increase the size of your arcane powers' blasts and bursts by 1.

Energetic Flight
Sorcerer Utility 6

You hurtle forward on wings shaped from streamers of dancing energy.

Daily ✦ Arcane
Minor Action   **Personal**
Effect: Until the end of your next turn, you gain a fly speed equal to your speed, and you can hover.

Sudden Scales
Sorcerer Utility 6

Dragon scales cover your form in reaction to an assault, as arcane power shields your mind and body from harm.

Encounter ✦ Arcane
Immediate Interrupt   **Personal**
Trigger: You are hit by an attack
Effect: You gain a +4 bonus to all defenses against the triggering attack.
    Dragon Magic: The bonus to all defenses equals 3 + your Strength modifier.

Swift Escape
Sorcerer Utility 6

A quick reaction saves you from the explosion.

Encounter ✦ Arcane, Teleportation
Immediate Interrupt **Personal**
Trigger: You are hit by an area or a close attack
Effect: You teleport 3 squares.
   Wild Magic: The number of squares you teleport equals 2 + your Dexterity modifier.

LEVEL 7 ENCOUNTER SPELLS

Chaos Storm
Sorcerer Attack 7

A storm of lightning pounds your enemies. When the storm clears, everyone has teleported to new positions by your magic.

Encounter ✦ Arcane, Implement, Lightning, Teleportation
Standard Action **Area** burst 1 within 10 squares
Target: Each creature in burst
Attack: Charisma vs. Reflex
Hit: 2d6 + Charisma modifier lightning damage.
Effect: You teleport each target hit by the attack so that it swaps positions with another target hit by the attack.
   Wild Magic: You instead teleport each target hit by the attack to any other space within the burst.

Crushing Sphere
Sorcerer Attack 7

A field of force contracts around your enemies, crushing them.

Encounter ✦ Arcane, Force, Implement
Standard Action **Area** burst 1 within 10 squares
Target: Each creature in burst
Attack: Charisma vs. Reflex
Hit: 2d6 + Charisma modifier force damage, and the target takes a -2 penalty to attack rolls until the end of your next turn.

Rimestorm
Sorcerer Attack 7

A wintry blast drives your enemies to their knees.

Encounter ✦ Arcane, Cold, Implement
Standard Action **Close** blast 3
Target: Each enemy in blast
Attack: Charisma vs. Fortitude
Hit: 2d8 + Charisma modifier cold damage, and you knock the target prone.
   Dragon Magic: The target also takes a -2 penalty to Fortitude until the end of your next turn.

Shout
Sorcerer Attack 7

A deafening shout leaves your enemies reeling.

Encounter ✦ Arcane, Implement, Thunder
Standard Action **Close** blast 5
Target: Each creature in blast
Attack: Charisma vs. Fortitude
Hit: 2d8 + Charisma modifier thunder damage, and the target is deafened until the end of your next turn.

LEVEL 9 DAILY SPELLS

Adamantine Echo
Sorcerer Attack 9

You unleash a thunderous roar to batter your enemies, and scales like those of an adamantine dragon cover your skin.

Daily ✦ Arcane, Implement, Thunder
Standard Action **Close** blast 3
Target: Each creature in blast
Attack: Charisma vs. Fortitude
Hit: 2d6 + Charisma modifier thunder damage, and ongoing 5 thunder damage (save ends).
Miss: Ongoing 5 thunder damage (save ends).
Effect: You gain a +2 power bonus to AC until the end of the encounter.
   Dragon Magic: The power bonus to AC equals your Strength modifier.

Contagious Curse
Sorcerer Attack 9

A cloud of poison gas coils around your foe, warding off help.

Daily ✦ Arcane, Implement, Poison
Standard Action **Ranged** 10
Target: One creature
Attack: Charisma vs. Fortitude
Hit: 2d10 + Charisma modifier poison damage.
Effect: You slide the target a number of squares equal to your Charisma modifier. The target is poisonous to your enemies (save ends). While the target is poisonous, any enemy that starts its turn adjacent to the target takes 1d10 poison damage.
   Wild Magic: If you rolled an even number on the attack roll, any enemy that starts its turn within 2 squares of the poisonous target takes 1d10 poison damage.

Prime the Fire
Sorcerer Attack 9

Flames wash over your foe and then subside, but they flare to life again if the enemy acts in hostility.

Daily ✦ Arcane, Fire, Implement
Standard Action **Area** burst 1 within 10 squares
Target: Each creature in burst
Attack: Charisma vs. Fortitude
Hit: 2d8 + Charisma modifier fire damage.
Effect: If the target attacks before the start of your next turn, the target takes 2d8 fire damage.

Staggering Blast
Sorcerer Attack 9

Your mental assault leaves your foe reeling. With a thought, you can force the foe to the ground if it tries to move.

Daily ✦ Arcane, Implement, Psychic
Standard Action **Ranged** 10
Target: One creature
Attack: Charisma vs. Will
Hit: 3d8 + Charisma modifier psychic damage. If the target moves before the end of your next turn, you can knock the target prone during that movement as an immediate interrupt.
Miss: Half damage, and you knock the target prone.

LEVEL 10 UTILITY SPELLS

Chaos Link
Sorcerer Utility 10

You bend the fabric of reality to bind an enemy's fate to yours.

Daily ✦ Arcane
Immediate Reaction   **Close** burst 5
Trigger: You are hit by an area or a close attack
Target: One creature in burst
Effect: The triggering attack also hits the target.

Devour Magic
Sorcerer Utility 10

You consume lingering magic to empower your own.

Daily ✦ Arcane, Implement
Standard Action   **Ranged** 5
Target: One conjuration or zone
Attack: Charisma + 2 vs. the Will of the target's creator
Hit: The target is destroyed. All its effects end, including those that a save can end.
 Dragon Magic: You gain the bonus from your Scales of the Dragon, whether or not you're bloodied.
 Wild Magic: Until the end of the encounter, the first time you attack during each of your turns, you can choose your Chaos Burst benefit, instead of having your attack roll determine it.

Invert Resistance
Sorcerer Utility 10

You twist the nature of your foes to turn their protection into a weakness.

Daily ✦ Arcane
Minor Action   **Close** burst 5
Target: Each enemy in burst
Effect: Each target loses its resistances and gains vulnerable 5 to the damage types it had resistance against (save ends both).

Narrow Escape
Sorcerer Utility 10

You teleport away from your foe and reduce the force of its attack.

Encounter ✦ Arcane, Teleportation
Immediate Reaction   **Personal**
Trigger: You are hit by an attack
Effect: You take half damage from the attack. You then teleport a number of squares equal to your Charisma modifier + your Dexterity modifier.

LEVEL 13 ENCOUNTER SPELLS

Chains of Fire
Sorcerer Attack 13

Fiery serpents wrap around your foes and drag them together, holding them close.

Encounter ✦ Arcane, Fire, Implement
Standard Action   **Ranged** 10
Target: One or two creatures
Attack: Charisma vs. Reflex
Hit: 2d8 + Charisma modifier fire damage. If you hit two targets with this power, you slide one of them to a space that must be adjacent to the other, and until the end of your next turn, the two targets take 1d10 fire damage the first time they are more than 3 squares apart.

Jaws of the Earth
Sorcerer Attack 13

The earth rises up like the maw of a hungry dragon to clamp around your foe and hold it in place.

Encounter ✦ Arcane, Implement
Standard Action   **Ranged** 10
Target: One creature
Attack: Charisma vs. Reflex
Hit: 3d6 + Charisma modifier damage, and the target is immobilized until the end of your next turn. While the target is immobilized by this power, you and your allies can move through the target's space and don't provoke opportunity attacks from it by leaving a square adjacent to it.

Mind Hammer
Sorcerer Attack 13

Howling chaos slams into your foe's mind and throws the creature to the ground.

Encounter ✦ Arcane, Implement, Psychic
Standard Action   **Ranged** 10
Target: One creature
Attack: Charisma vs. Will
Hit: 2d10 + Charisma modifier psychic damage, and you knock the target prone.
 Wild Magic: If you rolled an even number on the attack roll, the target can't stand up until the end of your next turn. If you rolled an odd number on the attack roll, you slide the target a number of squares equal to your Dexterity modifier.

Thunder Breath
Sorcerer Attack 13

A blast of thunder like a dragon's roar issues from your mouth, staggering your foes.

Encounter ✦ Arcane, Implement, Thunder
Standard Action   **Close** blast 3
Target: Each creature in blast
Attack: Charisma vs. Fortitude
Hit: 2d6 + Charisma modifier thunder damage, and the target is dazed until the end of your next turn.
 Dragon Magic: The target is also slowed until the end of your next turn.

LEVEL 15 DAILY SPELLS

Frost Eddies
Sorcerer Attack 15

Cold slams into your foe, leaving a whirling storm of frost lingering around it.

Daily ✦ Arcane, Cold, Implement
Standard Action   **Ranged** 10
Target: One creature
Attack: Charisma vs. Fortitude
Hit: 5d8 + Charisma modifier cold damage.
Effect: Until the end of the encounter, wherever the target moves, each square adjacent to it is difficult terrain for your enemies.

Hostility Charm
Sorcerer Attack 15

You cloud your foe's senses so that it questions which creatures are its allies.

Daily ✦ Arcane, Charm, Psychic, Implement
Standard Action   **Ranged** 10
Target: One creature
Attack: Charisma vs. Will
Hit: 5d6 + Charisma modifier psychic damage, and as a free action, the target charges your enemy nearest to it that it can charge and makes a melee basic attack.
  Wild Magic: If you rolled an even number on the attack roll, your enemies can provoke opportunity attacks from the target, and the target must make any opportunity attack that they provoke (save ends).
Miss: Half damage.

Scintillating Starburst
Sorcerer Attack 15

A brilliant mote of magic streaks toward your foe and explodes.

Daily ✦ Arcane, Implement, Radiant
Standard Action   **Ranged** 20
Target: One creature
Attack: Charisma vs. Reflex
Hit: 4d6 + Charisma modifier radiant damage, and the target is blinded (save ends).
Miss: Half damage.

Spitfire Furnace
Sorcerer Attack 15

After unleashing a blast of flames, you smolder with heat, and no one dares approach you.

Daily ✦ Arcane, Fire, Implement
Standard Action   **Close** blast 3
Target: Each creature in blast
Attack: Charisma vs. Reflex
Hit: 4d10 + Charisma modifier fire damage.
Effect: Until the end of the encounter, any enemy that starts its turn within 2 squares of you takes 3 fire damage.
  Dragon Magic: Until the end of the encounter, any enemy that starts its turn within 2 squares of you instead takes fire damage equal to 2 + your Strength modifier.

LEVEL 16 UTILITY SPELLS

Breath of the Desert Dragon
Sorcerer Utility 16

A gust of warm air lifts creatures skyward.

Encounter ✦ Arcane
Move Action   **Area** burst 3 within 10 squares
Target: Each creature in burst
Effect: Each target can fly a number of squares equal to 6 + your Strength modifier as an immediate reaction. Until the end of your next turn, each target can fly the same distance as a move action.

Chaos Echoes
Sorcerer Utility 16

You warp the natural laws of cause and effect to make an enemy feel the effects of an attack against you.

Daily ✦ Arcane
Immediate Reaction   **Close** burst 5
Trigger: You are hit or missed by an attack
Target: One enemy in burst
Effect: The triggering attack hits the target.

Chaos Sanctuary
Sorcerer Utility 16

You create small pockets of chaos to warp the energy of your next spell around your allies.

Encounter ✦ Arcane
Minor Action   **Close** burst 10
Effect: Choose a number of squares in the burst equal to your Dexterity modifier. Until the end of your turn, any creature whose space is entirely in those squares is not affected by your area or close arcane powers.

Comrades' Mantle
Sorcerer Utility 16

You share your resistance with your allies.

Daily ✦ Arcane
Minor Action   **Close** burst 5
Target: You and each ally in burst
Effect: Choose a damage type: acid, cold, fire, force, lightning, necrotic, poison, psychic, radiant, or thunder. Each target gains resist 5 to that damage type until the end of the encounter.

Draconic Majesty
Sorcerer Utility 16

As your foes draw near you, fear steals into their hearts.

Encounter ✦ Arcane, Fear, Zone
Minor Action   **Close** burst 3
Effect: The burst creates a zone of fear that lasts until the end of your next turn. When you move, the zone moves with you, remaining centered on you. The zone is difficult terrain for your enemies. While within the zone, any enemy takes a penalty to attack rolls equal to your Strength modifier.

LEVEL 17 ENCOUNTER SPELLS

Breath of Winter
Sorcerer Attack 17

You exhale a blast of freezing wind to slow your enemies' movement.

Encounter ✦ Arcane, Cold, Implement
Standard Action   **Close** blast 3
Target: Each creature in blast
Attack: Charisma vs. Fortitude
Hit: 2d8 + Charisma modifier cold damage, and the target is slowed until the end of its next turn.

Dragon Tail Meditation
Sorcerer Attack 17

A lashing tail of lightning protects you from a foe that thinks it has the advantage.

Encounter ✦ Arcane, Implement, Lightning
Immediate Reaction   **Melee** 1
Trigger: An enemy moves into a space where it flanks you
Target: The triggering creature
Attack: Charisma vs. Reflex
Hit: 2d10 + Charisma modifier lightning damage.
  Dragon Magic: You push the target a number of squares equal to your Strength modifier.

Poisonous Evasion — Sorcerer Attack 17

You disappear as your enemy misses, leaving a cloud of poison behind.

Encounter ✦ Arcane, Implement, Poison, Teleportation
Immediate Reaction   Close burst 1
Trigger: An enemy misses you with an attack
Target: Each creature in burst
Attack: Charisma vs. Fortitude
Hit: 3d10 + Charisma modifier poison damage.
Effect: You teleport 10 squares.

Thunder Summons — Sorcerer Attack 17

Thunderous crashes hurl your enemies around in a storm of chaos.

Encounter ✦ Arcane, Implement, Teleportation, Thunder
Standard Action   Ranged 10
Target: One, two, or three creatures
Attack: Charisma vs. Will
Hit: 3d8 + Charisma modifier thunder damage, and you teleport the target to a space adjacent to your enemy that is nearest to it.
Wild Magic: If you rolled an even number on the attack roll, you can teleport the target to a space adjacent to your ally, not your enemy, who is nearest to it.

LEVEL 19 DAILY SPELLS

Baleful Gaze of the Basilisk — Sorcerer Attack 19

You cast a toxic glance at your foe, leaving it paralyzed with fear.

Daily ✦ Arcane, Fear, Implement, Poison
Standard Action   Ranged 10
Target: One creature
Attack: Charisma vs. Fortitude
Hit: The target is stunned and takes ongoing 10 poison damage (save ends both).
Miss: Ongoing 10 poison damage (save ends).
Dragon Magic: When the target saves against the ongoing poison damage, you slide the target a number of squares equal to your Strength modifier.

Blackfire Serpent — Sorcerer Attack 19

A coiled serpent made of black flames appears among your enemies and unleashes a blast of fire.

Daily ✦ Arcane, Conjuration, Fire, Implement
Standard Action   Ranged 10
Effect: You conjure a blackfire serpent in an unoccupied square within range. The serpent lasts until the end of your next turn. The serpent occupies 1 square. Enemies cannot move through its space, but allies can.
  When it appears, the serpent makes the following attack, which is a close blast 3. As a move action, you can move the serpent a number of squares equal to your Strength modifier.
Target: Each creature in blast
Attack: Charisma vs. Reflex
Hit: 2d12 + Charisma modifier fire damage.
Sustain Minor: The snake persists, and it can repeat the attack.

Prismatic Explosion — Sorcerer Attack 19

You batter a group of enemies with dazzling colors, each color causing a different effect.

Daily ✦ Arcane, Implement; Varies
Standard Action   Area burst 1 within 10 squares
Target: Each creature in burst
Attack: Charisma vs. Reflex
Hit: 3d12 + Charisma modifier damage. Roll a d6 for each target to determine the attack's damage type and effect.
  1. Yellow: Radiant damage, and the target is blinded (save ends).
  2. Red: Fire damage, and the target is knocked prone and takes ongoing 10 fire damage (save ends).
  3. Green: Poison damage, and the target takes ongoing 15 poison damage (save ends).
  4. Turquoise: Lightning damage, and you knock the target prone and slide it a number of squares equal to your Dexterity modifier.
  5. Blue: Cold damage, and the target is stunned (save ends).
  6. Violet: Psychic damage, and the target takes a penalty to AC equal to your Dexterity modifier (save ends).
Miss: 2d12 damage. Roll a d6 for each target to determine the attack's damage type and effect, as above.

Split Strike — Sorcerer Attack 19

A bolt of lightning leaps from each of your hands.

Daily ✦ Arcane, Implement, Lightning
Standard Action   Ranged 10
Target: One or two creatures
Attack: Charisma vs. Reflex
Hit: 6d6 + Charisma modifier lightning damage.
  Wild Magic: If you rolled an even number on the attack roll, the target is immobilized (save ends). If you rolled an odd number on the attack roll, the target is dazed (save ends).
Miss: Half damage.

LEVEL 22 UTILITY SPELLS

Dragon Fear — Sorcerer Utility 22

You stop your enemy in its tracks.

Encounter ✦ Arcane, Fear
Immediate Interrupt   Ranged 5
Trigger: A creature moves closer to you during its turn
Target: The triggering creature
Effect: The target can't move closer to you until the end of its turn.

Platinum Scales — Sorcerer Utility 22

You gleam with platinum-tinted dragon scales of energy.

Daily ✦ Arcane
Immediate Interrupt   Personal
Trigger: You are hit by an attack
Effect: Until the end of the encounter, you gain a power bonus to all defenses equal to your Strength modifier.

Shared Sorcery
Sorcerer Utility 22

A shimmering emanation of sorcerous energy protects your friends from harm.

Daily ✦ Arcane
Minor Action　　Close burst 5
Target: You and each ally in burst
Effect: Choose a damage type: acid, cold, fire, force, lightning, necrotic, poison, psychic, radiant, or thunder. Each target gains resist 10 to that damage type until the end of the encounter.

Wind Shape
Sorcerer Utility 22

You become a creature of air and rushing wind.

Encounter ✦ Arcane, Polymorph
Minor Action　　Personal
Effect: Until the end of your next turn, you become insubstantial, you gain a fly speed equal to your speed, and you can hover.

LEVEL 23 ENCOUNTER SPELLS

Black Breath
Sorcerer Attack 23

You exhale a blast of acid, drawing on the power of the fearsome black dragon to sear your enemy and limit its vision.

Encounter ✦ Acid, Arcane, Implement
Standard Action　　Close blast 3
Target: Each creature in blast
Attack: Charisma vs. Reflex
Hit: 5d6 + Charisma modifier acid damage.
　Dragon Magic: Until the end of your next turn, the target doesn't have line of sight to any creature more than 3 squares away from it.

Chaos Orbs
Sorcerer Attack 23

You hurl two orbs of chaos at your foes.

Encounter ✦ Arcane, Implement, Psychic
Standard Action　　Ranged 10
Target: One or two creatures
Attack: Charisma vs. Will
Hit: 3d8 + Charisma modifier psychic damage, and the target is dazed until the end of your next turn.

Iron Chains
Sorcerer Attack 23

Smoking chains of black iron appear and wrap around your target, then snake outward to bind all nearby creatures.

Encounter ✦ Arcane, Implement
Standard Action　　Ranged 10
Target: One creature
Attack: Charisma vs. Fortitude
Hit: 2d6 + Charisma modifier damage, and the target and each creature adjacent to it are restrained until the end of your next turn.

Plates of Ice
Sorcerer Attack 23

Icy plates form over your enemy's body, draining its strength.

Encounter ✦ Arcane, Cold, Implement
Standard Action　　Ranged 20
Target: One creature
Attack: Charisma vs. Fortitude
Hit: 4d6 + Charisma modifier cold damage, and the target is weakened until the end of your next turn.
　Wild Magic: If you rolled an even number on the attack roll, each creature adjacent to the target takes 1d6 cold damage.

LEVEL 25 DAILY SPELLS

Draconic Incarnation
Sorcerer Attack 25

Calling on the full power of the arcane forces that flow through you, you stand within a vortex of devastating energy.

Daily ✦ Arcane, Implement; Varies
Standard Action　　Close blast 5
Target: Each creature in blast
Attack: Charisma vs. Reflex
Hit: 7d6 + Charisma modifier damage. Choose a damage type: acid, cold, fire, lightning, poison, or thunder. The attack deals damage of this type to each target.
Miss: Half damage.
Dragon Magic: Until the end of the encounter, once during each of your turns, you can slide one enemy within 3 squares of you 2 squares as a free action.

Force Storm
Sorcerer Attack 25

Bolts of force swirl in the area like a deadly tornado, stealing energy from each enemy to empower themselves.

Daily ✦ Arcane, Force, Implement
Standard Action　　Area burst 2 within 20 squares
Target: Each creature in burst
Attack: Charisma vs. Reflex
Hit: 3d6 + Charisma modifier force damage. The attack deals 5 extra force damage for each target it hits.
Miss: Half damage.

Words of Chaos
Sorcerer Attack 25

A wave of chaos assaults your enemy's mind. When the enemy attacks, you bend reality to redirect the attack.

Daily ✦ Arcane, Charm, Implement, Psychic
Standard Action　　Ranged 10
Target: One creature
Primary Attack: Charisma vs. Will
Hit: 4d12 + Charisma modifier psychic damage.
Effect: When the target makes an attack roll for a melee or a ranged attack, you can make a secondary attack against the target if it is within 10 squares of you (save ends).
　Immediate Interrupt　　Close burst 10
　Secondary Attack: Charisma vs. Will
　Hit: The target must choose a different creature to target with its attack if it can. Otherwise, its attack is unaffected by this secondary attack.
　Wild Magic: If you rolled an even number on the secondary attack roll, you choose the creature that the target attacks.

LEVEL 27 ENCOUNTER SPELLS

Lightning Eruption
Sorcerer Attack 27

Lightning crackles over your victim and arcs into nearby enemies.

Encounter ✦ Arcane, Implement, Lightning
Standard Action   Ranged 10
Target: One creature
Attack: Charisma vs. Reflex
Hit: 3d12 + Charisma modifier lightning damage, and each enemy adjacent to the target takes 1d12 + your Charisma modifier lightning damage.

Poison Ward
Sorcerer Attack 27

You lance a foe with poison, which coils in the foe's heart to punish any aggression against you.

Encounter ✦ Arcane, Implement, Poison
Standard Action   Ranged 10
Target: One creature
Attack: Charisma vs. Fortitude
Hit: 4d10 + Charisma modifier poison damage. If the target moves closer to you or hits or misses you during its next turn, the target takes 2d10 poison damage.

Thunder Pulse
Sorcerer Attack 27

You stomp a foot on the ground, and the resulting shock wave hurls your enemies away.

Encounter ✦ Arcane, Implement, Thunder
Standard Action   Close burst 3
Target: Each enemy in burst
Attack: Charisma vs. Fortitude
Hit: 3d6 + Charisma modifier thunder damage, and you push the target a number of squares equal to your Charisma modifier and knock it prone.

Wildfire Curse
Sorcerer Attack 27

As your foe bursts into flame, a fiery mote flies at another foe nearby.

Encounter ✦ Arcane, Fire, Implement
Standard Action   Ranged 10
Primary Target: One creature
Primary Attack: Charisma vs. Reflex
Hit: 4d6 + Charisma modifier fire damage. Make a secondary attack.
Secondary Target: One creature within 5 squares of the target last hit by this power
Secondary Attack: Charisma vs. Reflex
Hit: 4d6 + Charisma modifier fire damage. Repeat the secondary attack against a creature you haven't already targeted with this power during this encounter.

LEVEL 29 DAILY SPELLS

Endless Acid
Sorcerer Attack 29

Acid bubbles up from inside your foe, searing its flesh and resisting attempts to scrape it off.

Daily ✦ Acid, Arcane, Implement
Standard Action   Ranged 10
Target: One creature
Attack: Charisma vs. Fortitude
Hit: 1d6 + Charisma modifier acid damage, and ongoing 15 acid damage (save ends).
  Aftereffect: Ongoing 10 acid damage (save ends).
  Aftereffect: Ongoing 5 acid damage (save ends).
Miss: Ongoing 15 acid damage (save ends).

Entropic Whirlwind
Sorcerer Attack 29

Chaos swirls around you, opening and sealing holes in the fabric of reality to move your foes and allies as you wish.

Daily ✦ Arcane, Implement, Teleportation
Standard Action   Close burst 5
Target: Each enemy in burst
Attack: Charisma vs. Will
Hit: 3d8 + Charisma modifier damage, and you teleport the target a number of squares equal to your Dexterity modifier. The target again takes 3d8 + your Charisma modifier damage whenever it teleports (save ends).
Effect: Until the end of the encounter, when any creature ends its turn within 5 squares of you, you can teleport the creature to any space within 5 squares of you as an immediate reaction.

Prismatic Storm
Sorcerer Attack 29

The sky rains down a rainbow of destruction.

Daily ✦ Arcane, Implement; Varies
Standard Action   Area burst 3 within 20 squares
Target: Each creature in burst
Attack: Charisma vs. Reflex
Hit: 5d8 + Charisma modifier damage. Roll a d6 for each target to determine the attack's damage type and effect.
  1. Yellow: Radiant damage, and the target is blinded and takes a –2 penalty to saving throws (save ends both).
  2. Red: Fire damage, and the target is knocked prone and takes ongoing 15 fire damage (save ends).
  3. Green: Poison damage, and the target takes ongoing 20 poison damage (save ends).
  4. Turquoise: Lightning damage, and you knock the target prone and slide it a number of squares equal to your Dexterity modifier. In addition, the target is dazed (saved ends).
  5. Blue: Cold damage, and the target is stunned (save ends).
  6. Violet: Psychic damage, and the target takes a penalty to AC and Reflex equal to your Dexterity modifier (save ends).
Miss: 3d8 damage. Roll a d6 for each target to determine the attack's damage type and effect, as above.

PARAGON PATHS

ARCANE WELLSPRING

"I don't care why it works. I just know it does."

Prerequisite: Sorcerer

Arcane power flows in all sorcerers, an innate part of them. For you, however, that power is like a geyser building up beneath the earth before it finally erupts with devastating and glorious force. Your connection to that power has always been easy, almost instinctual. It's so much a part of you that it slowly transforms you, making you into a being as much of the forces you channel as of flesh and soul.

As you walk the path of the arcane wellspring, you master a second damage type. You learn spells that channel both damage types or that surround you with swirling arcane energy. Ultimately, you gain the ability to transform yourself into arcane energy for a brief time.

ARCANE WELLSPRING PATH FEATURES

Double Resistance (11th level): If you have Dragon Magic, choose a second damage type for your Dragon Soul class feature. If you have Wild Magic, roll twice on the Wild Soul table after each extended rest. (If you get the same result a second time, roll

again.) Whichever of these two Spell Source options you have, you gain resistance to both damage types, and your arcane powers ignore any target's resistance to both types up to the value of your resistance.

Split Spell Action (11th level): You can spend an action point to target an additional creature when you use an arcane power that normally targets only one, instead of taking an extra action.

Antagonistic Transposition (16th level): When you use an arcane power that is an area or a close attack, you can teleport two creatures hit by the attack, swapping their positions before resolving the attack.

ARCANE WELLSPRING SPELLS

Twin Bolt	Arcane Wellspring Attack 11

Summoning internal reserves, you hurl a bolt of magic that reflects the two forces that infuse you.

Encounter ✦ Arcane, Implement; Varies
Standard Action Ranged 10
Target: One creature
Attack: Charisma vs. Reflex
Hit: 3d10 + Charisma modifier damage. The damage is the two types you resist with your Dragon Soul or Wild Soul class feature and with your Double Resistance path feature.
Special: You can choose to lose both of the resistances provided by your Dragon Soul or Wild Soul class feature and by your Double Resistance path feature for the rest of the encounter. If you do so, you can make two attacks with this power, each against a different target. Each target the attack hits takes 3d12 + your Charisma modifier damage, instead of 3d10 + your Charisma modifier.

Sorcerous Wings	Arcane Wellspring Utility 12

Arcane power surrounds you and spreads out behind you to form wings.

Encounter ✦ Arcane; Varies
Minor Action Personal
Effect: Until the end of your next turn, you gain a fly speed of 6, and you can hover, and whenever an enemy makes an opportunity attack against you, that enemy takes 2d10 + your Charisma modifier damage. The damage is the two types you resist with your Dragon Soul or Wild Soul class feature and with your Double Resistance path feature.

Sorcerous Metamorphosis	Arcane Wellspring Attack 20

Your body becomes the energy that courses through you.

Daily ✦ Arcane, Implement; Varies
Standard Action Personal
Effect: Until the end of your next turn, you become insubstantial, and you gain phasing. In addition, when any creature makes a melee attack against you or when you first enter a creature's space on your turn, the creature takes 3d6 + your Charisma modifier damage. The damage is the two types you resist with your Dragon Soul or Wild Soul class feature and with your Double Resistance path feature.

DEMONSKIN ADEPT

"You see for yourself what becomes of my enemies."

Prerequisite: Sorcerer

Arcane magic is a form of power wielded for purposes both benevolent and malevolent. There is nothing inherently good or evil about it. Its moral value depends on the purpose to which it is put. At least, that is usually the case.

As a demonskin adept, you wield arcane power ripped from the depths of the Abyss, the home of demons. You incorporate the ritually treated skins of demons into your clothes and armor, and you use those skins to open conduits through which your spells are warped by the Abyss's unutterable evil. Perhaps you believe that good ends justify evil means, but how long can you maintain your desire for good when you allow such evil to touch your soul?

The power you wield is stolen, and the lords of the Abyss do not take kindly to being robbed. Although this path brings great power, it is power that comes at a sometimes terrible price. Count yourself lucky if the worst price you pay is your life.

DEMONSKIN ADEPT PATH FEATURES

Demon Fury (11th level): When you spend an action point to take an extra action, you and your allies gain a +3 bonus to attack rolls until the start of your next turn, and your enemies gain a +3 bonus to their attack rolls against you until the start of your next turn.

Variable Resistance (11th level): Once per encounter as a minor action, you can change the damage type that you resist through your Dragon Soul or Wild Soul class feature. Choose the new damage type from those available in the class feature.

Glimpse of the Abyss (16th level): When you score a critical hit, you and the target are blinded until the start of your next turn.

DEMONSKIN ADEPT SPELLS

Demon-Soul Bolts — Demonskin Adept Attack 11

You unleash a volley of howling, demonic souls torn from the Abyss to batter your foes.

Encounter ✦ Arcane, Implement, Thunder
Standard Action   **Ranged 10**
Target: One creature
Attack: Charisma vs. Fortitude
Hit: 1d8 + Charisma modifier thunder damage, and you slide the target 1 square.
Effect: Make the attack two more times against the same target or different ones.

Demonic Wrath — Demonskin Adept Utility 12

Like a howling demon, you channel your pain into greater power for your spells.

Daily ✦ Arcane
Minor Action   **Personal**
Requirement: You must be bloodied.
Effect: Until the end of the encounter, while you're bloodied, your arcane attacks deal 1d6 extra damage on a hit.

Swords of the Marilith — Demonskin Adept Attack 20

With a gesture, you fill the air about you with a marilith's slashing swords.

Daily ✦ Arcane, Implement, Zone
Standard Action   **Close burst 3**
Target: Each enemy in burst
Attack: Charisma vs. Reflex
Hit: 3d6 + Charisma modifier damage
Effect: The burst creates a zone of whirling blades that lasts until the end of your next turn. When the zone appears, choose its effect:
  ✦ Any enemy takes 3d6 + your Charisma modifier damage if it starts its turn within the zone.
  ✦ Any enemy takes 1d6 + your Charisma modifier damage if it starts its turn within the zone. While within the zone, you and your allies gain a +4 power bonus to AC.
Sustain Minor: The zone persists, and you can change its effect.

DRAGONSOUL HEIR

"That's no dragon—it's a slug, content to sleep on a pile of coins. See my power, the same power wielded by the dragon lords of ancient Arkhosia: I, my friend, am truly a dragon."

Prerequisite: Sorcerer, Dragon Magic class feature

In the early years of the world, the mightiest sorcerers were dragons, powerful spellcasters who used the elemental magic churning in their blood to create devastating spells that cemented their hold over vast empires. Even as recently as the dragonborn empire of Arkhosia, dragons were the exemplars of the draconic sorcerer's path. In the present age, however, few dragons practice the art that their ancestors created.

Your path follows in the ancient footsteps of the greatest sorcerers the world has ever known, drawing on the traditions preserved from Arkhosia's dragon lords and the sorcerers before them, back almost to the beginning of the world. Wielding the same power as the dragons of old, you inure yourself to the dangers of battle, making your mere presence a threat to your foes as you wreathe yourself in flames or lightning, acid or poison, cold or thunder, according to the nature of the draconic magic in your blood.

The dragons of old are alive in your soul, and their power is yours to command.

DRAGONSOUL HEIR PATH FEATURES

Draconic Durability (11th level): Your number of healing surges per day increases by two.

Draconic Resilience Action (11th level): When you spend an action point to take an extra action, you also gain a number of temporary hit points equal to one-half your level.

Dragon Soul Resistance (16th level): The resistance provided by your Dragon Soul class feature increases by 10.

DRAGONSOUL HEIR SPELLS

Breath of the Dragon Soul	Dragonsoul Heir Attack 11

You exhale a mighty blast of elemental essence.

Encounter ✦ Arcane, Implement; Varies
Standard Action   Close blast 5
Target: Each creature in blast
Attack: Charisma vs. Reflex
Hit: 2d8 + Charisma modifier damage. The damage is the type you resist with your Dragon Soul class feature.

Dragon's Revenge	Dragonsoul Heir Utility 12

Elemental power surrounds you and lashes out at those who attack you.

Daily ✦ Arcane; Varies
Minor Action   **Personal**
Effect: Until the end of the encounter, when any enemy hits or misses you with an attack against AC, that enemy takes 1d10 + your Strength modifier damage. The damage is the type you resist with your Dragon Soul class feature.

Veil of the Dragon	Dragonsoul Heir Attack 20

Elemental forces in the form of a dragon hover around you as you slash your foes with claws of magic.

Daily ✦ Arcane, Implement; Varies
Standard Action   Close burst 3
Target: Each enemy in burst
Attack: Charisma vs. Reflex
Hit: 6d6 + Charisma modifier damage.
Effect: Until the end of your next turn, any creature that makes a melee attack against you takes 2d6 + your Charisma modifier damage. In addition, you can make the following attack, which can be used as a melee basic attack.
   Standard Action   Melee 1
   Target: One creature
   Attack: Charisma vs. Reflex
   Hit: 4d6 + Charisma modifier damage.
Sustain Minor: The effect persists.
Special: The damage dealt by this power is the type you resist with your Dragon Soul class feature.

WILD MAGE

"If you can control your power, you don't have enough."

Prerequisite: Sorcerer, Wild Magic class feature

The entropy of the Elemental Chaos flows in your veins. Your spells open arcane conduits to that plane and draw energy through–whatever energy is convenient, impelled and empowered by the force of chaos itself. Your spells might be unpredictable, but their randomness gives them power.

WILD MAGE PATH FEATURES

Chaos Action (11th level): When you spend an action point to take an extra action, you can roll a d6 to also gain one of the benefits below.

d6	Chaos Action Effect
1	You become invisible until the start of your next turn.
2	You teleport a number of squares equal to 5 + your Dexterity modifier.
3	You gain temporary hit points equal to one-half your level.
4	Until the end of the encounter, each ally within 5 squares of you gains resist 10 to the damage type you resist with your Wild Soul.
5	You teleport an ally and an enemy within 10 squares of you, swapping their positions.
6	You and each ally within 5 squares of you each make a saving throw.

Wild Surge (11th level): When you roll a natural 1 on an attack roll for an arcane power, you can take the miss result and your Unfettered Power class feature, or you can roll a d6 to substitute one of the results below.

d6	Wild Surge Effect
1	The attack misses, and you and the target teleport, swapping positions after you resolve the rest of the attack.
2	The attack misses, and you drop prone and slide 3 squares away from the target.
3	The attack misses, and both you and the target are dazed (save ends).
4	Reroll the attack roll. If you roll a natural 1 again, you take 2d10 + your Charisma modifier damage, and you can't use Wild Surge again during this encounter.
5	The attack hits instead of misses, and you are stunned until the end of your next turn.
6	The attack hits instead of misses.

Critical Surge (16th level): When you score a critical hit, it deals 1d10 extra damage.

WILD MAGE SPELLS

Tempest Surge — Wild Mage Attack 11

Raw energy erupts from your outstretched palm, then curls into a whirling tempest.

Encounter ✦ Arcane, Implement
Standard Action Area burst 1d4 within 20 squares
Special: Pick the burst's origin square before rolling to determine the burst's size.
Target: Each creature in burst. Roll a d4, and you can exclude a number of targets equal to the result.
Attack: Charisma vs. Reflex
Hit: 3d8 + Charisma modifier damage.

Torrent of Power — Wild Mage Utility 12

You open a conduit to the Elemental Chaos. Its surging energy erupts uncontrollably.

Daily ✦ Arcane
Minor Action Personal
Effect: Until the end of the encounter, whenever you roll the highest number on any damage die, roll that die again and add its result to the damage total.

Prismatic Bolt — Wild Mage Attack 20

A beam of colorful light leaps from your hand to cause a debilitating effect.

Daily ✦ Arcane, Implement; Varies
Standard Action Ranged 10
Target: One creature
Attack: Charisma vs. Reflex
Hit: 5d8 + Charisma modifier damage. Roll a d6 to determine the attack's damage type and effect.
 1. **Yellow:** Radiant damage, and your ally nearest to the target can spend a healing surge.
 2. **Black:** Necrotic damage, and the target is weakened (save ends).
 3. **Green:** Poison damage, and the target takes ongoing 15 poison damage (save ends).
 4. **White:** Force damage, and the target is restrained (save ends).
 5. **Blue:** Cold damage, and the target is stunned (save ends).
 6. **Violet:** Psychic damage, and the target is dominated (save ends).
Miss: 3d8 damage. Roll a d6 to determine the attack's damage type and effect, as above.

WARDEN

"Get past me? You might as well try to push the mountains aside."

CLASS TRAITS

Role: Defender. You are sturdy and resilient, and you can assume bestial or treelike forms to destroy your foes. Depending on your choice of class features and powers, you lean toward either controller or striker as a secondary role.

Power Source: Primal. You are a primal champion, a guardian of the natural world and custodian of all living things.

Key Abilities: Strength, Constitution, Wisdom

Armor Proficiencies: Cloth, leather, hide; light shield, heavy shield

Weapon Proficiencies: Simple melee, military melee, simple ranged

Bonus to Defense: +1 Fortitude, +1 Will

Hit Points at 1st Level: 17 + Constitution score

Hit Points per Level Gained: 7

Healing Surges per Day: 9 + Constitution modifier

Trained Skills: Nature. From the class skills list below, choose three more trained skills at 1st level.
Class Skills: Athletics (Str), Dungeoneering (Wis), Endurance (Con), Heal (Wis), Intimidate (Cha), Nature (Wis), Perception (Wis)

Class Features: Font of Life, Guardian Might, Nature's Wrath

As mountains stand fast against the buffeting wind and trees bend but do not break in the storm, wardens are stalwart protectors who draw on the primal spirits of nature to defend the natural world from those who would corrupt or destroy it. Some wardens use the power of earth and stone to shield their allies from harm, whereas others summon the primal strength within themselves to increase their ferocity and tenacity.

As a warden, you might be the staunch defender of a tribe, chosen by the spirits to be your people's champion. Perhaps you were visited by spirits at a sacred grove and charged with protecting it against a spreading corruption. You might have been raised by a bear or nurtured by dryads, chosen from infancy to stand fast against nature's enemies.

Primal power waits in the ground beneath your feet, surges with every beat of your heart, and flows through your lungs with every breath. The world cries out to you, calling for a champion to defend it. Will you heed its call?

WARDEN CLASS FEATURES

Wardens have the following class features.

FONT OF LIFE

At the start of your turn, you can make a saving throw against one effect that a save can end. On a save, the effect immediately ends, preventing it from affecting you on your current turn. If you save against being stunned or dazed, you can act normally on your turn. If you save against ongoing damage, you avoid taking the damage.

If you fail the saving throw, you still make a saving throw against the effect at the end of your turn.

GUARDIAN MIGHT

Wardens connect with the natural world in a variety of ways to augment their fighting abilities. Choose one of the following options.

Earthstrength: While you are not wearing heavy armor, you can use your Constitution modifier in place of your Dexterity or Intelligence modifier to determine your AC.

In addition, when you use your second wind, you gain an additional bonus to AC equal to your Constitution modifier. The bonus lasts until the end of your next turn.

Wildblood: While you are not wearing heavy armor, you can use your Wisdom modifier in place of your Dexterity or Intelligence modifier to determine your AC.

In addition, when you use your second wind, each enemy marked by you takes an additional penalty to attack rolls for attacks that don't include you as a target. The penalty equals your Wisdom modifier and lasts until the end of your next turn.

NATURE'S WRATH

Once during each of your turns, you can mark each adjacent enemy as a free action. This mark lasts until the end of your next turn.

GUARDIAN FORM POWERS

Many of your daily powers are polymorph powers, which change your body into a guardian form, allowing you to take on the qualities of a beast spirit or a tree spirit. You remain in this form until the end of the encounter or until you choose to assume a new form. While you are in this form, you retain the ability to use your equipment and other powers.

In addition to a physical transformation, each guardian form power also grants you an attack you can make as a separate action (the action type is specified in the power description). You can use this attack once during the same encounter in which you use the guardian form power and only while you remain in that guardian form.

In addition, you gain the *warden's fury* and *warden's grasp* powers. You can use these powers against enemies to prevent them from harming those you protect.

CREATING A WARDEN

You can choose any warden powers you like for your character, though many wardens focus on powers that complement their choice of Guardian Might. All wardens rely on Strength. Wardens also benefit from a high Constitution or Wisdom, depending on which expression of warden they favor.

EARTH WARDEN

You draw primal power through a link with the land, and the power of the earth strengthens and sustains you. Make Strength your highest ability score, followed by Constitution, which increases your AC as well as your hit points if you choose the Earthstrength version of Guardian Might. Select powers that channel primal energy through the land around you, hindering your foes' movement or knocking them prone. You lean toward controller as a secondary role.

Suggested Class Feature: Earthstrength
Suggested Feat: Crushing Earthstrength
Suggested Skills: Athletics, Heal, Nature, Perception
Suggested At-Will Powers: *earth shield strike, strength of stone*
Suggested Encounter Power: *thunder ram assault*
Suggested Daily Power: *form of the willow sentinel*

WARDEN OVERVIEW

Characteristics: Boasting more hit points than most other characters of your level, you sometimes stand up to your foes by staunchly taking whatever punishment they throw at you. Thanks to the primal power coursing through you, you can throw it right back at them, manipulating the earth around you or altering your own form to hinder and punish your foes.

Religion: Like other primal classes, wardens generally disdain worship of the gods, which they view as interlopers in the natural world. Instead, they live in harmony with the spirits of beasts, trees, and stone that infuse the world. Some wardens, though, acknowledge some gods as peaceful partners of the primal spirits and look kindly upon such deities as Melora, Corellon, Kord, Moradin, and Pelor.

Races: Goliaths make ideal earth wardens, combining natural strength and endurance with a love of earth and stone. Longtooth shifters embody the ideals of the wild warden, channeling the beast within as a manifestation of the primal spirits. Humans, dwarves, dragonborn, and half-orcs are also commonly wardens.

WILD WARDEN

Your blood is a medium of primal power; nature's vigor pulses in your veins. Strength should be your highest ability score, followed by Wisdom, which increases your Armor Class if you choose the Wild-blood version of Guardian Might. Select powers that awaken the primal power within you, turning you into a vicious predator. You lean toward striker as a secondary role.

Suggested Class Feature: Wildblood

Suggested Feat: Wildblood Cunning

Suggested Skills: Athletics, Intimidate, Nature, Perception

Suggested At-Will Powers: *thorn strike, weight of earth*

Suggested Encounter Power: *wildblood frenzy*

Suggested Daily Power: *form of the relentless panther*

WARDEN POWERS

Your powers, called evocations, channel primal energy through your body. Some draw their strength from the earth, others call on primal beast spirits, and still others evoke the spirits of trees and other plants.

CLASS FEATURES

Each warden has the powers *warden's fury* and *warden's grasp*.

Warden's Fury	Warden Feature

You lash out with nature's wrath at a foe that has attacked your ally and diminish its defenses.

At-Will ✦ Primal, Weapon
Immediate Interrupt   Melee weapon
Trigger: An enemy marked by you makes an attack that does not include you as a target
Target: The triggering enemy
Attack: Strength vs. Fortitude
Hit: 1[W] + Strength modifier damage, and the target grants combat advantage to you and your allies until the end of your next turn.
  Level 21: 2[W] + Strength modifier damage.

Warden's Grasp	Warden Feature

Spectral vines clutch at a foe that has attacked your ally, impeding your enemy's movement.

At-Will ✦ Primal
Immediate Reaction   Close burst 5
Trigger: An enemy marked by you that is within 5 squares of you makes an attack that does not include you as a target
Target: The triggering enemy in burst
Effect: You slide the target 1 square. The target is slowed and cannot shift until the end of its turn.

LEVEL 1 AT-WILL EVOCATIONS

Earth Shield Strike	Warden Attack 1

Primal power flows from the ground to give the weight of stone to your strike and to your skin, shielding you from attack for a moment.

At-Will ✦ Primal, Weapon
Standard Action   Melee weapon
Target: One creature
Attack: Strength vs. AC
Hit: 1[W] + Strength modifier damage, and you gain a +1 power bonus to AC until the end of your next turn.
  Level 21: 2[W] + Strength modifier damage.

Strength of Stone	Warden Attack 1

Drawing power from the earth, you smash your weapon into your foe and bolster yourself against attack.

At-Will ✦ Primal, Weapon
Standard Action   Melee weapon
Target: One creature
Attack: Strength vs. AC
Hit: 1[W] + Strength modifier damage, and you gain temporary hit points equal to your Constitution modifier.
  Level 21: 2[W] + Strength modifier damage.

Thorn Strike	Warden Attack 1

Spectral thorns sprout from your weapon and grasp at your foe, pulling it closer.

At-Will ✦ Primal, Weapon
Standard Action   Melee 2
Target: One creature
Attack: Strength vs. AC
Hit: 1[W] + Strength modifier damage, and you pull the target 1 square.
  Level 21: 2[W] + Strength modifier damage.

Weight of Earth	Warden Attack 1

Your attack sends the primal energy of earth flowing into your enemy, slowing its movement.

At-Will ✦ Primal, Weapon
Standard Action   Melee weapon
Target: One creature
Attack: Strength vs. AC
Hit: 1[W] + Strength modifier damage, and the target is slowed until the end of your next turn.
  Level 21: 2[W] + Strength modifier damage.

Level 1 Encounter Evocations

Earth Spikes — Warden Attack 1

The earth rises in concert with your attack, driving sharp spikes of wood and stone up toward your foe even as your weapon slams down.

Encounter ✦ Primal, Weapon
Standard Action **Melee** weapon
Target: One creature
Attack: Strength vs. AC
Hit: 1[W] + Strength modifier damage. Until the end of your next turn, the target's space and each square adjacent to it are filled with spikes. Any enemy that enters this spike-filled area or starts its turn there takes 5 damage.

Hungry Earth — Warden Attack 1

You slam your weapon against the ground, bringing forth primal energy that causes the earth to batter your foes and churn beneath their feet.

Encounter ✦ Primal, Weapon
Standard Action **Close** burst 1
Target: Each enemy in burst
Attack: Strength vs. Fortitude
Hit: 1[W] + Strength modifier damage.
Effect: Until the end of your next turn, each square in the burst is difficult terrain for your enemies.

Thunder Ram Assault — Warden Attack 1

As your attack hits, you channel the spirit of the thunder ram to knock your foe and its companions away from you.

Encounter ✦ Primal, Thunder, Weapon
Standard Action **Melee** weapon
Primary Target: One creature
Primary Attack: Strength vs. AC
Hit: 1[W] + Strength modifier thunder damage. Make a secondary attack that is a close blast 3.
Earthstrength: You also push the primary target a number of squares equal to your Constitution modifier.
Secondary Target: Each creature in blast
Secondary Attack: Strength vs. Fortitude
Hit: 1d6 thunder damage, and you push the secondary target 1 square.

Wildblood Frenzy — Warden Attack 1

Primal power boils in your blood, and you surge into a frenzy, making two powerful attacks.

Encounter ✦ Primal, Weapon
Standard Action **Melee** weapon
Target: One creature
Attack: Strength vs. AC
Hit: 1[W] + Strength modifier damage.
Wildblood: The attack deals extra damage equal to your Wisdom modifier.
Effect: Make the attack one more time against the same target or a different one.

Level 1 Daily Evocations

Form of the Fearsome Ram — Warden Attack 1

You become mightier and faster, manifesting the horns and hooves of a ram. Your attacks push your foes around the battlefield, and you can make another attack to push a foe and knock it prone.

Daily ✦ Polymorph, Primal
Minor Action **Personal**
Effect: You assume the guardian form of the fearsome ram until the end of the encounter. While you are in this form, you gain a +2 power bonus to speed and a +2 bonus to charge attack rolls. In addition, when you hit a target with an at-will attack, you push the target 1 square. If the attack already pushes the target, the distance of the push increases by 1 square.

Once during this encounter, you can make the following weapon attack while you are in this form.
Standard Action **Melee** weapon
Effect: Before the attack, you shift your speed.
Target: One creature
Attack: Strength vs. Fortitude
Hit: 2[W] + Strength modifier damage, and you push the target 3 squares and knock it prone. You then shift into a space that must be adjacent to the target.
Miss: Half damage, and you push the target 1 square. You then shift into a square the target vacated.

Form of the Relentless Panther — Warden Attack 1

You take on the bestial fangs, sleek fur, and hunting grace of a panther. At the time you choose, you can make a nimble attack, darting across the battlefield to deal a bleeding wound to one of your foes.

Daily ✦ Polymorph, Primal
Minor Action **Personal**
Effect: You assume the guardian form of the relentless panther until the end of the encounter. While you are in this form, you gain a +2 bonus to Reflex and a +1 bonus to attack rolls against enemies marked by you. In addition, you can shift 2 squares as a move action.

Once during this encounter, you can make the following weapon attack while you are in this form.
Standard Action **Melee** weapon
Effect: Before the attack, you shift your speed.
Target: One creature
Attack: Strength vs. Reflex
Hit: 2[W] + Strength modifier damage, and ongoing 5 damage (save ends).
Miss: Half damage, and ongoing 2 damage (save ends).

Form of the Willow Sentinel — Warden Attack 1

Your skin takes on the appearance of smooth bark, and you draw strength from the earth. Your presence heightens your allies' endurance, and your viny branches help protect your nearby friends.

Daily ✦ Polymorph, Primal
Minor Action   **Personal**
Effect: You assume the guardian form of the willow sentinel until the end of the encounter. While you are in this form, you can negate being pulled, pushed, or slid. In addition, any ally gains a +2 power bonus to Fortitude while adjacent to you.
   Once during this encounter, you can make the following weapon attack while you are in this form.

Immediate Interrupt   Melee 1
Trigger: An enemy adjacent to you makes an attack roll against your ally
Target: The triggering enemy
Attack: Strength vs. AC
Hit: 1[W] + Strength modifier damage, and the target takes a –4 penalty to the triggering attack roll.
Miss: Half damage, and the target takes a –2 penalty to the triggering attack roll.

Form of Winter's Herald — Warden Attack 1

Ice as strong as steel forms over your armor, while frost on the ground around you hinders your enemies' movement. At the time you choose, you can swing your weapon in a freezing whirlwind that holds your enemies in place.

Daily ✦ Cold, Polymorph, Primal
Minor Action   **Personal**
Effect: You assume the guardian form of winter's herald until the end of the encounter. While you are in this form, you gain a +1 bonus to AC and resist 5 cold. In addition, each square within 2 squares of you, wherever you move, is difficult terrain for your enemies.
   Once during this encounter, you can make the following weapon attack while you are in this form.

Standard Action   Close burst 1
Target: Each enemy in burst
Attack: Strength vs. AC
Hit: 1[W] + Strength modifier cold damage, and the target is immobilized (save ends).
Miss: Half damage, and the target is immobilized until the end of your next turn.

Level 2 Utility Evocations

Eyes of the Hawk — Warden Utility 2

You call on the primal energy in your blood, allowing you to find your foes like a keen-eyed hawk.

Encounter ✦ Primal
Minor Action   **Personal**
Effect: You make a Perception check with a +10 power bonus.

Mountain Lion Step — Warden Utility 2

Like an agile mountain lion, you leap across difficult terrain with ease.

Encounter ✦ Primal
Minor Action   **Personal**
Effect: You ignore difficult terrain until the end of your next turn.

Nature's Abundance — Warden Utility 2

Plants burst into life around you. They sway back and forth to shield your allies, parting to allow attacks against your foes.

Daily ✦ Primal, Zone
Standard Action   Close burst 3
Effect: The burst creates a zone of plants that lasts until the end of the encounter. You and your allies have cover while within the zone.

Triumphant Vigor — Warden Utility 2

One victory gives you strength to achieve the next.

Daily ✦ Healing, Primal
Minor Action   **Personal**
Requirement: You must have reduced an enemy to 0 hit points during this turn.
Effect: You regain hit points equal to 1d6 + your Wisdom modifier + your Constitution modifier.

LEVEL 3 ENCOUNTER EVOCATIONS

Burst of Earth's Fury — Warden Attack 3

You slam your weapon into the ground, causing the earth to toss and churn as if from an earthquake.

Encounter ✦ Primal, Weapon
Standard Action   **Close** burst 1
Target: Each enemy in burst
Attack: Strength vs. AC
Hit: 1[W] + Strength modifier damage, and the target cannot shift until the end of your next turn.

Earthgrasp Strike — Warden Attack 3

The primal power of earth courses through your weapon and slams your foe to the ground, where rocks and roots hold it firm.

Encounter ✦ Primal, Weapon
Standard Action   **Melee** weapon
Target: One creature
Attack: Strength vs. AC
Hit: 1[W] + Strength modifier damage, and you knock the target prone. The first time the target stands up before the end of your next turn, it takes 1d10 + your Strength modifier damage.
  Earthstrength: The target can't stand up until the end of your next turn, and the first time it stands up before the end of the encounter, it takes 1d10 + your Strength modifier damage.

Predatory Guardian — Warden Attack 3

You press the attack, slicing into your foe and standing ready to pursue if it attempts to flee.

Encounter ✦ Primal, Weapon
Standard Action   **Melee** weapon
Target: One creature
Attack: Strength vs. AC
Hit: 2[W] + Strength modifier damage. If the target shifts before the start of your next turn, you shift 2 squares as an immediate reaction.
  Wildblood: The number of squares you shift equals 1 + your Wisdom modifier.

Thundering Strike — Warden Attack 3

You channel the essence of a storm into your weapon. As your strike hammers home, a peal of thunder crashes over your enemy.

Encounter ✦ Primal, Thunder, Weapon
Standard Action   **Melee** weapon
Target: One creature
Attack: Strength vs. AC
Hit: 1[W] + Strength modifier thunder damage, and the target is dazed and deafened until the end of your next turn.

LEVEL 5 DAILY EVOCATIONS

Storm Strike — Warden Attack 5

Whirling your weapon overhead, you create a storm of wind and lightning that you hurl at your enemies.

Daily ✦ Lightning, Primal, Weapon
Standard Action   **Close** blast 3
Target: Each creature in blast
Attack: Strength vs. AC
Hit: 1[W] + Strength modifier lightning damage, and you slide the target 3 squares.
Miss: Half damage, and you slide the target 1 square.

Hail of Thorns — Warden Attack 5

You sweep your weapon in a wide arc, drawing on primal energy to cast a hail of poisonous thorns at your foes.

Daily ✦ Poison, Primal, Weapon
Standard Action   **Close** blast 3
Target: Each creature in blast you can see
Attack: Strength vs. Reflex
Hit: 1[W] + Strength modifier poison damage, and the target takes ongoing 5 poison damage and is slowed (save ends both).
Miss: Half damage, and the target is slowed (save ends).

Thunder Step — Warden Attack 5

With a clap of thunder, you teleport next to an enemy and slam it with a thunderous blow.

Daily ✦ Primal, Teleportation, Thunder, Weapon
Standard Action   **Melee** weapon
Effect: Before the attack, you teleport 5 squares.
Target: One creature
Attack: Strength vs. Reflex
Hit: 2[W] + Strength modifier thunder damage, and the target is dazed (save ends).
Miss: Half damage, and the target is dazed until the end of your next turn.

Winter's Grip — Warden Attack 5

With a sweep of your weapon, a gale spawned from a blizzard blasts over your foes.

Daily ✦ Cold, Primal, Weapon, Zone
Standard Action   **Close** blast 3
Target: Each creature in blast
Attack: Strength vs. Fortitude
Hit: 1[W] + Strength modifier cold damage, and the target is slowed (save ends).
Miss: Half damage.
Effect: The blast creates a zone of frost that lasts until the end of your next turn. Any creature that enters the zone or starts its turn there takes 5 cold damage.
Sustain Minor: The zone persists.

LEVEL 6 UTILITY EVOCATIONS

Bear's Endurance — Warden Utility 6

Drawing on the boundless endurance of a bear, you regain a measure of your vitality.

Daily ✦ Healing, Primal
Immediate Interrupt   Personal
Trigger: You drop to 0 hit points or fewer
Effect: You regain hit points as if you had spent a healing surge.

Earthguard — Warden Utility 6

Primal power from the earth fortifies your body and mind.

Daily ✦ Primal, Stance
Minor Action   Personal
Effect: Until the stance ends, you gain a +1 power bonus to all defenses.

Sea Stride — Warden Utility 6

You draw on the strength of flowing water to glide through the waves with ease.

At-Will ✦ Primal
Minor Action   Personal
Effect: You gain a swim speed equal to your speed until the end of your turn.

Windborne Step — Warden Utility 6

A sudden gust of wind whips around you, lifting you into the fray.

Encounter ✦ Primal
Move Action   Personal
Effect: You shift 2 squares. You ignore difficult terrain during the shift.

LEVEL 7 ENCOUNTER EVOCATIONS

Earth Gift — Warden Attack 7

The spirits of earth reward your attack with a gift of health.

Encounter ✦ Healing, Primal, Weapon
Standard Action   Melee weapon
Target: One creature
Attack: Strength vs. AC
Hit: 2[W] + Strength modifier damage, and you regain 10 hit points.

Mountain Hammer — Warden Attack 7

You strike with the strength of a mountain: brutal and unforgettable.

Encounter ✦ Primal, Weapon
Standard Action   Melee weapon
Target: One creature
Attack: Strength vs. Fortitude
Hit: 2[W] + Strength modifier damage, and the target takes a -2 penalty to melee attack rolls until the end of your next turn.
Earthstrength: The penalty to melee attack rolls equals 1 + your Constitution modifier.

Stalker's Positioning — Warden Attack 7

Predatory instincts guide your attack as you position your prey exactly where you want it.

Encounter ✦ Fear, Primal, Psychic, Weapon
Standard Action   Melee weapon
Target: One creature
Attack: Strength vs. AC
Hit: 2[W] + Strength modifier damage, and you slide the target 1 square. You can slide the target into a second creature's space and then slide the second creature 1 square.
Wildblood: Both the target and the second creature take psychic damage equal to your Wisdom modifier.

Thorn Burst — Warden Attack 7

As you strike your foe, poisoned thorns burst from your weapon and lodge in your target's allies.

Encounter ✦ Poison, Primal, Weapon
Standard Action   Melee weapon
Primary Target: One creature
Primary Attack: Strength vs. Reflex
Hit: 1[W] + Strength modifier damage. Make a secondary attack.
Secondary Target: Each enemy adjacent to the primary target
Secondary Attack: Strength vs. Reflex
Hit: 5 poison damage.

LEVEL 9 DAILY EVOCATIONS

Form of the Oak Sentinel — Warden Attack 9

Your skin thickens into rough bark, and your hair becomes a mane of leaves. Your arms lengthen so that you can attack your foes and protect your allies from a distance.

Daily ✦ Polymorph, Primal
Minor Action   Personal
Effect: You assume the guardian form of the oak sentinel until the end of the encounter. While you are in this form, your melee reach increases by 1. In addition, any enemy that hits you with a melee attack takes damage equal to your Strength modifier. This damage increases to twice your Strength modifier at 21st level.
    Once during this encounter, you can make the following weapon attack while you are in this form.
Immediate Interrupt   Melee weapon
Trigger: An enemy within your reach makes a melee attack against your ally
Target: The triggering enemy
Attack: Strength vs. AC
Hit: 2[W] + Strength modifier damage.
Miss: Half damage.
Effect: You become the target of the triggering attack, even if you aren't within that attack's range.

Form of the Frenzied Wolverine · Warden Attack 9

You strike wounded foes with particular ferocity. When the time is right, you make a brutal attack against your chosen foe, opening a bleeding wound.

Daily ✦ Polymorph, Primal
Minor Action   **Personal**
Effect: You assume the guardian form of the frenzied wolverine until the end of the encounter. While you are in this form, you gain a +2 bonus to attack rolls against any enemy that is bloodied or taking ongoing damage. In addition, you can use your second wind as a minor action.
    Once during this encounter, you can make the following weapon attack while you are in this form.
Standard Action   **Melee** weapon
Target: One creature
Hit: 1[W] + Strength modifier damage, and ongoing 5 damage (save ends).
Miss: Half damage, and ongoing 2 damage (save ends).

Form of the Stone Sentinel · Warden Attack 9

Your body becomes a fusion of flesh and rough stone, invigorated by your connection to the earth.

Daily ✦ Healing, Polymorph, Primal
Minor Action   **Personal**
Effect: You regain hit points as if you had spent a healing surge. You also assume the guardian form of the stone sentinel until the end of the encounter. While you are in this form, you gain regeneration equal to your Constitution modifier.
    Once during this encounter, you can make the following weapon attack while you are in this form.
Standard Action   **Melee** weapon
Target: One creature
Attack: Strength vs. AC
Hit: 2[W] + Strength modifier damage.
Miss: Half damage.
Effect: You can spend a healing surge.

Form of the Storm Eagle · Warden Attack 9

Majestic feathered wings sprout from your back, and lightning crackles around your talonlike hands, as you leap into the air.

Daily ✦ Lightning, Polymorph, Primal
Minor Action   **Personal**
Effect: You assume the guardian form of the storm eagle until the end of the encounter. While you are in this form, you gain resist 5 lightning. You can fly your speed as a move action and must land at the end of the action.
    Once during this encounter, you can make the following weapon attack while you are in this form.
Standard Action   **Melee** weapon
Effect: Before the attack, you move your speed.
Target: One creature
Attack: Strength vs. AC
Hit: 1[W] + Strength modifier lightning damage, and the target is dazed (save ends).
Miss: Half damage, and the target is dazed until the end of your next turn.

LEVEL 10 UTILITY EVOCATIONS

Earthstride · Warden Utility 10

You meld into the ground and then emerge a short distance away.

Encounter ✦ Primal, Teleportation
Move Action   **Personal**
Effect: You teleport a number of squares equal to your Constitution modifier.

Returning Strength · Warden Utility 10

Just as primal energy grants life to the world, it lends strength and endurance to you.

Daily ✦ Healing, Primal
Minor Action   **Personal**
Effect: You spend a healing surge and regain additional hit points equal to your Strength modifier.

DEVON CADDY-LEE

Shield of Stone
Warden Utility 10

Earth carries your ally to safety while stone forms a protective barrier around him or her.

Daily ✦ Primal
Minor Action   Close burst 5
Target: One ally in burst
Effect: You slide the target 5 squares. Until the end of your next turn, the target gains resist 5 to all damage and a +2 power bonus to all defenses.

Warding Vines
Warden Utility 10

Spectral vines bloom around you to shield you and your allies.

Daily ✦ Primal, Zone
Minor Action   Close burst 2
Effect: The burst creates a zone of protective vines that lasts until the end of the encounter. While within the zone, you and your allies gain resistance to all damage equal to your Constitution modifier.

LEVEL 13 ENCOUNTER EVOCATIONS

Creeper's Grasp
Warden Attack 13

Tendrils cover the enemy you hit, stopping its movement.

Encounter ✦ Primal, Weapon
Standard Action   Melee weapon
Target: One creature
Attack: Strength vs. Reflex
Hit: 2[W] + Strength modifier damage, and the target is immobilized until the end of your next turn.

Icy Shards
Warden Attack 13

Ice crystals spread from your weapon to hinder your foe, then erupt to cut other nearby enemies.

Encounter ✦ Cold, Primal, Weapon
Standard Action   Melee weapon
Primary Target: One creature
Primary Attack: Strength vs. Fortitude
Hit: 2[W] + Strength modifier cold damage, and the primary target is slowed until the end of your next turn. Make a secondary attack.
    Secondary Target: Each enemy adjacent to the primary target
    Secondary Attack: Strength vs. Fortitude
    Hit: 5 cold damage.

Ponderous Strike
Warden Attack 13

Your weapon takes on the weight of stone as it smashes into your foe, knocking it off balance.

Encounter ✦ Primal, Weapon
Standard Action   Melee weapon
Target: One creature
Attack: Strength vs. AC
Hit: 3[W] + Strength modifier damage, and the target provokes an opportunity attack from you if it shifts before the end of your next turn.
Earthstrength: On a miss, the target provokes an opportunity attack from you if it shifts before the end of your next turn.

Sunburst Strike
Warden Attack 13

The light of the sun erupts around your enemy as you strike, blinding it for a moment.

Encounter ✦ Primal, Radiant, Weapon
Standard Action   Melee weapon
Target: One creature
Attack: Strength vs. AC
Hit: 1[W] + Strength modifier radiant damage, and the target is blinded until the end of your next turn.
    Wildblood: If the target is bloodied, you shift 2 squares.

LEVEL 15 DAILY EVOCATIONS

Form of Summer Fire
Warden Attack 15

A crown of flames on your head, a burst of fire around your weapon, and a smoldering inferno in your eyes mark your transformation, protecting you from fire as you later erupt in flames to sear your foes.

Daily ✦ Fire, Polymorph, Primal
Minor Action   Personal
Effect: You assume the guardian form of summer fire until the end of the encounter. While you are in this form, you gain resist 10 fire and a +3 bonus to damage rolls.
    Once during this encounter, you can make the following weapon attack while you are in this form.
Standard Action   Close burst 2
Target: Each enemy in burst
Attack: Strength vs. Reflex
Hit: 2[W] + Strength modifier fire damage.
Miss: Half damage.

Form of the Charging Boar
Warden Attack 15

Your features twist and contort as tusks push out from your jaw. The fury of the boar fills you when you choose to crash into your foe, knocking it across the battlefield.

Daily ✦ Polymorph, Primal
Minor Action   Personal
Effect: You assume the guardian form of the charging boar until the end of the encounter. While you are in this form, you gain resist 5 to all damage and a +2 power bonus to Fortitude and Will.
    Once during this encounter, you can make the following weapon attack while you are in this form.
Standard Action   Melee weapon
Effect: Before the attack, you move your speed.
Target: One creature
Attack: Strength vs. AC
Hit: 3[W] + Strength modifier damage, and you slide the target 2 squares.
Miss: Half damage, and you slide the target 1 square.

Form of the Rowan Sentinel — Warden Attack 15

Your skin becomes smooth bark that crackles with lightning. Your arms lengthen to complete your transformation. At the moment you choose, your attack delivers a barrage of lightning that staggers your foe.

Daily ✦ Lightning, Polymorph, Primal
Minor Action   **Personal**

Effect: You assume the guardian form of the rowan sentinel until the end of the encounter. While you are in this form, you gain resist 10 lightning, and your melee reach increases by 1. In addition, if any enemy starts its turn within 3 squares of you and you are able to take actions, that enemy is marked until the end of your next turn.

     Once during this encounter, you can make the following weapon attack while you are in this form.

Standard Action   **Melee** weapon

Target: One creature

Attack: Strength vs. AC

Hit: 2[W] + Strength modifier lightning damage, and the target is dazed and takes ongoing 5 lightning damage (save ends both).

Miss: Half damage, and the target is dazed until the end of your next turn.

Form of the Stonecrusher — Warden Attack 15

Stony plating spreads to armor your body and root you to the ground. When the time is right, you can swing your weapon in a great burst and smash your foes to the ground.

Daily ✦ Polymorph, Primal
Minor Action   **Personal**

Effect: You assume the guardian form of the stonecrusher until the end of the encounter. While you are in this form, you gain a +2 bonus to AC. If you are pulled, pushed, or slid, you can reduce the distance of the forced movement by 2 squares.

     Once during this encounter, you can make the following weapon attack while you are in this form.

Standard Action   **Close** burst 1

Target: Each enemy in burst you can see

Attack: Strength vs. AC

Hit: 1[W] + Strength modifier damage, and the target is immobilized (save ends).

Miss: Half damage.

Effect: You knock the target prone.

LEVEL 16 UTILITY EVOCATIONS

Cleansing Earth — Warden Utility 16

Even as harm befalls you, you draw on the earth for the strength to shrug it off.

Encounter ✦ Primal
Immediate Reaction   **Personal**

Trigger: You are subjected to an effect that a save can end

Effect: You make a saving throw against the triggering effect, with a power bonus to the saving throw equal to your Strength modifier.

Monkey's Grip — Warden Utility 16

Your grip is sure, allowing you to scramble up nearly any surface.

At-Will ✦ Primal
Minor Action   **Personal**

Effect: Until the end of your turn, you gain a climb speed equal to half your speed.

Primal Leap — Warden Utility 16

You spring into the air, making a prodigious leap over the heads of your enemies.

Encounter ✦ Primal
Move Action   **Personal**

Effect: You jump a number of squares equal to your speed + your Strength modifier.

Verdant Life — Warden Utility 16

You tap into the essence of primal power, causing even your most horrid wounds to mend in an instant.

Daily ✦ Healing, Primal
Minor Action   **Personal**

Effect: You can spend two healing surges.

LEVEL 17 ENCOUNTER EVOCATIONS

Call Forth the Harvest — Warden Attack 17

A vicious swing causes the ground around you to erupt in entangling growth, interfering with your enemies' movement.

Encounter ✦ Primal, Weapon
Standard Action   **Melee** weapon

Primary Target: One creature

Primary Attack: Strength vs. AC

Hit: 3[W] + Strength modifier damage. Make a secondary attack that is a close burst 2.

     Secondary Target: Each enemy in burst

     Secondary Attack: Strength vs. Reflex

     Hit: The secondary target is marked and slowed until the end of your next turn.

Eager Vine Strike — Warden Attack 17

Bright green tendrils wrap around your foe and hold it fast.

Encounter ✦ Primal, Weapon
Standard Action   **Melee** weapon

Target: One creature

Attack: Strength vs. AC

Hit: 2[W] + Strength modifier damage, and the target is immobilized until the end of your next turn.

     Earthstrength: Until the end of your next turn, the target also takes a penalty to AC and Reflex equal to your Constitution modifier.

Earth Hold's Rebuke — Warden Attack 17

Emerald light swirls around you as primal spirits lend their strength to your attack.

Encounter ✦ Healing, Primal, Weapon
Standard Action   **Melee** weapon

Target: One creature

Attack: Strength vs. AC

Hit: 3[W] + Strength modifier damage, and you can spend a healing surge.

Razorleaf Cut | Warden Attack 17

Coils of vines adorned with razor-sharp leaves tear the flesh of your enemy and drain its strength.

Encounter ✦ Primal, Weapon
Standard Action   **Melee** weapon
Target: One creature
Attack: Strength vs. Fortitude
Hit: 2[W] + Strength modifier damage, and the target is weakened until the end of your next turn.
     Wildblood: The attack deals extra damage equal to your Wisdom modifier.

LEVEL 19 DAILY EVOCATIONS

Blizzard Strike | Warden Attack 19

The bitter cold of the frozen wastes spreads over your foe, encasing it in ice, and wintry winds whip around you to slow your other enemies.

Daily ✦ Cold, Primal, Weapon
Standard Action   **Melee** weapon
Target: One creature
Attack: Strength vs. AC
Hit: 4[W] + Strength modifier cold damage, and the target is slowed (save ends).
     First Failed Saving Throw: The target is immobilized instead of slowed (save ends).
     Second Failed Saving Throw: The target is restrained instead of immobilized (save ends).
Miss: Half damage, and the target is slowed until the end of your next turn.
Effect: Each enemy within 3 squares of you, other than the target, is slowed until the end of your next turn.

Dire Beast Assault | Warden Attack 19

Like a great dire bear or tiger, you relentlessly pursue your foes and inflict bleeding wounds on them.

Daily ✦ Primal, Weapon
Standard Action   **Melee** weapon
Effect: Before and after the attack, you shift 1 square.
Target: One creature
Attack: Strength vs. AC
Hit: 3[W] + Strength modifier damage, and ongoing 10 damage (save ends).
Miss: Half damage, and ongoing 5 damage (save ends).

Lightning Barrage | Warden Attack 19

As you whirl your weapon, it draws lightning from the air and sends it cascading over the enemies around you.

Daily ✦ Lightning, Primal, Weapon
Standard Action   **Close** burst 1
Target: Each enemy in burst
Attack: Strength vs. Reflex
Hit: 1[W] + Strength modifier lightning damage, and the target is blinded and dazed (save ends both).
Miss: Half damage, and the target is dazed until the end of your next turn.

Thundering Bolts | Warden Attack 19

You smash your weapon into the earth, unleashing a wave of thunder that knocks your foes to the ground.

Daily ✦ Primal, Thunder, Weapon
Standard Action   **Close** blast 3
Target: Each enemy in blast
Attack: Strength vs. Fortitude
Hit: 2[W] + Strength modifier thunder damage.
Miss: Half damage.
Effect: You knock each target prone.

LEVEL 22 UTILITY EVOCATIONS

Eagle's Wings | Warden Utility 22

Black wings with white tips extend from your back, letting you catch the wind and fly.

Daily ✦ Polymorph, Primal
Minor Action   **Personal**
Effect: You sprout wings that last until the end of the encounter. While you have the wings, you have a fly speed equal to your speed, and you can hover.

Panacea | Warden Utility 22

You channel the protection of primal forces, warding yourself against harmful effects.

Daily ✦ Primal
Minor Action   **Personal**
Effect: You make a saving throw with a +4 power bonus. You also gain a +4 power bonus to saving throws until the end of the encounter.

DEVON CADDY-LEE

Renewal · Warden Utility 22

You draw nourishing energy from the earth and awaken reserves of power within yourself.

Daily ✦ Healing, Primal
Minor Action   **Personal**
Effect: You spend a healing surge. In addition, you regain the use of an encounter attack power you have already used during this encounter.

Wellspring of Life · Warden Utility 22

Your connection to the primal spirits sustains you.

Daily ✦ Healing, Primal
Minor Action   **Personal**
Effect: You spend a healing surge. In addition, you gain regeneration equal to 5 + your Strength modifier until the end of the encounter.

LEVEL 23 ENCOUNTER EVOCATIONS

Guardian's Wrath · Warden Attack 23

With a furious blow, you give your foe a painful reminder of the threat you pose, singling it out for wrath if it disregards you.

Encounter ✦ Primal, Weapon
Standard Action   **Melee** weapon
Target: One creature
Attack: Strength vs. AC
Hit: 4[W] + Strength modifier damage. Until the end of your next turn, the target is marked, and it provokes an opportunity attack from you if it makes an attack that does not include you as a target.

Nature's Ally · Warden Attack 23

The ground beneath your enemy's feet comes to life, shoving the foe into your vicious attack.

Encounter ✦ Primal, Weapon
Standard Action   **Close** burst 3
Target: One creature in burst
Primary Attack: Strength vs. Reflex
Hit: You pull the target 2 squares to a space that must be adjacent to you. Make a secondary attack that is a melee attack against the target.
    Secondary Attack: Strength + 2 vs. AC
    Hit: 3[W] + Strength modifier damage.
Earthstrength: If either attack hits, the target is also slowed until the start of your next turn.

Startling Savagery · Warden Attack 23

Your savage attack leaves your foe staggering, while power courses through your blood to enhance your next assault.

Encounter ✦ Primal, Weapon
Standard Action   **Melee** weapon
Target: One creature
Attack: Strength vs. AC
Hit: 3[W] + Strength modifier damage, and the target is dazed until the end of your next turn.
    Wildblood: Until the end of your next turn, you gain a power bonus to attack rolls equal to your Wisdom modifier.

Whirlwind Assault · Warden Attack 23

As you swing your weapon, it stirs up an encircling wind that lingers around you, protecting you from attacks.

Encounter ✦ Primal, Weapon
Standard Action   **Close** burst 1
Target: Each enemy in burst
Attack: Strength vs. AC
Hit: 2[W] + Strength modifier damage.
Effect: You gain a +2 power bonus to AC and Reflex until the end of your next turn.

LEVEL 25 DAILY EVOCATIONS

Form of the Blood Wolf · Warden Attack 25

Your body hunches forward and your legs grow longer as you take on the aspect of a wolf. You can make a single savage assault to throw your foe off balance, setting it up for you to knock it down with your next attack.

Daily ✦ Polymorph, Primal
Minor Action   **Personal**
Effect: You assume the guardian form of the blood wolf until the end of the encounter. While you are in this form, you gain a +2 bonus to speed and a +4 bonus to damage rolls for melee attacks against bloodied targets. In addition, if you have combat advantage against a target that you hit with a melee attack, you can knock that target prone.
    Once during this encounter, you can make the following weapon attack while you are in this form.
Standard Action   **Melee** weapon
Target: One creature
Attack: Strength vs. AC
Hit: 5[W] + Strength modifier damage, and the target grants combat advantage to you (save ends).
Miss: Half damage, and the target grants combat advantage to you until the end of your next turn.

Form of the Displacer Beast · Warden Attack 25

Your appearance shimmers as light warps around you, and you take on a feline aspect. At the time you choose, you can make a double attack.

Daily ✦ Polymorph, Primal
Minor Action   **Personal**
Effect: You assume the guardian form of the displacer beast until the end of the encounter. While you are in this form, roll a d20 whenever a melee attack hits you. On a roll of 10 or higher, you take half damage from the attack.
    Once during this encounter, you can make the following weapon attack while you are in this form.
Standard Action   **Melee** weapon
Target: One creature
Attack: Strength vs. AC
Hit: 2[W] + Strength modifier damage.
Miss: Half damage.
Effect: Make the attack one more time against the target.

Form of the Jungle Lord
Warden Attack 25

Your chest grows broader, your arms lengthen, and your legs shorten as you take on the aspect of a great ape. As you climb with ease, your powerful attacks position your enemies exactly where you want them.

Daily ✦ Polymorph, Primal
Minor Action   **Personal**

Effect: You assume the guardian form of the jungle lord until the end of the encounter. While you are in this form, you gain a climb speed equal to your speed and a +2 bonus to Reflex. In addition, whenever you hit a target with a melee attack, you slide the target 2 squares. If that attack already pulls, pushes, or slides the target, you slide the target 2 squares after that forced movement.

    Once during this encounter, you can make the following weapon attack while you are in this form.

Standard Action   **Melee** weapon
Target: One creature
Attack: Strength vs. AC
Hit: 4[W] + Strength modifier damage, and you slide the target 1 square.
Miss: Half damage.

Form of the Autumn Reaper
Warden Attack 25

Your body becomes like the dry form of a tree in late autumn, and death clings to you. Your attacks drain the life from your foes, and in one great blow, you can sap the strength from an enemy.

Daily ✦ Necrotic, Polymorph, Primal
Minor Action   **Personal**

Effect: You assume the guardian form of the autumn reaper until the end of the encounter. While you are in this form, you gain resist 10 necrotic, and your melee reach increases by 1. In addition, your melee attacks deal extra necrotic damage equal to your Strength modifier.

    Once during this encounter, you can make the following weapon attack while you are in this form.

Standard Action   **Melee** weapon
Target: One creature
Attack: Strength vs. Fortitude
Hit: 2[W] + Strength modifier necrotic damage, and the target is weakened (save ends).
Miss: Half damage, and the target is weakened until the end of your next turn.

LEVEL 27 ENCOUNTER EVOCATIONS

Earth Tomb
Warden Attack 27

Such is the force of your attack that the ground opens beneath your enemy and holds it down.

Encounter ✦ Primal, Weapon
Standard Action   **Melee** weapon
Target: One creature
Attack: Strength vs. AC
Hit: 3[W] + Strength modifier damage, and the target is knocked prone and can't stand up until the end of your next turn.

    Earthstrength: You also slide the target a number of squares equal to your Constitution modifier.

Guardian's Storm
Warden Attack 27

As you strike your foe, you call on storm spirits to surround it in a cage of lightning.

Encounter ✦ Lightning, Primal, Weapon
Standard Action   **Melee** weapon
Target: One creature
Attack: Strength vs. AC
Hit: 4[W] + Strength modifier damage, and the target takes 15 lightning damage if it moves before the end of your next turn.

    Wildblood: The lightning damage equals 15 + your Wisdom modifier.

Screaming Wind Strike
Warden Attack 27

Howling winds swirl around your foe and trap it in a whirling prison.

Encounter ✦ Primal, Weapon
Standard Action   **Melee** weapon
Target: One creature
Attack: Strength vs. Reflex
Hit: 2[W] + Strength modifier damage, and the target is stunned until the end of your next turn.

Weight of the Mountain
Warden Attack 27

Your weapon crashes onto your foe like an avalanche, and the earth shudders in response.

Encounter ✦ Primal, Weapon
Standard Action   **Melee** weapon
Primary Target: One creature
Primary Attack: Strength vs. AC
Hit: 2[W] + Strength modifier damage. Make a secondary attack that is a close burst 5.

    Secondary Target: Each enemy in burst
    Secondary Attack: Strength vs. Fortitude
    Hit: 2d6 damage.
    Effect: Each secondary target is slowed until the end of your next turn.

Level 29 Daily Evocations

Form of the Chimera
Warden Attack 29

As your head takes on a leonine aspect, two additional heads sprout from your shoulders: a ram's and a dragon's.

Daily ✦ Fire, Polymorph, Primal
Minor Action　　　　　**Personal**
Effect: You assume the guardian form of the chimera until the end of the encounter. While you are in this form, flanking enemies don't gain combat advantage against you. In addition, whenever you hit a target with a charge attack, you can either push the target 1 square or knock it prone.

　　Once during this encounter, you can make the following attack while you are in this form.
Standard Action　　　　**Close** blast 5
Target: Each creature in blast
Attack: Strength + 6 vs. Reflex
Hit: 2d10 fire damage, and ongoing 5 fire damage (save ends).
Miss: Half damage.

Form of Spring Renewal
Warden Attack 29

Brilliant light surrounds you, lifting you up and filling you with vitality. You can gather this energy and unleash it in a burst of searing light, but doing so leaves you momentarily disoriented.

Daily ✦ Healing, Polymorph, Primal, Radiant
Minor Action　　　　　**Personal**
Effect: You assume the guardian form of spring renewal until the end of the encounter. While you are in this form, you gain resist 10 necrotic. In addition, you gain a fly speed of 8, and you can hover.

　　Once during this encounter, you can make the following attack while you are in this form.
Standard Action　　　　**Close** burst 2
Target: Each enemy in burst
Attack: Strength + 6 vs. Reflex
Hit: 4d10 radiant damage.
Miss: Half damage.
Effect: You regain all your hit points, but you are stunned until the end of your next turn.

Form of the Starmetal Warrior
Warden Attack 29

Your skin hardens into gleaming dark metal, and the ground shudders beneath your heavy tread. Cosmic winds swirl around you, hindering airborne foes. When you lash out in fury, you make a devastating attack against nearby enemies.

Daily ✦ Polymorph, Primal
Minor Action　　　　　**Personal**
Effect: You assume the guardian form of the starmetal warrior until the end of the encounter. While you are in this form, you gain a +3 bonus to AC. In addition, while any flying enemy is within 10 squares of you, its fly speed is 1.

　　Once during this encounter, you can make the following weapon attack while you are in this form.
Standard Action　　　　**Close** burst 2
Target: Each enemy in burst
Attack: Strength vs. AC
Hit: 3[W] + Strength modifier damage. This damage ignores any of the target's resistances.
Miss: Half damage. This damage ignores any of the target's resistances.

Form of the Soul Serpent
Warden Attack 29

You take on the aspect of the soul serpent, keeper of the gate of dreams. The world becomes a ghostly landscape in which you feel your foes as much as see them. Your eyes flash, and when you choose, you can dazzle nearby foes with a glance.

Daily ✦ Polymorph, Primal, Psychic
Minor Action　　　　　**Personal**
Effect: You assume the guardian form of the soul serpent until the end of the encounter. While you are in this form, you gain a +2 bonus to AC and Fortitude. You also gain tremorsense 5.

　　Once during this encounter, you can make the following attack while you are in this form.
Standard Action　　　　**Close** blast 5
Target: Each enemy in blast
Attack: Strength + 6 vs. Will
Hit: 2d10 psychic damage, and you slide the target 5 squares.
Miss: Half damage.
Effect: Each target is dazed (save ends).

BLOODWRATH GUARDIAN

"We are all animals. Only our arrogance separates us from our more wild kin."

Prerequisite: Warden

The primal power you wield has formed a bond between you and the natural creatures of the world. In their myriad forms, you see fractured reflections of a greater being: the Primal Beast, who was the world's first predator. All the hunting animals of the world—mighty lions and howling wolves, lowly ferrets and soaring eagles—hold a distant echo of the Primal Beast in their hearts.

In your commitment to protect the world from demons, aberrations, and other beings that would corrupt the balance of nature, you find yourself growing closer to the Primal Beast's perfection. That growth is reflected in your bloodwrath—the heightened speed you gain when you adopt a guardian form, and the fury that punishes the enemies you mark. At the pinnacle of your path, you at last gain the ability to take on the form of the Primal Beast.

BLOODWRATH GUARDIAN PATH FEATURES

Furious Action (11th level): You can spend an action point to gain a bonus to attack rolls equal to your Wisdom modifier until the end of your turn, instead of taking an extra action.

Bloodwrath Stride (11th level): While you are in a guardian form, you gain a +2 bonus to speed.

Bloodwrath Fury (16th level): When you hit an enemy with a melee attack and the enemy is marked by you, you gain a +2 bonus to the damage roll.

BLOODWRATH GUARDIAN EVOCATIONS

Bloodwrath Strike	Bloodwrath Guardian Attack 11

Primal fury wells within you as you slam your weapon into your foe.

Encounter ✦ Primal, Weapon
Standard Action   **Melee** weapon
Target: One creature
Attack: Strength vs. Fortitude
Hit: 3[W] + Strength modifier damage.

Warding Frenzy	Bloodwrath Guardian Utility 12

Your senses heightened by the primal spirits around you, you present a constant threat to enemies nearby and are ready to strike if they ignore you.

Daily ✦ Primal, Stance
Minor Action   **Personal**
Effect: Until the stance ends, any enemy that starts or ends its turn adjacent to you is marked until the end of its next turn.

Form of the Primal Beast	Bloodwrath Guardian Attack 20

Your body becomes a hunched thing of fur and shadow, an echo of the archetypal predator, the Primal Beast. When you muster your strength for a great attack, you deal a grievous wound to your foe.

Daily ✦ Polymorph, Primal
Minor Action   **Personal**
Effect: You assume the guardian form of the Primal Beast until the end of the encounter. While you are in this form, your melee reach increases by 1, and you gain threatening reach.
  Once during this encounter, you can make the following weapon attack while you are in this form.
Standard Action   **Melee** weapon
Target: One creature
Attack: Strength vs. AC
Hit: 3[W] + Strength modifier damage, and ongoing 10 damage (save ends).

HORNED CHAMPION

"Don't speak to me of your petty concerns—speak to me of the world's needs."

Prerequisite: Warden

You have communed with the spirits of the land and have been found worthy of the horned champion's mantle. You transcend the flesh you were born with to become the chosen vessel of nature's spirits. Your duty is to take up arms against the fell creatures of the land, to put an end to their destruction, and to restore the splendor of the untamed wilds.

Becoming a horned champion is a transformative experience. Gone are the simple concerns that bound you to the world. You see the world on a grander scale, as an organism that must be protected against the abominations that would siphon its strength for dark purposes. You appear to have no ties to people or places, only to your weighty mission, leading many to feel as though you lack understanding of the individual's plight. Although it's true that you care little for the individual's suffering, giving no more attention to a mortal's difficulties than one would show to an insect, your concern encompasses the natural world and all things living in it. Thus, in a way, your ties to others are deeper than friendship, for they are forged from the bonds that connect all living things.

ERIC BELISLE

HORNED CHAMPION PATH FEATURES

Vicious Action (11th level): When you spend an action point to make an attack and that attack misses, you can reroll that attack roll but must use the second result.

Fervent Pursuit (11th level): When you hit an enemy with an opportunity attack, that enemy is slowed until the end of its turn.

Blessing of Spring (16th level): Whenever you use a warden daily attack power that has the polymorph keyword, you can spend a healing surge as a free action.

HORNED CHAMPION EVOCATIONS

Zealous Strike — Horned Champion Attack 11

With a roar, you charge at your enemies to deliver an overwhelming attack.

Encounter ✦ Primal, Weapon
Standard Action   **Melee** weapon
Target: One creature
Attack: Strength vs. AC. If the target is bloodied, you gain a +2 bonus to the attack roll.
Hit: 1[W] + Strength modifier damage, and you knock the target prone.
Effect: Make the attack one more time against the same target or a different one.

Impetuous Stride — Horned Champion Utility 12

Primal energy surrounds you as you push through the enemies' ranks. Only a fool would dare strike you.

Encounter ✦ Primal
Move Action   **Personal**
Effect: You move your speed. If any creature makes an opportunity attack against you during this movement, that creature takes damage equal to 5 + your Wisdom modifier.

Form of the Leaping Stag — Horned Champion Attack 20

Great horns sprout from your head as primal power quickens your step. Your charging assault can leave an enemy senseless.

Daily ✦ Polymorph, Primal
Minor Action   **Personal**
Effect: You assume the guardian form of the leaping stag until the end of the encounter. While you are in this form, you gain a +4 bonus to speed. In addition, as a move action, you can move your speed and gain a +2 power bonus to AC against opportunity attacks until the end of your turn. During this movement, you can move through any enemy's space, marking that enemy until the end of your next turn.

Once during this encounter, you can make the following weapon attack while you are in this form.
Standard Action   **Melee** weapon
Effect: Before the attack, you move your speed.
Target: One creature
Attack: Strength vs. AC
Hit: 2[W] + Strength modifier damage, and the target is stunned until the end of your next turn.
Miss: Half damage, and the target is dazed until the end of your next turn.

Storm Sentinel

"Feel the wrath of the storm unleashed, for I am nature's champion and none shall stand against me."

Prerequisite: Warden

To many, there is no clearer expression of the power of nature than the raging fury of the storm. Churning clouds, crashing thunder, and blasting lightning are manifestations of the rage coursing through the world when its natural laws are violated and its purity corrupted. When gods or primordials overstep their bounds, when demons or aberrant beings try to tear the fabric of reality, the fury of a storm—and its cleansing rain—are part of nature's response.

Most wardens draw power from the earth. As an incarnation of the storm's wrath, your greatest primal power comes from the sky. Lightning flows in your veins, and thunder booms in your footsteps. As you advance along this path, you can transform yourself into wind and rain and can ultimately take on the aspect of storm's wrath.

Storm Sentinel Path Features

Invigorating Action (11th level): When you spend an action point to make an attack, you can spend a healing surge as a free action after the attack.

Critical Jolt (11th level): Whenever you score a critical hit, it deals extra lightning damage equal to your Strength modifier.

Undying Wind (16th level): Whenever you spend a healing surge, you regain additional hit points equal to your Constitution modifier.

Storm Sentinel Evocations

Thunder Smash	Storm Sentinel Attack 11

Your weapon rumbles with thunder as you swing it toward the earth in a tremendous smash that knocks your foes down.

Encounter ✦ Primal, Thunder, Weapon
Standard Action   Close burst 2
Target: Each enemy in burst
Attack: Strength vs. Fortitude
Hit: 1[W] + Strength modifier thunder damage, and you knock the target prone.

Storm Step	Storm Sentinel Utility 12

For a brief moment, you transform into wind and rain.

Encounter ✦ Primal
Move Action   Personal
Effect: You become insubstantial until the end of your next turn. In addition, you fly your speed; at the end of this movement, you must land in a space adjacent to an enemy.

Form of Storm's Wrath	Storm Sentinel Attack 20

Thunder crashes around you as your skin becomes the dark blue-gray of thunderclouds and your eyes flash with lightning.

Daily ✦ Lightning, Polymorph, Primal
Minor Action   Personal
Effect: You assume the guardian form of storm's wrath until the end of the encounter. While you are in this form, any enemy that starts its turn adjacent to you is marked until the end of your next turn and takes lightning damage equal to your Constitution modifier if you are able to take actions. In addition, at the start of each of your turns, choose one enemy that you can see within 3 squares of you. That enemy takes lightning damage equal to 5 + your Constitution modifier.

Verdant Lord

"I am one with the forest, and the forest is one with me."

Prerequisite: Warden

Like the trees of the forest, you draw strength from the loamy earth, from the water that spills from the sky and flows across the land, and from the radiance of the sun. You embrace the essence of the tree, becoming the forest's protector, its champion against those that would despoil it. When you use your primal powers, shoots of new growth emerge from the ground, flowers bloom, and trees straighten with renewed vigor.

You favor guardian form powers that let you take on treelike forms (such as *form of the willow sentinel*, *form of the oak sentinel*, and *form of the rowan sentinel*), but even when you take on other aspects, the earth responds with growth. As the culmination of this path, you can take on a form like that of a treant, smashing foes and objects alike with a weapon held in your branchlike fists.

Verdant Lord Path Features

Reaching Action (11th level): When you spend an action point to take an extra action while you are in a guardian form, your melee reach increases by 1 until the end of your turn.

Writhing Roots (11th level): While you are in a guardian form, enemies treat each square adjacent to you as difficult terrain, and each ally adjacent to you gains a +1 bonus to AC.

Iron Boughs (16th level): When you hit an enemy with a melee attack and the enemy is marked by you, you gain a +2 bonus to the damage roll.

Verdant Lord Evocations

Falling Tree Strike — Verdant Lord Attack 11

As the tree falls and crushes all beneath it, your weapon smashes down to knock your foe off its feet.

Encounter ✦ Primal, Weapon
Standard Action — **Melee** weapon
Target: One creature
Attack: Strength vs. Reflex
Hit: 2[W] + Strength modifier damage, and you knock the target prone.

Awaken the Forest — Verdant Lord Utility 12

Vines burst from the ground around you to hinder your foes.

Daily ✦ Primal, Zone
Standard Action — **Close** burst 3
Effect: The burst creates a zone of thick vines that lasts until the end of your next turn. The zone is difficult terrain for your enemies. In addition, your allies have cover while within the zone. As a move action, you can move the zone 5 squares.
Sustain Minor: The zone persists.

Form of the Verdant Lord — Verdant Lord Attack 20

You transform into a treant, sprouting roots that draw strength from the earth and growing branches that sap life from your foes.

Daily ✦ Healing, Polymorph, Primal
Minor Action — **Personal**
Effect: You assume the guardian form of the verdant lord. While you are in this form, your melee reach increases by 1, you gain a +5 bonus to Strength checks to break objects, and your attacks deal triple damage to objects. In addition, at the start of each of your turns, each ally within 2 squares of you regains 5 hit points.

Once during this encounter, you can make the following weapon attack while you are in this form.
Standard Action — **Melee** weapon
Target: One creature
Attack: Strength vs. Fortitude
Hit: 3[W] + Strength modifier damage, and the target is immobilized (save ends).
Miss: Half damage, and the target is immobilized until the end of your next turn.

When you reach 21st level, you can choose an epic destiny. You're free to delay your choice until a later level or to forgo an epic destiny altogether. If you choose an epic destiny after 21st level, you gain all of the epic destiny's benefits that are for your level and lower.

FATESINGER

The Song of Heroes resonates in your soul. Until you can join the chorus, you share the wonder of its music with the world.

Prerequisite: 21st-level bard

In the darkest days of the divine war against the primordials, when those agents of oblivion seemed fated to tear down the divine works and unravel creation itself, the gods' heralds joined voices and spurred mortal champions to fight back. Their song made heroes of common folk, giving them the resolve to stand fast against the tide of enemies around them. These early heralds live on still in the legends and tales of their descendants, and without their emboldening song, the world might have come to an end.

You have studied the Song of Heroes, and you know that all great champions still hear its melody. They might not be aware of it, but at some point they, like you, caught a faint note of it. The distant strains of this ancient song—hidden in an uplifting tune, perhaps, or half-remembered in a stirring call to action—provide the inspiration that mortals need to rise above the mundane and become legends.

IMMORTALITY

You have heard the haunting melody of that ancient song. In that moment, when the words of creation echoed in the harmony of the cosmos, your life's purpose and final fate became clear. Now, your course changed, you devote your time to teasing out the fragments of this ancient song and binding them into a single work, restoring the Song of Heroes to the world to stir new champions to fight against the enemies of creation and safeguard the world for the future.

The Eternal Chorus: When you complete your Destiny Quest, you unlock the fullness of the glorious work, each elusive note captured in the proper order, the music clear. For the first time, you can perform the Song of Heroes in its entirety. The song's purity dissolves your form until you join the singers of yore in body and voice, blending your resonant tones with the rest of the chorus to carry the song forward into eternity.

FATESINGER FEATURES

Destiny Fulfilled (21st level): You can spend an action point to allow an ally within 20 squares of you to make an attack as a free action, instead of taking an extra action yourself. If the ally's attack hits, you regain the action point.

Fate's Clarity (24th level): Whenever you use your *majestic word* power, the target can roll twice on all attack rolls, saving throws, skill checks, and ability checks and use the result he or she prefers until the start of your next turn.

Heroic Inspiration (30th level): Whenever an ally within 5 squares of you spends an action point to make an attack, you and all allies can spend a healing surge as a free action.

FATESINGER POWER

Fragment of the Song	Fatesinger Utility 26

You sing a verse of the Song of Heroes, honoring champions past, present, and yet to come. Surrounded by its melodies, you and your allies are spurred to incredible heroism.

Daily ✦ Arcane, Zone
Minor Action　　　　　　**Close** burst 5
Effect: The burst creates a zone of emboldening music that lasts until the end of your next turn. While within the zone, you and each ally can spend an action point to take two extra actions, instead of one. As a move action, you can move the zone 3 squares.
Sustain Minor: The zone persists.

VINCENT DUTRAIT

GLORIOUS SPIRIT

Glorious deeds live forever. You have been marked for immortality as a warrior spirit to guide future generations.

Prerequisite: 21st level, any primal class

Among the host of primal spirits that guard the world and maintain its natural order, the revered spirits of great mortal heroes stand as proud beacons guiding their living descendants to follow their paths. It is your destiny to stand with them, proving your worth by earning glory in battle. While you still live, you are not yet a Glorious Spirit, but your immortal kindred exult in your triumphs and strengthen you with some portion of their own power, awaiting the appointed day when you fight your last mortal battle and join them in the spirit world.

Battle against any worthy adversary fills your heart with joy and wins the acclaim of your unseen comrades. You harbor a special enmity for foes who would cheat death or inflict inglorious deaths on others. These foes above all you seek to send ahead of you into the dark.

IMMORTALITY

The great ancestral spirits you revere are those who take joy in mortal examples of valor and great endurance. Through your love of battle, you have won the approval of these spirits, and in return they offer you the chance to aid your descendants and those of like mind when your days are done.

Eternal Glory: You distinguish yourself during your final battle, fighting with unmatched valor. Whether you stand or fall, you finally behold the great company of Glorious Spirits, gathered to welcome you into their shining ranks. In a flight of wild joy, they lead you into the spirit world, where a great feast has been prepared in your honor. Leaving your mortal life behind, you become a true Glorious Spirit, an unseen presence on the battlefields of the world who fills living warriors with the courage and might needed to overcome their enemies.

GLORIOUS SPIRIT FEATURES

Worthy Foe (21st level): Once per encounter as a minor action, you can designate the enemy nearest to you as a worthy foe until the end of the encounter. Until the start of your next turn, your attacks against the worthy foe ignore any resistance and the insubstantial quality.

In addition, once per round, you can deal 2d8 extra damage to the worthy foe on a hit. If you can make multiple attacks against the worthy foe during your turn, you decide which attack to apply the extra damage to after all the attacks are rolled.

Finally, if you reduce the worthy foe to 0 hit points, you can spend a healing surge as a free action.

Seeker of Foes (24th level): Once per encounter as a move action, you can teleport to a space adjacent to any creature that you can see.

Bearer of Doom (30th level): If your worthy foe is the only target of your attack and that attack misses, you retain the use of that attack power. Any effect that normally occurs when you miss with the power still applies.

GLORIOUS SPIRIT POWER

Spirit Steed	Glorious Spirit Utility 26

Appearing from nowhere, a winged spirit steed carries you beside your foe.

At-Will
Immediate Reaction   Personal
Trigger: The enemy designated by your Worthy Foe feature ends its movement within 6 squares of you
Effect: You fly and land in a space adjacent to the triggering enemy. This movement doesn't provoke opportunity attacks.

HARBINGER OF DOOM

Ill fortune follows in your wake.

Prerequisite: 21st level

You are an omen of storms, a herald of destruction, a spreader of calamity—wherever you go, destinies are unraveled and woven anew. You have broken free of the bonds of fate, and for you, nothing is written. Every step along your path, every decision you make, forces the future to shape itself accordingly. The ripples spreading from your choices can topple kings, wake ancient terrors, ruin kingdoms, and thwart the designs of the gods themselves.

The most dire consequences of your choices befall those people, realms, or causes to which you choose to give battle. Misfortunes, accidents, and natural disasters gather around your enemies when you are near—minor flukes at first, such as a hailstorm that ruins a crop, a messenger delayed by a few important hours when his horse throws a shoe, or a servant who forgets to secure a gate. You can't control these happenings, or even guess how they might take shape. In fact, ill chance often falls upon those you do not wish to harm, although not in the same measure as your enemies suffer. You dare not linger in places you love, lest you inadvertently destroy the things you hold dear.

IMMORTALITY

No one can know for sure what doom your existence portends. You might battle a dark overlord as a valiant champion of good. Your failure might cause the destruction of the kingdom you fought to defend, and your success might lead to the rise of an inflexible tyranny every bit as dangerous as the dark overlord you overthrew. Only at the end of your mortal life does your true purpose become clear.

Doom Fulfilled: You are drawn irresistibly to fulfill some ultimate doom—usually the catastrophic destruction of a great creature, a mighty realm, or a legendary artifact. When you triumph, fate repairs itself around you, and a new skein of destiny takes shape. In such a weaving, you no longer have a place, and you are hurled out of existence. Nothing remains of you, but you are remembered in the world's myths and legends as an agent of change and destruction. In some future time and place, you awaken with the dreadful knowledge that once again you must serve as doom's harbinger.

HARBINGER OF DOOM FEATURES

Shield of Ill Fortune (21st level): Whenever you roll a natural 1 on an attack roll, you can reroll it. If you roll a second natural 1, you can't reroll it. In addition, when any enemy rolls a natural 1 on an attack roll against you, that enemy is stunned until the end of your next turn, and you can slide the enemy 3 squares as an immediate reaction.

Master of Ill Fortune (24th level): Once per encounter, when a creature within 10 squares of you drops to 0 hit points or fewer, you can make a saving throw or spend a healing surge.

Doom's Reward (30th level): Whenever you make an attack and miss every target, you gain temporary hit points equal to one-half your level.

HARBINGER OF DOOM POWER

Cloak of Doom	Harbinger of Doom Utility 26

A storm of disaster surrounds you, bringing doom to your foes.

Daily

Minor Action   **Personal**

Effect: Until the end of the encounter, any enemy within 3 squares of you grants combat advantage to your allies, cannot teleport, and takes 5 damage whenever it misses with an attack.

LOREKEEPER

All knowledge must be preserved. It must be saved and protected, for knowledge holds the key to who we are, what we were, and what we shall become.

Prerequisite: 21st level, Intelligence 21 or Wisdom 21, training in two knowledge skills

You are a font of knowledge, a peerless scholar, and a custodian of legends, myths, and, above all, truth. Though you content yourself with study and reflection, people come to you from all over the world, and beyond it, for an audience. They seek to apply your keen intellect and wisdom to any number of problems: locating a long-lost artifact, solving an impossible riddle, or devising a strategy to overcome a horde of raging berserkers. Others seek you out just to talk, learn, and expand their own understanding.

With such knowledge comes grave responsibility, for some truths are best kept secret. If you glibly reveal the location of a powerful weapon lost since the fall of an ancient civilization, you might very well doom the world to witnessing firsthand that weapon's power. If you withhold the cure to a plague, the deaths of its victims rest upon your shoulders. Ultimately, you must decide whether you hoard your knowledge or dispense it freely, and whether you have the wisdom to know what to reveal and what to hide.

IMMORTALITY

Lorekeepers are among the most learned people in the world, and they rely on their vast knowledge to battle those who embrace ignorance and reject civilization.

Grand Library: The ultimate expression of your temporal power is the construction of a grand library to hold your collection. By the time you complete your Destiny Quest, you have acquired more books, manuscripts, and other texts than you can catalog. The only way to prevent certain suspect writings from falling into the wrong hands is to construct a place to protect them. Whether you build your edifice in the mortal world, adrift in the Astral Sea, or hidden within the City of Brass, Sigil, or Gloomwrought, this grand library ensures your immortality. The library reminds all who behold its wonders of your single-minded commitment to preserving lore and your great deeds in pursuit of knowledge.

LOREKEEPER FEATURES

Lorekeeper's Wisdom (21st level): Whenever you make a knowledge check or a monster knowledge check, you can roll twice and use either result.

In addition, your attacks deal 2 extra damage on a hit against creatures whose origins are within the purview of your trained skills. For example, if you are trained in Arcana, your attacks deal 2 extra damage on a hit against elemental, fey, and shadow creatures.

Lorekeeper's Cunning (24th level): When you are making a skill check for any ritual, you can roll twice and use either result.

You can double the time it takes to perform a ritual to reduce the component cost of that ritual by half.

In addition, whenever you score a critical hit against a creature whose origin is within the purview of one of your trained skills, you gain a +2 bonus to attack rolls against that creature until the end of your next turn.

Lorekeeper's Revelation (30th level): Choose two of your daily utility powers. Those two powers are now encounter powers for you. If you do not have two daily utility powers, you can immediately retrain your utility powers until you have two daily utility powers that then become encounter powers.

LOREKEEPER POWER

True Name	Lorekeeper Utility 26

You speak your foe's true name, revealing its weaknesses to your allies.

Encounter
Standard Action   **Close** burst 10
Target: One creature in burst
Effect: Until the end of your next turn, you and your allies gain a bonus to damage rolls against the target equal to your Intelligence or Wisdom modifier.

Primal Avatar

You are the living embodiment of nature's power, a mighty primal spirit veiled in living flesh.

Prerequisite: 21st level, any primal class

You are one with the world around you. You hear the whispers of the trees as they speak of their ancient dreams, you taste the change of seasons carried on the four winds, and you understand the thoughts of beasts nearby. The world of spirit that exists alongside the physical world is as real to you as your own body; you perceive and move in both realms at the same time. Like the wisest and most powerful barbarians, druids, shamans, and wardens who have gone before you, you have no fear of death, for when you die, you will reside in the spirit world that you already know.

Many primal spirits are benign. Some are heedless of mortal concerns, and others are actively malevolent. Your power and attunement to their world draws these spirits' attention, for they perceive you even as you perceive them. Hostile spirits see you as a threat and seek to hamper your progress. But you have allies in the spirit realm too, friendly powers who nurture you, lending a measure of their own strength to support your cause. As your power grows, so too does your connection to the spirits of nature, until its sustaining power accompanies you wherever you go.

Your presence in the world has such resonance that a great primal spirit might seek you out to recruit you for a greater purpose. Whether you choose to bind yourself to the entity or not has no effect on your abilities, but service might result in physical manifestations that evoke qualities held by your patron. For example, if you ally yourself with a spirit of the woodlands, your hair might take on a leafy appearance that changes with the passing of the seasons; if you choose to serve a spirit of the hunt, you might acquire a bestial appearance and a shaggy mane; and if you serve an animal spirit of wisdom and guidance, you might grow a stag's antlers or develop hooves for feet.

Immortality

When your body's life comes to its end, you will continue to exist as one of the spirits of nature.

Mighty Among the Spirits: As you near the completion of your Destiny Quest, you feel the tug of something greater, some deeper force drawing you on and goading you to bring your mission to its conclusion quickly. Not long after finishing your final task, you walk from the world into the spirit realm, leaving your mortality behind. Freed from the bonds of your body, you join the host of spirits that protect the natural order and guide new champions to follow the trail you blazed.

Primal Avatar Features

Primal Travel (21st level): When any enemy hits you with a melee attack, you can teleport 3 squares as an immediate reaction.

Spirit Boon (24th level): After each extended rest, choose one ability score. Until the end of your next extended rest, you gain a +1 bonus to attack rolls, skill checks, and ability checks related to that ability.

Eternal Return (30th level): Once per day, when you die and have at least two healing surges remaining, you can will yourself back to life. At the start of one of your turns within 10 rounds of your death, you can spend two healing surges to return to life. You return with hit points equal to your bloodied value and free of any effects that a save can end. You then take your turn normally.

Primal Avatar Power

Walk with the Spirits	Primal Avatar Utility 26

Your spirit slips free from your body, revealing your true nature.

Daily ✦ Primal
Minor Action — Personal

Effect: Your body disappears, and you appear in spirit form in an adjacent space. While you are in this form, you are insubstantial and gain phasing. You also gain a fly speed equal to your speed, and you can hover. You can use at-will powers and encounter powers, but you cannot use daily powers, magic item powers, or rituals. You can remain in this form until you end it as a standard action, until you drop to 0 hit points or fewer, or until you take a short rest or an extended rest. When you leave this form, your body reappears, rejoined by your spirit, in your current space.

ERIC BELISLE

REVERED ONE

You peer beyond the mortal veil to apprehend a deeper, fundamental truth.

Prerequisite: 21st level, any divine class

As the result of long reflection, unflinching morals, and a lifetime of pious service to the gods, you have developed a powerful new philosophy of the mortal place in the cosmos. You have glimpsed the truth of the infinite, the timeless expanse to which mortal souls eventually go, and your insights have the power to change the world. Your teachings are destined to bring hope and enlightenment to people for centuries to come, for glimpses of truth lie within the words you have set down and within the story of your deeds.

Your philosophy might seem, at first glance, to trivialize the gods and their dominions, but you recognize that the gods are necessary intermediaries between mortals and the infinite. You therefore honor all deities as examples for mortals to learn from. Your sermons, your writings, or the stories of your life have the power to help followers of many different gods to understand the lessons of the mortal world.

The exact nature of your revelations is up to you. You might be a visionary who perceives the eventual fate of mortal souls and teaches others how their actions in this world influence their ultimate destinies. You might be a reformer whose teachings challenge inflexible, age-old doctrines of great temples. You might be a philosopher who maintains a creed of stoicism, a fiery condemnation of evil, or an ethical system of obligation to others. Or perhaps you instruct your initiates in darker truths that incite greed, hedonism, or tyranny—not all who follow this path find philosophies of peace and enlightenment, after all.

IMMORTALITY

The Revered One walks a perilous road, for not all powerful entities wish for enlightenment and understanding to dawn on the mortal world.

Truth Revealed: You have traveled to the farthest corners of the universe, stood fast against heavenly legions, battled armies of devils, and thwarted demonic hordes. You have traveled the Astral Sea's dominions and explored the Elemental Chaos in your search for understanding. At last you are within reach of the wellspring of all existence. Upon completing your Destiny Quest, you receive a vision, a golden path stretching into infinity. Unshakable in the power of your convictions, you take the first step on this final journey, slipping beyond this reality and vanishing from view. The road ahead is long and strange, but your journey is only beginning. For ages to come, mortals will follow in your footsteps, guided by your teachings and inspired by your example.

REVERED ONE FEATURES

Immortal Foe (21st level): Immortal creatures take a -2 penalty to attack rolls against you. In addition, you gain a bonus to damage rolls against immortal creatures equal to your Wisdom modifier.

Manifest the Divine (24th level): You can use each of your Channel Divinity powers once per encounter. In addition, you can select any Channel Divinity feat, even if you do not worship the required god.

Bestow Grace (30th level): When any ally within 20 squares of you drops to 0 hit points or fewer, you can spend a healing surge as an immediate interrupt. You regain no hit points from spending the surge, but the ally regains hit points as if he or she had spent a healing surge.

REVERED ONE POWER

Serene Protection	Revered One Utility 26

Once you understand a thing, it becomes a simple matter to ignore it. Sharing your understanding with your allies, you ward yourself and them from harm.

Daily ✦ Divine
Minor Action   **Close** burst 5
Target: You and each ally in burst
Effect: Choose a damage type: acid, cold, fire, force, lightning, necrotic, poison, psychic, radiant, or thunder. Each target gains resist 30 to that damage type until the end of your next turn.
Sustain Minor: The resistance persists.

MIKE MAY

CHAPTER 3

CHARACTER OPTIONS

TAKEN TOGETHER, class and race define most of your character's capabilities—but there's more to a character than capabilities. Your character's feats and equipment complement your powers and class features, while a developed background helps to flesh out your character into a three-dimensional person.

Backgrounds give only minor benefits in the game, but they're an important part of defining who your character is, not just what he or she can do. They suggest elements of personality and story that you can use while you play your character, and they're also a great hook your DM can use to connect your character to the adventures that await you.

Feats are a great way to customize your character, to tweak your abilities so they're just right for the character you want to play. The feats in this chapter are aimed primarily at the new classes and races that appear in this book.

Mundane and magic items guard your weaknesses and enhance your strengths. They ensure that your attacks and defenses keep pace with the increasingly dangerous monsters you face in your adventures.

Rituals extend your capabilities, giving you new ways to overcome obstacles and handle problems outside combat. A careful selection of rituals helps round off your character, making you ready to tackle whatever adversity comes your way.

This chapter includes the following sections.

✦ **Backgrounds:** Rules and extensive story ideas for fleshing out your character's past and its effect on the present.

✦ **Feats:** A wide selection of new feats for characters of every tier.

✦ **Adventuring Gear:** Basic equipment your character might need.

✦ **Magic Items:** New armor, weapons, implements, and other items geared toward the classes in this book.

✦ **Rituals:** New rituals, including some exclusively for bards and those that provide new options for all ritual casters.

HOWARD LYON

The *Player's Handbook* provides questions to help you think about your character's background. The suggestions here are resources you can use when you create a character, offering a wider variety of story hooks and adding a game benefit that reflects your character's history.

This section describes a number of background elements you can use as inspiration for fleshing out your character. You can choose any number of these background elements, but a good way to create a rich yet manageable background is to choose one element from each of three different categories. This book includes five categories: geography, society, birth, occupation, and racial backgrounds.

Regardless of how many background elements you use, when you create a character you can (with your DM's consent) select one of the following background benefits:

+ Gain a +2 bonus to checks with a skill associated with your background.

+ Add a skill associated with your background to your class's skills list before you choose your trained skills.

+ Choose one language connected to your background. You can speak, read, and write that language fluently.

+ If you are using a campaign setting that offers regional benefits (such as the FORGOTTEN REALMS setting), gain a regional benefit.

The background elements presented here are not the only ones possible. Use these ideas for inspiration in creating a background as unique as your character. Above all, remember that a background is more than a game benefit. It forms the foundation of your character, provides hints of what lies ahead in the campaign, and informs your character's personality.

GEOGRAPHY

This element describes the basic environment of the region in which you were raised.

Desert: You were raised in an arid wasteland, such as a sandy desert or rocky badlands. How did you and your family survive? Do you long for the simple life of the desert, or are you thankful to be free of its constant hardships? How do you cope with the overwhelming variety of sights and smells in urban environments?

Associated Skills: Endurance, Nature

Forest: You were raised in a wooded region, such as a forest or a jungle. Did you survive by foraging, or were you and your family hunters? Do you feel at one with the forest, or is it merely a source of food to be harvested?

Associated Skills: Nature, Perception

Mountains: You were raised among the cold, craggy peaks of a mountain range. How often did you visit the lowlands as you were growing up? What brought you out of the mountains to become an adventurer?

Associated Skills: Athletics, Dungeoneering

Urban: You were raised in a large city. What part of the city did you grow up in? Did you stick to that area, or did you explore all the quarters of the city? Do you still have ties to your old neighborhood, or are you happy to forget your childhood?

Associated Skills: History, Streetwise

Wetlands: You were raised in a swamp, a river delta, or another marshy area. Which did you learn first—to walk or to swim? Do you distrust the feel of solid ground, or are you happy finally to have dry feet?

Associated Skills: Athletics, Nature

SOCIETY

This background element indicates your social and economic standing.

Poor: You grew up without a steady income. Were your family members peasants, servants, or unskilled laborers? Did you and your family have to beg in the streets to stay fed? What was the biggest sacrifice you or your family had to make to survive? How did you come to own your starting possessions?

Associated Skill: Streetwise

Wealthy: You grew up rich, never wanting for anything. What was the source of this wealth? Was it inherited, or did your family work for its riches? Was it obtained legitimately, or through underhanded methods? What kind of home did you live in? Was there ever a time when you knew what it was like to be hungry or desperate?

Associated Skill: History

Noble: You are a member of the aristocracy. Does your family have a noble rank? Are you the heir to a title, and if so, how many people stand between you and that title? Under what circumstances did you become an adventurer?

Associated Skills: Diplomacy, Insight

BIRTH

If one background element is common to many heroes, it is an unusual birth circumstance.

Among Another Race: You were born among a race other than your own. Did you grow up among the trees of an elven forest, deep in a dwarven mountain fortress, or in a halfling caravan? Did your family live among that race when you were born, or did some other circumstance bring you there?

Associated Skill: A skill the other race gains a bonus to

Blessed: You received a great blessing from a complete stranger when you were born. What type of person blessed you? Was he or she associated with a particular religion? If so, are you a member of that faith? Did you stay in contact with this person, or do you distrust the motives behind the blessing? How does the blessing affect you?

Associated Skills: Insight, Religion

Cursed: You received a dire curse from a complete stranger when you were born. What type of person cursed you, and why? Did you ever see the stranger again? Were you shunned because of the curse? Do you carry an obvious mark of it? How does the curse affect you?

Associated Skills: Bluff, Religion

Omen: Your birth was marked by an unusual occurrence—perhaps a great storm, an eclipse, or the start or end of a battle. What was the omen? How was it interpreted? Were others born under the same omen, and if so, do you have any special relationships with them?

Associated Skills: Arcana, History

On Another Plane: You were not born in the world, but rather on another plane, such as the Feywild. What circumstances brought your ancestors to that plane? Were they natives of that plane, taken there against their will, or just visitors? When did you leave that plane, and what did you have to accomplish to escape it? Do you miss your birth plane, or do you dread returning to it?

Associated Skill: Arcana

Prophecy: Your birth was foretold in a prophecy. What does the prophecy say about you and about your future? Who, if anyone, believes the prophecy? Are you trying to fulfill the prophecy or to thwart it? The details of the prophecy might suggest further adventures to the DM.

Associated Skills: History, Religion

OCCUPATION

Before you became an adventurer, this was the way you earned your keep.

Artisan: You had a skilled occupation dedicated to a particular craft, such as baking, blacksmithing, carpentry, or cobbling. What did you make? Did you enjoy your work, or was it only a means of supporting yourself? What was your finest creation, and what happened to that item?

Associated Skills: Athletics, Diplomacy

Criminal: You lived on the wrong side of the law. What sorts of crimes did you commit? Did you enter a life of crime by necessity or by choice? Did you belong to a gang? Do you still engage in occasional wrongdoing, or have you left that life behind? If the latter, what caused you to give up your criminal ways? Do you still have contacts among the criminal underworld? Do your former associates now consider you an enemy?

Associated Skills: Stealth, Thievery

Entertainer: You were a dancer, a singer, an acrobat, a storyteller, or another kind of performer. Were you a solo entertainer, or did you perform as part of a group? Were you well known? If so, do you still encounter admirers?

Associated Skills: Bluff, History

Farmer: You worked on a farm, learning the ways of the natural world. Did you raise livestock, crops, or both? Did your farm have a specialty? Did you or your family own the farm, or were you a hired hand? Do you miss those days, or were you eager to escape?

Associated Skills: Endurance, Nature

BACKGROUND EXAMPLES

Following are two examples of how to use the material in this section to craft a cohesive background for a character.

Born and raised in the grimy streets of a large city, Neris developed a knack for getting others to follow her lead. Once she was old enough to help support her family, this talent enabled her to rise to the rank of sergeant in the city militia. With her parents and younger siblings taken care of and a little extra copper for herself, Nerys was more comfortable than she ever thought she would be. But when one of her childhood friends needed a favor, Nerys found herself on the wrong side of one of the city's smuggling syndicates. On the run from a crime boss with a grudge, Nerys has fallen in with a band of adventurers and is putting her street smarts to good use.

Nerys's player chose three background elements: urban (geography), poor (society), and military (occupation). Nerys added Streetwise to her class skills list.

Jahan is the only child of a noble house and was his parents' treasure from the day he was born. Indeed, at the moment of his birth, a pair of cranes appeared and circled the roof of his tower room three times. Jahan became a respected scholar while still young, focusing his studies on the history of his land. As dawn broke on the day when he would enter adulthood and become next in line for his family's title, the rising sun revealed a terrible scene: thousands of dead cranes lay strewn over the countryside. Weeks later, their crops mysteriously failing and their wells gone dry, commoners have begun to whisper that Jahan is the cause. The time has come for him to abandon his books and search for answers in the outside world.

Jahan's player chose three background elements: noble (society), omen (birth), and scholar (occupation). Jahan gains a +2 bonus to History checks.

Mariner: You worked aboard a ship. Was it a riverboat or a sailing ship? Were you a deckhand, a pilot, a marine, or an officer? How extensively did you travel? Where did you go? Was your vessel a merchant craft, a pleasure yacht, a transport vessel, or a pirate ship?

Associated Skills: Acrobatics, Perception

Merchant: You were engaged in the buying and selling of goods. What kinds of goods did you buy or sell? Were you an honest merchant, or did you take advantage of your customers? Did you or your family own the business, or did you work for someone else? Did you travel, or did you work at a shop or inn?

Associated Skills: Bluff, Diplomacy

Military: You served in a military organization, such as an army or a city guard. Were you conscripted, or did you volunteer? What was your rank? How did you leave the service? If you haven't left, describe the circumstances under which you still serve while also adventuring.

Associated Skills: Athletics, Endurance

Scholar: Your life once revolved around knowledge. What area of scholarship was your domain? Were you a teacher or a scribe, an architect or an astrologer, a barrister or a sage? Did others respect your theories, or did they scoff at your ideas? Do you still seek to learn and to teach, or have you given up academia for a life of adventure?

Skills: Arcana, Religion

Racial Backgrounds

Something in your background sets you apart from others of your race.

Deva

Brink of Enlightenment: You were an incredibly advanced soul during your most recent past life, close to achieving the epic transcendence that your spirit has sought through a thousand lifetimes. What interrupted your spiritual journey and led to your rebirth as an adventurer?

Associated Skill: Arcana

Brink of Corruption: In your most recent past life, your spirit was corrupted. Your evil was so great that you were nearly reborn as a rakshasa. Although your rebirth washed most of the taint from your soul, you still experience flashes of violent anger or sadistic thoughts. What led to your corruption? Were you tempted by power, or were you seeking to avert a larger evil by your actions?

Associated Skills: Intimidate, Stealth

Forgotten Lifetime: Although your memory of your past lives is vague, there is one—your most recent—that you can't remember at all. As far as you can tell, there is a gap of nearly a century during which you didn't exist. Did something interfere with your reincarnation, or did something happen during that lifetime that prevents you from remembering it?

Associated Skills: Endurance, Thievery

Dragonborn

Dishonored: Some magnificent failure on your part resulted in the utter loss of your honor. Many dragonborn in your position would seek death, but you have not. Why? Were you wrongly accused? If not, what did you do that cost you your honor? Would you do it again? How might you regain your honor?

Associated Skills: Bluff, Streetwise

Rare Egg: The egg that you hatched from was unusual in a way that dragonborn consider auspicious. It might have had the appearance of burnished gold, carried a pattern that resembled a significant symbol, or broken cleanly into two pieces when you emerged. How much weight do you attach to this phenomenon? What do you think it means, and what did your parents think?

Associated Skills: Arcana, Religion

Brush with the Past: At some point in your life, you encountered some element of dragonborn history. You might have found a weapon forged in the lost empire of Arkhosia, discovered a fragment of parchment dating from that age, or dreamed of an ancient battle as if you had been there. How much of an impact did this encounter have on you? How does it motivate you now? Are you driven to rebuild the ancient glory of your race? Or are you embittered by the fall of Arkhosia and prepared to carve yourself a place in a new empire?

Associated Skills: History, Insight

Drow

Outcast: You were cast out from the city of your birth, most likely because of your failure to comply with the evil customs of your people or the terrible whims of Lolth's priests. Do you dream of returning and gaining revenge, or are you fleeing for your life?

Associated Skills: Dungeoneering, Perception

Orphan: The drow community in which you were born no longer exists. Perhaps an army of dwarves or elves wiped it from the Underdark, or it was exterminated by another drow city. Somehow, you survived this event. Did something about you prompt a member of the invading force to spare you and bring you to the surface?

Associated Skills: Dungeoneering, Endurance

Dwarf

Outcast: Your family and clan have cast you out, severing the ties that are so important to the members of your race. What did you do to deserve this fate? Are you trying to earn your way back into your clan, or to make a great name for yourself and establish a new clan of your own? Are your fellow adventurers a surrogate family for you, or are you a loner at heart?

Associated Skill: Bluff

Dedicated to an Ancestor: You were born on the same day of the year as one of your clan's ancestral heroes, and your parents dedicated you to that hero, whose name you share. What was that hero known for? Do you feel called to emulate your namesake's great deeds, or are you driven to make a name for yourself in a different way? Do you ever dream of your ancestor, or have feelings of déjà vu, as if you're walking in that hero's footsteps?

Associated Skills: Diplomacy, History

Ancestral Home Lost: During your youth, your clan's ancestral home was conquered by enemies or destroyed in a natural disaster. You were among the displaced survivors who built a new life, most likely in a nearby human settlement. Did your parents survive the disaster? If not, who raised you? Were the survivors welcomed into the new community, or were you ostracized? Do you dream of someday rebuilding your ancestral home?

Associated Skills: Nature, Perception

Eladrin

Noble Birth: One of your parents is a noble eladrin. What was your noble parent's title? (Bralani of autumn winds, ghaele of winter, and coure of mischief and strife are examples of the many possible titles.) Do you feel a special affinity for a season, passion, or other natural or emotional phenomenon associated with your parent's title? You probably have much stronger ties to the Feywild than to the world. Why are you now adventuring in the world? When was the first time you visited the world, and what was your reaction to it?

Associated Skills: Intimidate, Nature

Estranged Fey: You were born in the world and never visited the Feywild before the start of your adventuring career. Were your parents exiled or killed? Were you raised by members of another race? Perhaps your trance is haunted by visions of the Feywild's lush landscapes. Or is the Feywild foreign to you, as strange as some distant nation?

Associated Skills: Endurance, Nature

Drowscarred: You carry a personal mark of an encounter with the drow—perhaps a physical scar, but more likely an emotional one. What happened? No doubt this encounter intensified your hatred of the drow. But is your hatred now mixed with fear? Or is it a burning drive to exact revenge? Perhaps something about the encounter gave you a trace of compassion for the drow. Do you hope that they might one day be redeemed and rejoin the eladrin fold?

Associated Skills: Dungeoneering, Heal

Elf

Fey Ally: You are very familiar with the Feywild and have close ties to your eladrin cousins or to other fey creatures. How did you end up with such ties? Perhaps invaders destroyed your family or your home, forcing you to flee to the Feywild. Did the eladrin take you in? It is possible that you have never lived among other elves. Why did you leave the Feywild? Were you cast out, or did you strike out on your own to see the world?

Associated Skills: Arcana, Insight

Wild Elf: You come from a particularly wild tribe, considered primitive by other elves. Why is your tribe so isolated? Did you lose contact with the outside world, or did your people shun civilization? Have you ever been to a city, or are such places the stuff of campfire tales?

Associated Skills: Acrobatics, Athletics

Urban Elf: You were raised in a city where another race was dominant. What drove your family to the city? Do your people live as humans do, or did you grow up in an elven enclave? Are you happy there, or do you long to return to the wild?

Associated Skills: Streetwise, Thievery

Genasi

Chaos Born: You spent some part of your early life in the Elemental Chaos—perhaps living in the efreets' City of Brass or in a githzerai monastery. Fond of traveling in the Elemental Chaos, you recently found yourself thrust through a portal into the world. Are you stranded in the world, or have you decided to stay for a while? Are you eager to return, or enjoying a life less plagued by elemental dangers?

Associated Skills: Arcana, Endurance

Academic Exhibit: Perhaps they created you, perhaps they summoned you, or perhaps they simply found you—however they acquired you, a cabal of arcane scholars treated you as the subject of fascinating study. You might have been on display, or you might have been kept hidden away from everyone except members of the cabal. Were you well treated, or were you locked in a cage? Did some catastrophe befall the scholars, allowing you to escape? Were you the catastrophe?

Associated Skills: Arcana, Thievery

GNOME

Fomorian Captivity: You were the captive of a fomorian overlord. Was your family captured, or were you born into captivity? How did you escape? Are you driven by revenge, or by a deep desire to stay as far away from fomorians as possible?

Associated Skills: Endurance, Stealth

Estranged Fey: Your parents abandoned the Feywild before your birth and never returned. Did your family leave the Feywild by choice or through necessity? Do you plan to return to the homeland you have never seen, or are you content with the place you have found in the world?

Associated Skills: Endurance, Nature

GOLIATH

Skywatcher: You were a respected advisor to your tribe. You helped your people avoid overhunting and overharvesting, scouted new territory, and oversaw seasonal celebrations. Now you are separated from your tribe, either by choice or by necessity. What happened? Did you make a decision that earned you bitter enemies in your tribe? Did a younger member rise to favor over you? Or did you feel a call to the world beyond your tribal lands?

Associated Skills: History, Religion

Lightlost: Your tribe members, brought near starvation by drought, followed a mountain spring to an underground river and found the food they needed to survive. Eventually forging an alliance with a nearby clan of dwarves, they adapted to a subterranean life and haven't emerged since. You are the first member of your tribe to see the sun in generations. Why have you emerged from the caves?

Associated Skills: Athletics, Dungeoneering

HALF-ELF

Wanderer: You have never lived in one place for more than a few months at a time. Why do you travel so much? Are you and your family on the run from something? Or were you a foundling who was raised by another wayfarer? Do you know where your family members are now, or have you lost touch with them in your travels?

Associated Skill: Streetwise

Cultural Half-Elf: Unlike most half-elves, you were raised as part of a half-elf community. Your parents were half-elves, and the mingling of elf and human blood in your veins goes back generations. Why did this community form? Did your people face prejudice from humans, elves, or both? Or have you had almost no contact with either race until now?

Associated Skill: History

Outcast: You were born in circumstances that made you unwelcome—in a community of elves where humans were hated, for example, or vice versa. What was the circumstance of your birth? How did your parents fit into the community? Did you leave by choice, or were you forced out? Do any lingering rivalries or enemies from your home still plague you?

Associated Skills: Endurance, Nature

HALF-ORC

Orc Birth: The child of an orc and a half-orc, you were born and spent your early years among orcs. You might have been destined for greatness, but something happened. Perhaps the tribe was slaughtered in an ill-fated raid or by a group of adventurers. Or perhaps a full-blooded orc challenged your half-orc parent's leadership, and you fled to avoid certain death. How do you feel about orcs now?

Associated Skill: Athletics

Stormtouched: Many half-orcs hold Kord in particular respect, even if they don't acknowledge him as the creator of their race. You had a brush with

---

OTHER BENEFITS IN PLAY

Your DM might decide to give your character a bonus to certain skill checks or other rolls in situations when your character's background could conceivably provide an edge. If your character's background includes an apprenticeship to a blacksmith, for example, the DM might give a bonus to Diplomacy checks when your character interacts with the baron's blacksmith, or a bonus to a Perception check when particular training could help your character notice something awry. Feel free to ask the DM about a "background bonus" if you see a possible connection.

Your character's background might also mean that he or she knows how to do certain things that have nothing to do with the game's skill system or other rules elements. If your character worked as a blacksmith, you don't need to make a skill check for your character to produce a horseshoe, or to earn a subsistence living as a blacksmith. There might be circumstances in which a well-defined background can give your character an edge in the game, even when the rules don't cover the situation.

Details of your background almost always involve other people—such as friends, enemies, family members, and former teachers. These bits of history offer a good opportunity for the DM to create nonplayer characters and situations that can be used later in the campaign.

a storm; perhaps you were born during a thunderstorm, or maybe you were struck by lightning as a young adult. Now Kord's touch is on you, and it's clear that he has some particular destiny in mind for you. But what is it?

Associated Skills: Nature, Religion

First Generation: One of your parents was a human, and the other was an orc. What circumstances brought them together? Who raised you? Were you welcome in your home village or city, or treated as an outcast?

Associated Skill: Bluff

HALFLING

Storyteller: You are a font of halfling folklore, able to spin fables and legends relevant to virtually any situation. Hidden in these tales is a wealth of useful information about halfling history and culture. How did you learn them? Which of the stories do you consider most important? Did the stories spur you to a life of adventure, and if so, why?

Associated Skills: History, Religion

Avandra's Kiss: Your birth was accompanied by an unusual occurrence that your family regarded as a sign of Avandra's favor. Perhaps a bird perched on the windowsill of the room where you were born, or you have a birthmark resembling Avandra's holy symbol. What is the mark or occurrence that reveals this favor? How did it affect your childhood and training? Does it affect your plans for the future?

Associated Skills: Acrobatics, Heal

Banned: You have been cast out of your community, and members of your own family are forbidden to speak to you or even breathe your name. What did you do to earn this shame? Does anyone back home miss you or sympathize with your plight? Is there a price on your head, or does your past otherwise threaten to overshadow your future?

Associated Skills: Bluff, Stealth

HUMAN

Ancestral Holdings: Your family carried a significant noble title during the height of the empire of Nerath, but the lands your family once held are now a dangerous wilderness. Do you dream of clearing the lands and making them fit for human habitation once again? Or are you fleeing the ever-shabbier pretensions of your family of nobles-in-exile?

Associated Skills: Diplomacy, History

Heir of the Forgotten Gods: A sign at your birth or some event in your life pointed to the influence of a god that is either dead or forgotten. Are you destined to revive the worship of this long-forgotten deity, or to take the place of a god that has lain dead since the dawn of time? Do you view the other gods as potential allies or as dangerous competitors?

Associated Skills: Insight, Religion

SHIFTER

Moonspeaker: You were a moonspeaker, a religious leader who traveled among different shifter communities. That background gave you a much broader experience of the world than most shifters enjoy. Do you plan to return to your tribe one day, or is the endless variety of a life of adventure what you seek?

Associated Skills: Heal, Religion

City Shifter: Your tribe was forced off its lands at some point during the last century, and you were born and raised in a large human city. You might have been born to a life of crime, or your family might have established itself in a prominent position. How do you feel about urban life? Do you dream of open fields and untamed forests, or are the twisting alleys and crowded markets your true home?

Associated Skills: Acrobatics, Streetwise

Persecution: You or your family endured a period of persecution, during which shifters were imprisoned or killed because of their perceived ties to lycanthropes. Were you arrested? Did you live in hiding? Has the experience made you ashamed of your origin, or defiantly proud?

Associated Skills: Bluff, Stealth

TIEFLING

Merchant Dynasty: You grew up in a conclave of other tieflings, part of a large merchant family, surrounded by wealth if not prestige. It was a sheltered life, and you're unaccustomed to either hardship or prejudice. Why did you leave the comforts of your home to become an adventurer?

Associated Skill: Streetwise

Dark Secret: At some point in your past, you did something truly evil. You escaped punishment, but if you were ever to be identified as the perpetrator of that deed, you could still be put to death for it. Are you adventuring to forget the horror of your deed and stay away from those who still hunt you, or to try to atone for the wrong you committed? Whatever your crime, it was a clear demonstration of the evil of which you are capable because of the infernal taint in your soul. Will you transcend that evil, or will it ultimately claim you?

Associated Skills: Arcana, Dungeoneering

Infernal Nightmares: You are plagued by nightmarish visions that haunt your sleep. In your dreams, you have vivid glimpses of the Nine Hells and the torments they offer, as well as of the splendor of Asmodeus's palace and the luxurious lives of his most favored servants. What message do you take from these visions? What connection, if any, do you feel to the Nine Hells and their denizens? Does some infernal patron want something from you, or is some divine force reminding you of the punishment you risk if you stray from the path of righteousness?

Associated Skills: Bluff, Religion

FEATS

Feats are useful tools to customize your character, covering weaknesses or enhancing strengths. The feats presented here focus on the new races and classes in this book, but many of the feats are open to any character.

You must meet a feat's prerequisites, if any, to take the feat. If you ever lose a prerequisite for a feat, you can't use the feat until you meet the prerequisite again. A feat that has a class as a prerequisite is available only to members of that class, including characters who have joined the class through a class-specific multiclass feat.

HEROIC TIER FEATS

Any feat in this section is available to a character of any level who meets the prerequisites. Heroic tier feats and multiclass feats are the only feats you can take if you are 10th level or lower.

ADVANTAGE OF CUNNING

Prerequisite: Bard, Virtue of Cunning class feature

Benefit: When you slide an ally with your Virtue of Cunning, you can also slide an enemy that was adjacent to that ally into the space the ally vacated.

ANGER UNLEASHED

Prerequisite: Half-orc

Benefit: The first time you are bloodied during an encounter, you gain a +2 bonus to attack rolls until the end of your next turn.

ARCANE SPELLFURY

Prerequisite: Sorcerer

Benefit: When you hit any enemy with a sorcerer at-will attack power, you gain a +1 bonus to attack rolls against that enemy until the end of your next turn.

AUSPICIOUS LINEAGE

Prerequisite: Deva

Benefit: When you use your *memory of a thousand lifetimes* racial power, you add 1d8 to the triggering roll, instead of 1d6.

BARDIC KNOWLEDGE

Prerequisite: Bard

Benefit: You gain a +2 feat bonus to Arcana, Dungeoneering, History, Nature, Religion, and Streetwise checks.

BLURRING CLAWS

Prerequisite: Razorclaw shifter

Benefit: While you are under the effect of your *razorclaw shifting* racial power, you gain a +2 bonus to melee weapon damage rolls against any target granting combat advantage to you.

COMBAT MEDIC

Prerequisite: Trained in Heal

Benefit: You administer first aid to stabilize the dying as a minor action, instead of a standard action.

You also gain a +2 feat bonus to Heal checks.

COORDINATED EXPLOSION

Benefit: When you use any implement power that creates a burst or a blast, you gain a +1 bonus to attack rolls against the power's targets if at least one ally is within the burst or the blast.

CRUSHING EARTHSTRENGTH

Prerequisite: Warden, Earthstrength class feature

Benefit: When you use your second wind, you gain a bonus to weapon damage rolls equal to your Constitution modifier until the end of your next turn.

DEADLY RAGE

Prerequisite: Barbarian

Benefit: You gain a +1 bonus to damage rolls while raging. The bonus increases to +2 at 11th level and +3 at 21st level.

DISCIPLINED WILD SOUL

Prerequisite: Sorcerer, Wild Magic class feature

Benefit: When determining your Wild Soul damage type, roll twice and use either result.

DISTANT ADVANTAGE

Benefit: You gain combat advantage for ranged or area attacks against any enemy flanked by your allies.

ECHOES OF THUNDER

Benefit: When you hit with any thunder attack power, you gain a +1 bonus to damage rolls until the end of your next turn. The bonus increases to +2 at 11th level and +3 at 21st level.

ENRAGED BOAR FORM

Prerequisite: Druid, *wild shape* power

Benefit: While you are in beast form, you gain a +1 bonus to attack rolls and a +2 bonus to damage rolls with charge attacks.

EXPERT RITUALIST

Prerequisite: Ritual Caster feat

Benefit: You gain a +2 bonus to skill checks that you make while performing a ritual.

FEROCIOUS TIGER FORM

Prerequisite: Druid, *wild shape* power

Benefit: While you are in beast form, you gain a +2 bonus to damage rolls against enemies granting combat advantage to you.

FEY TRICKSTER

Prerequisite: Gnome

Benefit: You gain the wizard cantrips *mage hand* and *prestidigitation* (*Player's Handbook*, pages 158 and 159) as encounter powers.

GOLIATH GREATWEAPON PROWESS

Prerequisite: Goliath

Benefit: You gain proficiency with all simple and military two-handed melee weapons and a +2 feat bonus to damage rolls with such weapons. The bonus increases to +3 at 11th level and +4 at 21st level.

GOREBRUTE CHARGE

Prerequisite: Longtooth shifter

Benefit: While you are under the effect of your *longtooth shifting* racial power, you gain a +3 bonus to damage rolls with charge attacks.

GROUP STEALTH

Prerequisite: Gnome

Benefit: Allies within 10 squares of you gain a +2 racial bonus to Stealth checks.

GUARANTEED RETRIBUTION

Prerequisite: Avenger, Censure of Retribution class feature, *oath of enmity* power

Benefit: When any enemy other than your *oath of enmity* target hits you, you gain a +1 feat bonus to attack rolls against your *oath of enmity* target until the end of your next turn.

IMPLEMENT EXPERTISE

Benefit: Choose a type of implement. You gain a +1 bonus to attack rolls with any implement power you use through that type of implement. The bonus increases to +2 at 15th level and +3 at 25th level.

Special: You can take this feat more than once. Each time you take this feat, choose a different type of implement.

IMPROVED ARMOR OF FAITH

Prerequisite: Avenger, *armor of faith* power

Benefit: While you are neither wearing heavy armor nor using a shield, you gain a +1 bonus to AC. The bonus increases to +2 at 11th level and +3 at 21st level.

IMPROVED BULL RUSH

Prerequisite: Str 13, Con 13

Benefit: When you use the bull rush action, you gain a +4 feat bonus to the attack roll. The bonus increases to +6 at 11th level and +8 at 21st level.

IMPROVED DRAGON SOUL

Prerequisite: Sorcerer, Dragon Magic class feature

Benefit: The resistance granted by your Dragon Soul increases by 2. The increase changes to 5 at 11th level and 10 at 21st level.

Any Class	Prerequisites	Benefit
Anger Unleashed	Half-orc	+2 attack for 1 round after becoming bloodied
Auspicious Lineage	Deva	Roll d8 instead of d6 for *memory of a thousand lifetimes*
Blurring Claws	Razorclaw shifter	+2 damage with combat advantage during *razorclaw shifting*
Combat Medic	Trained in Heal	Stabilize the dying as minor action, +2 to Heal checks
Coordinated Explosion	–	+1 to attack rolls with blast or burst if ally is in area
Distant Advantage	–	Gain combat advantage with ranged and area attacks against flanked enemies
Echoes of Thunder	–	+1 damage after you hit with thunder power
Expert Ritualist	Ritual Caster	+2 bonus to ritual skill checks
Fey Trickster	Gnome	Gain *mage hand* and *prestidigitation* as encounter powers
Goliath Greatweapon Prowess	Goliath	Gain proficiency, +2 damage with two-handed melee weapons
Gorebrute Charge	Longtooth shifter	+3 damage on charge attacks during *longtooth shifting*
Group Stealth	Gnome	Nearby allies gain +2 to Stealth checks
Implement Expertise	–	+1 to attack rolls with chosen implement
Improved Bull Rush	Str 13, Con 13	+4 to bull rush attacks
Improved Grab	Str 13	+4 to grab attacks
Markings of the Blessed	Goliath	Roll twice for first saving throw each encounter
Markings of the Victor	Goliath	Roll twice for first attack roll each encounter
Melee Training	–	Change ability used for melee basic weapon attacks
Oncoming Storm	–	Hit with lightning power to gain +1 on thunder attacks
Potent Rebirth	Deva	+2 to attack and damage if reduced to 0 hp
Radiant Power	Deva	+2 damage with implement power for –2 to attack
Restful Healing	–	Maximize healing between encounters
Savage Assault	Half-orc	Target of *furious assault* takes –1 to defenses
Shadow Skulk	Gnome	Stay hidden when you miss with area or ranged attack
Speed Loader	–	Load crossbow as free action instead of minor
Surging Flame	–	Fire-resistant target takes extra damage from fire powers
Thirst for Battle	Half-orc	+3 to initiative and one additional healing surge
Timely Respite	–	Second wind or total defense grants saving throw
Two-Weapon Threat	Dex 13, Two-Weapon Fighting	+3 damage on opportunity attacks with two melee weapons
Weapon Expertise	–	+1 to attacks with weapon group
Wild Senses	Shifter	Roll twice when following tracks, +3 to initiative

Continued on page 187

IMPROVED GRAB

Prerequisite: Str 13

Benefit: When you use the grab action, you gain a +4 feat bonus to the attack roll. The bonus increases to +6 at 11th level and +8 at 21st level.

IMPROVED MAJESTIC WORD

Prerequisite: Bard, *majestic word* power

Benefit: When you use *majestic word*, the target of the power gains temporary hit points equal to your Charisma modifier.

IMPROVED RAGEBLOOD VIGOR

Prerequisite: Barbarian, Rageblood Vigor class feature

Benefit: You gain 5 additional temporary hit points from your Rageblood Vigor.

IMPROVED ROAR OF TRIUMPH

Prerequisite: Barbarian, Thaneborn Triumph class feature

Benefit: When you use *roar of triumph* while raging, *roar of triumph* becomes a close burst 5 + your Charisma modifier, instead of a close burst 5, and you gain a +2 power bonus to weapon damage rolls until the end of your next turn.

INSIGHTFUL PRESERVATION

Prerequisite: Invoker, Covenant of Preservation class feature

Benefit: When you use your *preserver's rebuke* power, one ally hit by the triggering attack gains temporary hit points equal to 3 + your Intelligence modifier.

Avenger Feat	Prerequisites	Benefit
Guaranteed Retribution	Avenger, Censure of Retribution, *oath of emnity*	+1 to next attack roll against *oath of enmity* target when when another enemy hits you
Improved Armor of Faith	Avenger, *armor of faith*	Increases *armor of faith* bonus to AC
Invigorating Pursuit	Avenger, Censure of Pursuit, *oath of enmity*	Gain +2 AC and damage when you charge *oath of enmity* target

Barbarian Feat	Prerequisites	Benefit
Deadly Rage	Barbarian	+1 damage while raging
Improved Rageblood Vigor	Barbarian, Rageblood Vigor	Gain 5 extra temporary hp from Rageblood Vigor
Improved Roar of Triumph	Barbarian, Thaneborn Triumph	*Roar of triumph* burst is larger, grants you +2 damage
Rising Fury	Barbarian	+2 damage when you reduce enemy to 0 hp

Bard Feat	Prerequisites	Benefit
Advantage of Cunning	Bard, Virtue of Cunning	Slide enemy into ally's vacated space
Bardic Knowledge	Bard	+2 bonus to several skill checks
Improved Majestic Word	Bard, *majestic word*	Target of *majestic word* gains temporary hp
Strength of Valor	Bard, Virtue of Valor	Virtue of Valor also grants +2 damage

Druid Feat	Prerequisites	Benefit
Enraged Boar Form	Druid, *wild shape*	+1 attack, +2 damage when charging in beast form
Ferocious Tiger Form	Druid, *wild shape*	+2 damage with combat advantage in beast form
Primal Fury	Druid, Primal Predator	+1 to attacks with primal powers against bloodied enemies
Primal Instinct	Druid, Primal Guardian	Ally can reroll initiative

Invoker Feat	Prerequisites	Benefit
Insightful Preservation	Invoker, Covenant of Preservation	*Preserver's rebuke* grants temporary hp
Invoker Defense	Invoker	+2 AC when you hit nearby enemy
Resonating Covenant	Invoker, Divine Covenant	+1 attack with at-will after using encounter or daily power
Scouring Wrath	Invoker, Covenant of Wrath	*Armor of wrath* gives target vulnerable 2

Continued on page 188

INVIGORATING PURSUIT

Prerequisite: Avenger, Censure of Pursuit class feature, *oath of enmity* power

Benefit: When you hit your *oath of enmity* target with a charge attack, you gain a +2 bonus to AC and damage rolls until the end of your next turn.

INVOKER DEFENSE

Prerequisite: Invoker

Benefit: When you hit an enemy within 3 squares of you with an invoker power, you gain a +2 feat bonus to AC until the start of your next turn.

MARKINGS OF THE BLESSED

Prerequisite: Goliath

Benefit: The first time you make a saving throw during each encounter, you can roll twice and use either result.

MARKINGS OF THE VICTOR

Prerequisite: Goliath

Benefit: The first time you make an attack roll during each encounter, you can roll twice and use either result.

MELEE TRAINING

Benefit: Choose an ability other than Strength. When you make a melee basic attack using a weapon you are proficient with, you can use that ability instead of Strength for the attack roll and the damage roll.

ONCOMING STORM

Benefit: When you hit with any lightning attack power, you gain a +1 bonus to attack rolls with thunder powers until the end of your next turn.

Shaman Feat	Prerequisites	Benefit
Protector Spirit Adept	Shaman, Protector Spirit	Allies adjacent to spirit companion gain +1 Fort, Ref, Will
Shared Healing Spirit	Shaman, *healing spirit*	Change recipient of additional hit points
Spirit Speaker	Shaman, Speak with Spirits	*Speak with spirits* grants skill bonus to ally
Stalker Spirit Adept	Shaman, Stalker Spirit	Allies adjacent to spirit companion can shift as a free action

Sorcerer Feat	Prerequisites	Benefit
Arcane Spellfury	Sorcerer	+1 to attack rolls after hitting with sorcerer at-will attack
Disciplined Wild Soul	Sorcerer, Wild Magic	Roll twice to determine Wild Soul damage type
Improved Dragon Soul	Sorcerer, Dragon Magic	Increase Dragon Soul resistance by 2
Sorcerous Blade Channeling	Sorcerer	Use dagger to make ranged attacks as melee attacks

Warden Feat	Prerequisites	Benefit
Crushing Earthstrength	Warden, Earthstrength	Add Constitution modifier to damage after second wind
Revitalizing Font of Life	Warden, Font of Life	Successful Font of Life saving throw grants +2 bonus to other saving throws
Sudden Roots	Warden	Enemy hit by opportunity attack is slowed
Wildblood Cunning	Warden, Wildblood	Shift when you use second wind

POTENT REBIRTH

Prerequisite: Deva

Benefit: When you drop to 0 hit points or fewer, you gain a +2 bonus to attack rolls and damage rolls until the end of the encounter.

PRIMAL FURY

Prerequisite: Druid, Primal Predator class feature

Benefit: You gain a +1 bonus to attack rolls with primal powers against bloodied enemies.

PRIMAL INSTINCT

Prerequisite: Druid, Primal Guardian class feature

Benefit: When you roll initiative at the start of any encounter, one ally within 5 squares of you can reroll his or her initiative.

PROTECTOR SPIRIT ADEPT

Prerequisite: Shaman, Protector Spirit class feature

Benefit: Your allies gain a +1 bonus to Fortitude, Reflex, and Will while adjacent to your spirit companion.

RADIANT POWER

Prerequisite: Deva

Benefit: When you make an implement attack, you can take a -2 penalty to the attack roll. If you do so and the attack hits, it deals 2 extra radiant damage. The extra radiant damage increases to 4 at 11th level and 6 at 21st level.

RESONATING COVENANT

Prerequisite: Invoker, Divine Covenant class feature

Benefit: Whenever you use a divine encounter or daily attack power on your turn, you gain a +1 feat bonus to your next attack roll with an at-will divine power before the end of your next turn.

RESTFUL HEALING

Benefit: After you take a short rest or an extended rest, any healing power you use before the start of your next encounter restores the maximum number of hit points possible.

For example, if a 6th-level cleric with Wisdom 18 and this feat uses *healing word* after a rest, that power allows the target to regain hit points equal to his or her healing surge value plus 16 (the maximum result of 2d6 + 4).

REVITALIZING FONT OF LIFE

Prerequisite: Warden, Font of Life class feature

Benefit: If you succeed on a saving throw granted by Font of Life, you gain a +2 bonus to all other saving throws during or at the end of your current turn.

RISING FURY

Prerequisite: Barbarian

Benefit: When you reduce an enemy to 0 hit points, you gain a +2 feat bonus to weapon damage rolls until the end of your next turn. The bonus increases to +3 at 11th level and +4 at 21st level.

SAVAGE ASSAULT

Prerequisite: Half-orc

Benefit: When you use your *furious assault* racial power, the enemy you hit also takes a -1 penalty to all defenses until the end of your next turn.

SCOURING WRATH

Prerequisite: Invoker, Covenant of Wrath class feature

Benefit: When you use your *armor of wrath* power, the target gains vulnerable 2 to all other damage until the end of your next turn.

SHADOW SKULK

Prerequisite: Gnome

Benefit: Whenever you miss with a ranged or an area attack while hidden, you remain hidden.

SHARED HEALING SPIRIT

Prerequisite: Shaman, *healing spirit* power

Benefit: When you use *healing spirit*, you can choose one ally within 2 squares of the target to regain the additional hit points, instead of an ally adjacent to your spirit companion.

SORCEROUS BLADE CHANNELING

Prerequisite: Sorcerer

Benefit: When you use any ranged sorcerer attack power through a dagger, you can use the power as a melee attack. If you do so, the power's range equals your melee reach.

SPEED LOADER

Benefit: As a free action, you can reload a crossbow you're wielding that has the load minor property.

SPIRIT SPEAKER

Prerequisite: Shaman, *speak with spirits* power

Benefit: When you use *speak with spirits*, you can grant the power's effect to an ally within 5 squares of you, rather than to yourself.

STALKER SPIRIT ADEPT

Prerequisite: Shaman, Stalker Spirit class feature

Benefit: Any ally who starts his or her turn adjacent to your spirit companion can shift 1 square as a free action, as the first action during his or her turn.

STRENGTH OF VALOR

Prerequisite: Bard, Virtue of Valor class feature

Benefit: When you grant an ally temporary hit points with your Virtue of Valor, that ally also gains a +2 bonus to the next damage roll he or she makes before the end of your next turn.

SUDDEN ROOTS

Prerequisite: Warden

Benefit: Whenever you hit an enemy with an opportunity attack, that enemy is slowed until the end of its turn.

SURGING FLAME

Benefit: When you hit a target that has fire resistance with a fire power, any fire power deals 5 extra fire damage against that target until the end of your next turn.

THIRST FOR BATTLE

Prerequisite: Half-orc

Benefit: You gain a +3 feat bonus to initiative checks, and your number of healing surges increases by one.

TIMELY RESPITE

Benefit: When you use your second wind or use the total defense action, you can make a saving throw.

TWO-WEAPON THREAT

Prerequisite: Dex 13, Two-Weapon Fighting feat

Benefit: While you are wielding two melee weapons, you gain a +3 bonus to damage rolls with opportunity attacks.

WEAPON EXPERTISE

Benefit: Choose a weapon group. You gain a +1 bonus to attack rolls with any weapon power you use with a weapon from that group. The bonus increases to +2 at 15th level and +3 at 25th level.

Special: You can take this feat more than once. Each time you select this feat, choose another weapon group.

WILDBLOOD CUNNING

Prerequisite: Warden, Wildblood class feature

Benefit: When you use your second wind, you can shift a number of squares equal to your Wisdom modifier as a free action.

WILD SENSES

Prerequisite: Shifter

Benefit: Whenever you make a Perception check to find tracks, you roll twice and use either result.

You also gain a +3 feat bonus to initiative checks.

PARAGON TIER FEATS

Any feat in this section is available to a character of 11th level or higher who meets the feat's other prerequisites.

AGILE OPPORTUNIST

Prerequisite: 11th level

Benefit: When you are pulled, pushed, or slid into a square adjacent to an enemy, you can use an opportunity action to make a melee basic attack against that enemy.

ARCANE FLEXIBILITY

Prerequisite: 11th level, sorcerer, Spell Source class feature

Benefit: When you score a critical hit with a sorcerer power, you can change the damage type dealt by the power to a damage type you have resistance or immunity to.

ASCENDANT LINEAGE

Prerequisite: 11th level, deva

Benefit: When you use your *memory of a thousand lifetimes* racial power and the triggering roll still fails, you don't expend the use of *memory of a thousand life-*

times. However, you can't use the power again until the start of your next turn.

ASTRAL RENEWAL

Prerequisite: 11th level, deva

Benefit: Whenever your Astral Resistance racial trait reduces the damage you take from an enemy's attack, you gain a +2 bonus to the next attack roll you make before the end of your next turn.

BEASTHIDE SHIFTING

Prerequisite: 11th level, shifter

Benefit: While you are under the effect of your *razorclaw shifting* or *longtooth shifting* racial power, you gain resist 2 to all damage.

CHARGING RAMPAGE

Prerequisite: 11th level, barbarian, Rampage class feature

Benefit: When you score a critical hit with a barbarian attack power while you are raging, you can charge as a free action, instead of making a melee basic attack as a result of Rampage.

CLIFFWALK SHIFTING

Prerequisite: 11th level, shifter

Benefit: While you are under the effect of your *razorclaw shifting* or *longtooth shifting* racial power, you gain a climb speed equal to your speed.

DRACONIC SPELLFURY

Prerequisite: 11th level, sorcerer, Dragon Magic class feature

Benefit: Whenever you hit an enemy with a sorcerer at-will attack power, you gain temporary hit points equal to your Strength modifier.

EARTHSTRENGTH RESOLVE

Prerequisite: 11th level, warden, Earthstrength class feature

Benefit: When any enemy marked by you makes an attack that doesn't include you as a target, you gain temporary hit points equal to your Constitution modifier.

ENHANCED FONT OF LIFE

Prerequisite: 11th level, warden, Font of Life class feature

Benefit: You gain a +1 bonus to saving throws granted by your Font of Life.

FADE ALLY

Prerequisite: 11th level, gnome

Benefit: Your *fade away* racial power is a close burst 5, instead of a personal power, and it can target you or one of your allies in the burst. The target is invisible until he or she attacks or until the end of his or her next turn.

Guardian Spirit

Prerequisite: 11th level, shaman, Protector Spirit class feature

Benefit: While any unconscious ally is adjacent to your spirit companion, he or she gains resist 20 to all damage and a +2 bonus to death saving throws.

Hunting Wolf Form

Prerequisite: 11th level, druid, *wild shape* power

Benefit: While you are in beast form, you gain a +5 feat bonus to Perception checks and a +1 feat bonus to speed.

Inexorable Pursuit

Prerequisite: 11th level, avenger, Censure of Pursuit class feature, *oath of enmity* power

Benefit: When you charge your *oath of enmity* target, you can ignore difficult terrain and move through enemies' spaces during the charge.

Improved Cunning

Prerequisite: 11th level, bard, Virtue of Cunning class feature

Benefit: When you use Virtue of Cunning to slide an ally, you can slide the ally 2 squares instead of 1.

Improved Valor

Prerequisite: 11th level, bard, Virtue of Valor class feature

Benefit: The number of temporary hit points granted by your Virtue of Valor increases by 3.

Lyric of Rejuvenation

Prerequisite: 11th level, bard, Song of Rest class feature

Benefit: Each ally affected by your Song of Rest regains 2 additional hit points with each healing surge he or she spends at the end of the rest.

Nimble Spirit

Prerequisite: 11th level, shaman, Companion Spirit class feature

Benefit: You can use *call spirit companion* as a free action during your turn.

Onslaught of Enmity

Prerequisite: 11th level, avenger, *oath of enmity* power

Benefit: When you use *oath of enmity*, you can shift 2 squares closer to the target as a free action.

Overbearing Retribution

Prerequisite: 11th level, invoker, Covenant of Wrath class feature

Benefit: When you use your *armor of wrath* power, the target falls prone after you push it.

Paragon Defenses

Prerequisite: 11th level

Benefit: You gain a +1 feat bonus to Fortitude, Reflex, and Will.

Preserver's Vengeance

Prerequisite: 11th level, invoker, Covenant of Preservation class feature

Benefit: You gain a +2 bonus to damage rolls with divine attack powers while a bloodied ally is within 5 squares of you.

Protected Isolation

Prerequisite: 11th level, avenger, Censure of Retribution class feature, *oath of enmity* power

Benefit: While you are adjacent to your *oath of enmity* target, you gain a +1 bonus to AC.

Quick Recovery

Prerequisite: 11th level

Benefit: Whenever you spend a healing surge at the end of a short rest or an extended rest, you regain 5 additional hit points.

Quick Wild Shape

Prerequisite: 11th level, druid, *wild shape* power

Benefit: You can use your *wild shape* power as a free action during your turn.

Rageblood Recovery

Prerequisite: 11th level, barbarian, Rageblood Vigor class feature

Benefit: When you hit with the charge attack granted by *swift charge* while you are raging, you can spend a healing surge as a free action.

Reserve Maneuver

Prerequisite: 11th level

Benefit: Choose an encounter attack power from your class. The power must be your level or lower and one that you don't already have. When you regain the use of your powers at the end of any rest, you can gain the use of the chosen power instead of regaining the use of an encounter attack power of the same level or higher.

Special: Each time you gain a level, you can exchange the power you chose for this feat for another encounter attack power from your class. The power must be your level or lower and one that you don't already have.

Speaker of the Gods

Prerequisite: 11th level, invoker

Benefit: When you use any Channel Divinity power, you can score a critical hit on a roll of 18–20 with the next divine attack power that you use before the end of your next turn.

PARAGON TIER FEATS

Any Class	Prerequisites	Benefit
Agile Opportunist	—	Use opportunity action to attack when subjected to forced movement
Ascendant Lineage	Deva	*Memory of a thousand lifetimes* not expended on failed roll
Astral Renewal	Deva	+2 to next attack when Astral Resistance reduces damage
Beasthide Shifting	Shifter	Gain resist 2 to all damage during racial power
Cliffwalk Shifting	Shifter	Gain climb speed during racial power
Fade Ally	Gnome	*Fade away* can affect nearby ally instead of you
Paragon Defenses	—	+1 to Fortitude, Reflex, and Will
Quick Recovery	—	Regain additional hp after resting
Reserve Maneuver	—	Swap encounter powers during rest
Strength from Pain	Half-orc	+5 damage for 1 round after becoming bloodied
Surprising Disappearance	Gnome	*Fade away* gives combat advantage against attacker
Two-Weapon Opening	Two-Weapon Fighting	Critical hit with main weapon grants free attack with off-hand weapon
Unrelenting Assault	Half-orc	Trigger *furious assault* on miss
Unyielding Stone	Goliath	*Stone's endurance* grants temporary hp
Versatile Master	Half-elf	Improved Dilettante and paragon multiclassing
Vexing Flanker	—	Targets you flank grant combat advantage to your allies

Avenger Feat	Prerequisites	Benefit
Inexorable Pursuit	Avenger, Censure of Pursuit, *oath of enmity*	Ignore difficult terrain and move through enemies' spaces when you charge your *oath of enmity* target
Onslaught of Enmity	Avenger, *oath of enmity*	Shift toward target when you use *oath of enmity*
Protected Isolation	Avenger, Censure of Retribution, *oath of enmity*	Gain +1 AC when adjacent to *oath of enmity* target

Barbarian Feat	Prerequisites	Benefit
Charging Rampage	Barbarian, Rampage	Charge when you score a critical hit
Rageblood Recovery	Barbarian, Rageblood Vigor	Spend healing surge when you hit with *swift charge*
Thaneborn Advance	Barbarian, Thaneborn Triumph	Shift when you use *roar of triumph*

STALKING PANTHER FORM
Prerequisite: 11th level, druid, *wild shape* power
Benefit: While you are in beast form, you gain a +5 feat bonus to Stealth checks and a +4 feat bonus to initiative checks.

STRENGTH FROM PAIN
Prerequisite: 11th level, half-orc
Benefit: The first time you are bloodied during an encounter, you gain a +5 bonus to damage rolls until the end of your next turn.

SURPRISING DISAPPEARANCE
Prerequisite: 11th level, gnome
Benefit: When you use your *fade away* racial power, the creature that dealt the triggering damage to you grants combat advantage to your allies until the end of its next turn.

THANEBORN ADVANCE
Prerequisite: 11th level, barbarian, Thaneborn Triumph class feature
Benefit: When you use your *roar of triumph* power while you are raging, you can shift a number of squares equal to your Charisma modifier and use your new position as the origin square of the burst.

TWO-WEAPON OPENING
Prerequisite: 11th level, Two-Weapon Fighting feat
Benefit: When you are wielding two melee weapons and score a critical hit with your main weapon, you can make a melee basic attack with your off-hand weapon against the same target as a free action.

UNRELENTING ASSAULT
Prerequisite: 11th level, half-orc
Benefit: You can use your *furious assault* racial power when you miss with an attack. If you do so, the attack deals 1[W] damage if it's a weapon attack or 1d10 damage if it isn't.

PARAGON TIER FEATS cont.

Bard Feat	Prerequisites	Benefit
Improved Cunning	Bard, Virtue of Cunning	Slide ally 2 squares instead of 1
Improved Valor	Bard, Virtue of Valor	Virtue of Valor grants +3 temporary hp
Lyric of Rejuvenation	Bard, Song of Rest	Song of Rest grants extra healing

Druid Feat	Prerequisites	Benefit
Hunting Wolf Form	Druid, *wild shape*	+5 to Perception, +1 to speed in beast form
Quick Wild Shape	Druid, *wild shape*	Use *wild shape* as a free action
Stalking Panther Form	Druid, *wild shape*	+5 to Stealth, +4 to initiative in beast form

Invoker Feat	Prerequisites	Benefit
Overbearing Retribution	Invoker, Covenant of Wrath	*Armor of wrath* target knocked prone
Preserver's Vengeance	Invoker, Covenant of Preservation	+2 to damage when bloodied ally is nearby
Speaker of the Gods	Invoker	Score critical hit on 18–20 after Channel Divinity power

Shaman Feat	Prerequisites	Benefit
Guardian Spirit	Shaman, Protector Spirit	Spirit companion protects unconscious allies
Nimble Spirit	Shaman, Companion Spirit	Conjure spirit companion as a free action

Sorcerer Feat	Prerequisites	Benefit
Arcane Flexibility	Sorcerer, Spell Source	Change damage type of your critical hits
Draconic Spellfury	Sorcerer, Dragon Magic	Gain temporary hp when you hit with at-will sorcerer attack
Wild Spellfury	Sorcerer, Wild Magic	Adjacent enemies take damage when you hit with at-will sorcerer attack

Warden Feat	Prerequisites	Benefit
Earthstrength Resolve	Warden, Earthstrength	Gain temporary hp when marked enemy attacks an ally
Enhanced Font of Life	Warden, Font of Life	+1 to saving throws from Font of Life
Wildblood Speed	Warden, Wildblood	Shift when marked enemy attacks an ally

UNYIELDING STONE

Prerequisite: 11th level, goliath

Benefit: When you use your *stone's endurance* racial power, you gain temporary hit points equal to one-half your level + your Constitution modifier.

VERSATILE MASTER

Prerequisite: 11th level, half-elf

Benefit: You can use the power you chose through your Dilettante racial trait as an at-will power.

If you choose the paragon multiclassing option (see the *Player's Handbook*, page 209), you can choose powers at 11th level, 12th level, and 20th level from any class, instead of only from your second class. You can also spend an action point to regain the use of an encounter attack power that you have already used during this encounter, instead of taking an extra action.

VEXING FLANKER

Prerequisite: 11th level

Benefit: While you are flanking an enemy, that enemy grants combat advantage to your allies.

WILD SPELLFURY

Prerequisite: 11th level, sorcerer, Wild Magic class feature

Benefit: Whenever you hit an enemy with a sorcerer at-will attack power, each enemy adjacent to you takes damage equal to your Dexterity modifier.

WILDBLOOD SPEED

Prerequisite: 11th level, warden, Wildblood class feature

Benefit: When any enemy marked by you makes an attack that doesn't include you as a target, you can shift a number of squares equal to your Wisdom modifier as a free action.

Epic Tier Feats

Any feat in this section is available to a character of 21st level or higher who meets the feat's other prerequisites.

Ancient Stone

Prerequisite: 21st level, goliath
Benefit: When your *stone's endurance* racial power ends, you gain resist 10 to all damage until the end of your next turn.

Bow Mastery

Prerequisite: 21st level
Benefit: When you make a ranged attack with a bow or a crossbow, you can score a critical hit on a roll of 19–20.

Burst of Savagery

Prerequisite: 21st level, shifter
Benefit: While you are under the effect of your *razorclaw shifting* or *longtooth shifting* racial power, you can end that power's effects as a free action in order to deal 2d6 extra damage to one target you hit. When you do so, you also gain 10 temporary hit points.

Enduring Font

Prerequisite: 21st level, warden, Font of Life class feature
Benefit: Your Font of Life grants you two saving throws instead of one. You must make the saving throws against two different effects.

Enduring Rage

Prerequisite: 21st level, barbarian, Rageblood Vigor class feature
Benefit: While you are raging, you do not fall unconscious as a result of the dying condition.

Epic Fortitude

Prerequisite: 21st level
Benefit: You gain a +4 bonus to Fortitude.

Epic Reflexes

Prerequisite: 21st level
Benefit: You gain a +4 bonus to Reflex.

Epic Will

Prerequisite: 21st level
Benefit: You gain a +4 bonus to Will.

Ferocious Critical

Prerequisite: 21st level, half-orc
Benefit: Whenever you score a critical hit with a melee weapon attack, you gain a +4 bonus to attack rolls and damage rolls until the end of your next turn.

Indomitable Will

Prerequisite: 21st level
Benefit: You gain a +2 feat bonus to Will and saving throws against effects that make you dazed, dominated, or stunned.

Invoked Devastation

Prerequisite: 21st level, invoker
Benefit: You can increase the size of any blast or burst you create with an invoker power by 1 (from blast 3 to blast 4, for example).

Long Arm of Virtue

Prerequisite: 21st level, bard, Bardic Virtue class feature
Benefit: The range of your Bardic Virtue increases by 5 squares.

Mighty Enmity

Prerequisite: 21st level, avenger, *oath of enmity* power
Benefit: The first time you use *oath of enmity* during an encounter, you can target two enemies you can see in the burst, instead of one.

Mighty Spirit

Prerequisite: 21st level, shaman, Companion Spirit class feature
Benefit: Any benefits granted to allies adjacent to your spirit companion apply to all allies within 2 squares of your spirit companion.

Opportune Reflexes

Prerequisite: 21st level
Benefit: You gain a +2 feat bonus to Reflex and saving throws against ongoing damage.

Primal Aspect Form

Prerequisite: 21st level, druid, *wild shape* power
Benefit: While you are bloodied in beast form, you gain regeneration 2.

Primal Resurgence

Prerequisite: 21st level, any primal class
Benefit: Once per day, when you become bloodied, as a free action you can regain the use of a primal daily power you have already used today.

Robust Defenses

Prerequisite: 21st level
Benefit: You gain a +2 feat bonus to Fortitude, Reflex, and Will.

Sorcerous Flux

Prerequisite: 21st level, sorcerer
Benefit: When you attack at least two enemies with a sorcerer power, you can swap the attack rolls against two of the targets after you make all the attack rolls for that power.

Any Class	Prerequisites	Benefit
Ancient Stone	Goliath	Gain resist 10 to all damage when *stone's endurance* ends
Bow Mastery	–	Score critical hit on a 19-20 with a bow or a crossbow
Burst of Savagery	Shifter	End racial power for extra damage and temporary hp
Epic Fortitude	–	+4 to Fortitude
Epic Reflexes	–	+4 to Reflex
Epic Will	–	+4 to Will
Ferocious Critical	Half-orc	+4 to attack and damage after a critical hit
Indomitable Will	–	+2 to Will, +2 to saving throws against dazed, dominated, or stunned
Opportune Reflexes	–	+2 to Reflex, +2 to saving throws against ongoing damage
Primal Resurgence	–	Regain primal daily power when bloodied 1/day
Robust Defenses	–	+2 to Fortitude, Reflex, and Will
Transcendent Lineage	Deva	Roll twice for *memory of a thousand lifetimes*
Unyielding Fortitude	–	+2 to Fortitude, +2 to death saving throws
Vanishing Act	Gnome	Teleport when you use *fade away*

Avenger Feat	Prerequisites	Benefit
Mighty Enmity	Avenger, *oath of enmity*	Pick two *oath of enmity* targets the first time you use the oath

Barbarian Feat	Prerequisites	Benefit
Enduring Rage	Barbarian, Rageblood Vigor	Remain conscious at 0 hp or lower while raging
Thaneborn Conqueror	Barbarian, Thaneborn Triumph	*Roar of triumph* reduces damage dealt by foes

Bard Feat	Prerequisites	Benefit
Long Arm of Virtue	Bard, Bardic Virtue	Increase range of Bardic Virtue by 5 squares

Druid Feat	Prerequisites	Benefit
Primal Aspect Form	Druid	Gain regeneration 2 while bloodied in beast form

Invoker Feat	Prerequisites	Benefit
Invoked Devastation	Invoker	Expand size of blast or burst

Shaman Feat	Prerequisites	Benefit
Mighty Spirit	Shaman, Companion Spirit	Spirit companion effects extend to 2 squares

Sorcerer Feat	Prerequisites	Benefit
Sorcerous Flux	Sorcerer	Swap attack rolls of multitarget sorcerer power

Warden Feat	Prerequisites	Benefit
Enduring Font	Warden, Font of Life	Font of Life grants two saving throws per turn

THANEBORN CONQUEROR

Prerequisite: 21st level, barbarian, Thaneborn Triumph class feature

Benefit: When you use your *roar of triumph* power while raging, any enemy affected by the power's penalty to defenses also takes a -5 penalty to damage rolls until the end of your next turn.

TRANSCENDENT LINEAGE

Prerequisite: 21st level, deva

Benefit: When you use your *memory of a thousand lifetimes* racial power, you can reroll the die and add either result to the triggering roll.

UNYIELDING FORTITUDE

Prerequisite: 21st level

Benefit: You gain a +2 feat bonus to Fortitude and death saving throws.

VANISHING ACT

Prerequisite: 21st level, gnome

Benefit: Whenever you use your *fade away* racial power, you can also teleport a number of squares equal to your speed. The power gains the teleportation keyword.

MULTICLASS FEATS

Name	Prerequisites	Benefit
Acolyte of Divine Secrets	Wis 13	Invoker: Religion skill, invoker at-will 1/encounter
Arcane Prodigy	Cha 13	Sorcerer: Arcana skill, bonus damage 1/encounter
Bardic Dilettante	Cha 13	Bard: skill training, *majestic word* 1/day
Berserker's Fury	Str 13, Con 13	Barbarian: skill training, bonus damage 1/day
Defender of the Wild	Str 13	Warden: skill training, mark adjacent enemies 1/encounter
Divine Bloodline	Wis 13	Avenger: Religion skill, *oath of enmity* 1/encounter
Initiate of the Old Faith	Wis 13	Druid: Nature skill, *wild shape*, at-will beast form power 1/encounter
Spirit Talker	Wis 13	Shaman: Nature skill, *call spirit companion*, *spirit's fangs* or *spirit's shield* 1/encounter, *speak with spirits* 1/day

MULTICLASS FEATS

The following class-specific multiclass feats allow you to dabble in the classes presented in this book. See pages 208 and 209 in the *Player's Handbook* for rules on multiclassing.

If you take a class-specific multiclass feat, you count as a member of that clas for the purpose of meeting prerequisites, including prerequisites for feats, paragon paths, epic destinies, and rituals.

ACOLYTE OF DIVINE SECRETS [MULTICLASS INVOKER]

Prerequisite: Wis 13

Benefit: You gain training in Religion.

Choose a 1st-level invoker at-will attack power. You can use that power once per encounter.

In addition, you can wield invoker implements.

ARCANE PRODIGY [MULTICLASS SORCERER]

Prerequisite: Cha 13

Benefit: You gain training in Arcana.

Once per encounter as a free action, you can gain a +2 bonus to your next damage roll. The bonus increases to +3 at 11th level and +4 at 21st level.

In addition, you can wield sorcerer implements.

BARDIC DILETTANTE [MULTICLASS BARD]

Prerequisite: Cha 13

Benefit: You gain training in one skill from the bard's class skills list.

Once per day, you can use the bard's *majestic word* power.

In addition, you can wield bard implements.

BERSERKER'S FURY [MULTICLASS BARBARIAN]

Prerequisite: Str 13, Con 13

Benefit: You gain training in one skill from the barbarian's class skills list.

Once per day as a free action, you can gain a +2 bonus to damage rolls until the end of the encounter.

DEFENDER OF THE WILD [MULTICLASS WARDEN]

Prerequisite: Str 13

Benefit: You gain training in one skill from the warden's class skills list.

Once per encounter as a free action, you can mark each enemy adjacent to you until the end of your next turn.

DISCIPLE OF DIVINE WRATH [MULTICLASS AVENGER]

Prerequisite: Wis 13

Benefit: You gain training in Religion.

Once per encounter, you can use the avenger's *oath of enmity* power. The effect lasts until the end of your next turn.

In addition, you can wield avenger implements.

INITIATE OF THE OLD FAITH [MULTICLASS DRUID]

Prerequisite: Wis 13

Benefit: You gain training in Nature.

You gain the druid's *wild shape* power.

Choose a 1st-level druid at-will attack power that has the beast form keyword. You can use that power once per encounter.

In addition, you can wield druid implements.

SPIRIT TALKER [MULTICLASS SHAMAN]

Prerequisite: Wis 13

Benefit: You gain training in Nature.

You gain the shaman's *call spirit companion* power, but you use it as a standard action.

You gain either *spirit's fangs* or *spirit's shield* as an encounter power.

You gain *speak with spirits* as a daily power.

In addition, you can wield shaman implements.

ADVENTURING GEAR

In addition to the gear presented in the *Player's Handbook* and in the *Adventurer's Vault* supplement, musical instruments and totems are available for purchase.

ADVENTURING GEAR

Item	Price	Weight
Musical instrument		
Drum	3 gp	1 lb.
Flute	5 gp	1 lb.
Harp	15 gp	4 lb.
Horn	7 gp	3 lb.
Lute	12 gp	2 lb.
Lyre	9 gp	2 lb.
Woodwind	10 gp	1 lb.
Totem	5 gp	2 lb.

Musical Instrument: Bards and other characters use instruments for art and entertainment. A nonmagical musical instrument confers no game benefit but can be enchanted later. The instruments on the table are portable instruments.

Totem: Druids and shamans use totems as focuses for their evocations. A totem is a short length of wood or bone, similar to a rod, which is carved to resemble a nature spirit and is adorned with feathers, fur, leaves, bones, teeth, and the like. A nonmagical totem confers no game benefit but can be enchanted later.

MAGIC ITEMS

The magic items presented in this chapter use the same rules as those in the *Player's Handbook* and in the *Adventurer's Vault* supplement.

This chapter introduces two kinds of magic items: totems and musical instruments. Totems (page 207) are implements for certain primal classes, and musical instruments are wondrous items (page 209) that are especially useful to bards.

ARMOR

Magic armor increases your Armor Class by adding an enhancement bonus to the armor's armor bonus.

Masterwork Armor: Masterwork armor grants a higher armor bonus than non-masterwork armor and is always magical. The type and level of magic armor determines if it can be masterwork, as detailed in the tables below. The cost of masterwork armor is included in the cost of magic armor, so higher-level characters should seek out masterwork armor instead of normal magic armor. Some masterwork armor grants a resistance or an armor bonus to Fortitude, Reflex, or Will, instead of granting a higher armor bonus to AC. The *Player's Handbook* and *Adventurer's Vault* describe various types of masterwork armor.

MAGIC CLOTH ARMOR

Lvl	Masterwork Type	Armor Bonus	Enhancement Bonus	Total AC Bonus
1-5	–	+0	+1	+1
6-10	–	+0	+2	+2
11-15	Githweave*	+0	+3	+3
16-20	Feyweave	+1	+4	+5
21-25	Efreetweave*	+1	+5	+6
26-30	Starweave	+2	+6	+8

*This armor, detailed in *Adventurer's Vault*, grants you a +1 armor bonus to Will.

MAGIC LEATHER ARMOR

Lvl	Masterwork Type	Armor Bonus	Enhancement Bonus	Total AC Bonus
1-5	–	+2	+1	+3
6-10	–	+2	+2	+4
11-15	Drowmesh*	+2	+3	+5
16-20	Feyleather	+3	+4	+7
21-25	Anathema*	+3	+5	+8
26-30	Starleather	+4	+6	+10

*This armor, detailed in *Adventurer's Vault*, grants you a +1 armor bonus to Reflex.

MAGIC HIDE ARMOR

Lvl	Masterwork Type	Armor Bonus	Enhancement Bonus	Total AC Bonus
1-5	–	+3	+1	+4
6-10	–	+3	+2	+5
11-15	Earthhide*	+3	+3	+6
16-20	Darkhide	+4	+4	+8
21-25	Stalkerhide*	+4	+5	+9
26-30	Elderhide	+5	+6	+11

*This armor, detailed in *Adventurer's Vault*, grants you a +1 armor bonus to Fortitude.

MAGIC CHAINMAIL

Lvl	Masterwork Type	Armor Bonus	Enhancement Bonus	Total AC Bonus
1-5	–	+6	+1	+7
6-10	Finemail	+7	+2	+9
11-15	Braidmail	+8	+3	+11
16-20	Forgemail	+9	+4	+13
21-25	Weavemail*	+10	+5	+15
26-30	Spiritmail	+12	+6	+18

*This armor, detailed in *Adventurer's Vault*, grants you a +1 armor bonus to Will.

MAGIC SCALE ARMOR

Lvl	Masterwork Type	Armor Bonus	Enhancement Bonus	Total AC Bonus
1-5	–	+7	+1	+8
6-10	Drakescale	+8	+2	+10
11-15	Wyvernscale	+9	+3	+12
16-20	Wyrmscale	+10	+4	+14
21-25	Nagascale*	+11	+5	+16
26-30	Elderscale	+13	+6	+19

*This armor, detailed in *Adventurer's Vault*, grants you a +1 armor bonus to Fortitude.

MAGIC PLATE ARMOR

Lvl	Masterwork Type	Armor Bonus	Enhancement Bonus	Total AC Bonus
1–5	–	+8	+1	+9
6–10	Layered plate	+9	+2	+11
11–15	Gith plate	+10	+3	+13
16–20	Warplate	+11	+4	+15
21–25	Legion plate	+12	+5	+17
26–30	Godplate	+14	+6	+20

MAGIC ARMOR

Lvl	Name	Price (gp)	Categories
2	Agile resolve vestments +1	520	Cloth
2	Astral fire +1	520	Chain
2	Enduring spirit vestments +1	520	Cloth
2	Horn tusk +1	520	Hide
2	Hunting beast +1	520	Hide
2	Indomitable resolve vestments +1	520	Cloth
2	Luring withdrawal +1	520	Leather, chain
2	Vigorous resolve vestments +1	520	Cloth
2	Warding spirit +1	520	Leather
3	Divine retribution +1	680	Chain
3	Life vine +1	680	Hide
3	Predator +1	680	Hide
3	Skald's +1	680	Leather, chain
4	Bear spirit +1	840	Leather
4	Bold victory +1	840	Leather, Chain
4	Pouncing beast +1	840	Hide
4	Rebuking +1	840	Chain
5	Enduring beast +1	1,000	Hide
5	Panther spirit +1	1,000	Leather
7	Agile resolve vestments +2	2,600	Cloth
7	Astral fire +2	2,600	Chain
7	Enduring spirit vestments +2	2,600	Cloth
7	Horn tusk +2	2,600	Hide
7	Hunting beast +2	2,600	Hide
7	Indomitable resolve vestments +2	2,600	Cloth
7	Luring withdrawal +2	2,600	Leather, chain
7	Vigorous resolve vestments +2	2,600	Cloth
7	Warding spirit +2	2,600	Leather
8	Divine retribution +2	3,400	Chain
8	Life vine +2	3,400	Hide
8	Predator +2	3,400	Hide
8	Shared valor +2	3,400	Leather, chain
8	Skald's +2	3,400	Leather, chain
9	Bear spirit +2	4,200	Leather
9	Bold victory +2	4,200	Leather, chain
9	Inner warmth +2	4,200	Hide
9	Pouncing beast +2	4,200	Hide
9	Rebuking +2	4,200	Chain
10	Enduring beast +2	5,000	Hide
10	Lifeblood +2	5,000	Hide
10	Panther spirit +2	5,000	Leather

MAGIC ARMOR CONT.

Lvl	Name	Price (gp)	Categories
12	Agile resolve vestments +3	13,000	Cloth
12	Astral fire +3	13,000	Chain
12	Enduring spirit vestments +3	13,000	Cloth
12	Horn tusk +3	13,000	Hide
12	Hunting beast +3	13,000	Hide
12	Indomitable resolve vestments +3	13,000	Cloth
12	Luring withdrawal +3	13,000	Leather, chain
12	Vigorous resolve vestments +3	13,000	Cloth
12	Warding spirit +3	13,000	Leather
13	Desperate resolve vestments +3	17,000	Cloth
13	Divine retribution +3	17,000	Chain
13	Life vine +3	17,000	Hide
13	Predator +3	17,000	Hide
13	Rageblood +3	17,000	Hide
13	Shared valor +3	17,000	Leather, chain
13	Skald's +3	17,000	Leather, chain
13	Spirit shield +3	17,000	Leather
13	Warding light +3	17,000	Chain
14	Bear spirit +3	21,000	Leather
14	Bold victory +3	21,000	Leather, chain
14	Inner warmth +3	21,000	Hide
14	Legendmaker +3	21,000	Leather, chain
14	Pouncing beast +3	21,000	Hide
14	Rebuking +3	21,000	Chain
15	Bloodvine +3	25,000	Hide
15	Enduring beast +3	25,000	Hide
15	Lifeblood +3	25,000	Hide
15	Panther spirit +3	25,000	Leather
15	Penance +3	25,000	Chain
17	Agile resolve vestments +4	65,000	Cloth
17	Astral fire +4	65,000	Chain
17	Enduring spirit vestments +4	65,000	Cloth
17	Horn tusk +4	65,000	Hide
17	Hunting beast +4	65,000	Hide
17	Indomitable resolve vestments +4	65,000	Cloth
17	Luring withdrawal +4	65,000	Leather, chain
17	Vigorous resolve vestments +4	65,000	Cloth
17	Warding spirit +4	65,000	Leather
18	Desperate resolve vestments +4	85,000	Cloth
18	Divine retribution +4	85,000	Chain
18	Life vine +4	85,000	Hide
18	Predator +4	85,000	Hide
18	Rageblood +4	85,000	Hide
18	Roc +4	85,000	Hide
18	Shared valor +4	85,000	Leather, chain
18	Skald's +4	85,000	Leather, chain
18	Spirit shield +4	85,000	Leather

Lvl	Name	Price (gp)	Categories
18	Warding light +4	85,000	Chain
19	Bear spirit +4	105,000	Leather
19	Bold victory +4	105,000	Leather, Chain
19	Inner warmth +4	105,000	Hide
19	Legendmaker +4	105,000	Leather, Chain
19	Pouncing beast +4	105,000	Hide
19	Rebuking +4	105,000	Chain
20	Bloodvine +4	125,000	Hide
20	Enduring beast +4	125,000	Hide
20	Lifeblood +4	125,000	Hide
20	Panther spirit +4	125,000	Leather
20	Penance +4	125,000	Chain
20	Perpetual resolve vestments +4	125,000	Cloth
22	Agile resolve vestments +5	325,000	Cloth
22	Astral fire +5	325,000	Chain
22	Enduring spirit vestments +5	325,000	Cloth
22	Horn tusk +5	325,000	Hide
22	Hunting beast +5	325,000	Hide
22	Indomitable resolve vestments +5	325,000	Cloth
22	Luring withdrawal +5	325,000	Leather, chain
22	Vigorous resolve vestments +5	325,000	Cloth
22	Warding spirit +5	325,000	Leather
23	Desperate resolve vestments +5	425,000	Cloth
23	Divine retribution +5	425,000	Chain
23	Life vine +5	425,000	Hide
23	Predator +5	425,000	Hide
23	Rageblood +5	425,000	Hide
23	Roc +5	425,000	Hide
23	Shared valor +5	425,000	Leather, chain
23	Skald's +5	425,000	Leather, chain
23	Spirit shield +5	425,000	Leather
23	Warding light +5	425,000	Chain
24	Bear spirit +5	525,000	Leather
24	Bold victory +5	525,000	Leather, chain
24	Inner warmth +5	525,000	Hide
24	Legendmaker +5	525,000	Leather, chain
24	Pouncing beast +5	525,000	Hide
24	Rebuking +5	525,000	Chain
25	Bloodvine +5	625,000	Hide
25	Enduring beast +5	625,000	Hide
25	Lifeblood +5	625,000	Hide
25	Panther spirit +5	625,000	Leather
25	Penance +5	625,000	Chain
25	Perpetual resolve vestments +5	625,000	Cloth
27	Agile resolve vestments +6	1,625,000	Cloth
27	Astral fire +6	1,625,000	Chain
27	Enduring spirit vestments +6	1,625,000	Cloth

Lvl	Name	Price (gp)	Categories
27	Horn tusk +6	1,625,000	Hide
27	Hunting beast +6	1,625,000	Hide
27	Indomitable resolve vestments +6	1,625,000	Cloth
27	Luring withdrawal +6	1,625,000	Leather, chain
27	Vigorous resolve vestments +6	1,625,000	Cloth
27	Warding spirit +6	1,625,000	Leather
28	Desperate resolve vestments +6	2,125,000	Cloth
28	Divine retribution +6	2,125,000	Chain
28	Life vine +6	2,125,000	Hide
28	Predator +6	2,125,000	Hide
28	Rageblood +6	2,125,000	Hide
28	Roc +6	2,125,000	Hide
28	Shared valor +6	2,125,000	Leather, chain
28	Skald's +6	2,125,000	Leather, chain
28	Spirit shield +6	2,125,000	Leather
28	Sudden escape +6	2,125,000	Chain
28	Warding light +6	2,125,000	Chain
29	Bear spirit +6	2,625,000	Leather
29	Bold victory +6	2,625,000	Leather, chain
29	Inner warmth +6	2,625,000	Hide
29	Legendmaker +6	2,625,000	Leather, chain
29	Pouncing beast +6	2,625,000	Hide
29	Rebuking +6	2,625,000	Chain
30	Bloodvine +6	3,125,000	Hide
30	Enduring beast +6	3,125,000	Hide
30	Lifeblood +6	3,125,000	Hide
30	Panther spirit +6	3,125,000	Leather
30	Penance +6	3,125,000	Chain
30	Perpetual resolve vestments +6	3,125,000	Cloth

Agile Resolve Vestments
Level 2+

These embroidered vestments channel your resolve to imbue you with agility.

Lvl		Price	Lvl		Price
Lvl 2	+1	520 gp	Lvl 17	+4	65,000 gp
Lvl 7	+2	2,600 gp	Lvl 22	+5	325,000 gp
Lvl 12	+3	13,000 gp	Lvl 27	+6	1,625,000 gp

Armor: Cloth
Enhancement: AC
Property: While you are bloodied, you gain a +2 item bonus to Reflex.

Astral Fire Armor
Level 2+

The small crystals in the links of this armor glitter like stars, and when exposed to divine energy, they flare and fill you with defensive power.

Lvl		Price	Lvl		Price
Lvl 2	+1	520 gp	Lvl 17	+4	65,000 gp
Lvl 7	+2	2,600 gp	Lvl 22	+5	325,000 gp
Lvl 12	+3	13,000 gp	Lvl 27	+6	1,625,000 gp

Armor: Chain
Enhancement: AC
Property: When you use any Channel Divinity power, you gain a +2 item bonus to AC and Fortitude until the end of your next turn.

Bear Spirit Armor — Level 4+

Crafted from bear hide and stitched with invocations to the beast's spirit, this armor rewards fury with a bear's endurance.

Lvl 4	+1	840 gp	Lvl 19	+4	105,000 gp
Lvl 9	+2	4,200 gp	Lvl 24	+5	525,000 gp
Lvl 14	+3	21,000 gp	Lvl 29	+6	2,625,000 gp

Armor: Leather
Enhancement: AC
Power (Daily ✦ Spirit): Immediate Reaction. *Trigger:* An ally within 5 squares of your spirit companion hits an enemy. *Effect:* You and each ally within 5 squares of your spirit companion gain temporary hit points equal to 5 + your Constitution modifier.
Level 14 or 19: 10 + your Constitution modifier temporary hit points.
Level 24 or 29: 15 + your Constitution modifier temporary hit points.

Bloodvine Armor — Level 15+

Embedded beneath this armor's surface are rootlike tendrils. When you are hit, these tendrils expand and harden, providing superior protection.

Lvl 15	+3	25,000 gp	Lvl 25	+5	625,000 gp
Lvl 20	+4	125,000 gp	Lvl 30	+6	3,125,000 gp

Armor: Hide
Enhancement: AC
Power (Daily): Immediate Reaction. *Trigger:* An enemy hits you. *Effect:* You gain a +1 power bonus to AC until the end of the encounter. Whenever an enemy hits you, the bonus increases by 1 to a maximum power bonus of +2.
Level 20: Maximum power bonus of +3.
Level 25 or 30: Maximum power bonus of +4.

Bold Victory Armor — Level 4+

The magic that flows through this impressive armor bolsters you or your friend as you turn a battle toward victory.

Lvl 4	+1	840 gp	Lvl 19	+4	105,000 gp
Lvl 9	+2	4,200 gp	Lvl 24	+5	525,000 gp
Lvl 14	+3	21,000 gp	Lvl 29	+6	2,625,000 gp

Armor: Leather, chain
Enhancement: AC
Power (Encounter): Free Action. *Trigger:* You or an ally within 5 squares of you bloodies an enemy. *Effect:* The attacker gains a +2 power bonus to AC until the end of his or her next turn.

Desperate Resolve Vestments — Level 13+

The divine power within these vestments turns the deadliest attack into a glancing blow.

Lvl 13	+3	17,000 gp	Lvl 23	+5	425,000 gp
Lvl 18	+4	85,000 gp	Lvl 28	+6	2,125,000 gp

Armor: Cloth
Enhancement: AC
Power (Daily ✦ Healing): Immediate Interrupt. *Trigger:* You take damage from an attack. *Effect:* You become insubstantial until the end of your next turn. You can spend a healing surge.

Divine Retribution Armor — Level 3+

When you are hit, the divine power imbuing the links of this armor flares and empowers your attacks against those that harm you.

Lvl 3	+1	680 gp	Lvl 18	+4	85,000 gp
Lvl 8	+2	3,400 gp	Lvl 23	+5	425,000 gp
Lvl 13	+3	17,000 gp	Lvl 28	+6	2,125,000 gp

Armor: Chain
Enhancement: AC
Power (Encounter): Immediate Reaction. *Trigger:* An enemy hits you with a melee or a close attack. *Effect:* Until the end of your next turn, you gain a bonus to damage rolls against the triggering enemy equal to the armor's enhancement bonus.

Enduring Beast Armor — Level 5+

The spirit within this glistening armor grants you the fortitude to replenish your energy even after the most grievous wounds.

Lvl 5	+1	1,000 gp	Lvl 20	+4	125,000 gp
Lvl 10	+2	5,000 gp	Lvl 25	+5	625,000 gp
Lvl 15	+3	25,000 gp	Lvl 30	+6	3,125,000 gp

Armor: Hide
Enhancement: AC
Property: While you are in beast form, you regain 2 additional hit points whenever you spend a healing surge.
Level 15 or 20: 4 additional hit points.
Level 25 or 30: 6 additional hit points.
Power (Daily ✦ Healing): Minor Action. You spend a healing surge.

Enduring Spirit Vestments — Level 2+

The divine power imbued in these vestments inures you to damage.

Lvl 2	+1	520 gp	Lvl 17	+4	65,000 gp
Lvl 7	+2	2,600 gp	Lvl 22	+5	325,000 gp
Lvl 12	+3	13,000 gp	Lvl 27	+6	1,625,000 gp

Armor: Cloth
Enhancement: AC
Power (Daily ✦ Healing): Free Action. *Trigger:* You use a Channel Divinity power. *Effect:* You gain a +2 bonus to AC until the end of the encounter. You also regain 5 hit points.
Level 12 or 17: Regain 10 hit points.
Level 22 or 27: Regain 15 hit points.

Horn Tusk Armor — Level 2+

Short tusks protrude from this armor's shoulder guards. The armor gives you the resilience of a boar, allowing you to attack even as a foe drops you.

Lvl 2	+1	520 gp	Lvl 17	+4	65,000 gp
Lvl 7	+2	2,600 gp	Lvl 22	+5	325,000 gp
Lvl 12	+3	13,000 gp	Lvl 27	+6	1,625,000 gp

Armor: Hide
Enhancement: AC
Power (Encounter): Immediate Interrupt. *Trigger:* An enemy reduces you to 0 hit points or fewer. *Effect:* You make a melee basic attack with a bonus to the attack roll and the damage roll equal to the armor's enhancement bonus.

Hunting Beast Armor — Level 2+

This armor carries within it the spirit of a hunting beast. When you change into beast form, that spirit guides your movements.

Lvl 2	+1	520 gp	Lvl 17	+4	65,000 gp
Lvl 7	+2	2,600 gp	Lvl 22	+5	325,000 gp
Lvl 12	+3	13,000 gp	Lvl 27	+6	1,625,000 gp

Armor: Hide

Enhancement: AC

Property: While you are in beast form, you gain a +2 item bonus to Reflex.

Power (Encounter ✦ Beast Form): Move Action. You shift 2 squares.

Indomitable Resolve Vestments — Level 2+

These embroidered vestments channel your resolve and imbue you with willpower and determination.

Lvl 2	+1	520 gp	Lvl 17	+4	65,000 gp
Lvl 7	+2	2,600 gp	Lvl 22	+5	325,000 gp
Lvl 12	+3	13,000 gp	Lvl 27	+6	1,625,000 gp

Armor: Cloth

Enhancement: AC

Property: While you are bloodied, you gain a +2 item bonus to Will.

Inner Warmth Armor — Level 9+

Created from the hide of elemental beasts, this armor exudes an aura of comforting warmth.

Lvl 9	+2	4,200 gp	Lvl 24	+5	525,000 gp
Lvl 14	+3	21,000 gp	Lvl 29	+6	2,625,000 gp
Lvl 19	+4	105,000 gp			

Armor: Hide

Enhancement: AC

Property: You gain resist 5 cold and resist 5 necrotic.
Level 19 or 24: Resist 10 cold and resist 10 necrotic.
Level 29: Resist 15 cold and resist 15 necrotic.

Power (Daily): Minor Action. Until the end of the encounter, any ally adjacent to you gains the resistances granted by this armor.

Legendmaker Armor — Level 14+

Wearing this impressive armor, you can inspire your allies to help create the stuff of legends.

| Lvl 14 | +3 | 21,000 gp | Lvl 24 | +5 | 525,000 gp |
| Lvl 19 | +4 | 105,000 gp | Lvl 29 | +6 | 2,625,000 gp |

Armor: Leather, chain

Enhancement: AC

Property: If you have the *majestic word* power, you are not restricted to using it only once per round.

Power (Daily): Immediate Reaction. *Trigger:* An ally within 5 squares of you reduces an enemy to 0 hit points. *Effect:* The triggering ally can take an extra standard action before the end of his or her turn.

Lifeblood Armor — Level 10+

This armor is infused with primal spirits that sustain and shield you from your enemies' attacks.

Lvl 10	+2	5,000 gp	Lvl 25	+5	625,000 gp
Lvl 15	+3	25,000 gp	Lvl 30	+6	3,125,000 gp
Lvl 20	+4	125,000 gp			

Armor: Hide

Enhancement: AC

Property: You gain 5 temporary hit points after each rest. If you remove the armor, you lose these temporary hit points.
Level 15 or 20: 10 temporary hit points.
Level 25 or 30: 15 temporary hit points.

Life Vine Armor — Level 3+

This armor is woven with an intricate lattice of living vines that form a symbiotic relationship with the wearer.

Lvl 3	+1	680 gp	Lvl 18	+4	85,000 gp
Lvl 8	+2	3,400 gp	Lvl 23	+5	425,000 gp
Lvl 13	+3	17,000 gp	Lvl 28	+6	2,125,000 gp

Armor: Hide

Enhancement: AC

Power (Daily ✦ Healing): Immediate Interrupt. *Trigger:* An enemy scores a critical hit against you. *Effect:* You spend a healing surge and regain additional hit points equal to the armor's enhancement bonus.

Luring Withdrawal Armor — Level 2+

Crafted from the essence of wind elementals, this armor allows you to withdraw from a foe and lure it into a trap.

Lvl 2	+1	520 gp	Lvl 17	+4	65,000 gp
Lvl 7	+2	2,600 gp	Lvl 22	+5	325,000 gp
Lvl 12	+3	13,000 gp	Lvl 27	+6	1,625,000 gp

Armor: Leather, chain

Enhancement: AC

Power (Daily): Immediate Reaction. *Trigger:* An enemy misses you with a melee attack. *Effect:* You shift 1 square and slide the triggering enemy into the space you vacated.

Panther Spirit Armor — Level 5+

Crafted of supple leather from a noble panther's hide, this armor is imbued with the panther spirit's power and resilience.

Lvl 5	+1	1,000 gp	Lvl 20	+4	125,000 gp
Lvl 10	+2	5,000 gp	Lvl 25	+5	625,000 gp
Lvl 15	+3	25,000 gp	Lvl 30	+6	3,125,000 gp

Armor: Leather

Enhancement: AC

Power (Daily ✦ Healing): Immediate Reaction. *Trigger:* An ally within 5 squares of you hits an enemy with a melee attack and is flanking that enemy. *Effect:* The triggering ally regains hit points equal to half the attack's damage.

Penance Armor — Level 15+

Intricate runes of rebuke are scribed into this armor's links, promising divine punishment for those that dare harm you.

| Lvl 15 | +3 | 25,000 gp | Lvl 25 | +5 | 625,000 gp |
| Lvl 20 | +4 | 125,000 gp | Lvl 30 | +6 | 3,125,000 gp |

Armor: Chain

Enhancement: AC

Power (Daily): Immediate Interrupt. *Trigger:* An enemy hits you with a melee or a close attack. *Effect:* The triggering enemy is weakened until the end of its next turn.

Perpetual Resolve Vestments — Level 20+

The divine power in these vestments shields you from ongoing damage.

| Lvl 20 | +4 | 125,000 gp | Lvl 30 | +6 | 3,125,000 gp |
| Lvl 25 | +5 | 625,000 gp | | | |

Armor: Cloth
Enhancement: AC
Property: You take ongoing damage at the end of your turn, instead of at the start. At the end of your turn, you make saving throws against ongoing damage before taking the damage.

Pouncing Beast Armor — Level 4+

When you wear this armor, you can feel the beast spirit within you urging you to leap forward and attack.

Lvl 4	+1	840 gp	Lvl 19	+4	105,000 gp
Lvl 9	+2	4,200 gp	Lvl 24	+5	525,000 gp
Lvl 14	+3	21,000 gp	Lvl 29	+6	2,625,000 gp

Armor: Hide
Enhancement: AC
Property: When you use *wild shape* to change into beast form, you can shift 1 square.
Power (Daily ✦ Beast Form): Move Action. You shift 5 squares and must end in a space adjacent to an enemy.

Predator Armor — Level 3+

When you change into beast form, the primal spirit within this armor grants you the power to bring down an escaping foe.

Lvl 3	+1	680 gp	Lvl 18	+4	85,000 gp
Lvl 8	+2	3,400 gp	Lvl 23	+5	425,000 gp
Lvl 13	+3	17,000 gp	Lvl 28	+6	2,125,000 gp

Armor: Hide
Enhancement: AC
Property: While you are in beast form, you gain a +1 item bonus to Fortitude and Will.
Power (Daily ✦ Beast Form): Immediate Reaction. *Trigger:* An enemy adjacent to you shifts. *Effect:* Until the end of your next turn, you gain a bonus to attack rolls and damage rolls against the triggering enemy equal to the armor's enhancement bonus.

Rageblood Armor — Level 13+

This armor was crafted from the hide of a ferocious behemoth. That creature's blood rage now enhances your own fury.

| Lvl 13 | +3 | 17,000 gp | Lvl 23 | +5 | 425,000 gp |
| Lvl 18 | +4 | 85,000 gp | Lvl 28 | +6 | 2,125,000 gp |

Armor: Hide
Enhancement: AC
Property: When you use any barbarian rage power, you regain hit points equal to 10 + your Constitution modifier.
Power (Daily): Free Action. *Trigger:* You make a damage roll and dislike the result. *Effect:* You reroll the damage and use either result.

Rebuking Armor — Level 4+

This silver chainmail glimmers as the divine magic within it bolsters your defenses against a foe that feels your wrath.

Lvl 4	+1	840 gp	Lvl 19	+4	105,000 gp
Lvl 9	+2	4,200 gp	Lvl 24	+5	525,000 gp
Lvl 14	+3	21,000 gp	Lvl 29	+6	2,625,000 gp

Armor: Chain
Enhancement: AC
Property: When you hit an enemy with any divine attack power, you gain a +1 bonus to all defenses against that enemy's attacks until the end of your next turn.

Roc Armor — Level 18+

This armor is decorated with roc feathers. When you enter beast form, you can tap into the great beast's spirit to adopt its shape.

| Lvl 18 | +4 | 85,000 gp | Lvl 28 | +6 | 2,125,000 gp |
| Lvl 23 | +5 | 425,000 gp | | | |

Armor: Hide
Enhancement: AC
Power (Daily): Free Action. Until the end of the encounter, you can use your *wild shape* power to assume the form of a roc that is your size. In this form, you gain a fly speed of 6, and you can hover. You can't use daily attack powers or manipulate objects.
Until this power ends, you can use *wild shape* to change among this form, another beast form, and your humanoid form.

Shared Valor Armor — Level 8+

The verses and images inlaid into this armor's surface are a source of inspiration for the wearer as much as for those who behold the armor.

Lvl 8	+2	3,400 gp	Lvl 23	+5	425,000 gp
Lvl 13	+3	17,000 gp	Lvl 28	+6	2,125,000 gp
Lvl 18	+4	85,000 gp			

Armor: Leather, chain
Enhancement: AC
Property: Whenever you grant temporary hit points to an ally, you gain temporary hit points equal to half the number you granted to that ally.

Skald's Armor — Level 3+

A favorite item of wandering bards, this armor enhances your ability to talk your way out of tight situations.

Lvl 3	+1	680 gp	Lvl 18	+4	85,000 gp
Lvl 8	+2	3,400 gp	Lvl 23	+5	425,000 gp
Lvl 13	+3	17,000 gp	Lvl 28	+6	2,125,000 gp

Armor: Leather, chain
Enhancement: AC
Property: You gain a +2 item bonus to Bluff checks and Diplomacy checks.
Level 13 or 18: +4 item bonus.
Level 23 or 28: +6 item bonus.
Power (Daily): Immediate Interrupt. *Trigger:* An enemy targets you with a melee attack. *Effect:* The triggering enemy instead targets a creature of your choice adjacent to you.

Spirit Shield Armor
Level 13+

This leather armor is engraved with images of beast spirits, and their power flows through your spirit companion to your allies.

Lvl 13	+3	17,000 gp		Lvl 23	+5	425,000 gp
Lvl 18	+4	85,000 gp		Lvl 28	+6	2,125,000 gp

Armor: Leather

Enhancement: AC

Power (Daily): Minor Action. Until the end of your next turn, you lose the armor's enhancement bonus, and each ally adjacent to your spirit companion gains a bonus to AC equal to the armor's enhancement bonus.

Sudden Escape Armor
Level 28

This shimmering armor allows you to invoke astral energy to spirit yourself away from an attack.

Lvl 28	+6	2,125,000 gp

Armor: Chain

Enhancement: AC

Power (Daily ✦ Teleportation): Immediate Interrupt.
Trigger: An enemy hits you with a melee or a close attack.
Effect: You teleport 5 squares and become insubstantial until the start of your next turn.

Vigorous Resolve Vestments
Level 2+

These embroidered vestments channel your resolve and imbue you with resilience.

Lvl 2	+1	520 gp		Lvl 17	+4	65,000 gp
Lvl 7	+2	2,600 gp		Lvl 22	+5	325,000 gp
Lvl 12	+3	13,000 gp		Lvl 27	+6	1,625,000 gp

Armor: Cloth

Enhancement: AC

Property: While you are bloodied, you gain a +2 item bonus to Fortitude.

Warding Light Armor
Level 13+

White and yellow fire plays over this armor's links. When a foe strikes you, these flames erupt in a punishing flare.

Lvl 13	+3	17,000 gp		Lvl 23	+5	425,000 gp
Lvl 18	+4	85,000 gp		Lvl 28	+6	2,125,000 gp

Armor: Chain

Enhancement: AC

Power (Daily ✦ Radiant): Immediate Reaction. *Trigger:* An enemy hits you. *Effect:* The triggering enemy takes 1d8 + your Wisdom modifier radiant damage.
Level 18 or 23: 2d8 + your Wisdom modifier radiant damage.
Level 28: 3d8 + your Wisdom modifier radiant damage.

Warding Spirit Armor
Level 2+

The primal power infused within this leather armor draws power from your spirit companion to shield you from attack when your guard is down.

Lvl 2	+1	520 gp		Lvl 17	+4	65,000 gp
Lvl 7	+2	2,600 gp		Lvl 22	+5	325,000 gp
Lvl 12	+3	13,000 gp		Lvl 27	+6	1,625,000 gp

Armor: Leather

Enhancement: AC

Property: You gain a +4 power bonus to AC against opportunity attacks while your spirit companion is present in the encounter.

WEAPONS

You add a magic weapon's enhancement bonus to your attack rolls and damage rolls when you attack with it using a weapon power.

MAGIC WEAPONS

Lvl	Name	Price (gp)	Categories
2	Wyrmtooth dagger +1	520	Dagger
3	Harsh songblade +1	680	Heavy blade, light blade
4	Tooth of chaos +1	840	Dagger
5	Winged dagger +1	1,000	Dagger
7	Wyrmtooth dagger +2	2,600	Dagger
8	Harsh songblade +2	3,400	Heavy blade, light blade
9	Tooth of chaos +2	4,200	Dagger
10	Elemental twist dagger +2	5,000	Dagger
10	Winged dagger +2	5,000	Dagger
12	Wyrmtooth dagger +3	13,000	Dagger
13	Harsh songblade +3	17,000	Heavy blade, light blade
13	Piercing songblade +3	17,000	Heavy blade, light blade
14	Tooth of chaos +3	21,000	Dagger
15	Elemental twist dagger +3	25,000	Dagger
15	Winged dagger +3	25,000	Dagger
17	Wyrmtooth dagger +4	65,000	Dagger
18	Harsh songblade +4	85,000	Heavy blade, light blade
18	Piercing songblade +4	85,000	Heavy blade, light blade
19	Tooth of chaos +4	105,000	Dagger
20	Elemental twist dagger +4	125,000	Dagger
20	Lilting songblade +4	125,000	Heavy blade, light blade
20	Winged dagger +4	125,000	Dagger
22	Wyrmtooth dagger +5	325,000	Dagger
23	Harsh songblade +5	425,000	Heavy blade, light blade
23	Piercing songblade +5	425,000	Heavy blade, light blade
24	Tooth of chaos +5	525,000	Dagger
25	Elemental twist dagger +5	625,000	Dagger
25	Lilting songblade +5	625,000	Heavy blade, light blade
25	Winged dagger +5	625,000	Dagger
27	Wyrmtooth dagger +6	1,625,000	Dagger
28	Harsh songblade +6	2,125,000	Heavy blade, light blade
28	Piercing songblade +6	2,125,000	Heavy blade, light blade
29	Tooth of chaos +6	2,625,000	Dagger
30	Elemental twist dagger +6	3,125,000	Dagger
30	Lilting songblade +6	3,125,000	Heavy blade, light blade
30	Winged dagger +6	3,125,000	Dagger

Using a Weapon as an Implement: Some classes can use certain magic weapons as implements. If you're able to wield a magic weapon as an implement and use an implement power through it, you add the weapon's enhancement bonus to the power's attack rolls and damage rolls, but you do not use the weapon's proficiency bonus. If you score a critical hit with the magic weapon when using it as an implement, you use the weapon's critical hit effect.

Elemental Twist Dagger · Level 10+

This dagger allows you to twist your foes' resistances to your advantage.

Lvl 10	+2	5,000 gp	Lvl 25	+5	625,000 gp
Lvl 15	+3	25,000 gp	Lvl 30	+6	3,125,000 gp
Lvl 20	+4	125,000 gp			

Weapon: Dagger
Enhancement: Attack rolls and damage rolls
Critical: +1d6 damage per plus
Property: When any enemy's resistances or immunities reduce the damage of any sorcerer attack power you use through this dagger, you gain 5 temporary hit points.
Level 15 or 20: 10 temporary hit points.
Level 25 or 30: 15 temporary hit points.
Power (Daily): Free Action. *Trigger:* You hit an enemy with a sorcerer attack power using this dagger. *Effect:* Choose a damage type. The triggering enemy loses resistance or immunity to that damage type until the end of the encounter.

Harsh Songblade · Level 3+

As this blade channels your bardic magic, the blade unleashes a wail that leaves your foes senseless.

Lvl 3	+1	680 gp	Lvl 18	+4	85,000 gp
Lvl 8	+2	3,400 gp	Lvl 23	+5	425,000 gp
Lvl 13	+3	17,000 gp	Lvl 28	+6	2,125,000 gp

Weapon: Heavy blade, light blade
Enhancement: Attack rolls and damage rolls
Critical: +1d8 damage per plus
Property: Bards can use this blade as an implement for bard powers and bard paragon path powers.
Power (Daily): Free Action. *Trigger:* You hit an enemy with a bard thunder power using this blade. *Effect:* Each enemy within 2 squares of the triggering enemy is dazed until the end of your next turn.

Lilting Songblade · Level 20+

When swung in an arc, this blade unleashes an inspiring ode to victory that increases in intensity with each defeated enemy.

Lvl 20	+4	125,000 gp	Lvl 30	+6	3,125,000 gp
Lvl 25	+5	625,000 gp			

Weapon: Heavy blade, light blade
Enhancement: Attack rolls and damage rolls
Critical: +1d10 damage per plus
Property: Bards can use this blade as an implement for bard powers and bard paragon path powers.
Power (Daily): Minor Action. Each ally within 20 squares of you gains a +4 item bonus to damage rolls until the end of the encounter. Whenever you or an ally reduces an enemy to 0 hit points before the end of the encounter, the bonus increases by 2.

Piercing Songblade · Level 13+

Silent until it lands a crucial blow, this blade sends forth a piercing note that rends your target's armor.

Lvl 13	+3	17,000 gp	Lvl 23	+5	425,000 gp
Lvl 18	+4	85,000 gp	Lvl 28	+6	2,125,000 gp

Weapon: Heavy blade, light blade
Enhancement: Attack rolls and damage rolls
Critical: +1d10 damage per plus
Property: Bards can use this blade as an implement for bard powers and bard paragon path powers.
Power (Daily): Free Action. *Trigger:* You hit an enemy with a bard attack power using this blade. *Effect:* Until the end of the encounter, that enemy takes a -2 penalty to AC.

Tooth of Chaos · Level 4+

This dagger seems to change shape in your hand, becoming precisely what you need to strike your enemy.

Lvl 4	+1	840 gp	Lvl 19	+4	105,000 gp
Lvl 9	+2	4,200 gp	Lvl 24	+5	525,000 gp
Lvl 14	+3	21,000 gp	Lvl 29	+6	2,625,000 gp

Weapon: Dagger
Enhancement: Attack rolls and damage rolls
Critical: +1d8 damage per plus
Power (Daily): Free Action. *Trigger:* You hit an enemy with a sorcerer attack power using this dagger. *Effect:* Whenever you hit that enemy with a sorcerer attack power before the end of the encounter, you can treat your attack roll as even or odd.

Winged Dagger · Level 5+

This dagger can take to the air to deliver your spells and protect you from harm.

Lvl 5	+1	1,000 gp	Lvl 20	+4	125,000 gp
Lvl 10	+2	5,000 gp	Lvl 25	+5	625,000 gp
Lvl 15	+3	25,000 gp	Lvl 30	+6	3,125,000 gp

Weapon: Dagger
Enhancement: Attack rolls and damage rolls
Critical: +1d6 damage per plus
Power (At-Will): Free Action. *Trigger:* An enemy hits you with an opportunity attack when you use a sorcerer ranged or area attack power through this dagger. *Effect:* The triggering enemy takes 5 damage.
Level 15 or 20: 10 damage.
Level 25 or 30: 15 damage.
Power (Daily): Minor Action. Choose one enemy within 10 squares of you that you can see. The next sorcerer close attack power you use through this dagger before the end of the encounter treats a square adjacent to that enemy as its origin square.

Wyrmtooth Dagger · Level 2+

Carved from a dragon's tooth, this dagger can strip away a creature's elemental defenses.

Lvl 2	+1	520 gp	Lvl 17	+4	65,000 gp
Lvl 7	+2	2,600 gp	Lvl 22	+5	325,000 gp
Lvl 12	+3	13,000 gp	Lvl 27	+6	1,625,000 gp

Weapon: Dagger
Enhancement: Attack rolls and damage rolls
Critical: +1d6 damage per plus, and the target loses its resistances (save ends).
Power (Daily): Free Action. Until the end of the encounter, sorcerer attack powers you use through this dagger ignore the resistances of any enemy within 10 squares of you.

Rods

A rod is a short, heavy cylinder, typically covered in mystic runes or inscribed crystals. You can't make melee attacks with a rod.

If you can wield a rod as an implement, you can add its enhancement bonus to the attack rolls and the damage rolls of implement powers you use through the rod, and you can use its properties and powers. Otherwise, you gain no benefit from wielding a rod.

RODS

Lvl	Name	Price (gp)
2	Rod of hope triumphant +1	520
4	Rod of forceful invocation +1	840
4	Rod of wrathful dismissal +1	840
7	Rod of binding awe +2	2,600
7	Rod of hope triumphant +2	2,600
8	Rod of resurgent valor +2	3,400
9	Rod of forceful invocation +2	4,200
9	Rod of wrathful dismissal +2	4,200
12	Rod of binding awe +3	13,000
12	Rod of hope triumphant +3	13,000
13	Rod of resurgent valor +3	17,000
13	Rod of scouring justice +3	17,000
14	Rod of brilliant wrath +3	21,000
14	Rod of forceful invocation +3	21,000
14	Rod of wrathful dismissal +3	21,000
17	Rod of binding awe +4	65,000
17	Rod of hope triumphant +4	65,000
18	Rod of resurgent valor +4	85,000
18	Rod of scouring justice +4	85,000
19	Rod of brilliant wrath +4	105,000
19	Rod of forceful invocation +4	105,000
19	Rod of wrathful dismissal +4	105,000
20	Rod of retributive justice +4	125,000
22	Rod of binding awe +5	325,000
22	Rod of hope triumphant +5	325,000
23	Rod of resurgent valor +5	425,000
23	Rod of scouring justice +5	425,000
24	Rod of brilliant wrath +5	525,000
24	Rod of forceful invocation +5	525,000
24	Rod of wrathful dismissal +5	525,000
25	Rod of retributive justice +5	625,000
27	Rod of binding awe +6	1,625,000
27	Rod of hope triumphant +6	1,625,000
28	Rod of resurgent valor +6	2,125,000
28	Rod of scouring justice +6	2,125,000
29	Rod of brilliant wrath +6	2,625,000
29	Rod of forceful invocation +6	2,625,000
29	Rod of wrathful dismissal +6	2,625,000
30	Rod of dual invocation +6	3,125,000
30	Rod of retributive justice +6	3,125,000

Rod of Binding Awe — Level 7+

Divine power channeled through this rod overwhelms your foe with awe, rooting it in place.

Lvl 7	+2	2,600 gp	Lvl 22	+5	325,000 gp
Lvl 12	+3	13,000 gp	Lvl 27	+6	1,625,000 gp
Lvl 17	+4	65,000 gp			

Implement (Rod)
Enhancement: Attack rolls and damage rolls
Critical: +1d6 damage per plus
Power (Daily): Free Action. *Trigger:* You hit an enemy with a divine attack power using this rod. *Effect:* That enemy is immobilized until the end of its next turn.

Rod of Brilliant Wrath — Level 14+

When you invoke radiant power with this rod, you can intensify its power to daze or blind your foes.

Lvl 14	+3	21,000 gp	Lvl 24	+5	525,000 gp
Lvl 19	+4	105,000 gp	Lvl 29	+6	2,625,000 gp

Implement (Rod)
Enhancement: Attack rolls and damage rolls
Critical: +1d8 radiant damage per plus
Power (Daily): Free Action. *Trigger:* You hit an enemy and deal radiant damage to it using this rod. *Effect:* That enemy and any creature adjacent to it are dazed until the end of your next turn.
Level 24 or 29: That enemy and any creature adjacent to it are also blinded until the end of your next turn.

Rod of Dual Invocation — Level 30

When unleashed, the mighty divine power contained within this rod allows you to echo your first attack with another devastating attack.

Lvl 30	+6	3,125,000 gp

Implement (Rod)
Enhancement: Attack rolls and damage rolls
Critical: +1d6 damage per plus
Power (Daily): Free Action. *Trigger:* You hit an enemy with an invoker attack power using this rod. *Effect:* You use an invoker at-will or encounter attack power that must include the triggering enemy as a target.

Rod of Forceful Invocation — Level 4+

When your prayer smites your foes, they stagger backward under the weight of this rod's power.

Lvl 4	+1	840 gp	Lvl 19	+4	105,000 gp
Lvl 9	+2	4,200 gp	Lvl 24	+5	525,000 gp
Lvl 14	+3	21,000 gp	Lvl 29	+6	2,625,000 gp

Implement (Rod)
Enhancement: Attack rolls and damage rolls
Critical: +1d6 damage per plus
Power (Daily): Free Action. *Trigger:* You hit an enemy with a divine attack power using this rod. *Effect:* You push that enemy 2 squares and knock it prone. If the triggering attack already pushes the target, you apply this push after that.
Level 14 or 19: Push 4 squares.
Level 24 or 29: Push 6 squares.

Rod of Hope Triumphant

Level 2+

As your foe falls, the divine power of this rod invigorates you, for justice has been served.

Lvl 2	+1	520 gp	Lvl 17	+4	65,000 gp
Lvl 7	+2	2,600 gp	Lvl 22	+5	325,000 gp
Lvl 12	+3	13,000 gp	Lvl 27	+6	1,625,000 gp

Implement (Rod)

Enhancement: Attack rolls and damage rolls

Critical: +1d6 damage per plus

Property: When you reduce any enemy to 0 hit points with a divine attack power using this rod, you gain temporary hit points equal to the rod's enhancement bonus.

Rod of Resurgent Valor

Level 8+

Divine wrath channeled through this rod empowers your prayers against those who dare to attack you.

Lvl 8	+2	3,400 gp	Lvl 23	+5	425,000 gp
Lvl 13	+3	17,000 gp	Lvl 28	+6	2,125,000 gp
Lvl 18	+4	85,000 gp			

Implement (Rod)

Enhancement: Attack rolls and damage rolls

Critical: +1d6 damage per plus

Property: When any creature attacks you, you gain a +1 item bonus to attack rolls with this rod against that creature until the end of your next turn.

Rod of Retributive Justice

Level 20+

As you clutch this rod, words of divine power spring to your lips to smite those who harm you.

| Lvl 20 | +4 | 125,000 gp | Lvl 30 | +6 | 3,125,000 gp |
| Lvl 25 | +5 | 625,000 gp | | | |

Implement (Rod)

Enhancement: Attack rolls and damage rolls

Critical: +1d6 damage per plus, and the target takes a -1 penalty to all defenses until the end of your next turn.

Power (Daily): Immediate Reaction. *Trigger:* An enemy hits you. *Effect:* You use an invoker at-will or encounter attack power that must include the triggering enemy as a target.

Rod of Scouring Justice

Level 13+

The divine wrath channeled through this rod cascades doom upon your foe.

| Lvl 13 | +3 | 17,000 gp | Lvl 23 | +5 | 425,000 gp |
| Lvl 18 | +4 | 85,000 gp | Lvl 28 | +6 | 2,125,000 gp |

Implement (Rod)

Enhancement: Attack rolls and damage rolls

Critical: +1d6 damage per plus

Power (Daily): Free Action. *Trigger:* You hit an enemy with a divine attack power using this rod. *Effect:* That enemy takes a -2 penalty to saving throws and ongoing 5 damage (save ends both).
Level 23 or 28: Ongoing 10 damage.

Rod of Wrathful Dismissal

Level 4+

This rod's power lets you move a foe into a position where your allies can deal with it.

Lvl 4	+1	840 gp	Lvl 19	+4	105,000 gp
Lvl 9	+2	4,200 gp	Lvl 24	+5	525,000 gp
Lvl 14	+3	21,000 gp	Lvl 29	+6	2,625,000 gp

Implement (Rod)

Enhancement: Attack rolls and damage rolls

Critical: +1d6 damage per plus

Power (Daily): Immediate Reaction. *Trigger:* An enemy hits you. *Effect:* You slide the triggering enemy 3 squares to a space that must be adjacent to one of your allies.

STAFFS

A staff is a shaft of wood as tall or slightly taller than you are, sometimes crowned with a decorative crystal or some other symbol of power. A staff is an implement that can also be used as a weapon.

If you can wield a staff as an implement, you can add its enhancement bonus to the attack rolls and the damage rolls of implement powers you use through the staff, and you can use its properties and powers. Otherwise, you treat a staff as a magic quarterstaff and cannot use its properties or powers.

Using a Staff as a Weapon: When you use a melee weapon power through a staff, the staff functions as a magic quarterstaff, and you add the staff's enhancement bonus to the power's attack rolls and damage rolls. You add the weapon's proficiency bonus to the attack rolls if you're proficient with quarterstaffs. If you score a critical hit with the staff when using it as a weapon, you use the staff's critical hit effect.

STAFFS

Lvl	Name	Price (gp)
7	Staff of distant shielding +2	2,600
8	Staff of provocation +2	3,400
12	Staff of distant shielding +3	13,000
13	Staff of provocation +3	17,000
14	Staff of the sunburst +3	21,000
17	Staff of distant shielding +4	65,000
18	Staff of provocation +4	85,000
19	Staff of the sunburst +4	105,000
22	Staff of distant shielding +5	325,000
23	Staff of provocation +5	425,000
24	Staff of the sunburst +5	525,000
27	Staff of distant shielding +6	1,625,000
28	Staff of provocation +6	2,125,000
29	Staff of the sunburst +6	2,625,000

Staff of Distant Shielding
Level 7+

With a word, you ward an ally against a foe's attack, promising swift retribution if harm comes to your companion.

Lvl 7	+2	2,600 gp	Lvl 22	+5	325,000 gp
Lvl 12	+3	13,000 gp	Lvl 27	+6	1,625,000 gp
Lvl 17	+4	65,000 gp			

Implement (Staff)
Enhancement: Attack rolls and damage rolls
Critical: +1d6 damage per plus
Power (Daily ✦ Radiant): Minor Action. Choose one ally within 10 squares of you. The next enemy to make an attack roll against that ally before the end of the encounter takes 10 radiant damage.
Level 12 or 17: 15 radiant damage.
Level 22 or 27: 20 radiant damage.

Staff of Provocation
Level 8+

The enemy you smite with your attack is momentarily marked as anathema, provoking even its own allies to bring it down.

Lvl 8	+2	3,400 gp	Lvl 23	+5	425,000 gp
Lvl 13	+3	17,000 gp	Lvl 28	+6	2,125,000 gp
Lvl 18	+4	85,000 gp			

Implement (Staff)
Enhancement: Attack rolls and damage rolls
Critical: +1d6 damage per plus
Power (Daily ✦ Charm): Free Action. *Trigger:* You hit an enemy with an attack power using this staff. *Effect:* One creature of your choice makes a melee basic attack against that enemy as a free action. The attacking creature gains a bonus to the attack roll and the damage roll equal to your Intelligence modifier.

Staff of the Sunburst
Level 14+

Adorned with a gleaming solar disk, this staff can erupt with radiant power when you are hit.

Lvl 14	+3	21,000 gp	Lvl 24	+5	525,000 gp
Lvl 19	+4	105,000 gp	Lvl 29	+6	2,625,000 gp

Implement (Staff)
Enhancement: Attack rolls and damage rolls
Critical: +1d6 damage per plus
Power (Daily ✦ Radiant): Immediate Reaction. *Trigger:* An enemy damages you with an attack. *Effect:* Each enemy within 5 squares of you takes 5 radiant damage and is knocked prone.
Level 24 or 29: 10 radiant damage.

TOTEMS

A totem is a short length of wood or bone carved to resemble a patron animal or a nature spirit. One end is typically adorned with feathers, teeth, small bones, scraps of hide, leaves, or other symbols of primal power. You can't make melee attacks with a totem.

If you can wield a totem as an implement, you can add its enhancement bonus to the attack rolls and the damage rolls of implement powers you use through the totem, and you can use its properties and powers. Otherwise, you gain no benefit from wielding a totem.

TOTEMS

Lvl	Name	Price (gp)
1	Magic totem +1	360
2	Autumn harvest totem +1	520
2	Hungry spirits totem +1	520
3	Summer growth totem +1	680
3	Watchful spirit totem +1	680
4	Winter's Grasp Totem +1	840
5	Pure spirit totem +1	1,000
5	Spring renewal totem +1	1,000
6	Magic totem +2	1,800
7	Autumn harvest totem +2	2,600
7	Hungry spirits totem +2	2,600
8	Feral spirit totem +2	3,400
8	Summer growth totem +2	3,400
8	Watchful spirit totem +2	3,400
9	Winter's grasp totem +2	4,200
10	Pure spirit totem +2	5,000
10	Spring renewal totem +2	5,000
11	Magic totem +3	9,000
12	Autumn harvest totem +3	13,000
12	Hungry spirits totem +3	13,000
13	Feral spirit totem +3	17,000
13	Summer growth totem +3	17,000
13	Watchful spirit totem +3	17,000
14	Winter's grasp totem +3	21,000
15	Pure spirit totem +3	25,000
15	Spring renewal totem +3	25,000
16	Magic totem +4	45,000
17	Autumn harvest totem +4	65,000
17	Hungry spirits totem +4	65,000
18	Feral spirit totem +4	85,000
18	Summer growth totem +4	85,000
18	Watchful spirit totem +4	85,000
19	Winter's grasp totem +4	105,000
20	Pure spirit totem +4	125,000
20	Spring renewal totem +4	125,000
21	Magic totem +5	225,000
22	Autumn harvest totem +5	325,000
22	Hungry spirits totem +5	325,000
23	Feral spirit totem +5	425,000
23	Summer growth totem +5	425,000
23	Watchful spirit totem +5	425,000
24	Winter's grasp totem +5	525,000
25	Pure spirit totem +5	625,000
25	Spring renewal totem +5	625,000
26	Magic totem +6	1,125,000
27	Autumn harvest totem +6	1,625,000
27	Hungry spirits totem +6	1,625,000
28	Feral spirit totem +6	2,125,000
28	Summer growth totem +6	2,125,000
28	Watchful spirit totem +6	2,125,000
29	Winter's grasp totem +6	2,625,000
30	Pure spirit totem +6	3,125,000
30	Spring renewal totem +6	3,125,000

Autumn Harvest Totem

Level 2+

This totem is fashioned from leaves and bone shards. It embodies the spirit of autumn and the inevitability of death.

Lvl 2	+1	520 gp	Lvl 17	+4	65,000 gp
Lvl 7	+2	2,600 gp	Lvl 22	+5	325,000 gp
Lvl 12	+3	13,000 gp	Lvl 27	+6	1,625,000 gp

Implement (Totem)

Enhancement: Attack rolls and damage rolls

Critical: +1d6 damage per plus, or +1d10 damage per plus against a bloodied creature

Property: Attacks made through this totem deal extra damage against bloodied creatures equal to 1 + one-half the totem's enhancement bonus.

Feral Spirit Totem

Level 8+

When the wild spirits stream forth from their homes to hunt, they won't be satisfied with only one victim.

Lvl 8	+2	3,400 gp	Lvl 23	+5	425,000 gp
Lvl 13	+3	17,000 gp	Lvl 28	+6	2,125,000 gp
Lvl 18	+4	85,000 gp			

Implement (Totem)

Enhancement: Attack rolls and damage rolls

Critical: +1d6 damage per plus to the target or to one enemy adjacent to your spirit companion

Power (Daily): Free Action. *Trigger:* You bloody an enemy with a primal ranged attack power using this totem. *Effect:* One enemy adjacent to your spirit companion takes 1d6 damage per plus.

Hungry Spirits Totem

Level 2+

The appearance of this totem changes week by week, depending on which spirits are hungriest.

Lvl 2	+1	520 gp	Lvl 17	+4	65,000 gp
Lvl 7	+2	2,600 gp	Lvl 22	+5	325,000 gp
Lvl 12	+3	13,000 gp	Lvl 27	+6	1,625,000 gp

Implement (Totem)

Enhancement: Attack rolls and damage rolls

Critical: +1d10 damage per plus, and you can move your spirit companion to a space adjacent to the target.

Power (Daily ✦ Healing, Spirit): Free Action. *Trigger:* You hit an enemy adjacent to your spirit companion with a primal attack power using this totem. *Effect:* You and one ally within 2 squares of the enemy can spend a healing surge.

Magic Totem

Level 1+

This item is a simple totem that channels primal energy.

Lvl 1	+1	360 gp	Lvl 16	+4	45,000 gp
Lvl 6	+2	1,800 gp	Lvl 21	+5	225,000 gp
Lvl 11	+3	9,000 gp	Lvl 26	+6	1,125,000 gp

Implement (Totem)

Enhancement: Attack rolls and damage rolls

Critical: +1d6 damage per plus

Pure Spirit Totem

Level 5+

Interwoven vines carved on this totem symbolize the primal magic of healing and growth held within it.

Lvl 5	+1	1,000 gp	Lvl 20	+4	125,000 gp
Lvl 10	+2	5,000 gp	Lvl 25	+5	625,000 gp
Lvl 15	+3	25,000 gp	Lvl 30	+6	3,125,000 gp

Implement (Totem)

Enhancement: Attack rolls and damage rolls

Critical: +1d8 damage per plus

Power (Daily ✦ Healing): Minor Action. One ally within 5 squares of you regains 1d6 hit points per plus.

Spring Renewal Totem

Level 5+

This totem carries the primal magic of spring. It represents the power to restore life.

Lvl 5	+1	1,000 gp	Lvl 20	+4	125,000 gp
Lvl 10	+2	5,000 gp	Lvl 25	+5	625,000 gp
Lvl 15	+3	25,000 gp	Lvl 30	+6	3,125,000 gp

Implement (Totem)

Enhancement: Attack rolls and damage rolls

Critical: +1d6 damage per plus, and one ally within 5 squares of you regains hit points equal to twice the totem's enhancement bonus.

Power (Daily ✦ Healing): Free Action. *Trigger:* You hit an enemy with a primal attack power using this totem. *Effect:* One ally within 5 squares of you gains regeneration equal to twice the totem's enhancement bonus until the end of the encounter.

Summer Growth Totem

Level 3+

Summer brings growth, and the primal energy channeled through this item helps spawn vines that hinder your foes.

Lvl 3	+1	680 gp	Lvl 18	+4	85,000 gp
Lvl 8	+2	3,400 gp	Lvl 23	+5	425,000 gp
Lvl 13	+3	17,000 gp	Lvl 28	+6	2,125,000 gp

Implement (Totem)

Enhancement: Attack rolls and damage rolls

Critical: +1d6 damage per plus, and the target is restrained until the end of your next turn.

Power (Daily): Minor Action. Each square within 5 squares of you is difficult terrain for your enemies until the end of your next turn.

Watchful Spirit Totem

Level 3+

Several animal faces seem to look out from this totem with wide eyes. Its magic, channeled through your spirit companion, lashes out at those who harm your allies.

Lvl 3	+1	680 gp	Lvl 18	+4	85,000 gp
Lvl 8	+2	3,400 gp	Lvl 23	+5	425,000 gp
Lvl 13	+3	17,000 gp	Lvl 28	+6	2,125,000 gp

Implement (Totem)

Enhancement: Attack rolls and damage rolls

Critical: +1d6 damage per plus, or +1d12 damage per plus against a bloodied creature

Property: You gain an item bonus to Perception checks equal to the totem's enhancement bonus.

Power (Daily): Minor Action. Until the end of your next turn, any enemy that damages an ally adjacent to your spirit companion takes damage equal to twice this totem's enhancement bonus.

Winter's Grasp Totem — Level 4+

This totem is fashioned from dry wood and white fur. It embodies the spirit of winter and a time when nature sleeps and life grows weak.

Lvl 4	+1	840 gp	Lvl 19	+4	105,000 gp
Lvl 9	+2	4,200 gp	Lvl 24	+5	525,000 gp
Lvl 14	+3	21,000 gp	Lvl 29	+6	2,625,000 gp

Implement (Totem)

Enhancement: Attack rolls and damage rolls

Critical: +1d10 cold damage per plus

Power (Daily): Free Action. *Trigger:* You hit an enemy with a primal attack power using this totem. *Effect:* That enemy is weakened until the end of your next turn.

WONDROUS ITEMS

The wondrous items in this chapter are musical instruments. Any class can use musical instruments, but the items are particularly appealing to bards. A bard can use certain instruments as implements for bard powers as well as bard paragon path powers. A few instruments also have powers that are enhanced if used by a bard who has the Song of Rest class feature.

Using a Musical Instrument: Like other wondrous items, a musical instrument doesn't take up an item slot. However, to use an instrument's properties and powers, you must be holding and playing the instrument as appropriate: strumming a lute, sounding a horn, and so on.

WONDROUS ITEMS

Lvl	Name	Price (gp)
3	Fochlucan bandore	680
3	Harp of deeper slumber	680
5	Mac-Fuirmidh cittern	1,000
6	Flute of the dancing satyr	1,800
7	Doss lute	2,600
9	Watcher's horn	4,200
12	Cli lyre	13,000
17	Canaith mandolin	65,000
18	Fire horn	85,000
22	Horn of Baldagyr	325,000
23	Anstruth harp	425,000
29	Ollamh harp	2,625,000

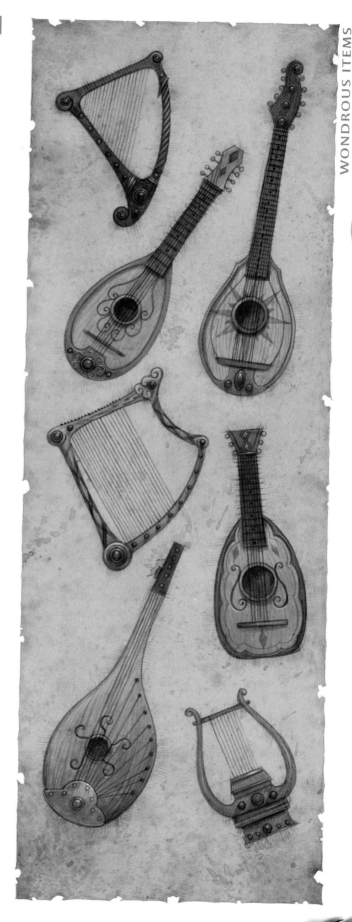

Anstruth Harp
Level 23

Named for an ancient college of bardic learning, this small, elegant harp holds mighty powers of healing.

Wondrous Item   425,000 gp

Property: Bards can use this item as an implement for bard powers and bard paragon path powers. As an implement, it grants a +5 enhancement bonus to attack rolls and damage rolls, and it deals 5d6 extra damage on a critical hit.

Power (Daily ✦ Healing): Standard Action. Use this power during a short rest. At the end of the short rest, one ally who remained within 20 squares of you during the rest regains all of his or her hit points.

Song of Rest: The ally also regains a healing surge.

Canaith Mandolin
Level 17

The life-giving music of this lutelike instrument revitalizes a listener.

Wondrous Item   65,000 gp

Property: Bards can use this item as an implement for bard powers and bard paragon path powers. As an implement, it grants a +4 enhancement bonus to attack rolls and damage rolls, and it deals 4d6 extra damage on a critical hit.

Power (Daily ✦ Healing): Standard Action. Use this power during a short rest. At the end of the short rest, choose yourself or an ally who remained within 20 squares of you during the rest. Until the end of that character's next short rest or extended rest, he or she regains an additional 5 hit points when spending a healing surge.

Song of Rest: The additional hit points equal 10.

Cli Lyre
Level 12

The graceful, rounded body of this magic lyre produces resonant tones that imbue listeners with increased presence.

Wondrous Item   13,000 gp

Property: Bards can use this item as an implement for bard powers and bard paragon path powers. As an implement, it grants a +3 enhancement bonus to attack rolls and damage rolls, and it deals 3d6 extra damage on a critical hit.

Power (Daily): Standard Action. You and each ally within 20 squares of you gain a +5 power bonus to his or her next Bluff, Diplomacy, or Intimidate check before the end of his or her next short rest or extended rest.

Song of Rest: The power bonus equals +10.

Doss Lute
Level 7

The dulcet music of this lute imbues its listeners with resilience and quiet resolve.

Wondrous Item   2,600 gp

Property: Bards can use this item as an implement for bard powers and bard paragon path powers. As an implement, it grants a +2 enhancement bonus to attack rolls and damage rolls, and it deals 2d6 extra damage on a critical hit.

Power (Daily): Standard Action. Use this power during a short rest. At the end of the short rest, choose yourself or an ally who remained within 20 squares of you during the rest. Until the end of that character's next short rest or extended rest, he or she gains a +1 power bonus to saving throws.

Song of Rest: The power bonus equals +2.

Fire Horn
Level 18

This brass horn is warm to the touch. Fire symbols are carved along its length.

Wondrous Item   85,000 gp

Power (Daily): Minor Action. Each enemy in a close blast 5 is affected by this power. An affected enemy that does not have resistance or immunity to fire gains vulnerable 10 fire (save ends). An affected enemy that has resistance or immunity to fire loses that resistance or immunity (save ends).

Flute of the Dancing Satyr
Level 6

Carved from wood and inscribed with arcane glyphs, this flute can play a tune of speed and elegance.

Wondrous Item   1,800 gp

Power (Encounter): Move Action. You shift 2 squares, and each ally within 5 squares of your destination space can shift 1 square as a free action.

Fochlucan Bandore
Level 3

This instrument's song imbues listeners with fervor and strength.

Wondrous Item   680 gp

Property: Bards can use this item as an implement for bard powers and bard paragon path powers. As an implement, it grants a +1 enhancement bonus to attack rolls and damage rolls, and it deals 1d6 extra damage on a critical hit.

Power (Daily): Standard Action. Use this power during a short rest. At the end of the short rest, one ally who remained within 20 squares of you during the rest gains a +1 power bonus to weapon damage rolls until the end of his or her next short rest or extended rest.

Song of Rest: The power bonus equals +2.

Harp of Deeper Slumber
Level 3

A single tone from this small harp leaves creatures briefly inattentive.

Wondrous Item   680 gp

Power (Daily): Minor Action. Each creature within 20 squares of you takes a -15 penalty to Perception checks until the end of your next turn.

Horn of Baldagyr — Level 22

This horn is crafted from the scales of Baldagyr, an astral dragon sworn to watch over the resting place of a mighty primordial until the end of time.

Wondrous Item   325,000 gp

Power (Daily): No Action. *Trigger:* You roll initiative at the beginning of an encounter. *Effect:* You and each ally within 10 squares of you gain a +5 item bonus to initiative checks and a +2 power bonus to attack rolls on his or her first turn during the encounter.

Mac-Fuirmidh Cittern — Level 5

The music of this magic lute lingers in the mind, providing vigor long after its tones have ceased.

Wondrous Item   1,000 gp

Property: Bards can use this item as an implement for bard powers and bard paragon path powers. As an implement, it grants a +1 enhancement bonus to attack rolls and damage rolls, and it deals 1d6 extra damage on a critical hit.

Power (Daily ✦ Healing): Standard Action. Use this power during a short rest. At the end of the short rest, choose yourself or an ally who remained within 20 squares of you during the rest. Until the end of that character's next short rest or extended rest, he or she regains an additional 2 hit points when spending a healing surge.

Song of Rest: The additional hit points equal 4.

Ollamh Harp — Level 29

This harp calls down the fury of the storm and grants it to all listeners.

Wondrous Item   2,625,000 gp

Property: Bards can use this item as an implement for bard powers and bard paragon path powers. As an implement, it grants a +6 enhancement bonus to attack rolls and damage rolls, and it deals 6d6 extra damage on a critical hit.

Power (Daily): Standard Action. Use this power during a short rest. At the end of the short rest, you and each ally who remained within 20 squares of you during the rest are affected by this power. Until the end of each affected character's next short rest or extended rest, his or her attacks deal 5 extra lightning damage.

Watcher's Horn — Level 9

This small black horn produces no noise when sounded, but it awakens your slumbering friends and makes them ready to fight.

Wondrous Item   4,200 gp

Power (Daily): Minor Action. The horn silently awakens each sleeping ally within 10 squares of you. Each ally is not surprised when he or she wakes up.

RITUALS

From ancient rites and ceremonies to arcane forces bound to music, rituals have many forms and functions in the DUNGEONS & DRAGONS game. Rituals create magical effects through the recitation and performance of magical formulas drawn from ritual scrolls and books. This section provides a variety of rituals, many of which are tailored for the new classes in this book. Although these rituals evoke arcane, divine, and primal themes, any adventurer who has the Ritual Caster feat can master and perform most of them.

PREREQUISITE

Some rituals in this chapter include a "Prerequisite" entry. You must meet a ritual's prerequisite to master or perform the ritual, although you can assist another character in performing a ritual even if you don't meet the prerequisite.

CATEGORY

Each ritual category in the *Player's Handbook* is associated with one or more key skills. Some of the rituals in this book have key skills other than the ones normally associated with some ritual categories.

VARIANT RITUAL BOOKS

Although the ritual books described in the *Player's Handbook* contain all the instructions necessary to master and perform a ritual, their form may be unappealing to characters who have forsaken the traditional trappings of civilization. Variant ritual book options can reconcile a character's background with his or her desire to use ritual magic.

Some ritual casters record their rituals in an unorthodox manner. They inscribe rituals on cured hides, etch them into stone tablets, or paint them onto armor or weapons. Remote cultures and isolated ritual casters have even more esoteric methods of storing and encoding their rituals, from patterns of knots tied in rope to tiny statuettes displaying the required body motions, or even tubes of glass that convey the ritual through shape and color. No matter what form it takes, a variant ritual book still requires a 50 gp investment. In addition, a ritual caster must spend the same amount of time to create it and to master the rituals within it as described in "Creating a Ritual Book" on page 298 of the *Player's Handbook*. Each of these unusual methods of storing rituals contains the same amount of space for recording rituals as a traditional ritual book.

RITUAL DESCRIPTIONS

AFFECT NORMAL FIRE

Fire leaps and dances at your command, brightening or dimming.

Level: 3
Category: Exploration
Time: 1 minute
Duration: 8 hours
Component Cost: 25 gp
Market Price: 125 gp
Key Skill: Arcana or Nature (no check)

You gain mastery over nonmagical fire. For the ritual's duration, or until you take an extended rest, you can manipulate nonmagical flames within 10 squares of you as a minor action. You can make a fire that normally provides dim light produce an equal amount of bright light, or you can double the radius of bright light a fire produces. Alternatively, you can diminish a fire's light, reducing its area of bright light to an equal amount of dim light, or reducing its area of dim light to darkness. Reducing a fire's light to produce no light does not extinguish the flame. You can extinguish 1 square of nonmagical fire as a minor action.

ANIMAL FRIENDSHIP

The animal nuzzles your hand, returning the friendship you offer.

Level: 5
Category: Binding
Time: 1 minute
Duration: Special
Component Cost: 50 gp
Market Price: 250 gp
Key Skill: Nature

When you perform this ritual, choose a nonhostile Tiny natural beast, such as a cat, a fox, a fish, a mouse, or a sparrow. This animal must remain within 5 squares of you for the time necessary to perform the ritual. Once the ritual is complete, the animal regards you as a friend and performs simple tasks on your behalf. The tasks are limited to the options below, and assigning a task requires a standard action.

Fetch: The animal retrieves a Tiny object of 10 pounds or less that you and it can see. If the animal is unable to carry the object due to the item's size or weight, the animal enlists the aid of other creatures of its kind to fulfill the task.

Perform: The animal performs a simple trick, such as rolling over or playing dead.

Seek: The animal scouts ahead and examines an area for anything that's alive or animate. The animal can travel up to 20 squares away from you and uses your passive Perception check to determine if it notices hidden creatures in the area. When the animal returns, you learn from it whether a creature occupies the area. The animal cannot communicate any other information aside from the presence or absence of a creature.

Watch: The animal remains in its current location and watches that area. When you assign the animal the task, you designate creatures that are allowed to enter the location. If a creature that you have not designated enters the location, the watching animal informs you by coming to you and making a noise. If you move more than 20 squares away from the area, the animal leaves its post and rejoins you.

Unless otherwise commanded, the animal accompanies you for the ritual's duration, perching on your shoulder, hiding in your pocket, or walking alongside you. The animal has AC 14, Fortitude 12, Reflex 12, and Will 12. The animal has 1 hit point, and a missed attack never damages the animal.

Your Nature check determines the length of time the animal remains in your service, but you can release an animal from your service as a minor action.

Nature Check Result	Duration
19 or lower	1 hour
20–29	8 hours
30–39	1 day
40 or higher	1 week

At the heroic tier, you can have one animal at a time bound to your service using the ritual. At the paragon tier, you can have two animals bound using the ritual. At the epic tier, you can have three animals bound using the ritual. You must complete a separate ritual for each animal you bind.

ARIA OF REVELATION

Your operatic notes spark new ideas, helping your allies overcome a challenging problem.

Level: 10
Category: Divination
Time: 10 minutes
Duration: Instantaneous
Prerequisite: Bard
Component Cost: 400 gp, plus a focus worth 1,000 gp
Market Price: 1,000 gp
Key Skill: Arcana

When you finish performing the ritual, each ally who heard it can make an Arcana, a Dungeoneering, a History, a Nature, or a Religion check to uncover a clue or recall a bit of useful information. The ally must be trained in the skill and gains a bonus to the check based on your Arcana check result.

Arcana Check Result	Bonus
19 or lower	+5
20–29	+10
30–39	+15
40 or higher	+20

The information learned is equivalent to that gained from a successful knowledge check or monster knowledge check.

Focus: A musical instrument you play as part of performing the ritual.

BLOOM

Grass grows, trees bear fruit, and the land's bounty is available to all.

Level: 2   **Component Cost:** 20 gp
Category: Exploration   **Market Price:** 100 gp
Time: 10 minutes   **Key Skill:** Nature (no check)
Duration: Instantaneous

Upon completion of the ritual, you cause all outdoor terrain within 20 squares of you to bloom with new growth and foliage. The entire area becomes difficult terrain.

Alternatively, the ritual causes crops and fruit-bearing plants within 20 squares of you to yield food. The plants produce enough food to feed five people for a week.

CALL WILDERNESS GUIDE

An animal native to the local wilderness answers your call, approaching you and then walking away. A moment later it pauses, looking over its shoulder as if to make sure you are following.

Level: 6   **Component Cost:** 144 gp
Category: Exploration   **Market Price:** 360 gp
Time: 30 minutes   **Key Skill:** Nature
Duration: Special

You call a nature spirit into your service to act as a guide. The guide takes the form of a Medium or smaller natural beast, with defenses equal to yours at the time you perform the ritual. The guide has 1 hit point, and a missed attack never damages it. It has a speed of 8, but it measures its pace so that you and your party can keep up with it.

The guide leads you to a location you name as you perform the ritual. The destination must be a specific place, such as Shathrax's Lair or the Tower of Kettenor. The guide cannot lead you to a general location, such as "a cave full of treasure," or to an unknown place, such as "the secret lair of the dragon Arrythis." For the ritual's duration, the guide leads you to the destination by the shortest (although not necessarily the safest) route.

Your Nature check determines how long the guide serves you. If you can't reach the specified destination within the allotted time, the guide leads you as far as it can along the way and then vanishes.

Nature Check Result	Duration
19 or lower	1 hour
20–29	4 hours
30–39	8 hours
40 or higher	16 hours

RITUALS BY LEVEL

Lvl	Ritual	Key Skill
1	Create Campsite	Nature
1	Glib Limerick*	Arcana
1	Traveler's Chant*	Arcana
2	Bloom	Nature
2	Pyrotechnics	Arcana
2	Tree Shape	Nature
3	Affect Normal Fire	Arcana or Nature
3	Lullaby*	Arcana
4	Snare	Nature
5	Animal Friendship	Nature
5	Speak with Nature	Nature
6	Call Wilderness Guide	Nature
6	Fool's Speech*	Arcana
6	Ironwood	Nature
6	Tree Stride	Nature
6	Wyvern Watch	Arcana
8	Song of Sustenance*	Arcana
9	Tune of Merriment*	Arcana
10	Aria of Revelation*	Arcana
10	Chorus of Truth*	Arcana
10	Song of Restfulness*	Arcana
12	Reverse Portal	Arcana
14	Control Weather	Nature

***This ritual is usable only by bards.**

CHORUS OF TRUTH

Falsehood rings like dissonance against the beautiful harmonies of your instrument.

Level: 10   **Component Cost:** 200 gp,
Category: Exploration   plus a focus worth 1,000 gp
Time: 10 minutes   **Market Price:** 1,000 gp
Duration: 30 minutes **Key Skill:** Arcana
Prerequisite: Bard

Make an Arcana check. Creatures within 5 squares of you while you perform the ritual take a penalty to Bluff checks determined by your check result. The penalty lasts for the duration of the ritual.

Arcana Check Result	Penalty
19 or lower	–2
20–29	–4
30–39	–6
40 or higher	–10

Focus: A musical instrument you play as part of performing the ritual.

CONTROL WEATHER

Thunderheads form on the horizon and race across the sky, bringing with them curtains of rain and slashing lightning.

Level: 14
Category: Exploration
Time: 1 hour
Duration: Special

Component Cost: 1,800 gp
Market Price: 4,500 gp
Key Skill: Nature

You change the weather outside in a 2-mile radius centered on you. The change is limited by the current season. Choose from the options below based on the season.

Season	Weather Results
Spring	Heat wave, sleet storm, or thunderstorm
Summer	Hailstorm, heat wave, or rainstorm
Autumn	Cold snap, fog, sleet, or windstorm
Winter	Blizzard, windstorm, or thaw

You control the weather's general tendencies, such as the direction and intensity of the wind or the degree of obscurity from fog, hail, rain, and snow. You cannot control specific applications of the weather, such as where lightning strikes. You can alter the weather among the available options as a standard action for the duration of the ritual, which is determined by your Nature check. Each time you choose to change the weather result, the new weather conditions take 10 minutes to manifest.

Nature Check Result	Duration
19 or lower	2 hours
20–29	4 hours
30–39	16 hours
40 or higher	24 hours

CREATE CAMPSITE

A crackling fire, a hot meal, and a warm bedroll await you after a long day of adventuring.

Level: 1
Category: Exploration
Time: 10 minutes
Duration: 8 hours

Component Cost: 15 gp
Market Price: 50 gp
Key Skill: Nature

You summon hundreds of diminutive nature spirits to assemble a campsite in a 5-square radius around you. The spirits clear the area, set up tents, unroll bedrolls, gather water, and prepare a nourishing meal. They also conceal the campsite, with your Nature check result serving as the DC for Perception checks to notice the hidden camp.

The spirits utilize your and your allies' gear to make the campsite. If you and your allies lack the appropriate gear, the spirits gather raw materials from the environment to make the campsite.

At the end of the ritual's duration, the spirits break down the campsite, pack up your gear, and restore the site to its original state, removing evidence that you and your allies camped there.

DEVON CADY-LEE

FOOL'S SPEECH

What did you say?

Level: 6
Category: Deception
Time: 10 minutes
Duration: 1 hour
Prerequisite: Bard

Component Cost: 50 gp, plus a focus worth 360 gp
Market Price: 360 gp
Key Skill: Arcana (no check)

When you finish performing the ritual, you and up to five allies who heard it can use a secret language to communicate with each other. To other creatures, your speech is incomprehensible, a string of nonsense words. Affected characters can speak in Fool's Speech or another language at their discretion.

Focus: A musical instrument you play as part of performing the ritual.

GLIB LIMERICK

You recite a short rhyme and feel your tongue loosen so the lies can flow freely.

Level: 1
Category: Deception
Time: 1 minute
Duration: 10 minutes
Prerequisite: Bard

Component Cost: 10 gp, plus a focus worth 5 gp
Market Price: 50 gp
Key Skill: Arcana (no check)

For the ritual's duration, whenever you make a Bluff check, you can roll twice and use either result. The ritual's effect automatically ends when you roll initiative.

Focus: A musical instrument you play as part of performing the ritual.

IRONWOOD

The wood beneath your hand hardens, assuming an almost metallic sheen.

Level: 6
Category: Creation
Time: 1 hour
Duration: Permanent

Component Cost: 75 gp
Market Price: 360 gp
Key Skill: Nature

You alter a quantity of wood to have the strength and consistency of steel. The DC to burst or break the wood increases by 5. The wood also gains resist 10 to all damage.

Your Nature check determines the amount of wood you can affect with this ritual.

Nature Check Result	Size
19 or lower	Medium object
20–29	Large object
30–39	Huge object
40 or higher	Gargantuan object

LULLABY

Your audience grows sleepy with your soothing performance.

Level: 3
Category: Exploration
Time: 10 minutes
Duration: As long as you play plus 10 minutes
Prerequisite: Bard

Component Cost: 25 gp, plus a focus worth 20 gp
Market Price: 125 gp
Key Skill: Arcana

Your performance makes your audience drowsy. Make an Arcana check. The result determines the penalty to Insight checks and Perception checks of each creature that can hear you other than you and your allies.

Arcana Check Result	Penalty
19 or lower	–2
20–29	–4
30–39	–6
40 or higher	–10

Affected creatures are also considered distracted, which might allow an ally (or you, after you stop playing) to make Stealth checks to hide from them even without superior cover or total concealment.

Focus: A musical instrument you play as part of performing the ritual.

PYROTECHNICS

A flare soars into the night sky and explodes with brilliant color.

Level: 2
Category: Creation
Time: 1 minute
Duration: 10 minutes

Component Cost: 20 gp
Market Price: 50 gp
Key Skill: Arcana (no check)

You send a barrage of small, colorful explosions into the sky. The explosions blossom into whatever color or shape you choose for 1 minute. At the end of each minute of the ritual's duration, you can choose a new color and shape. At night, the lights are visible within a 10-mile radius. During the day, the lights are visible within a 1-mile radius.

REVERSE PORTAL

You open a portal not from here to there, but from there to here.

Level: 12
Category: Travel
Time: 10 minutes
Duration: Special

Component Cost: 500 gp
Market Price: 2,600 gp
Key Skill: Arcana

You create a shortcut across the fabric of the world, linking your location with a permanent teleportation circle elsewhere on the same plane (see the Linked Portal ritual, *Player's Handbook*, page 307). As part of performing this ritual, you sketch out a 10-foot-diameter circle in rare chalks and inks. Alternatively, you can use a permanent teleportation circle, which reduces the component cost to 150 gp and grants you a +5 bonus to your Arcana check.

At the ritual's completion, make an Arcana check. The result determines the duration that the portal remains open.

Arcana Check Result	Portal Duration
19 or lower	1 round
20–39	3 rounds
40 or higher	5 rounds

The portal displays views of the other location in the same way as that created by the Linked Portal ritual, but creatures cannot enter the origin point and appear at the other location. Instead, creatures can only step into the distant end of the portal to appear at the origin point with you.

SNARE

A barely visible circle appears on the ground, ready to entrap any enemies that enter the area.

Level: 4
Category: Warding
Time: 10 minutes
Duration: 8 hours or until discharged

Component Cost: 25 gp
Market Price: 150 gp
Key Skill: Nature

You create a magical snare in a 2-square-by-2-square area adjacent to you. When you complete the ritual, make a Nature check. The check result is the Perception DC to detect the snare and the Thievery DC to disable it. As part of the ritual, you can name creatures that can pass freely through the snare's area, and you can set conditions that allow a creature to bypass the snare. Any other creature that enters the snare's area is subject to an attack equal to your level + 4 vs. Reflex. On a hit, the target is immobilized (save ends). When the snare is triggered, you become aware that it has been triggered regardless of your distance from it. The ritual is also discharged.

SONG OF RESTFULNESS

As you play your instrument, your allies nod off one by one. When you finish, they awaken, refreshed and filled with resolve to continue the quest.

Level: 10
Category: Exploration
Time: 10 minutes
Duration: Instantaneous
Prerequisite: Bard

Component Cost: 400 gp, plus a focus worth 1,000 gp
Market Price: 1,200 gp
Key Skill: Arcana (no check)

When you perform this ritual at the beginning of an extended rest, you reduce the time needed for the extended rest by 2 hours for yourself and any allies who hear the performance. A character can benefit from this ritual only once during any 24-hour period.

Focus: A musical instrument you play as part of performing the ritual.

SONG OF SUSTENANCE

Your audience finds your dulcet tones as nourishing as the finest fare.

Level: 8
Category: Exploration
Time: 10 minutes
Duration: 48 hours
Prerequisite: Bard

Component Cost: 135 gp, plus a focus worth 680 gp
Market Price: 680 gp
Key Skill: Arcana (no check)

Your performance nourishes up to ten Small or Medium creatures for the duration, as if they had enjoyed a great feast. The creatures also gain a +5 bonus to Endurance checks for the duration. You designate the affected creatures as part of performing the ritual, and they must hear all of it.

Focus: A musical instrument you play as part of performing the ritual.

SPEAK WITH NATURE

Animals and plants respond to your queries, revealing what they have seen and what they know.

Level: 5
Category: Divination
Time: 10 minutes
Duration: 10 minutes

Component Cost: 80 gp
Market Price: 250 gp
Key Skill: Nature

For the ritual's duration, you can communicate with natural beasts and mundane plants (but not plant creatures). The ritual does not make animals friendly, and the animals or plants are limited in their knowledge by their experiences and mobility. For example, a plant knows only about its immediate surroundings, and a fish can describe only what it has seen or experienced underwater.

Your Nature check result determines the number of questions you can ask.

Nature Check Result	Number of Questions
9 or lower	Zero
10–19	One
20–29	Two
30 or higher	Three

TRAVELER'S CHANT

Your chant lifts your allies' steps and helps take their minds off the drudgery of the journey.

Level: 1
Category: Exploration
Time: 10 minutes
Duration: 8 hours
Prerequisite: Bard

Component Cost: 10 gp, plus a focus worth 5 gp
Market Price: 75 gp
Key Skill: Arcana (no check)

For the ritual's duration, you and up to eight allies who heard the whole performance of the ritual can travel farther than normal. For the purpose of determining how far you and the allies can travel in an hour or a day, treat the group's speed as the slowest member's speed + 2.

Focus: A musical instrument you play as part of performing the ritual.

TREE SHAPE

You assume the form of a tree, blending into the forest around you.

Level: 2
Category: Exploration
Time: 10 minutes
Duration: 6 hours

Component Cost: 20 gp
Market Price: 100 gp
Key Skill: Nature (no check)

You transform into a Large tree or shrub. While you are in this state, you perceive everything around you as normal. You retain all of your statistics, though you cannot use powers or perform rituals. All your clothing and gear transforms along with you. The ritual ends and you revert to your normal form if you take any damage or take an action, or at the end of the ritual's duration.

TREE STRIDE

Stepping into one plant, you instantly emerge from another some distance away.

Level: 6
Category: Travel
Time: 30 minutes
Duration: Special

Component Cost: 50 gp
Market Price: 360 gp
Key Skill: Nature

You open a magical portal in a tree adjacent to you, connecting it to a second tree that you can see. You and up to eight allies can move through the portal and emerge instantly from the second tree, and return by stepping into the second tree. The portal remains in place for a duration determined by your Nature check result, but only you and the designated allies can pass through the portal in either direction.

Nature Check Result	Duration
19 or lower	1 hour
20–29	4 hours
30–39	12 hours
40 or higher	24 hours

TUNE OF MERRIMENT

Your songs and rhymes intoxicate the gathered crowd with laughter, making it susceptible to your and your friends' influence.

Level: 9
Category: Exploration
Time: 10 minutes
Duration: 10 minutes
Prerequisite: Bard

Component Cost: 160 gp, plus a focus worth 840 gp
Market Price: 900 gp
Key Skill: Arcana (no check)

For the ritual's duration, you and any ally who heard the whole performance of the ritual can roll twice and use either result when making Diplomacy checks to influence anyone else who heard all of it.

Focus: A musical instrument you play as part of performing the ritual.

WYVERN WATCH

A wyvern-shaped presence formed from mist fills the area, promising doom to those who stumble into its demesne.

Level: 6
Category: Warding
Time: 1 hour
Duration: 8 hours or until discharged

Component Cost: 100 gp
Market Price: 360 gp
Key Skill: Arcana

You place a ward in a 4-square-by-4-square area. The ghostly form of a wyvern appears in that area. Your Arcana check determines the Perception DC to notice the wyvern's presence.

As part of the ritual, you can name creatures that can pass freely through the warded area, and you can set conditions that allow a creature to bypass the ward. Any other creature that enters the area is subject to an attack equal to your level + 4 vs. Will. On a hit, the target is immobilized (save ends). When the attack is triggered, you become aware that it has been triggered regardless of your distance from the ritual's area. The ritual is also discharged.

APPENDIX: RULE UPDATES

This appendix contains rule updates for powers and the Stealth skill. Visit the Wizards of the Coast website for other updates.

READING A POWER

The *Player's Handbook* introduces how to read a power, starting on page 54 of that book. This section touches on some of the information discussed there: the format of player character powers and their keywords. The information here incorporates clarifications and new rules, and it supersedes previous sources.

THE POWER FORMAT

Player character powers are designed to be easily referenced during play. Even though other kinds of powers, such as monster powers, have different formats, many of the guidelines here also apply to them.

Sequence: The order of information in a power description is a general guide to the sequence in which the power's various effects occur. For example, an "Effect" entry might appear above attack information in a power description to indicate that something happens before you make the attack.

Indentation: When information is indented in a power description, that means the information is contingent on the information directly above it. For example, a "Secondary Attack" entry indented below a "Hit" entry is a reminder that you can make the secondary attack only if you hit with the primary attack.

THE POWER DESCRIPTION

A power description contains various entries, some of which appear in every power description, whereas other entries appear only when needed by a particular power. Here are explanations of the various entries, presented in their typical order.

Power Name and Level: The name of a power and the power's level appear in a colored bar on the first line of the power's description. The color of the bar indicates how often you can use the power; green means the power is an at-will power, red means it's an encounter power, and black means it's a daily power.

Flavor Text: The next line, in italicized text, briefly explains what the power does, from the perspective of your character in the world. The rest of the power description is rules text, but this material is intended to help you narrate what your character is doing.

Usage: The first word on the next line tells you how often you can use the power, that is, whether it is an at-will, an encounter, or a daily power.

Keywords: The power's keywords appear next. The keywords tell you the power source, any damage types associated with the power, accessories you can use with it, and other associated effects. If "Varies" appears among the keywords, that means the power has variable keywords, which you or circumstances determine.

Action Type: The next line begins with the type of action required to use the power: standard, move, minor, free, immediate reaction, immediate interrupt, or opportunity. Some powers require no action to use. See the *Player's Handbook*, page 267, for more information about action types.

Trigger: Powers that are immediate actions (interrupts or reactions) or opportunity actions have a trigger, which defines when you're allowed to use the power. Some powers that are free actions, or that require no action to use, have a trigger as well.

Attack Type and Range: The power's attack type and range appear on the same line as its action type. The attack types are melee, ranged, area, and close. Each attack type has rules for range and targeting, detailed on pages 270-273 of the *Player's Handbook*.

Prerequisite or Requirement: Some powers are usable only if you meet a precondition. You must meet a *prerequisite* to select a power. You must meet a *requirement* to use a power.

Target: If a power directly affects one or more creatures or objects, it has a "Target" entry, specifying whom and what the power affects.

Attack: A power's attack entry specifies the ability score you use to make the attack, any special modifiers that apply to the attack roll, and which of the target's defenses you check against.

Hit: This entry describes what happens to each target that you hit with the power's attack.

Miss: This entry describes what happens to each target that you miss with the power's attack. In

---

THE MARKED CONDITION

When you mark a creature, you force it to engage you or suffer the consequences. While that creature is marked by you, it takes a -2 penalty to attack rolls for any attack that doesn't include you as a target. In addition, powers, class features, magic item properties, and feats might have effects that trigger when the creature takes certain actions.

A creature can be subject to only one mark at a time, and a new mark supersedes a mark that was already in place. The effect you use to mark a creature determines how long the creature remains marked by you. Regardless of the mark's duration, it ends if someone else marks that creature, unless an effect says otherwise.

contrast to the *Player's Handbook*, the "Miss" entries in this book specify only what happens when you miss, not what doesn't happen.

"Half damage" in this entry refers to rolled damage. Roll the damage specified in the "Hit" entry and deal half of that damage to each target you miss. "Half damage" does not apply to ongoing damage or any other damaging effects in the "Hit" entry.

Effect: Anything that appears in an "Effect" entry occurs when you use the power, whether or not you hit with it, if it is an attack power.

Secondary Target and Secondary Attack: Some powers allow you to make secondary (or even tertiary) attacks. A "Hit," a "Miss," or an "Effect" entry tells you when to make a secondary attack. Unless otherwise noted, the attack type and the range of a secondary attack are the same as the power's, and the secondary attack doesn't require a separate action.

Some powers give you the ability to make a secondary attack at a point later in an encounter, after the initial effect takes place. These powers include information about the secondary attack's action type, attack type, range, and effect.

Sustain: If a power has a "Sustain" entry, you can keep that power active by taking a specified action during your turn. See "Durations," page 278 in the *Player's Handbook*, for more about sustaining a power.

Class Feature Names: When a class feature name appears as a header in a power description, the associated entry describes an additional or a replacement effect that applies if you have that class feature.

Aftereffect: An aftereffect automatically occurs after another effect ends. An "Aftereffect" entry is beneath the effect it applies to, which is typically in a "Hit" or an "Effect" entry.

A target is sometimes subject to an aftereffect after a save. If that save occurs when the target is making multiple saving throws, the aftereffect takes effect after the target has made all of them.

MOVEMENT EFFECTS

Many powers allow you and your allies to move or allow you to move your enemies forcibly. If a power notes a distance that you or an ally moves (for example, "you shift 2 squares"), the character allowed to move can decide to move all, some, or none of that distance. Similarly, if a power forcibly moves an enemy (for example, "you push the target 3 squares"), you can decide to move the enemy all, some, or none of that distance.

If a power notes the destination for your or an ally's move (for example, "a space adjacent to the target"), the character allowed to move decides either to move to that destination or not. You can't move partway. Similarly, if a power specifies where you force an enemy to move, you decide either to move the enemy there or not.

Failed Saving Throw: Sometimes an effect changes as a target fails saving throws against it. The new effect, specified in a "First Failed Saving Throw" or a "Second Failed Saving Throw" entry, takes effect after the target fails a saving throw against the previous effect at the end of the target's turn. The effect doesn't change if the creature fails a saving throw against it at a time other than the end of its turn.

Special: Any unusual information about the use of a power appears in this entry. For example, some powers can be used as basic attacks, which is noted in a "Special" entry.

Level: This entry tells you if some part of the power—often its damage—increases at a specific level.

KEYWORDS

Here is a list of keywords currently used in PC powers. Some of these keywords—beast form, rage, spirit, and summoning—are introduced in this book. Others are used in books, like *Martial Power*, that have been published since the *Player's Handbook*. Following the list are keywords that have special rules.

KEYWORDS

Power Sources	Effect Types
Arcane	Beast*
Divine	Beast Form*
Martial	Charm
Primal	Conjuration*
Damage Types	Fear
Acid	Healing
Cold	Illusion
Fire	Invigorating*
Force	Poison
Lightning	Polymorph*
Necrotic	Rage
Poison	Rattling*
Psychic	Reliable*
Radiant	Sleep
Thunder	Spirit*
Accessories	Stance*
Implement*	Summoning*
Weapon*	Teleportation*
	Zone*

*Indicates special rules.

BEAST

A power that has the beast keyword can be used only while your beast companion is conscious and present in an encounter.

BEAST FORM

You can use a beast form power only while you are in beast form.

CONJURATION

Powers that have the conjuration keyword create conjurations, objects or creatures of magical energy.

CONJURATION

A conjuration you create uses these rules, unless a power description says otherwise.

- ✦ **Occupies No Squares:** The conjuration occupies no squares.
- ✦ **Unaffected by the Environment:** Terrain and environmental phenomena have no effect on the conjuration. For example, a conjuration that is an icy hand functions in an inferno without penalty. The conjuration does not need to be supported by a solid surface, so it can float in the air.
- ✦ **Your Defenses:** Normally, a conjuration cannot be attacked or physically affected. If a conjuration can be attacked or physically affected, it uses your defenses. Unless an attack specifically targets conjurations, only the attack's damage (not including ongoing damage) affects the conjuration.
- ✦ **Attacking with a Conjuration:** If you can attack with a conjuration, you make the attack. You determine line of sight normally, but you determine line of effect from the conjuration.
- ✦ **Movable Conjurations:** If the power you use to create a conjuration allows you to move it, it's a movable conjuration. At the end of your turn, the movable conjuration ends if you are not within range of at least 1 square it's in (using the power's range) or if you don't have line of effect to at least 1 square it's in.

  When you move a conjuration, you can't move it through a solid obstacle.
- ✦ **Death Ends:** If you die, the conjuration ends immediately.

IMPLEMENT

Implements are items wielded by certain characters to channel their powers. Your class description or a feat tells you which implements you can wield, if any. To use the powers and the properties of a magic implement, you must be able to wield that implement.

The implement keyword identifies a power that can be used through an implement, and the implement must be a type wielded by the power's class. You can use implement powers without an implement, and wielding a nonmagical implement confers no benefit. If you wield a magic implement, you can add its enhancement bonus to the attack rolls and the damage rolls of implement powers you use through it (Chapter 3 contains various magic implements, as does Chapter 7 in the *Player's Handbook*).

INVIGORATING

If you are trained in Endurance, you gain temporary hit points equal to your Constitution modifier when you hit with a power that has the invigorating keyword. No invigorating power grants temporary hit points more than once during a turn, even if you hit more than once with that power.

POLYMORPH

Polymorph powers change a target's physical form in some way.

POLYMORPH

You use these rules when you're affected by a polymorph power.

- ✦ **One Polymorph at a Time:** If you are affected by more than one polymorph power, only the most recent one has any effect. The other powers' effects remain on you and their durations expire as normal, but those effects don't apply. However, when the most recent effect ends, the next most recent one that is still active applies to you.
- ✦ **Changing Size:** If a polymorph power reduces your space, you do not provoke opportunity attacks for leaving squares as you shrink.

  If a polymorph effect makes you too large to fit in the available space, the effect fails against you, but you are stunned (save ends). For example, if you are crawling through a narrow tunnel and a polymorph effect tries to turn you into a creature that is too large for the tunnel, the effect fails, but you are stunned until you save.
- ✦ **Death Ends:** If you die, polymorph effects end on you immediately.

RAGE

A rage power allows you to enter a rage specified in the power. A rage lasts until you enter a new rage or until the end of the encounter.

RATTLING

If you are trained in Intimidate and deal damage with a power that has the rattling keyword, the target takes a –2 penalty to attack rolls until the end of your next turn. A creature that is immune to fear is not subject to this penalty.

RELIABLE

If you miss every target when using a reliable power, you don't expend the use of that power.

SPIRIT

You can use a spirit power only if your spirit companion is present in the encounter. If a spirit power includes "spirit" in its range, you determine line of sight and line of effect from your spirit companion's space, which is the power's origin square.

STANCE

When you use a stance power, you assume a stance that lasts until you assume another stance or until the end of the encounter.

SUMMONING

Powers that have the summoning keyword bring creatures from elsewhere, often other planes, to serve you in a variety of ways.

SUMMONED CREATURE

A creature you summon uses these rules, unless a power description says otherwise.

✦ **Allied Creature:** When you use a summoning power, you create a creature that is an ally to you and your allies. The power determines where the summoned creature appears.

✦ **Your Defenses:** The summoned creature's defenses equal yours when you summon it, not including any temporary bonuses or penalties.

✦ **Hit Points:** The summoned creature's maximum hit points equal your bloodied value. When the summoned creature drops to 0 hit points, it is destroyed, and you lose a healing surge. If you have no healing surges left, you instead take damage equal to half your bloodied value.

✦ **No Healing Surges:** The summoned creature lacks healing surges, but if a power allows it to spend a healing surge, you can spend a healing surge for it. The summoned creature then gains the benefit of the healing surge, instead of your gaining it.

✦ **Speed:** The summoning power determines the summoned creature's speed.

✦ **Commanding the Creature:** The summoned creature has no actions of its own; you spend actions to command it mentally. You can command the creature only if you have line of effect to it. When you command the creature, the two of you share knowledge but not senses.

  As a minor action, you can command the summoned creature to take one of the following actions, if it is physically capable of taking that action: crawl, escape, fly, open or close a door or a container, pick up or drop an item, run, stand up, shift, squeeze, or walk.

  The summoning power determines any special commands you can give the summoned creature and gives an action type for each command. If a special command is a minor action, you can give that command only once during each of your turns.

✦ **Attacks and Checks:** If a summoning power allows the summoned creature to attack, you make an attack through the creature, as specified in the power description. If the summoned creature can make a skill check or an ability check, you make the check. Attacks and checks you make through the creature do not include temporary bonuses or penalties to your statistics.

✦ **Duration:** Unless the summoning power states otherwise, the summoned creature lasts until the end of the encounter and then disappears. As a minor action, you can dismiss the summoned creature.

TELEPORTATION

A teleportation power transports creatures or objects instantaneously from one location to another.

TELEPORTATION

You use these rules when you use a teleportation power.

✦ **Line of Sight:** You must have line of sight to the destination space.

✦ **No Line of Effect:** Neither you nor the creature or object being teleported needs line of effect to the destination space.

✦ **Destination Space:** The destination must be a space that the creature or object being teleported can occupy without squeezing.

✦ **Instantaneous:** Teleportation is instantaneous. The creature or object being teleported disappears and immediately appears in the destination space you choose. The movement is unhindered by intervening creatures, objects, or terrain.

✦ **No Opportunity Actions:** The creature or object being teleported doesn't provoke opportunity actions for leaving its space.

✦ **Immobilized or Restrained:** Being immobilized or restrained doesn't prevent a creature from teleporting. If a creature teleports away from a physical restraint, a monster's grasp, or some other immobilizing effect that is located in a specific space, the creature is no longer immobilized or restrained. Otherwise, the creature teleports but is still immobilized or restrained when it reaches the destination space.

WEAPON

The weapon keyword identifies a power that is used with a weapon, including an improvised weapon such as an unarmed strike (see "Weapons," *Player's Handbook*, page 215). The range and the damage of a weapon power is usually determined by the weapon you use with it. A [W] in a power's damage expression stands for your weapon's damage dice (see "Damage," *Player's Handbook*, page 276).

If you use a weapon power with a weapon you're proficient with, you add the weapon's proficiency bonus to the attack rolls of that power. Your class and feats determine your weapon proficiencies. If you use a weapon power with a magic weapon, you can

---

EXTRA DAMAGE

Many effects grant you the ability to deal extra damage, including powers, feats, and magic item properties. Extra damage is always in addition to other damage. For example, if you have a feat that causes your area attacks to deal extra damage, the extra damage doesn't apply when you use an area attack that deals no damage, such as the wizard's *sleep* power.

add the magic weapon's enhancement bonus to the power's attack rolls and damage rolls.

ZONE

Powers that have the zone keyword create zones, magical areas that last for a round or more.

ZONE

A zone you create uses these rules, unless a power description says otherwise.

- ✦ **Fills an Area of Effect:** The zone is created by an area of effect and fills each square in the area that is within line of effect of the origin square.
- ✦ **Unaffected by Attacks and the Environment:** The zone cannot be attacked or physically affected, and terrain and environmental phenomena have no effect on it. For example, a zone that deals fire damage is unaffected by cold damage.
- ✦ **Movable Zones:** If the power you use to create a zone allows you to move it, it's a movable zone. At the end of your turn, the movable zone ends if you are not within range of at least 1 square of it (using the power's range) or if you don't have line of effect to at least 1 square of it.
    When you move a zone, you can't move it through a solid obstacle.
- ✦ **Overlapping Zones:** If zones overlap and impose penalties to the same roll or game statistic, a creature affected by the overlapping zones is subject to the worst penalty. Similarly, a creature in the overlapping area takes damage only from the zone that deals the most damage, regardless of damage type.
- ✦ **Death Ends:** If you die, the zone ends immediately.

NEW STEALTH RULES

This section presents updates to the Stealth skill and to rules related to that skill, as presented in the first printing of the *Player's Handbook*.

BLUFF

The following paragraph replaces the "Create a Diversion to Hide" paragraph in the Bluff skill's shaded box (*Player's Handbook*, page 183).

- ✦ **Create a Diversion to Hide:** Once per combat encounter, you can create a diversion to hide. As a standard action, make a Bluff check opposed by the passive Insight check of any enemy that can see you. If you succeed, make a Stealth check opposed by the passive Perception check of any enemy present. If the Stealth check succeeds against an enemy, you are hidden from that enemy until the end of your turn or until you attack.

STEALTH

The following shaded box replaces the Stealth skill's shaded box and the table underneath it (*Player's Handbook*, page 188).

Stealth: At the end of a move action.

- ✦ **Opposed Check:** Stealth vs. passive Perception. If multiple enemies are present, your Stealth check is opposed by each enemy's passive Perception check. If you move more than 2 squares during the move action, you take a -5 penalty to the Stealth check. If you run, the penalty is -10.
- ✦ **Becoming Hidden:** You can make a Stealth check against an enemy only if you have superior cover or total concealment against the enemy or if you're outside the enemy's line of sight. Outside combat, the DM can allow you to make a Stealth check against a distracted enemy, even if you don't have superior cover or total concealment and aren't outside the enemy's line of sight. The distracted enemy might be focused on something in a different direction, allowing you to sneak up.
- ✦ **Success:** You are hidden, which means you are silent and invisible to the enemy (see "Concealment" and "Targeting What You Can't See," page 281).
- ✦ **Failure:** You can try again at the end of another move action.
- ✦ **Remaining Hidden:** You remain hidden as long as you meet these requirements.
    Keep Out of Sight: If you no longer have any cover or concealment against an enemy, you don't remain hidden from that enemy. You don't need superior cover, total concealment, or to stay outside line of sight, but you do need some degree of cover or concealment to remain hidden. You can't use another creature as cover to remain hidden.
    Keep Quiet: If you speak louder than a whisper or otherwise draw attention to yourself, you don't remain hidden from any enemy that can hear you.
    Keep Still: If you move more than 2 squares during an action, you must make a new Stealth check with a -5 penalty. If you run, the penalty is -10. If any enemy's passive Perception check beats your check result, you don't remain hidden from that enemy.
    Don't Attack: If you attack, you don't remain hidden.
- ✦ **Not Remaining Hidden:** If you take an action that causes you not to remain hidden, you retain the benefits of being hidden until you resolve the action. You can't become hidden again as part of that same action.
- ✦ **Enemy Activity:** An enemy can try to find you on its turn. If an enemy makes an active Perception check and beats your Stealth check result (don't make a new check), you don't remain hidden from that enemy. Also, if an enemy tries to enter your space, you don't remain hidden from that enemy.

PERCEPTION

Using the Perception skill actively is a minor action, not a standard action (*Player's Handbook*, page 186).

TARGETING WHAT YOU CAN'T SEE

The following paragraphs replace the second and third paragraphs in the "Targeting What You Can't See" sidebar (*Player's Handbook*, page 281).

Invisible Creatures and Stealth: If an invisible creature is hidden from you ("Stealth," page 188), you can neither hear nor see it, and you have to guess what space it occupies. If an invisible creature is not hidden from you, you can hear it or sense some other sign of its presence and therefore know what space it occupies, although you still can't see it.

Make a Perception Check: On your turn, you can make a Perception check as a minor action (page 186) to try to determine the location of an invisible creature that is hidden from you.

GLOSSARY

This brief glossary contains game terms that appear in this book and are defined in a book other than a *Player's Handbook*.

attacking objects: With your DM's permission, you can use a power that normally attacks creatures to attack objects. See the *Dungeon Master's Guide*, page 65, for how to damage objects.

blindsight: If you have blindsight, you can clearly see creatures or objects within a specified range and within line of effect, even if they are invisible or obscured. You otherwise rely on your normal vision.

fly speed: If you have a fly speed, you can fly a number of squares up to that speed as a move action. To remain in the air, you must move at least 2 squares during your turn, or you crash at the end of your turn. While flying, you can't shift or make opportunity attacks, and you crash if you're knocked prone. See the *Dungeon Master's Guide*, page 47, for more about flying.

hover: If you have a fly speed and can hover, you can remain in the air without moving during your turn. You can also shift and make opportunity attacks while flying.

overland flight: An overland flight speed works like a fly speed with one exception: While you are in the air using your overland flight speed, you crash if you take any action other than a move action to use overland flight or a free action.

tremorsense: If you have tremorsense, you can clearly see creatures or objects within a specified range, even if they are invisible, obscured, or outside line of effect, but you and they must be in contact with the ground or the same substance, such as water or a web. You otherwise rely on your normal vision.

INDEX

WHEN THERE'S A FIGHT WITH A DRAGON, IT'S MORE FUN TO BE ON *HIS* SIDE.

As Dungeon Master, you get to control the monsters, craft the challenges, and create the stories that get retold. Expand your imagination beyond your character sheet and into a D&D® campaign of your own.

Pick up a copy of the *Dungeon Master's Guide*® and *Dungeon Master's Guide 2* — and share the experience.

CREATE AN ACCOUNT AT:
DNDINSIDER.COM